EUI—Series D—2

Groß, The Role of the Current Account in Asset Market Models of Exchange Rate Determination

European University Institute
Institut Universitaire Européen
Europäisches Hochschulinstitut
Istituto Universitario Europeo

Series D

Economics/Economiques/Wirtschaft/Economia

2

Badia Fiesolana — Firenze

The Role of the Current Account in Asset Market Models of Exchange Rate Determination

by

Alexander Groß

1987

Walter de Gruyter · Berlin · New York

Library of Congress Cataloging-in-Publication Data

Gross, Alexander, 1953-
The role of the current account in asset market models of exchange rate determination.
(Series D--Economics = Economiques = Wirtschaft = Economia ; 2)
Based on the author's thesis (doctoral)--European University Institute, Florence, Italy.
Bibliography: p.
1. Balance of payments--Econometric models. 2. Foreign exchange--Econometric models. I. Title. II. Title: Current account in asset market models of exchange rate determination. III. Series: Series D--Economics ; 2.
HG3882.G75 1987 332.4'56 87-8852
ISBN 0-89925-373-0 (U.S.)

CIP-Kurztitelaufnahme der Deutschen Bibliothek

Gross, Alexander:
The role of the current account in asset market models of exchange rate determination / by Alexander Gross. — Berlin ; New York : de Gruyter, 1987.
(European University Institute : Ser. D, Economics ; 2)
ISBN 3-11-011346-5
NE: Istituto Universitario Europeo <Fiesole>: European University Institute / D

Dust Cover Design: Rudolf Hübler, Berlin.
Printing: Hildebrand, Berlin. — Binding: Verlagsbuchbinderei Dieter Mikolai, Berlin.
Printed in Germany

Für Waltraud

Acknowledgements

This book originated from my doctoral thesis written during a three-year stay at the European University Institute, Florence, Italy. While working and living in Florence, I have incurred many debts of all kinds to people both inside and outside the Institute. My generic thanks go to all those who made these three years in Florence such a unique professional and personal experience.

In particular, I would like to thank Professor Marcello De Cecco who, as my supervisor, provided the scientific freedom and benevolence which made it possible to achieve this dissertation. I also very much appreciated Professor Manfred Streit's steady interest in my work. His ideas on the formation of expectations will certainly have left their marks on this thesis.

Among my colleagues and friends at the Institute I owe particular thanks to Dr. Filip Keereman (for some relaxed discussions on general problems of portfolio models) and to Dr. Sabine Lessmann (for valuable comments on the rationality problem). Dr. Stefan Flätgen's critical remarks on earlier drafts of this thesis have been very helpful.

Without the technical assistance of the staff of the computer center at the European University Institute I probably would have been lost in the computer operation. My special thanks here go to Dr. Robert Danziger.

Professor Wolfgang Harbrecht gave the initial impulse for writing this dissertation, and Professor Manfred Neumann invested five years of patience, encouragement and support which made it possible to complete it. He has been of constant help in all aspects of this dissertation so that my greatest thanks go to him.

Unfortunately, none of the above-mentioned persons is responsible for the remaining errors and shortcomings. As for the most obvious weakness, namely the style of presentation, the reader is asked to be indulgent to the linguistic slips of a German writing in English while living in Italy.

Firenze/Nürnberg
April 1985

Alexander Groß

CONTENTS

ABBREVIATIONS

BHM	-	Branson, Halttunen and Masson (1977, 1979)
CA	-	Current Account
IFS	-	International Financial Statistics, International Monetary Fund
MEI	-	Main Economic Indicators, OECD
MD	-	Murphy and Van Duyne (1980)
MM	-	Martin and Masson (1979)
NFP	-	Net Foreign Asset Position
SDR	-	Special Drawing Rights

"There are three problems which drive mankind crazy: love, ambition, and the study of currency problems."

George Schartz, quoted according to Caspers (1977, p.9).

Outline

As the title suggests, this thesis attempts to analyse different approaches to a reintroduction of the current account (CA) into asset market orientated models of exchange rate determination. The idea that there is a need for such a reintroduction will seem strange to anyone concerned with exchange rates in practice: in public discussions and political decisions the CA has always been recognized as an important determinant of exchange rates. Nevertheless, in the theoretical field the still prevailing monetary approach to exchange rate determination ignores the CA in its explanation of exchange rate behaviour.

The discrepancy between theoretical and practical assessments of the importance of the CA in exchange rate determination has led to an increasing number of recent publications and represents also the starting point of this thesis. In accordance with some of these studies, we will argue that the pivotal importance of international financial markets in exchange rate determination does not lessen the importance of the CA. In the following chapters we attempt to analyse some theoretical and empirical reasons which justify the reinstallment of the CA as an important factor in exchange rate movements.

The first part of the thesis is devoted to a theoretical investigation of the role of the CA in asset market approaches to exchange rate determination. Since the monetary approach can be taken as the currently prevailing theory, a more extensive work on exchange rate determination must first examine this approach. This examination will be carried out in a fairly condensed form in the second chapter. It will be concluded that recent exchange rate behaviour cannot be fully explained only in terms of relative supplies of and demand for money. In particular, we will attempt to show that one of the basic assumptions underlying all monetary models - perfect asset substitutability - may be inadequate in a world of uncertainty and risk aversion.

In the sections following we investigate the ways possible of implementing the CA in a more complete portfolio balance framework assuming imperfect asset substitutability. This theoretical approach is based on Tobin's (1969) general equilibrium approach to monetary theory and McKinnon's (1969) work on portfolio balance and payment adjustment.

In the third and fourth chapter some of the already existing applications and extensions of this approach will be discussed. The CA enters portfolio balance models of exchange rate determination in essentially two ways.

First, CA imbalances involve changes in net foreign asset stocks. Hence, there exists a direct relationship between the CA and relative asset supplies, portfolio dispositions and the exchange rate. The third chapter focuses on the various implications of this wealth redistribution effect.

Sencond, rational asset holders will take CA developments into account when forming their exchange rate expectations if they consider the CA as an important exchange rate determinant. Possible links between the CA, exchange rate expectations and the actual exchange rate will be described in chapter four.

Apart from some extensions and modifications, chapters three and four serve more as a survey than as a new contribution to the investigated subject. Considering the host of publications over the last years, the selection of models and arguments (though hopefully taking into account the major developments) must necessarily be eclectic and, of course, subjective.

Our exposition focuses on the causality direction from the CA to the exchange rate. The inverse relationship, important as it is, will be dealt with only insofar as dynamic adjustment processes are concerned.

Since we concentrate on financial portfolio analysis, problems which may arise in connection with real capital stocks will not be discussed. While this is certainly a shortcoming, it is doubtful whether an inclusion of real growth and capital accumulation would be essential for short and medium run exchange rate determination.[1)]

---

1) Support for this view is provided by McKinnon (1969), Isard (1978, pp. 20), Kouri (1980) and Baltensperger and Böhm (1982). Portfolio models which include real capital can be found in Tobin and De Macedo (1980), and Dornbusch (1980a, pp. 206).

Mathematical derivations and stability proofs are omitted where unnecessary to clear understanding. Rigorous formal treatments of the models presented in the third and the fourth chapter can be found in the literature quoted. In some cases, the formulas and equations given are the result of my own simple calculations and hence they may differ from the exposition in the cited sources.

In chapter five we address a special problem which is closely related to the wealth redistribution effect of CA imbalances. Most portfolio models in which the exchange rate effect of CA imbalances is explicitly dealt with proceed from the assumption that domestic assets are not held by foreigners. The only internationally accepted asset is a standard foreign-currency denominated asset issued by a foreign authority. This common assumption makes it possible to identify any CA imbalance with a corresponding change in the stock of net foreign-currency denominated assets. In chapter five we drop this assumption and allow for international trade in domestic and foreign-currency denominated assets. In such a setting CA transactions can be financed with domestic and/or foreign assets (diversified CA financing). Accordingly, we try to clarify whether the currency of denomination of CA induced wealth shifts is relevant to the exchange rate effect of CA imbalances. This analysis will be conducted in a small-country framework as well as in a two-country portfolio model. Both models are designed for an investigation of financial asset markets in a short run partial-equilibrium context. Their basic structure resembles the models developed by Branson (1976), Girton and Henderson (1977), and Martin and Masson (1979).

In the second part of the thesis we turn to an empirical investigation of the role of the CA in exchange rate determination. Chapters seven and eight contain a critical review of econometric tests of standard portfolio models. We refer in particular to the estimations of Branson, Halttunen, and Masson (1977, 1979), Martin and Masson (1979), and Murphy and Van Duyne (1980). All these estimations proceed from models which include only one internationally traded asset.

This discussion provides the point of departure for the empirical investigation which will be presented in chapter nine. As in the studies quoted above, a stationary-expectations portfolio model will be estimated in which only one internationally traded asset is assumed. The theory is applied to three different exchange rates: the Deutsche mark/US dollar rate, the Japanese yen/US dollar rate, and the Pound Sterling/US dollar rate. This allows for a broader scope compared with previous tests. The complete sample period runs from early 1973 to late 1982. Besides a conventional regression analysis, we perform exchange rate forecasts for the subperiod from November 1978 to August 1982.

Chapter ten deals with the empirical application of the portfolio balance model in the case of diversified CA financing. Following the theoretical model layed down in chapter five we leave aside the assumption of only one internationally traded asset and allow for bilateral trade in assets denominated in two different currencies. Empirical evidence concerning the relevance of diversified CA financing will be presented for the DM/dollar rate.

The last section of the thesis, chapter eleven, is devoted to a special, but nevertheless crucial problem inherent in many stationary-expectations portfolio balance models. In some recent papers it has been suggested that negative holdings of foreign-currency denominated assets cause dynamic instability in flexible exchange rate regimes. We first investigate this problem from a theoretical point of view. Subsequently, we report statistical data and estimates for private and total net foreign asset positions of those countries to which the portfolio model has been applied over the last chapters. The figures for the United States, Germany, Japan, and the United Kingdom provide some empirical clues for an assessment of the practical importance of negative net foreign asset positions as a source of exchange rate instability.

The following definitions and symbols will be used throughout the thesis unless indicated otherwise.

The exchange rate is defined as the domestic currency price of one unit of foreign currency. In some places the term "spot rate" is used synonymously.

The CA records the value of all exports and imports of goods (trade account) and services (service account) as well as the value of unilateral payments within a certain period. In the theoretical part of the thesis the CA will be reduced to the trade account or, depending on the model structure, to the trade account plus the service account which includes as only item international interest payments.

Numbers of equations, figures, and tables in the text refer to the respective section.

An asterisk * indicates a foreign variable; a dot ˙ above a variable denotes the derivative with respect to time; a hat ^ denotes the rate of change; + or - above a variable indicates the sign of the partial derivative.

PART I:

THEORETICAL FOUNDATIONS

"While 'monetarists' from Hume to Friedman stressed the asset aspects of the problem, their opponents from Malthus to Keynes emphasized output flows, but the fundamental problem was always the interaction between stocks and flows during the dynamic adjustment process."

Niehans (1977, p. 1245)

1. Introduction: Exchange Rate Theories and the Current Account

There is nothing new in investigating the role of the CA in exchange rate determination. In fact, research on the interaction between the CA and the exchange rate is one of the oldest and at the same time most durable topics within the balance of payments and exchange rate theory.[1)] Nevertheless, since the revival of the monetary approach to exchange rate determination little attention has been paid to research in the influence of the CA on exchange rates. In most of the recent macroeconomic exchange rate models the CA appears, if at all, only as a supernumerary.[2)] This, however, stands in clear contradiction to the importance attributed to the CA as an exchange rate determinant by central bank officials and within the public discussion.[3)]

Waning scientific interest in the CA as an exchange rate determinant, however, might be regarded almost as a trend in the theoretical development-line starting from the elasticity and absorbtion approach and leading via the macroeconomic Mundell-Fleming approach and the microeconomic "modern theory" of exchange markets to the current monetary approach. Although it is not intended to provide a history of this development, a short description of the role of the CA within these different theoretical frameworks may be useful as starting point for the subsequent analysis.

Since the system of fixed parities was dominant over the period after World War II, the exchange rate/current account discussion has centered on the question under which conditions a discrete devaluation produces an improvement of the CA. The capital account was taken as predetermined while imports and exports were assumed as functions of the exchange rate. As analytical tools, price and quantity elasticities of

---

1) The dominant influence of export and import flows on the exchange rate was, according to Einzig (1970, p. 141), already stressed by the English economist Gresham in a memorandum for Elisabeth I in 1559.

2) There are, of course, some important exceptions to which we will refer later on. Nonetheless, main stream exchange rate theories consider the CA mostly as a reacting variable and not as an acting one.

3) See, for example, Gleske (1982), Williamson (1983, p. 53).

trade flows were introduced and the famous "Marshall-Lerner" condition and the more sophisticated "Robinson" condition were derived as conditions for a "normal" reaction of the CA to exchange rate changes.[1] In the discussion about the performance of a flexible rate system, it seemed obvious to apply the elasticity approach in an inverted fashion to the analysis of exchange rate movements: with sufficient export and import elasticities, and therefore sufficient elasticities of flow supply and demand for foreign exchange, an exogenous shift in the CA towards a deficit (surplus) was expected to bring about a depreciation (appreciation).

Although this approach was sharply attacked, in particular because of its partial-equilibrium character and its total neglect of capital flows,[2] elasticitiy considerations are still used as a foundation for popular exchange rate analyses and for some recent macroeconomic models.[3]

With increasing freedom in capital movements, development of non-national currency markets and internationalization of the banking system, the attention switched more and more to the analysis of capital movements.

In the macroeconomic context these developments were reflected in comparative-static, multi-equation models based on Mundell's and Fleming's seminal work.[4] The exchange rate was simultaneously determined by a macoreconomic market system consisting of equilibrium conditions for

---

1) Although Marshall (1923, pp. 161, 337, 341, 353) is, in general, credited for the derivation of the basic elasticity condition, it should be mentioned that he deals with a real barter economy. Therefore, he concentrates on the determination of the terms-of-trade on the basis of total supply and demand elasticities, whereas the monetary elasticity approach is based on partial price elasticities. See also Jacob (1972) on this point. Bickerdike (1920) seems to has been the first who applied a formal elasticity analysis to exchange rate determination. Important contributions can be found in Robinson (1947), Machlup (1966), and Stackelberg (1949). A good historical exposition is provided by Meyer (1961) and Jacob (1972).

2) For a detailed critizism see Alexander (1952), Kleinewefers (1969), Cézanne (1974), Dornbusch (1975).

3) See, for example, Michaely (1980), Branson (1976, 1979, 1981).

4) See Mundell (1963) and Fleming (1962). An earlier attempt leading in the same direction is Meade's (1951).

goods and money markets and the overall balance of payments. It was shown that the flow equilibrium solution for the exchange rate and the performance of fiscal and monetary policy depends essentially on the assumptions about the degree of capital mobility. Consequently, further research focused chiefly on international capital flows.[1)]

On the microeconomic side, the "modern theory" of foreign exchange markets tried to clarify the role of speculation and arbitrage in exchange rate determination.[2)] One of the main contributions of this branch of exchange rate theory consists in emphasizing exchange rate expectations. Flow equilibrium in foreign exchange markets is not brought about merely by variations of the spot rate but by the simultaneous interaction of spot rate, forward rate, and exchange rate expectations. This relationship was totally neglected by standard Mundell-Fleming models because of the static-expectations assumption.

Given all this, these developments did not lead to the conclusion that the CA does not matter. The strong emphasis on the capital account simply reflected the upswing in international capital movements due to changed economic conditions. The backbone of all these models was still the traditional conception of the foreign exchange market as a market for flow-demand and flow-supply of different currencies resulting from current account and capital account transactions. Accordingly, the equilibrium exchange rate was derived from the condition of flow equilibrium in the exchange market.

---

1) Extensive elaborations of this approach can now be found in every textbook on international economics, see, for example, Rose (1978), Neumann (1973); for a comprehensive description see Dornbusch and Krugman (1976), and Dornbusch (1978). For a recent application to the European Currency System see Harbrecht (1979). Despit all critizism, Mundell's model approach remains popular, as Dornbusch puts it, as "the Volkswagen of the field - easy to drive, reliable and sleek", Dornbusch (1980a, p. 4). For critizism see Myhrmann (1977), Hammann (1980, pp. 84), Ingram (1978).

2) The "modern theory" goes back at least to Keynes (1923). Important contributions can be found in Tsiang (1959/60), Sohmen (1966), Grubel (1966). For a detailed exposition see Graf (1971), Cézanne (1974).

The treatment of capital movements as pure flows, in particular, was sharply attacked by proponents of a stock approach to exchange rate determination. It was argued that capital flows could be better analysed when seen as adjustments to desired asset stocks. With a high speed of adjustment in capital markets it would be more appropriate to explain the underlying stocks of assets and, in particular, portfolio behaviour of agents rather than mere stock adjustments.[1)]

One of the outcomes of this debate was the emergence of the monetary approach to exchange rate determination which was, at least in the beginning, closely related to the monetarist school of thought. The monetary approach considers the exchange rate as the relative price of two different moneys: "...the equilibrium exchange rate is attained when the existing stocks of the two moneys are willingly held. It is reasonable, therefore, that a theory of the determination of the relative price of two moneys could be stated conveniently in terms of supply of and the demand for these moneys." [2)] The theoretical core of this approach consists in an restatement and merger of the quantity theory of money with the purchasing power parity theory (PPP). As a result of the pure monetary stock-approach, the CA as a typical flow variable was totally neglected.

Similar to the monetary approach, portfolio balance models consider the exchange rate as a relative price of domestic and foreign financial assets denominated in different currencies. The equilibrium exchange rate is determined in asset markets by the demand for and the supply of stocks of assets: if the desired asset stocks are brought in line with the actual stocks - by exchange and interest rate movements - international portfolio equilibrium is attained. Thus, both approaches determine the exchange rate by a stock-equilibrium condition. And both the monetary and the portfolio balance approach share the assumption of perfect capital mobility. In the absence of substantial

---

1) For a detailed description of the stock-flow debate see Mussa (1976), Bender (1977), Myhrmann (1977). For a comprehensive view on the different implications see also Foley (1975), Allen and Kenen (1976).

2) Frenkel (1976, p. 201).

transaction costs and capital controls the exchange rate must adjust instantly to equilibrate the international demand for stocks of national assets. Perfect capital mobility implies the validity of covered interest rate parity: the interest rate on domestic bonds must be equal to the interest rate on similar foreign bonds plus the forward premium.

Despite this common foundation, monetary and portfolio models show several important differences. One of the most important distinguishing characteristics with regard to the role of the CA is related to the assumption about the degree of substitutability of domestic and foreign interest-bearing assets.
Uncovered foreign-currency denominated assets are considered as perfect substitutes for domestic assets if differences in interest returns are exactly matched by the expected rate of depreciation of the home currency. The validity of this "uncovered interest rate parity" requires the absence of any risk difference between domestic and foreign assets or risk neutral agents. If this is taken for granted, the money market equilibrium conditions together with the uncovered IRP condition describe a complete asset market equilibrium and hence, they are sufficient to determine the exchange rate.
The assumption of perfect substitutability is one of the crucial characteristics of the monetary approach: since domestic and foreign bonds must be identical with respect to the expected net returns their existence is sufficiently taken into account by the uncovered IRP condition. Shifts in relative asset supplies, others than money, do not affect the exchange rate.

Contrary to the monetary approach, portfolio balance models consider imperfect asset substitutability as a more realistic assumption. Mainly because of the risk involved in holding assets denominated in different currencies, expected net returns of domestic and foreign bonds may differ from each other in equilibrium. Hence, uncovered IRP does not hold. This assumption opens up for a broader conception of asset market and portfolio equilibrium in which monetary disturbances are not the only source of exchange rate fluctuations. Asset market equilibrium has to be defined in terms of relative supplies of and demands for all domestic and foreign assets. A change in the actual asset stocks of an economy, e.g., an increase in net foreign assets by a CA surplus attains, through induced portfolio adjustments, direct influence on interest rates and exchange rates. Since the CA indicates the rate at which the economy in the aggregate is adding to its net external assets it becomes an important portfolio and, hence, exchange rate determinant.

However, before we investigate the link between the CA, portfolio equilibrium and the exchange rate in more detail it is necessary to examine the validity of the simple monetary approach first.

2. The Monetary Approach

2.1. Long Run: Purchasing Power Parity

The monetary approach to exchange rate determination is based on the fundamental idea that the "valuation of a foreign currency in terms of our own ... mainly depends on the relative purchasing power of the two currencies in their respective countries."[1] This classical definition of absolute purchasing power parity by Cassel builds the foundation of monetarist exchange rate theories. The monetary approach adds to that statement the equally classical proposition that the quantity of money simultaneously determines the overall price level and the exchange rate. Prices and exchange rates are both considered as endogenous variables. This way of thinking leads directly to the definition of the exchange rate as the relative price of domestic and foreign currencies which is determined by the relative supply of and demand for money.[2]

To illustrate the role of real variables within this framework, we start off with the law of one price.[3]

---

1) Cassel (1922, p. 138). Although Cassel is credited for inventing the term "purchasing power parity", the roots of this theory go back, according to Einzig (1970, p. 145), to Spanish economists writting in the 16th and 17th century.

2) For a detailed description of different versions of PPP see Officer (1976a). The monetary approach is explicitly derived from PPP theory by Frenkel (1976, 1978), Myhrmann (1976), and Mussa (1976).

3) The following exposition is taken from Claassen (1980, pp. 423). For a similar presentation see Dornbusch (1976a), for a graphical analysis Clements (1981).
It is not intended to define PPP only in terms of traded goods, which is done sometimes. We focus on the overall price level. But this approach has some advantages over usual presentations which derive PPP theory and the monetary approach, respectively, directly from conditions of money market equilibrium:

- monetarist arguments concerning the role of real factors and the CA can be illustrated better in this framework;
- it provides an explanation for the causality connection between money supply and the exchange rate, namely commodity arbitrage.

If, in the case of a small country, the law of one price is assumed to hold, then the exchange rate e equals the ratio between the domestic price level of internationally traded goods P_T and the given foreign price level of traded goods P_T^*.

(1) $e = P_T / P_T^*$

The overall domestic price level can be defined as

(2) $P = \alpha P_T + (1 - \alpha) P_N$

where P_N is the domestic price level of nontraded goods and α denotes the relative expenditure share on traded goods.

Defining $\beta = P_N / P_T$ as the equilibrium relative price between traded and nontraded goods (equilibrium internal price ratio)[1], combining eqs. (1) and (2), and extending to two countries yields for the equilibrium exchange rate

(3) $e = ({}^{P}/_{P^*}) \, ({}^{\gamma^*}/_{\gamma})$ with $\gamma = \alpha + (1 - \alpha)\beta$.

Next we introduce the equilibrium conditions for the respective money markets. Real demands for the exogenously given money supplies are defined in the usual way as stable functions of real incomes Y and nominal interest rates r.

(footnote 3. last page continued) It should be stressed, however, that the law of one price is often not regarded as a necessary part of PPP theory or the monetary approach, see Frenkel (1978, 1981b) or Niehans (1980). But if it is abstracted from commodity arbitrage, the adjustment mechanism remains unexplained and PPP is simply an assumed equilibrium condition or a "doctrine" but not a theory of exchange rate determination; see on this point Frenkel (1976), Harbrecht and Neumann (1979, PP. 18), Dornbusch and Krugman (1976).

1) This ratio is determined by relative costs of production and consumers' relative valuations of both goods. The aggregation of exportable and importable goods to the class of tradeable goods and the analysis of the equilibrium internal price ratio was introduced by Salter (1959). For further elaborations see also Claassen (1978, pp. 121), Hammann (1980, pp. 50).

(4) $M / P = L(r, Y)$ and $M^* / P^* = L^*(r^*, Y^*)$

with $\partial L/\partial r = L_r < 0$, $\partial L/\partial Y = L_Y > 0$ for both countries.

Solving eq. (4) for the price level and substituting the result in eq. (3) yields the central statement of the monetary approach

(5) $$e = [{}^{M}/_{M^*}] \left[\frac{L^*(r^*, Y^*)}{L(r, Y)}\right] [{}^{\gamma^*}/_{\gamma}] .$$

The exchange rate determinants included in eq. (5) can now be divided in real and monetary factors.

Real variables affect the exchange rate through the money demand function as well as through the internal expenditure division α and the internal price ratio β, both included in γ.

From eq. (5) it can be seen that a change in the equilibrium exchange rate, at constant money stocks, could be brought about by:[1)]

- nonproportional changes in money demands, due, for example, to different speeds of real income growth or alterations in the real interest rate;
- shifts in the relative equilibrium internal price ratio β/β^* or shifts in the relative internal expenditure share on traded and nontraded goods α/α^*. Changes in these real variables attain direct influence on the nominal exchange rate even if the overall price level is kept constant by monetary measures. International differences in the level and the change of the equilibrium internal price ratios β, β^* may result, e.g., from exogenous shifts in the domestic demand for traded and nontraded goods, from different income elasticities for both goods, or from unequal technical progress in both goods sectors.[2)]

1) These effects are elaborated in more detail in Dornbusch (1976a), Claassen (1980), Clements (1981), Baltensperger and Böhm (1982).

2) This is the basis of Balassa's (1964) argument for a systematic productivity bias in PPP. He argues that nontraded goods are relatively more expensive in high productivity (rich) countries. Thus, a PPP calculation based on overall price levels and not only on prices for traded goods would indicate that the rich country's currency is overvalued. Empirical support for this hypothesis is provided by Clements and Semudram (1983); see also the mixed empirical evidence of Officer (1979b).

Nevertheless, the conventional monetarist version of the monetary approach abstracts from changes in relative prices. They are assumed to be determined in the real sector by factors which can be taken as given without loss of essential information.[1)]

The monetarist argument takes the law of one price as well as a stable relationship between prices of traded and nontraded goods as a good approximation to reality. Hence, an increase in the price level, triggered off by monetary measures has no lasting influence on the terms of trade and thus on the CA. While the exchange rate reflects primarily international differences in money growth, the CA is determined by real factors. Therefore, the CA and the exchange rate are mutually independent.

The abstraction from terms of trade effects and the dominant influence of monetary variables are the main characteristics of the monetary approach.[2)] For this reason eq. (5) is reduced to money supply and demand.

$$(5') \qquad e = \left[{}^{M}/_{M^*}\right] \left[\frac{L^*(r^*, Y^*)}{L(r, Y)}\right]$$

Equation (5') states that an increase in the domestic money supply leads, ceteris paribus, to an equiproportional depreciation of the domestic currency. An increase in relative domestic real income induces an appreciation because of the higher demand for real balances and, finally, a positive nominal interest differential reduces the demand for real balances and leads to a depreciation.

---

1) This is not to say that these influences are not seen by proponents of the monetary approach, see, for example, Frenkel (1976, p. 219), Niehans (1979, 1980), Mussa (1976). A good example for the monetarist electicism, used in stating a "monetary impulse theory" is given by Myhrmann (1976, pp. 185). Frenkel (1981b) attempts to test the hypothesis of stable internal price ratios. In his test the ratio of the cost of living to the wholesale price index is used as proxy for the internal price ratio P_N/P_T. He concludes that over the period from June 1973 to July 1979 the internal relative prices "have not changed much in the U.S. and the U.K., they have changed somewhat in Germany and have changed dramatically in France." Frenkel (1981b, p. 153)

2) See, among others, Bilson (1979a), Myhrmann (1976).

Before we examine the functional relationship described by eq. (5') further, we attempt to show that even in a such restrictive setting the CA may gain influence on the exchange rate. When we accept the framework given by eq. (5'), the only way in which the CA can affect the exchange rate is by affecting the money market variables. The following reasons can be put forward for such an influence.

First, CA developments may lead to shifts in relative money demand functions. This point can be illustrated by referring to the function of the US dollar as international vehicle currency for trade transactions. With a large part of world trade denominated in US dollars, an increase in the volume of international trade can raise the demand for dollars relative to other currencies and thus induce a dollar appreciation. Likewise, we may start by observing that over the last decade oil has played a pivotal role in the CA development of many countries. World oil trade is transacted in dollars. A sharp rise in oil prices should, therefore, raise the relative demand for dollars. On the other hand, a reduction in national oil bills should lower the demand for dollars.[1)]

The second line of argument is more often mentioned in the literatur. It is based on the fact that a domestic CA surplus is associated with a transfer of wealth from foreign residents to domestic residents. This wealth transfer can increase the relative demand for domestic money directly if wealth enters money demand functions and domestic residents have a stronger preference for domestic money than foreign residents.[2)] If wealth is an argument in consumption functions a domestic CA surplus raises domestic expenditures and thus domestic income and the transaction demand for domestic money.[3)]

---

1) On this argument see Frankel (1983, p. 95).

2) This effect is considered in Porter (1979), Dornbusch (1980b, p. 164), and Frankel (1983). Bilson (1979b, p. 63) too acknowledges wealth effects in money demands, though only in a casual remark. Recent empirical evidence supporting the importance of wealth in determining the demand for money is quoted in United Kingdom Central Statistical Office (1981, p. 111). This relationship is discussed further in connection with the portfolio balance approach in chapters 3. and 5.

3) See, for example, Dornbusch (1980b, pp. 154), Frankel (1983). The role of CA induced wealth effects in the consumption function will be discussed in section 3.4.

Although these effects are normally not considered in monetary models, they show that it is possible to rationalize a relation between the CA and the exchange rate while adhering to the fundamentals of the monetary approach.

We return to eq. (5'). The assumed relationship between real income, interest rates and the exchange rate stands in apparent contradiction to the traditional Keynesian assumptions as used, e.g., in Mundell-Fleming models. According to the Keynesian view, a change in the nominal money supply is always associated with a change in real balances and hence with movements in the real interest rate. Thus, the liquidity-preference function describes a negative relationship between money supply and the (real) interest rate. Consequently, an increase in the domestic interest rate is explained by a tight monetary policy. The induced higher demand for domestic financial assets leads to an appreciation of the home currency. Thus, Keynesian analysis refers implicitly to times of relatively stable prices during which inflationary expectations, reflected in nominal interest rates, can be neglected.[1)]

The monetary approach, on the other hand, refers to times of full employment with perpetual inflation. If agents are used to permanent price increases, a rise in nominal money supply leads quickly to higher goods prices and inflationary expectations and hence has no influence on the real sector even in the short run. The Keynesian assumption of money illusion is rejected as unrealistic and the real interest rate is taken as independent of monetary disturbances. With freedom from money illusion and efficient money markets, an increase in the nominal interest rate reflects increased inflationary expectations caused by an expansive monetary policy. It follows that a higher nominal interest differential $(r - r^*)$ indicates an expected reduction in the value of the home currency and is connected, therefore, with a decline in the domestic money demand and an immediate depreciation of the home currency.

---

1) While the assumption of relatively rigid prices and price expectations over a longer period seems to be reasonable only in situations of protracted unemployment, it can be justified also in full employment situations for the short run as long as agents are taken by surprise by monetary measures or entrepreneurs do not see possibilities for an immediate price adjustment, see McKinnon (1979, pp. 177). For a theoretical analysis of differences between nominal and real interest rates in periods of inflation see Claassen (1978, pp. 7), Neumann (1973, pp. 272).

Hence the nominal interest rate is positively related to the domestic nominal money supply.[1)]

In Keynesian models, an increase in the level of real income leads by means of an induced CA deficit to a depreciation whereas in monetary models the appreciation effect follows from an "incipient capital account surplus brought about by the increase in the demand for money"[2)] which dominates any CA deficit.[3)]

Theoretical arguments for and against the validity of the monetary approach and PPP theory are by now almost a special discipline within the field of international economics. The discussion is mainly concerned with index problems,[4)] the validity of the law of one price,[5)] the direction of causality between exchange rates and prices,[6)] and the overlapping general problem of long run neutrality of monetary measures.

---

1) For further analyses of these different views see Bilson (1979a), Frenkel (1976). An attempt to connect both views can be found in Frankel (1979a). His empirical test on the DM/US dollar rate for the period 1974 - 1978 supports the Keynesian view with respect to the three-month money market nominal interest differential and the monetarist view with respect to long run interest rates. In an update of his test through December 1980 this evidence was confirmed. His results, however, for the money supplies and relative income do not support the monetary theory for the extended period. See Frankel (1983).

2) Bilson (1979a, p. 203)

3) For a short discussion of this relationship see Branson (1980) and the literature quoted there. This view has become increasingly popular over the last years also outside the economic theory. For example Steuer (1983, p. 88) writes in "Wirtschaftswoche": "Denn über den Leistungsbilanzsaldo entscheiden bei freien Wechselkursen ... nicht die Wettbewerbsfähigkeit, der Entwicklungsgrad oder das Inflationstempo einer Volkswitschaft, sondern der Saldo des Geld- und Kapitalverkehrs mit dem Ausland."

4) For a general discussion on this point see Frenkel (1978). A monetarist solution of the index problem is provided by Bilson (1979a, p. 206): "the 'true' price index is an unobservable variable whose ratio is defined to be the exchange rate - the exchange rate is, by definition, the correct relative price with which to measure the relative purchasing power of two currencies."

5) The law of one price was attacked on empirical grounds by Isard (1977, 1978) and Magee (1979) among others. It should be noted that this is not an argument against PPP theory or the monetary approach as long as commodity arbitrage is not quoted as the adjustment mechanism, see Frenkel (1976, p. 203), Niehans (1980, p. 214). But it is an argument against the assumption of constant relative prices.

6) See next page.

An exposition of this discussion is beyond the scope of this thesis. The literature developed the following three conditions under which the PPP theory and the monetary approach, respectively, may yield reasonable results in explaining actual exchange rate movements.[1)]

a. Changes in real variables are of low importance relative to monetary disturbances.

b. Money is the only asset exogenously supplied by the government. Strict validity of the monetary approach cannot be assumed in the presence of nonmonetary government debt.[2)]

c. The time period under consideration is long enough to allow for temporary adjustments.

One of the most important shortcomings of the monetary approach is its long run orientated, comparative-static character. Thus, in most cases it is not possible to derive meaningful results for the short run and the dynamic exchange rate behaviour in the medium run from PPP considerations. As it can be often found in economics, it is hard to say how long the "long run" actually is. The monetarist side, sometimes referring to times of hyperinflation, regards the transitional adjustment period as rather short whereas Keynesian economists

---

(footnote 6. last page). See, for example, Laidler (1976), Hammann (1980, p. 109). Proponents of the monetary approach have always argued that "the PPP-principle does not depend on direct causation", Niehans (1980, p. 214); see also Frenkel (1978, 1981b). This, however, renders PPP theory a "black box" model.

1) For a more detailed discussion on the following three conditions see, for example, Hammann (1980, pp. 106), Niehans (1980, p. 214).

2) This argument, well known since Metzler (1951), is stressed by Niehans (1980) and can also be found in Roper (1975), Kouri (1980, pp. 100), and Baltensperger and Böhm (1982, p. 20) as one of the conditions for long run neutrality of monetary measures.
Isard (1978, p. 26) concludes that "most models in which the menue of outside (or exogenously controlled) financial assets extends beyond money will not exhibit long-run neutrality." Later on we refer to this point in more detail.

stress the hypothetical character of the PPP equilibrium.[1)]

Finally, the question whether the monetary approach and PPP theory, respectively, provide reasonable explanations for the actual exchange-rate behaviour should also be judged from an empirical point of view. Although results of econometric tests are rather controversial because of the chosen sample period, the method of analysis and different data sets, three conclusions have been supported by most investigations.[2)]

a. There is a long run tendency of the exchange rate in the PPP direction. Thus, the monetary approach might be a useful tool in analyzing long run exchange rate behaviour.[3)]

b. Within the short period, roughly up to three years, large deviations from PPP are possible and most likely to occur in periods with strong influences from changes in real factors.
Referring to the exchange rate behaviour over the last years, the empirical content of the simple monetary approach is extremely poor. This is admitted by proponents of the monetary approach too: "... the monetary models appear to be incapable of explaining the volatile behaviour of exchange rates during the current float."[4)]

---

1) Niehans (1979, p. 204) estimates two or three years for the adjustment period, Claassen (1978, p. 40) one or two years, Isard (1978, p. 8) "several years". Lee (1976) analyses the price/exchange rate deviations for nine countries during the period 1900 - 1972 by a cross-average method. His results indicate that a change in exchange rates, larger than 10 per cent, produced PPP deviations for about two years. Based on Swiss and US data over the period from 1973 to 1977, Driskill (1981) calculated the long run to be approximately two to three years.

2) We draw here on results collected in Kohlhagen (1978) and Isard (1978) as well as on empirical studies quoted below.

3) It is interesting that Bilson (1978, p. 64) concludes from his test results for the DM/Pound Sterling rate over the period from 1970 to 1977: "The harsh truth is, consequently, that the monetary model does not improve upon a sophisticated PPP model as an exchange rate forecasting tool."

4) Bilson (1979, p. 205). The poor performance of the monetary model is also documented in Niehans (1979, p. 202), Genberg (1978), Black (1977, pp.37), Frenkel (1981b), Meese and Rogoff (1981), Gaab (1982), Frankel (1983), among others.

In a recent study, Dornbusch (1980b) tests the PPP theory directly and by estimating an equation similar to eq. (5') in this section for some major industrial countries over the period from 1973 to 1979. He concludes: "Not only does the short-term exchange rate deviate from a PPP path, but there are also cumulative deviations from that path that show substantial persistence."[1] Similar evidence in a number of other studies has led to conclusions like Machlup's (1980, p. 101): "The survival of the purchasing-power-parity in present-day discussions among international monetary economists is a sorry reflection of their critical judgment."

c. Exchange rate changes lead to changes in relative prices and competitiveness and hence they have considerable influence on the CA. This effect can last for a relatively long period.[2]

In the light of these results, Dornbusch's conclusion seems reasonable: "The evidence on PPP and the econometric evidence reported here leave little doubt that the monetary approach in the form of equation 3 (equation 5' in this section - the author) is an unsatisfactory theory of exchange rate determination. The key link between the exchange rate and PPP fails to hold, and any reasonable model must include a theory of real exchange rate determination."[3]

---

1) Dornbusch (1980b, p. 146), see also Dornbusch (1978) and Frenkel (1981a, 1981b) for similar results.

2) See Dornbusch and Krugman (1976), Dornbusch (1978, pp. 45), Artus and Young (1979, pp. 659), Frenkel (1981b, pp. 152), and also the short collection of real-exchange rate studies included in Harbrecht and Neumann (1979). Further empirical evidence for the 70's is quoted in Frankel (1983).

3) Dornbusch (1980b, p. 151).

2.2. Short Run: Interest Rate Parity

The inability of the long run orientated monetary approach to explain the volatile behaviour of exchange rates during the current float led to the development of short run theories which put special emphasis on the determination of interest rates and exchange rate expectations. Most of these theories take as a common starting-point the well-known interest rate parity (IRP) condition:[1)]

$$(1) \qquad r - r^{*} = \frac{f - e}{e}$$

f : forward exchange rate of one-period maturity;
e : spot exchange rate
r, r^{*} : domestic and foreign interest rate, respectively.

As a statement of covered IRP, eq. (1) assumes that in efficient financial markets in which capital is perfectly mobile and assets issued in different countries are free of default risk, the forward premium on the foreign currency must always equal the nominal interest differential. Any deviation from coverd IRP would imply unexploited profits and hence triggers off an off-setting adjustment process.[2)]

If it is now assumed that the forward exchange market is dominated by profit maximizing, risk neutral speculators who prevent any discrepancy between the forward rate and the expected future spot rate $\tilde{e}$, eq. (1) can be transformed to the condition for uncovered IRP. The forward rate becomes the market forecast of the expected future spot rate and, therefore, the forward premium is equivalent to the expected

---

1) Ignoring the term $1/(1 + r^{*})$ which is small for normal values of r^{*}. r, r^{*}, and f are defined over the same time interval.

2) Reviewing empirical evidence on covered IRP, Kohlhagen (1978,p. 9) concludes: "the covered interest differential is zero in the long run, or any deviations from interest parity are adequately explained by transaction costs or the non comparability of assets...". Isard (1978) mentions the importance of capital controls. For empirical evidence supporting covered IRP see Frenkel and Levich (1975, 1979), Niehans (1979).

rate of depreciation of the domestic currency d within the considered period:

$$(2) \qquad r - r^* = \frac{\tilde{e} - e}{e} = d$$

This equilibrium relationship has been applied in two quite different ways to determine the short run equilibrium exchange rate.

Within the monetarist equilibrium rational expectations approach (ERE) the forward premium, that is the expected rate of depreciation, determines the nominal interest differential.[1)] The theory starts with the assumption of perfectly flexible prices which preserve money market equilibrium at every point in time. But since the "true" price index is regarded as an unobservable variable, the exchange rate is taken as the correct relative price and hence as the right deflator in the money market equilibrium condition. PPP is guaranteed by definition and the exchange rate has to adjust at every moment to maintain money market equilibrium. This approach, however, leaves the interest differential exogenous. Through the IRP condition it is now possible to explain the interest rate differential by the expected rate of depreciation.[2)] The model is closed by the rational expectations assumption: the expected future spot rate and hence the expected rate of depreciation is defined by the spot rate predictions of the model itself.
The main results and implications of standard ERE models can be summarized as follows.

---

1) The term "equilibrium rational expectations approach" was created by Bilson (1979a, p. 206). Referring to the most popular advocates of the ERE theory, Frenkel and Bilson, Frankel (1979a, p. 610) uses the term "Chicago theorie". For a detailed description and empirical evidence see, for example, Frenkel (1976, 1981a), Bilson (1978, 1979a, 1979b), Hoffman and Schlagenhauf(1983). A rigouros mathematical treatment of a stochastic ERE model can be found in Mussa (1976).

2) Analogous arguments for a causality direction from the forward premium to interest rates were developed in the microeconomic theory of spot and forward rate determination. Kohlhagen (1978, p. 8), quoting Roll and Solnik (1975), reports: "dealers in Eurocurrency markets actually used (the interest rate parity 'theorem') to establish their prices." See also Isard (1978).

Since the actual spot rate is influenced largely by the expected rate of depreciation, defined by the model itself, it depends upon the current and expected future values of all exogenous variables. These variables are all included in the money market equilibrium condition. At constant real income, therefore, no room is left for real variables. The short run equilibrium is a discounted prediction of the long run equilibrium and, hence, there is no need to describe transitory adjustments.

The positive relationship between the domestic interest rate and the exchange rate follows from the assumption of perfectly flexible prices. It is built-in through the direct transmission of inflationary expectations from the expected rate of depreciation to the interest differential.[1)] Seen from this point of view, short run fluctuations in exchange rates must be the result of an unstable monetary policy. An increase in the money supply influences the exchange rate in two different ways at the same time: by an immediate and proportional depreciation effect, as it was shown in our discussion on the long run monetary approach, and by an induced additional expectations effect which depends on the expected future monetary growth. It is obvious that in ERE models exchange rate "overshooting" occures with respect to the actual increase in the money supply if speculators expect further increases. But "overshooting" with respect to the long run equilibrium exchange rate is ruled out by the rational expectations assumption.[2)]

---

1) That is assuming perfectly Fisherian expectations: the interest differential equals the forward premium which in turn equals the expected change in the exchange rate. See critical on that point Aliber (1975, pp. 369), Kohlhagen (1978, p. 9).

2) A consistent description of "destabilizing speculation" in this sense is given by Bilson (1979a, pp. 209): "If the central bank follows a strict monetary rule, then rational speculators will tend to enforce the equality between the actual exchange rate and the equilibrium rate defined by the monetary rule. On the other hand, if the exchange rate is fixed at a level that conflicts with the domestic monetary policies of the central bank, then rational speculators will appear to be destabilizing with respect to the parity, although they will not be destabilizing with respect to the equilibrium exchange rate."

In contrast to the ERE approach, Keynesian IRP models start with the assumption of sticky prices in the short run.[1] If the real income is pegged to the full employment level, the interest rate has to adjust to maintain continuous money market equilibrium. Since domestic and foreign bonds are assumed to be perfect substitutes on an uncovered basis, the exchange rate has to adjust continuously in order to balance expected net returns, that is, to preserve uncovered IRP.[2] The model can be closed with different assumptions about expectations formation. To allow for a consistent comparison with the ERE approach we refer to the case of rational expectations.[3]

Contrary to ERE models, a nonanticipated, once-for-all increase in the domestic money supply leads to an instantaneous depreciation which exceeds the depreciation necessary in long run equilibrium. The increase in the money stock causes an immediate fall in the interest rate. Thus, uncovered IRP requires an equiproportional reduction in the forward premium, that is, a reduction in the expected rate of depreciation. Since in the new long run equilibrium the exchange rate and the price level will exactly reflect the increase in the money supply according to PPP, the rationally expected spot rate (the forward rate) rises immediately and anticipates the long run depreciation.[4] Therefore, the short run depreciation must exceed ("overshoot") the long run equilibrium depreciation. In other words "... the extent of that depreciation has to be sufficient to give rise to the anticipation of appreciation at a just sufficient a rate to offset the reduced domestic interest rate."[5] Since prices adjust over time to the

---

1) The Keynesian approach described here is closely associated with the seminal works of Dornbusch. We refer especially to Dornbusch (1976a, 1976b). A similar model can be found in Claassen (1980, pp. 429). For an extensive discussion of model properties and good critizism see Ingram (1978). Roots of this approach lie first of all in Mundell (1963) and in the expectations augmented versions Niehans (1975) and Argy and Porter (1972).

2) In models of the Dornbusch-type the uncovered IRP becomes a complete equilibrium condition for the market of domestic and foreign interest-bearing assets.

3) For an adaptive expectations mechanism see Dornbusch (1976a, 1978), Ingram (1978).

4) The long run homogeneity result follows from the complete model structure, see Dornbusch (1976b).

5) Dornbusch (1976b, p. 1168).

the increased money supply, the interest rate rises and the exchange appreciates on the way to the long run equilibrium. The ultimate effect consists in an equiproportional increase in prices and the exchange rate.

Having described the fundamental mechanisms underlying Keynesian and monetarist applications of uncovered IRP, we summarize in a short comparison of both standard models.

In Dornbusch's model overshooting occurs because of the delayed price adjustment in the goods market.[1] Since the price index for domestic output is used as deflator for money balances and PPP does not continuously hold on that basis, the negative liquidity effect of the increased money stock on the interest rate plays the crucial part in determinig the impact effect on the exchange rate.
In the ERE model the liquidity effect is ruled out by the assumption of perfectly elastic prices. At constant real interest rates, therefore, differences in nominal interest rates can reflect only differences in expected inflation rates.

In the ERE model the entire adjustment process which follows an unexpected exogenous disturbance takes place at a point in time. Hence, expectations are mainly directed towards future monetary policies.
In Dornbusch's model, on the other hand, expectations are orientated towards the price adjustment period (which does not exist in the ERE approach) and, therefore, they depend on structural parameters of the economy like the interest elasticity of money demand or the price elasticity of the demand for domestic output.[2]
According to the different conceptions of the adjustment period, the monetary approach abstracts from changes in real variables in the long run as well as in the short run ERE version. In the Keynesian version, however, changes in real variables are considered as an important part of the dynamic adjustment process. "In the short run ..

1) Dornbusch's overshooting hypothesis constitudes the point of departure for many subsequent exchange rate models. A comprehensive presentation of the overshooting discussion is given by Levich (1981), and Frenkel and Rodríguez (1982).

2) An extension of this expectations horizon in an Keynesian framework is provided by McKinnon (1979, 1980).

... the monetary expansion does exert real effects on interest rates, the terms of trade, and aggregate demand."[1] Nevertheless, the analysis of the adjustment process confines itself to an explanation of the price movements towards the long run equilibrium. No attention is paid to the CA.[2]

---

1) Dornbusch (1976b, p. 1171).

2) Although Dornbusch notes short-term changes in the terms of trade, the CA contributes to his analysis only in so far as the instantaneous depreciation following a monetary shock leads to a rise in the demand for domestic output and hence to a subsequent price increase. But it is not clear if this effect works by means of a domestic substitution effect between imports and domestic goods or by a CA surplus induced by a rise in exports. See on this point Claassen (1978, p. 173), Ingram (1978).

2.3. Summary and Some Remarks on Asset Substitutability and Wealth Effects

In the last two sections we attempted to give a short overview of standard versions of currently prevailing exchange rate theories: the long run monetary approach and short run IRP theories.

The monetarists regard the exchange rate as a pure monetary variable. As relative price of different currencies the exchange rate is determined in the short run as well as in the long run exclusively by the relative supplies of and demands for these currencies. The short run ERE approach may be considered by virtue of the rational expectations assumption as a discounted long run model. Exchange rate expectations are related only to variables included in the money market equilibrium condition. Thus, an analysis of exchange rate behaviour can be conducted independently of CA and goods market considerations. Real factors obtain influence on the exchange rate only if they work through changes in the money demand. According to the basic monetarist hypothesis of the dominance of monetary impulses, alterations in real variables, however, are considered subordinate and of negligible importance compared with relative rates of money growth. The empirical evidence on PPP and real exchange rate movements does not appear to support a pure monetary explanation of exchange rate behaviour over the last years.[1)]

The dominant role of asset markets in Dornbusch's Keynesian model, on the other hand, is merely the result of an assumed higher adjustment speed in asset markets than in goods markets. A pure stock equilibrium approach is therefore applied only in the short run: with

---

1) It should be mentioned, however, that there are almost no empirical tests on complete monetarist rational expectations models. An exception is Gaab (1982). His test on the DM/US dollar rate from 1974.10 to 1981.5 suggests that the relative money supplies and real income levels follow approximately a random walk. The estimation of the ERE model based on this finding, however, yields rather poor results. Hoffman and Schlagenhauf(1983) find that the relevant monetary variables for the US dollar/DM, US dollar/French franc, and US dollar/Pound Sterling generally followed a differenciated AR(1) process with an autoregressive parameter greater than zero for the absolute change in the variables for the period from 1974.6 to 1979.12. Their subsequent test on the ERE model seems to support the model.

sticky prices and quantities in goods markets and well-developed, efficient capital markets with a high degree of capital mobility, asset stock-equilibrium is reached much faster than flow equilibrium in the market of goods. Hence it is possible to ignore the goods sector while analyzing the short run determination of exchange rates. Although the money market plays a central role also in this approach, money market equilibrium is considered only as one part of the complete asset market equilibrium. But since domestic and foreign interest-bearing assets are assumed to be perfect substitutes, their influence on the exchange rate is sufficiently taken into account by the uncovered IRP condition.[1)]

In the medium run, Keynesian full employment models focus on the dynamic price adjustment which is regarded as the most important factor in the transition from the short to the long perspective. Since a long run stationary state requires both stock and flow equilibrium, that is equilibrium in goods and asset markets, interactions between the financial and the real sector are taken into account. Nevertheless, the role of the CA is limited to a component of goods demand which has some influence on the dynamic price adjustment but no direct influence on asset markets and hence on the exchange rate. Accordingly, research on the CA focuses on the causality direction from the exchange rate to the CA. This research is especially engaged in investigations on the relationship between exchange rates, relative prices and competitiveness, and the relevance of "J-curve" and "ratchet" effects.[2)]

Empirical evidence on price adjustments in goods markets and the efficiency of capital markets supplies some justification for an emphasis on asset markets in the short run.[3)] The Keynesian assumption, therefore, constitutes an adequate background for a more detailed short run asset market analysis. On the other hand, the subordinate role of the CA is not a mandatory conclusion of every asset

---

1) Yet, this can be regarded as an extension of pure money market models toward a broader portfolio view.

2) For a good discussion on these points see Artus and Crockett (1978), Artus and Young (1979), Goldstein (1980), and Ueda (1983).

3) The sticky-price assumption is by now almost generally accepted in the literature. For empirical evidence see Frenkel (1981b, p. 161), Frankel (1979, 1983), Gaab (1982), and Artus (1981, 1982).

asset market approach. As we now attempt to show, this outcome is largely due to the assumption of perfect substitutability between domestic and foreign interest-bearing assets and to the neglect of wealth effects in asset demands.

Perfect substitutability of domestic and foreign interest-bearing assets is necessary for the validity of uncovered IRP, which builds the backbone of the short run theories described above. Uncovered foreign-currency denominated assets are considered as perfect substitutes for domestic assets if differences in interest returns are exactly matched by the expected rate of depreciation of the home currency. In extension to the case of covered IRP, perfect substitutability of uncovered assets requires the absence of any currency risk or risk neutral agents.[1)] Perfect substitutability implies that asset holders are indifferent with respect to the composition of their portfolios as long as expected net returns are equal. The slightest change in net returns would produce indefinite capital movements which, in the extreme case, lead to a complete switch from domestic to foreign assets and vice versa.

The implications of this assumption are well known.[2)] With perfect substitutability between domestic and foreign interest-bearing assets the relative supply of nominal outside assets others than monies has no direct influence on the exchange rate. At a given foreign interest rate, an increase in net domestic assets by a bond financed government deficit, or a rise in domestic holdings of net foreign assets by a CA surplus, can be neglected; equilibrium in the portfolio of interest-bearing assets is fully described by the demand side represented by the uncovered IRP rule.

If it is furthermore assumed that the supply of outside assets does not affect the demand for money, shifts in international wealth due to CA imbalances are irrelevant for the exchange rate.[3)]

---

1) Other reasons for deviations from uncovered IRP, like transaction costs, default or country risk, influence both covered and uncovered IRP and reduce the substitutability of covered assets as well, see Kohlhagen (1978), Solnik (1980).

2) See, for example, Dornbusch (1982a), Frankel (1983).

3) Based on these relationships, Eaton and Turnovsky (1983, p. 557) point at some furthergoing implications: "Thus when uncovered IRP obtains a small country can run a perpetual current account deficit without affecting its exchange rate or its interest rate. If, in (continued next page)

With a view to economic policy, the perfect substitutability assumption implies that any attempt to influence the exchange rate by direct foreign exchange market intervention while pursuing at the same time an independent interest rate policy is futile.

But perfect substitutability seems to be more the limiting case than an adequate description of the reality. The abstraction from risk by assuming perfect foresight or risk neutral agents has been frequently attacked in the literature.[1] Since future exchange rate movements can not be known with certainty, exchange rate risk is inherent in any uncovered asset position denominated in foreign currency. Even in the case of perfect foresight with respect to future exchange rates, large deviations of the actual exchange rate from PPP give rise to relative inflation risk.[2]

"At the limit, if the exchange rate has been fluctuating widely, the degree of risk (uncertainty) may be so high that an increase in the expected relative yield on domestic bonds caused by a rise in the domestic interest rate will have only a small effect on foreigners' willingness to buy such bonds. High risk could isolate the various financial markets more efficiently than would capital controls.
In such a case, an increase in the domestic interest rate may fail to have much effect on the spot exchange rate, whether or not it has any effect on the expected future rate." Artus (1976, p. 316).

Currency risk results from the variability of real return due to uncertain inflation and fluctuations in exchange rates and gives rise to portfolio diversification between assets denominated in different currencies. Consequently, many multinational enterprises and banks hold large volumes of bonds denominated in various currencies. These bonds are rarely viewed as perfect substitutes but as components of an optimal portfolio.[3]

(footnote 3. last page continued) addition to uncovered IRP, asset supplies do not affect the demand for money, the exchange rate and the price level evolve independently of the government deficit and the balance of payments on current account outside of steady state.

1) See, for example, Artus and Crockett (1978), Aliber (1975, 1976), Black (1977, pp. 35), Fellner (1980), Solnik (1979).

2) For a detailed classification of various risks involved in international financial transactions see Wihlborg (1978), Kohlhagen(1978).

3) This perception has led to the development of a wide range of models dealing with optimal mean-variance portfolios based on utility maximisation with risk averse agents. The classical reference is Markowitz (1970). For a recent application see Kouri and De Macedo (1978). The microeconomic mean-variance approch has been applied to a macroeconomic portfolio model by Dornbusch (1980c); see also Dornbusch (1982b).

If asset holders regard bonds denominated in different currencies as imperfect substitutes one should expect a risk premium in uncovered IRP. On an econometric level, however, it is very difficult to find clear evidence for the existence or nonexistence of risk premiums. The main problem in empirical testings is that the risk premium assumption cannot be tested separately but only jointly with assumptions about exchange rate expectations. Since this is an important point for the relevance of portfolio balance models, we elaborate this argument somewhat further.

Imperfect substitutability implies the existence of a risk premium so that uncovered IRP does not hold. As expectations are not observeable, it is not possible to test uncovered IRP directly. The conventional way of testing the risk premium assumption, therefore, consists in testing (Fama) market efficiency. Consider the following efficiency equation:[1)]

$$E_t\,(e_{t+1}/I_t) = f_t^{t+1} + \varphi_t = e_{t+1} + u_{t+1} \tag{1}$$

$E_t\,(e_{t+1}/I_t)$	: Market expectations in time t about the exchange rate in t+1, based on the set of information available in time t (I_t). E_t denotes a general expectations operator.
f_t^{t+1}	: Forward rate in time t for delivery in time t+1.
e_{t+1}	: Actual exchange rate in time t+1.
φ_t	: Risk premium.
u_{t+1}	: Error term.

1) The concept of efficient markets traces back to Fama (1970, 1976). More detailed descriptions of the different forms of Fama efficiency and further implications of this conception can be found in Kohlhagen (1978), Sweeny (1978), and Isard (1978).

In a Fama-efficient exchange market,[1] expectations about the future exchange rate incorporate all available information, and these expectations are fully reflected in the forward rate. Thus, Fama-efficiency presumes the absence of a risk premium.

$$(2) \qquad E_t\ (e_{t+1}/I_t) \ = \ f_t^{t+1}$$

Furthermore, in an efficient market it is not possible for a single speculator to use existing information in such a way that his predictions are systematically superior to the market predictions.
The market forecast, f_t^{t+1}, is the best possible prediction of the future exchange rate. This, however, requires that the market uses all relevant, available information and processes this information by applying the best possible model. The best model is the "true" model and only rational expectations are truly unbiased estimations for the future exchange rate: "The virtue of the rational expectations assumption is that it is the only assumption which eliminates consistent profits from foreign exchange speculation."[2]

In this case, the forward rate is an unbiased prediction of the future exchange rate. Deviations of f_t^{t+1} from e_{t+1} are possible only through nonanticipated, stochastic disturbances occurring in the time between t and t+1. The error term u_{t+1} reflects the exchange rate impact of such stochastic news and thus is white noise.

$$(3) \qquad f_t^{t+1} \ = \ e_{t+1} + u_{t+1}$$

As exchange rate expectations are not observable, empirical tests of the efficient market hypothesis concentrate on econometric tests of the relationship between f_t^{t+1} and e_{t+1}. Such estimations, however,

---

1) Conventionally, Fama market efficiency is subdivided in weak-form, semi strong-form, and strong-form efficiency. This distinction defines the different information sets - past prices, public information and all available information - on which expectations are based. Our presentation may refer to strong or semi strong efficiency.

2) Bilson (1979b, p. 62).

neglect the assumption made in eq. (2) and, therefore, test a joint hypothesis.[1)] Thus, it is theoretically inconsistent to interpret empirical support for the efficient market hypothesis as support for the rational expectations assumption or as support for the assumption of a nonexistence of risk premiums. This can be illustrated if we assume risk averse agents. In this case,exchange rate expectations are not fully incorporated in the forward rate. The difference between $E_t\ (e_{t+1}/I_t)$ and f_t^{t+1} defines the risk premium φ.

$$(2') \qquad E_t\ (e_{t+1}/I_t) \;=\; f_t^{t+1} + \varphi_t$$

Applying eq. (2') to eq. (3) yields

$$(3') \qquad f_t^{t+1} \;=\; e_{t+1} \;+\; (u_{t+1} - \varphi_t)$$

The error term in paranthesis includes now a news component u_{t+1} and the risk component φ_t. Even if the complete term is estimated as white noise, this does not necessarily imply that both components are separately serially uncorrelated. Thus, it is in general not possible to conclude backwards from an empirically unbiased forward rate to the nonexistence of a risk premium or to rational exchange rate expectations. Likewise, empirical evidence on market inefficiency can be viewed as an indication of nonrational expectations and/or as an indication of imperfect substitutability due to risk aversion. This argument suggests that the interpretation of market efficiency tests either as evidence on rational expectations (assuming that assets are perfect substitutes) or as evidence on substitutability (assuming that expectations are formed rationally) depends to a large extent on the theoretical outlook of the judge.[2)]

---

1) This relationship is also reckognized by Frenkel (1981a, pp. 670), Levich (1981, pp. 17), and Frankel (1983, footnote 3.).

2) According to the Jurgensen Report, such difficulties in interpreting market efficiency tests arose in the US Treasury Working Group on Exchange Market Intervention too, see Jurgensen Report quoted in Williamson (1983, p. 50). See also Frankel (1983, footnote 3.).

Nevertheless, there seems to be little reason to attribute the existence of systematic and exploitable prediction errors to a systematic and consistent ignorance and/or misinterpretation of available (low-cost) information. Such errors would be easy to detect for speculators by observing actual exchange rate developments.[1)] Therefore, we consider the risk argument and hence, imperfect substitutability of assets as a more convincing explanation of potential market inefficiencies.

The empirical evidence on efficiency in foreign exchange markets is mixed. Over the last years, however, there has been an increasing number of studies indicating that market inefficiency is indeed observable in foreign exchange markets. These studies generally support the hypothesis of time-varying risk premiums and thus indicate that it is justified to consider assets denominated in different currencies as imperfect substitutes.[2)]

With imperfect substitutability expected rates of return on domestic and foreign bonds can differ so that the uncovered IRP condition ceases to characterize portfolio equilibrium. This provides some scope for an independent domestic interest rate: to some extent the central bank may influence the exchange rate and the interest rate separately.

---

1) The important point of this argument is that nonrationality which causes market inefficiency will be perceivable by the agents. On the other hand, it is possible to show that nonrational expectations are compatible also with (econometric) market efficiency. In this case, there are no forecasting errors to perceive and thus there is no incentive to correct expectations. This second line of argument is discussed under the headings of "extraneous beliefs", "the peso problem", and "rational bubbles". A comprehensive view on these three issues is provided by Dornbusch (1982a, pp. 13, 1983, pp. 18).

2) The earlier literature on market efficiency in foreign exchange markets is surveyed by Kohlhagen (1978, pp. 25). According to Kohlhagen, risk premiums were found by Solnik (1974), Roll and Solnik (1975), Grauer, Litzenberger, and Stehle (1978). More recent empirical evidence and further literature supporting the risk premium view is given in Stockmann (1978), Solnik (1979), Meese and Singleton (1980), Stein (1980, pp. 530), Dooley and Isard (1982, p. 274), Eaton and Turnovsky (1983, p. 556). An excellent presentation supporting the view that foreign exchange markets exhibit inefficiencies is provided by the study of the US Treasury Working Group on Exchange Market Intervention (Jurgensen Report, 1983). The relevant parts of this study are quoted in Williamson (1983, pp. 49). For an opposite view on market efficiency see Frenkel (1981a), Bilson (1979b).

Furthermore, not all exchange rate movements need to be related to monetary disturbances. For example, "if money demand is independent of wealth and expected yields on foreign assets, shifts in asset preferences between domestic and foreign securities will alter exchange rates with no effect whatsoever on the monetary sector."[1)]
Asset market equilibrium has to be defined not only in terms of relative demands but also in terms of relative supplies of outstanding domestic and foreign interest-bearing assets. Changes on the supply side brought about, for example, by a bond financed government budget deficit or a domestic CA surplus achieve through induced portfolio adjustments direct influence on interest rates and exchange rates. Since the CA indicates the rate at which the economy in the aggregate is adding to its net external assets it becomes an important portfolio and hence exchange rate determinant. Moreover, if it can be shown that the international redistribution of wealth through CA imbalances constitutes an important factor of exchange rate determination, then it seems reasonable to assume that exchange rate expectations will also be influenced by the CA. If, for example, asset holders expect the CA position of a country to deteriorate, that is, they expect a decrease in the country's net stock of foreign assets, this may generate expectations of a certain influence on the exchange rate. Since anticipated exchange rate movements have an important impact on expected net returns and thus on portfolio dispositions, the effect on expectations can constitute another channel for the CA to influence the exchange rate.

In the next chapter we investigate possible interactions between asset markets and the CA in some more detail. During this analysis we abstract largely from effects of expectations and concentrate on the wealth redistribution effect of the CA. The relationship between the CA and exchange rate expectations will be considered explicitly in chapter 4.

---

1) Dornbusch and Krugman (1976, p.556).

3. Portfolio Balance and Wealth Redistribution Effects of the Current Account

3.1. The Basic Structure

Over the next four sections our discussion will focus on the exchange rate impact of CA induced wealth effects. All of the following models start from a basic accounting identity: imbalances in a country's CA correspond to changes in the country's net foreign asset position. The only way to change the level of net foreign claims and liabilities is by running an imbalanced CA. Since net claims and liabilities to the foreign sector can be regarded as wealth components, the counterpart of a CA surplus is a transfer of wealth from foreign residents to domestic residents. International shifts in wealth due to CA imbalances, however, can be embodied in various sorts of assets denominated in various currencies.

In the simplest case, one can make the assumption that there is only one internationally traded asset. From the point of view of a small country it is reasonable to assume further that this asset is denominated in foreign currency and thus, for reasons discussed above, represents an imperfect substitute for domestic currency assets. The assumption of only one internationally traded asset also implies that residents of the small country "... are the only ones who wish to hold domestically denominated assets. The domestic country is assumed to be too small for its assets to be of interest to foreign residents." [1] Consequently, the net stocks of foreign-currency assets held by domestic residents can be changed only by means of an imbalanced CA. There is no international trade in assets denominated in different currencies, and the problem of currency of denomination of CA transactions is assumed away. Although this assumption is in most cases rather unrealistic, it allows a clear exposition of the basic relationships and, therefore, it has been applied in the vast majority of portfolio balance models. The presentation over the following four sections, too, proceeds from the supposition of only one internationally traded asset. In chapter 5., however, we will drop this assumption.

---

1) Frankel (1983, pp. 97-98).

To clarify the fundamental interactions between asset market equilibrium and the CA, it seems reasonable to start with a simple stock-flow model.[1)] The model is based on the following rather restrictive assumptions. Full employment is always guaranteed by flexible prices and wages. Since real investments are excluded and labour is fully employed, output is fixed at the full employment level Y.
All goods produced and consumed are internationally traded. The"small" home country is a price taker, so that the overall price level P is equal to the exchange rate e.[2)]
The asset menue is restricted to domestic and foreign money. It is assumed that foreigners do not hold domestic money. Since there are no interest-bearing assets, the only rate of return relevant in this model is the expected rate of depreciation (inflation) of the home currency π.[3)]

Domestic absorbtion is equal to the sum of private consumption C and government expenditure G

$$(1) \qquad A = C + G = C(\overset{+}{Y-T}, \overset{+}{W}) + T + m\, M/P$$

An increase in real disposable income Y-T or in the stock of real financial wealth W increases private consumption. Government real expenditure G is determined by the sum of real tax revenues T and the growth of the money stock $\dot{M}/P$ where $\dot{M}/P$ is equal to the real government budget deficit.[4)] The government fixes the rate of change in the money stock $m = \dot{M}/M$ and the real tax revenue, and adjusts real expenditure accordingly. It follows for the government expenditure function $G=T+m\, M/P$.

---

1) Although some variations are included, the following model is identical to the model of Kouri (1976). Good descriptions and extensions can be found in Schadler (1977), Black (1977), Kouri (1980, 1983). See also the similar models Niehans (1977) with slow portfolio adjustment, Rodríguez (1980) with trade flows incorporated in an rational expectations mechanism, Calvo and Rodríguez (1977) for a treatment with traded and nontraded goods, and Frenkel and Rodríguez (1982) who stress the degree of substitution among assets.

2) The foreign price of traded goods is in the following normalized to 1. Hence, $P = eP_T^*$ and, with a given $P_T^* = 1$, $e = P$.

3) π = expected $\dot{P}/P$ = expected $\dot{e}/e$.

4) Kouri assumes that the central bank acquires all government debt so that the nominal budget deficit is equal to the change in the money supply.

Real wealth consists of domestic real balances M/P and foreign assets (money) F.[1)]

$$(2) \qquad W = M/P + F$$

In this framework the CA reduces to the trade account B. The trade account surplus corresponds to the excess of domestic output over domestic absorbtion.

$$(3) \qquad B = Y - A = Y - C(Y-T, W) - T - m\,M/P$$

At given real income, the change in the trade balance is defined by the change in absorbtion. Substituting eq. (2) in eq. (1) and differentiating the result yields [2)]

$$(4) \qquad \dot{A} = \dot{T}(1 - \overset{+}{C}_{Y-T}) + (\overset{+}{C}_W + m)\,M/P\,(\hat{M} - \hat{P}) + C_W\,\dot{F}$$

For given values of M, T, and F, absorbtion can be described as a decreasing function of the exchange rate. The slope is given by

$$dA/de = -(C_W + m)(M/P^2) < 0$$

An increase in the exchange rate (a devaluation) leads to a lower value of real wealth and hence reduces absorbtion and improves the trade account.[3)] This relationship is shown by the DD curve in figure 1.

---

1) The real value of F is defined in terms of purchasing power. Since the exchange rate and the price level move strictly together, a change in the exchange rate does not alter the purchasing power real value of F. This can be seen when we write for the nominal domestic wealth $PW = M + eF$ with $e = P$.

2) A subscript denotes a partial derivative $dY/dX = Y_X$. Mathematical symbols are explained on page 5.

3) The slope of the DD curve can be derived from eq. (1) as follows. $dA/de = C_W\,(dW/de) + m\,(-M/P^2)$ where $dW/de = -M/P^2$. This yields $dA/de = (C_W + m)(-M/P^2)$ which corresponds to the equation given above. As can be seen by the slope of DD, the reduction in absorbtion is not only due to the reduction in private consumption but also to the lower value of government debt issues and hence to a fall in real government expenditure.

At the point of intersection of the DD curve with the vertical line for the fixed output the trade account is in balance.
An increase in e reduces real wealth and absorbtion and leads to a trade account surplus. Since foreign residents do not hold domestic money, a trade account surplus is not only equal to a net accumulation of foreign assets, it constitutes also the only way in which foreign assets can be acquired. The trade account establishes the connection between the real and the financial sector. Equation (4) is used to determine the change in the stock of foreign assets.

Asset market equilibrium is described by the following market clearing conditions.

(5) $L(\overset{-}{\pi}, \overset{+}{Y}, \overset{+}{W}) = M/P$ money market

(6) $f(\overset{+}{\pi}, \overset{+}{Y}, \overset{+}{W}) = F$ foreign asset market

Portfolio equilibrium is reached when the domestic demand for money equals the stock of real balances, and when the demand for foreign assets equals the stock of foreign assets. Both asset demands are defined as positive functions of real income and real wealth. An increase in the expected rate of depreciation of the domestic currency increases the demand for foreign assets and reduces the demand for domestic money. Asset holders are assumed to adjust instantaneously to changes in the portfolio determinants so that financial markets equilibrate very fast. Because of the wealth constraint only one of these equations is independent. Substituting the definition of real wealth from eq. (2) in eq. (6) yields

(7) $f(\overset{+}{\pi}, \overset{+}{Y}, M/P \overset{+}{+} F) = F$

It follows for the equilibrium change in the demand for foreign assets

(8) $\dot{f} = 1/L_W \, [\, f_\pi \, \dot{\pi} + f_W \, M/P \, (\hat{M} - \hat{P}) \,]$

Given π, F, and M, the exchange rate has to adjust to preserve portfolio equilibrium.[1] Equation (7) is used to determine the exchange rate.

Asset market equilibrium is illustrated in figure 1. by the MM curve. An increase in the exchange rate lowers the stock of real balances; the demand for foreign assets declines and a lower stock of foreign assets is required for portfolio equilibrium. The slope of the MM curve is therefore negative and depends on the desired ratio of real balances and foreign assets in the portfolio.[2]

$$df/de \;=\; -\, f_W \,/\, L_W \;\; (M/P^2) \;<\; 0$$

Equilibrium in goods and asset markets is shown in figure 1:

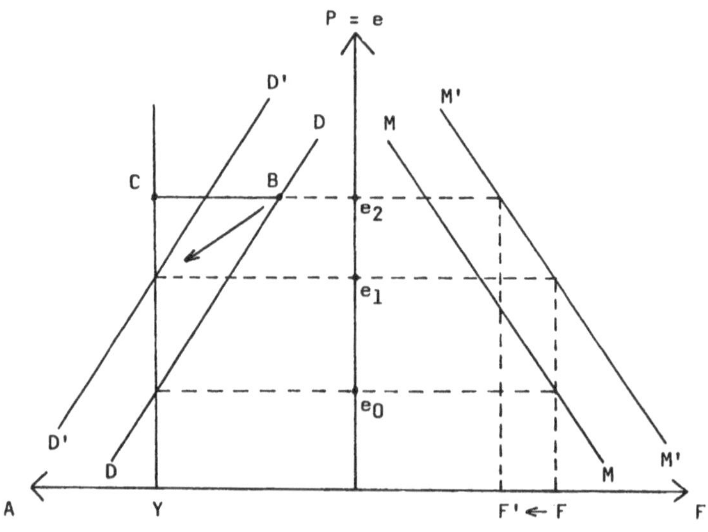

---

1) The wealth constraint given by eq. (2) implies $L_W + f_W = 1$; it follows $1 - f_W = L_W$. This expression is used in equation (8).

2) The slope of the MM curve can be derived from eq. (7) as follows. $dF/de = f_W\,(dW/de) = f_W\,(-M/P^2) + f_W\,(dF/de)$; in equilibrium dF=df, thus, $(df/de)\,(1-f_W) = f_W\,(-M/P^2)$. Substituting $L_W = 1-f_W$ yields the expression given above.

At the exchange rate e_0 absorbtion equals domestic output; the trade account is balanced and the stock of foreign assets remains at the initial level F which equals the domestic demand for foreign assets.[1)]

To point out clearly the dynamic interactions between the trade account and asset equilibrium, expectations are assumed to be stationary, that is, the expected future spot rate is set equal to the current spot rate. Furthermore, it is assumed that asset markets adjust instantaneously to exogenous disturbances whereas the reaction in goods markets takes time.

We consider first an exogenous, once-for-all increase in the domestic money supply by the central bank.[2)]
The rise in the money supply shifts the MM curve rightwards to M'M' and causes at the initial exchange rate e_0 portfolio disequilibrium: a higher stock of real balances would require a higher stock of foreign assets. Since F is fixed at the time of the disturbance, the exchange rate has to rise in order to reduce real balances to the initial level to keep real wealth unchanged and thereby preserve portfolio equilibrium. The immediate depreciation to e_1 has to be equal to the increase in money supply.
The increase in M shifts also the DD curve outwards. But since real wealth stays unchanged in the new asset equilibrium, absorbtion keeps unchanged too and the trade account remains balanced. The new equilibrium is reached at once.

This description seems to conform to traditional results of pure monetary analyses: PPP is guaranteed by assumption, and since the terms of trade remain constant and real wealth keeps unchanged no effects are spread to the real sector. Overshooting does not occur. This result follows from the assumption of a slow adjustment of the

---

1) A constant slope of the MM curve, as assumed in the diagram, presupposes that asset demand functions are linear homogeneous in wealth so that a change in W does not alter the desired proportions of both assets in the portfolio. In this case, f_W / L_W is constant for every W.

2) This disturbance, caused by "helicopter money", is not included in Kouri's paper.

goods market and the trade account to changes in wealth, but also from the restricted asset menue.[1)]

We assume now that the increase in the money supply is not autonomous but is the result of a central bank purchase of foreign exchange (central bank intervention in the foreign exchange market).
Kouri shows that this operation leads to different results compared to the case analysed above. An increase in M which is equiproportional to a decline in the stock of foreign assets shifts the MM curve to the right to M'M'. The higher stock of money requires at the given exchange rate a higher stock of foreign assets to keep portfolios in equilibrium: since overall wealth has not changed, the initial proportion between M/P and F has to be reestablished. Since F' is lower now than the initial stock F, the exchange rate has to depreciate to lower also real balances below the initial level. This means that the exchange rate depreciation must exceed the increase in the money supply. Therefore, the impact effect is a rise in the exchange rate to e_2.[2)]
At first, the proportional shift between money and foreign assets has no influence on absorbtion since at the initial exchange rate wealth is unchanged. Hence, the DD curve does not shift. After the instantaneous depreciation to e_2 real wealth has declined and absorbtion is reduced. Thus, at e_2 the trade account shows a surplus, $\overline{CB}$ in figure 1., which leads to an inflow of foreign assets and the stock of foreign assets begins to rise. It follows a dynamic interaction of asset and goods markets: when F rises the exchange rate declines again to keep portfolios in balance. The increased stock of real wealth increases absorbtion, reduces the trade account surplus and decelerates the further accumulation of foreign assets.

---

1) It is interesting that overshooting occurs if the trade account reacts quickly and the exchange rate adjustment takes time. If the increase in M leads only over time to a higher exchange rate, real balances will increase and absorbtion increases accordingly. This leads to a trade account deficit and hence to a reduction in foreign assets. Since F declines, the exchange rate has to depreciate overproportionally to the increase in M.

2) By solving eq. (8) for the change in the exchange rate it can be shown that the extent of overshooting depends essentially on the initial amount of both assets in the portfolios and on the relative response of both demand functions to wealth changes:

$$(de/dM)\Big|_{dM=-dF} = 1/M\ (1 + L_W / f_W) \quad \text{for } p = 1$$

(continued next page).

The dynamic adjustment consists in a movement along the M'M' curve and a gradual outwards shift of the DD curve to D'D' as the increase in F (with a declining rate during the adjustment) increases absorbtion and reduces the trade account surplus. During the adjustment the economy stays always on the M'M' schedule and on the shifting DD curve.

The final equilibrium is reached at the exchange rate e_1 with a balanced trade account and the initial stocks of real balances and foreign assets. The ultimate devaluation is equiproportional to the initial increase in M.

Besides the fact that overshooting is partly due to the stationarity of expectations,[1)] another reason for this phenomenon lies in the assumption of different adjustment speeds in goods and asset markets. The slow reaction of domestic absorbtion to changes in the value of real wealth is essential for overshooting. If all adjustments in both markets would work at the same time, then the impact depreciation, necessary to keep portfolios balanced, would lead immediately to a trade account surplus and an increase in F. The outwards shift of the DD curve during the exchange rate depreciation would establish portfolio equilibrium by an increase in F and a (smaller) rise in the exchange rate.

Summing up, the following results and implications of the Kouri model seem interesting.

(footnote 2. last page continued) If asset demand functions are assumed to be linear homogeneous in wealth (L_W, f_W = constant) overshooting can be seen as a function of the desired shares of both assets in portfolios. It is remarkable that this simple model is capable of producing essentially the same results as more elaborated models; see, for example, Calvo and Rodríguez (1977), Frenkel and Rodríguez (1982).

1) It can be shown that the assumption of rational expectations reduces overshooting, but cannot eliminate it totally: at the moment when the depreciation exceeds the long run equilibrium rate e_1 expectations of a later appreciation would come into existence and reduce the impact effect (the M'M' curve shifts to the left). Hence, the impact portfolio equilibrium will be reached at an exchange rate between e_1 and e_2 depending on the substitutability between the two assets. The following appreciation reduces the expected decline in the exchange rate (M'M' shifts to the right again) so that the final equilibrium is reached in e_1. See Schadler (1977, p. 271).

It was shown that relative adjustment speeds in goods and asset markets play an important role in short run exchange rate analysis. At a high adjustment speed in asset markets relative to goods markets, the exchange rate is determined at every point in time exclusively by the portfolio equilibrium conditions.

Exchange rate movements may feed back on goods markets and absorbtion through wealth effects, that is through exchange rate induced alterations in the real value of assets. This valuation effect occurs, with the assumption of continuous PPP, in the form of a real balance effect. If prices are assumed to be fixed in the short run, this effect takes the form of a change in the value of holdings of foreign assets.[1)]

Since accumulations and decumulations of foreign assets are determined in goods markets by the evolution of the trade account, export or import surpluses can have an important direct influence on asset markets and, therefore, on the exchange rate. While changes in the exchange rate alter the value of real asset stocks, the trade account determines the change in the nominal stock of foreign assets.

This simple model supports the conventional view that a trade account surplus is combined with an appreciating exchange rate and a deficit with a depreciation.

---

1) On this point see Henderson (1977). In the second case, relative price effects would have to be taken into account.

3.2. Extension: Secondary Effects of Wealth Transfers

In the last section we discussed a small country model. It was assumed that residents of the "small" domestic country produce and consume only traded goods the price of which was exogenously given. As a result, interrelations with other countries could be neglected.

In the following, the view will be extended to two countries which produce two diversified goods. As in the preceding model, the CA plays also here a twofold part. CA induced wealth shifts have a direct influence on relative asset supplies and hence on portfolio and exchange rate equilibrium. On the other hand, wealth is regarded as a determinant of domestic and foreign consumption so that CA imbalances affect domestic and foreign absorbtion.The small country assumption excluded repercussions of changes in the international distribution of wealth on world income and the structure of world goods demand. This assumption will now be dropped and we attempt to give an answer to the following question: what are the consequences of an international redistribution of wealth through CA imbalances for the long run equilibrium exchange rate if countries show differences in savings behaviour and in the demand distribution between domestic and foreign products ?

The main idea underlying the following model can be summarized as follows.[1] Since marginal propensities to save and the distribution of demand between domestic and foreign goods will in general differ for different countries, an international shift of wealth affects the distribution and the level of global world demand and income. Long run equilibrium requires an international distribution of wealth which is compatible with balanced CAs and equilibrium in world goods markets. Thus, in the long run the exchange rate is determined by the equilibrium distribution of wealth as well as by portfolio equilibrium conditions.

Although the model highlights the role of real factors in exchange rate determination, it belongs to the vast group of asset market models: the short run equilibrium exchange rate is determined by

---

1) This section draws mainly on Kouri and De Macedo (1978) from where the structure of the model is taken. A more detailed exposition of the problem discussed in this section can be found in Lapan and Enders (1978).

the conditions of portfolio equilibrium including the relative supplies of domestic and foreign assets. Exchange rate changes in turn alter the real value of wealth and hence affect domestic and foreign consumption. These changes in wealth, however, may have different effects on national consumption functions and thus on absorbtion and national CAs. Since the change in stocks of foreign assets is determined by the CA, the exchange rate depends in the long run and over the dynamic adjustment period on consumption and savings behaviour in both countries.

In the following description of the static long run equilibrium all variables are expressed in nominal terms and denominated in foreign currency. The equilibrium level of nominal income in the world economy is given by eq. (1).

$$(1) \qquad Y^* + Y/e = c_y^* Y^* + c_y Y/e + c_w^* W^* + c_w W$$

Y^*, Y/e	: Nominal output of the foreign and the domestic country, respectively, expressed in foreign currency units.
c_y, c_w and c_y^*, c_w^*	: Propensity to consume from income and wealth, respectively, in the home country and abroad.
$W = F + M/e$	: Nominal wealth held by domestic residents, expressed in foreign currency.
$W^* = F^*$	: Nominal foreign wealth.

The equilibrium distribution of world demand on domestic and foreign goods is given by eq. (2).

$$(2) \qquad Y^* = \alpha\,(Y/e)$$

where α is a parameter which indicates the equilibrium distribution of nominal world demand between domestic output and foreign output. This parameter is assumed to be given. Shifts in demand can be interpreted as shifts in α.[1)]

---

1) See next page.

Domestic portfolio equilibrium is obtained when domestic money M/e and foreign assets F are held in the desired proportion m. m is assumed as function of the expected rate of depreciation of the foreign currency π^*.

(3) $F = m(\pi^*)(M/e)$ where $m_{\pi^*} < 0$

(footnote 1. last page) The major shortcoming of this model lies in the assumption of an exogenous α without giving any explanation for the behavioral relationship in the background.
Together with eq. (1) this assumption implies that monetary disturbances have no long run influence on the terms of trade.
To make this point clear, eq. (2) can be made explicit by the following two equations (2') and (2''):

(2') $Y^* = P^* D_2 + P^* D_2^*$

(2'') $Y/e = (P/e) D_1 + (P/e) D_1^*$

where D_1, D_1^* denote real domestic and foreign demand for good 1 produced at home; D_2, D_2^* denote real domestic and foreign demand for good 2 produced abroad; P, P^* denote the respective price levels.

Defining Y_r and Y_r^* as real output in both countries, eq. (2') and (2'') can be rearranged to a more precise version of eq.(2) above:

$$\frac{P^* Y_r^*}{(P/e) Y_r} = \underbrace{\left[\frac{e P^*}{P}\right] \left[\frac{D_2 + D_2^*}{D_1 + D_1^*}\right]}_{\alpha}$$

In this presentation, the assumption of a constant α can have two different meanings. An increase in the foreign price level P^*, for example, leaves α unchanged if:

a. the deterioration in the terms of trade for the home country leads to an equiproportional shift in the demand structure towards domestic goods;

b. price and exchange rate adjustments maintain constant terms of trade at an unchanged distribution of real demand.

Since real demand is independent of price changes in this model, the structure of real demand is, by assumption, constant. Therefore, changes in the terms of trade play no role for the international demand distribution. On this point see also Whitman (1978).

The CA surplus of the home country is defined by the excess of domestic production over domestic absorbtion.

$$(4) \qquad B = Y/e - c_y Y/e - c_w W$$

Combining equations (1) and (2), and solving for the equilibrium level of nominal income yields eq. (5).

$$(5) \qquad Y^* + Y/e = \frac{c_w^* (1+\alpha)}{\alpha s_y^* + s_y} W^* + \frac{c_w (1+\alpha)}{\alpha s_y^* + s_y} W$$

where $s_y = 1 - c_y$ and $s_y^* = 1 - c_y^*$

Eq. (5) shows that a shift of wealth from the foreign country to the home country due to a domestic CA surplus reduces the global level of nominal demand and output if the domestic propensity to consume from wealth c_w is lower than the foreign propensity c_w^*.[1)]
Substituting eq. (5) in eq. (4) yields for the CA surplus of the home country:

$$(6) \qquad B = \Phi^* W^* - \Phi W$$

where $\Phi^* = \dfrac{s_y c_w^*}{\alpha s_y^* + s_y}$ and $\Phi = \dfrac{\alpha s_y^* c_w}{\alpha s_y^* + s_y}$

Equation (6) illustrates that with international differences in savings and consumption behaviour ($\Phi \neq \Phi^*$) a mere shift of wealth ($dW^* = -dW$) cannot produce a balanced CA. An existing CA imbalance has to be eliminated by a wealth transfer and a change in the relative price of assets, that is, by a change in the exchange rate.

---

1) It is not clear, however, if this result is brought about by a decrease in the price level or by a reduction in real output.

Equation (6) cannow be used to derive the long run equilibrium distribution of assets consistent with a current account balance of zero.

$$(7) \qquad [W^*/W] = [s^*_y/s_y]\,[c_w/c^*_w]\,\alpha$$

From eq. (7) it can be infered that the equilibrium distribution of wealth depends on relative saving propensities and on the distribution of demand between domestic and foreign goods.
Using the accounting identity $W^* = F^*$, the definition of total supply of foreign currency $\bar{F} = F + F^*$, and the definition of domestic wealth $W = F + M/e$, the equilibrium condition $B = 0$ can also be written:

$$(8) \qquad F = \frac{\Phi^*}{\Phi^* + \Phi}\bar{F} - \frac{\Phi}{\Phi^* + \Phi}(M/e)$$

Equation (8) determines the equilibrium stock of domestically held foreign assets. The equilibrium stock of foreign assets, which keeps the CA in balance, depends on the total supply of domestic and foreign money and on the relative price between both: the exchange rate.

Holding $\bar{F}$ and M constant, the DD schedule in the figure below shows all combinations of e and F which keep the CA balanced. The DD curve is upward sloping: an increase in domestic holdings of foreign assets increases domestic wealth and absorbtion and causes a CA deficit. The domestic currency has to depreciate (e has to rise) to lower wealth and absorbtion again and, thus, to keep the CA in balance.

Assuming a constant π^* (stationary expectations), the FF curve represents instantaneous portfolio equilibrium, defined by eq. (3).
As in the model before, an increase in F must be accompanied by a rise in the exchange rate to maintain the desired relation m between F and M/e.

Instantaneous portfolio equilibrium and long run stock-flow equilibrium with a balanced CA is brought together in the following figure.

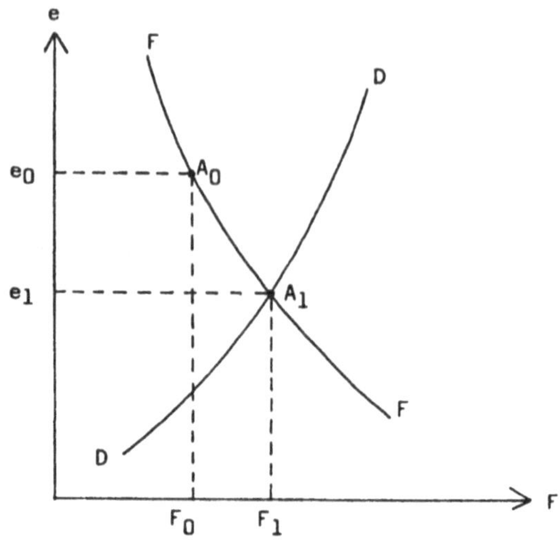

Every point above and to the left of the DD curve implies a CA surplus of the home country. At a given exchange rate the domestic stock of foreign assets lies below its equilibrium level so that domestic production exceeds domestic absorbtion. Consider the point A_0. At the initial combination (e_0, F_0) domestic portfolios are in equilibrium but the surplus in the domestic CA leads to an accumulation of foreign assets. The home country's stock of foreign assets increases while the foreign currency depreciates until long run equilibrium is reached at A_1 with a lower exchange rate and a higher stock of domestic holdings of foreign assets.

The long run equilibrium value of the exchange rate can be derived by combining the portfolio balance condition eq. (3) with the condition for a balanced CA, given by eq. (8).

$$(9) \qquad e = \frac{\Phi\,(1 + m) + \Phi^* m}{\Phi^*} \quad (M/\bar{F})$$

According to eq. (9), the long run equilibrium exchange rate depends not only on the relative supply of domestic and foreign assets but also on the international distribution of demand, on savings and consumption behaviour, and on portfolio preferences.[1)]
A demand shift in favour of domestic goods (a decrease in α) can be described as a shift of the DD curve to the right. The increase in the demand for domestic output leads to an appreciation of the domestic currency and increases the holdings of foreign assets in the home country in long run equilibrium. If the propensity to consum from wealth is lower in the home country than abroad ($c_w < c_w^*$) global nominal income is reduced. It is, however, not clear from this model whether the adjustment occurs through a reduction in prices or in employment. Given some rigidity in prices, full employment abroad is not guaranteed by the exchange rate adjustment.

It can also be seen from eq. (9) that an increase in the domestic propensity to save leads to an appreciation of the home currency and a higher equilibrium stock of foreign currency. The same is true for a shift in portfolio preferences in favour of domestic money (an increase in m).

---

1) It is interesting to consider PPP in the light of this equation. From eq. (9) follows, that an increase in M leads to an equiproportional long run depreciation only if the monetary change has no influence on Φ, Φ^*, and m. For this to hold, the following conditions must be fulfilled:

   a. Absence of money illusion with respect to consumption and savings.

   b. Changes in the money supply have no lasting influence on the real demand distribution and no effect on the terms of trade, which is, in this model, true by definition.

   If an increase in M generates lasting expectations of a depreciation of the home currency ($\dot{\pi}^* < 0$), asset holders shift towards foreign currency and the actual depreciation exceeds the increase in the money supply. This can be seen by the derivative of eq. (9):

$$\hat{e} = \hat{x} + \hat{M} - \hat{F}$$

$$\text{with} \quad x = \frac{\Phi(1+m) + \Phi^* m}{\Phi^*} \quad \text{and} \quad \hat{x} = \frac{\Phi + \Phi^*}{\Phi(1+m) + m\Phi^*} \, m_{\pi^*} \, \dot{\pi}^*$$

   If the increase in M creates lasting inflationary expectations ($\dot{\pi}^* < 0$) it follows $\hat{x} > 0$ and hence $\hat{e} > \hat{M}$.

3.3. Extension: Interest-Bearing Assets

In the preceding analysis the asset menue was restricted to domestic and foreign money. Hence the interest rate did not appear in portfolio considerations. The following exposition extends this view mainly with respect to two points.

First, we introduce domestic and foreign interest-bearing assets. Thus, the exchange rate is simultaneously determined with the interest rate by conditions of instantaneous portfolio equilibrium.
Second, the dynamic adjustment of the exchange rate as well as the long run equilibrium is governed not only by the trade account but by a more comprehensive version of the CA including international interest payments.

A very good example of this approach is given by Branson (1976) to which we refer.[1)] His small-country model is based on the usual assumptions of asset market analysis. Since goods prices and real variables are slow to adjust relative to asset variables, the model focuses on the equilibrium process in financial markets. At every point in time the price level, income and employment are taken as given and the stocks of financial assets are predetermined by past wealth accumulation. Thus, in the short run the exchange rate and the interest rate are determined by the requirements of financial portfolio (asset market) equilibrium. The exchange rate in turn is seen as a major determinant of the CA. In Branson's model it is not the exchange rate induced wealth effect on absorbtion which governs the development of the CA but the exchange rate impact on relative goods prices. Similar to the preceding models, however, the dynamic development of the exchange rate is determined by the interaction of exchange rate changes and CA balances.
The portfolio structure of the model is described by the following asset market equilibrium conditions.

---

1) See also Branson (1977, 1979, 1981, 1982), Branson, Halttunen, and Masson (1977), and the similar model by Riechel (1978, pp. 53).

(1)	$M = m(r, r^*)\, W$		money market
(2)	$B = b(r, r^*)\, W$		domestic bond market
(3)	$eF = f(r, r^*)\, W$		foreign bond market
(4)	$W = eF + B + M$		nominal wealth of the private sector (balance sheet constraint)

M : Domestic money, held only by domestic residents.

B : Private net holdings of assets denominated in domestic currency which earn an interest rate r (domestic bonds).

The foreign sector does not issue or hold bonds denominated in domestic currency. Thus, B is essentially government debt held by the domestic private sector.

F : Private net holdings of assets denominated in foreign currency which earn an interest rate r^* (foreign bonds).

r, r^* : Domestic and foreign interest rate, respectively. The foreign interest rate is assumed to be fixed in the world capital market and therefore exogenous for the small country.

The demand functions m, b, f are defined as linear homogeneous in wealth: a change in total wealth does not alter the desired proportions of each asset in the portfolio. Hence, m, b, and f can be interpreted as desired asset shares in the portfolio.[1)]

The balance sheet constraint eq. (4) implies

$$m + b + f = 1 \quad \text{and} \quad m_r + b_r + f_r = 0 .$$

Given eq. (4) and gross substitutability of the three assets, it follows further[2)]

$$m_r + f_r = - b_r < 0 .$$

1) Note further that specifying asset demand functions as linear homogeneous in wealth eliminates the price level from the asset market equilibrium conditions.

2) Gross substitutability means that an increase in the return on one asset, which raises the demand for this asset, reduces the demand for all other assets.

For the signs of the partial derivatives it is assumed:

$$b_r,\ f_r^* > 0$$

$$m_r,\ m_r^*,\ b_r^*,\ f_r < 0 \ .$$

The total supply of M, B, and F is given at any point in time. Since F is the only internationally traded asset there is no possibility of swapping M or B for F.[1)]

In the absence of central bank interventions in the foreign exchange market, the change in the stock of foreign assets F is equal to the balance of the CA. In fact, the only way for the private sector to change their stocks of F is by running an imbalanced CA. Likewise, a change in the net foreign asset position accrues always as a change in F.

The exchange rate e is used to translate F into home currency. Hence, exchange rate movements alter the domestic currency value of overall private wealth and thereby affect the demand for all other assets. This wealth effect is the channel through which the exchange rate influences private portfolio dispositions.

Equilibrium in each of the three asset markets can be defined in terms of a specific combination of the exchange rate and the domestic interest rate. The equilibrium curves are depicted in figure 1.

The MM curve shows combinations of e and r which produce equilibrium in the domestic money market. The slope of the curve is positive:

$$de/dr = -W\, m_r / m\, F > 0$$

An increase in the exchange rate increases the value of wealth and therefore money demand. The interest rate has to rise to preserve money market equilibrium.

---

1) In this model B and F are defined as fixed-price assets and hence, capital gains or losses resulting from interest rate changes are excluded. This assumption will be relaxed in the next section.

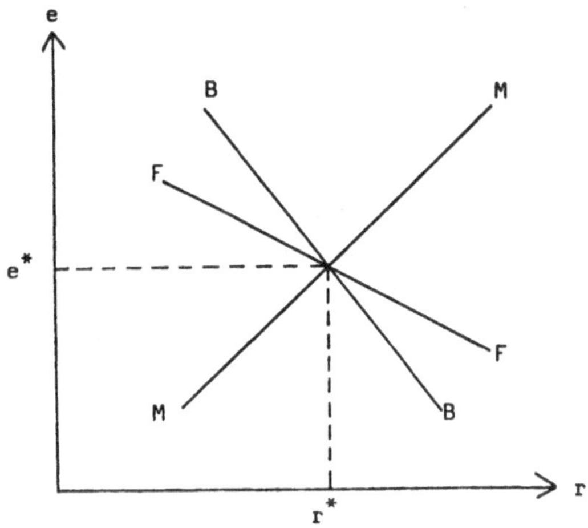

Figure 1.

The BB curve shows equilibrium in the market for domestic bonds.
The slope is negative:

$$de/dr = - W b_r / b F < 0$$

A depreciation rises the domestic-currency value of wealth and thus requires a fall in the domestic interest rate to keep bond demand in line with the given stock of B.

The slope of the equilibrium schedule for demand and supply of foreign bonds, given by the FF curve, is also negative but in absolute terms lower than the slope of the BB-curve:

$$de/dr = - W f_r / F (1 - f) < 0$$

A certain increase in r requires a smaller drop in the exchange rate to restore equilibrium in the market for foreign bonds than the drop which is necessary to restore equilibrium in the domestic bond market. This is also one of the conditions for stability of the asset market equilibrium. From a formal analysis of stability requirements the two conditions $1 - f > b$ and $b_r > - f_r$ can be derived. They are always fulfilled because of the wealth constraint $1 - f = m + b$ and the gross substitutability assumption $b_r = - f_r - m_r$.[1)]

It follows also from the wealth constraint eq. (4) that only two equations of eq. (1) to eq. (3) are necessary to determine the short run equilibrium values of e and r. If MM and BB equilibrium is chosen, the short run comparative statics can be obtained by the total differential of eqs. (1) and (2) and solving the system for changes in the equilibrium values of the exchange rate and the interest rate.
This yields:

$$\underbrace{\begin{pmatrix} \overset{-}{W m_r} & \overset{+}{m F} \\ \overset{+}{W b_r} & \overset{+}{b F} \end{pmatrix}}_{D} \begin{pmatrix} dr \\ de \end{pmatrix} = \begin{pmatrix} \overset{+}{1-m} & \overset{-}{-m} & \overset{-}{-me} & \overset{+}{-W m_r^*} \\ \overset{-}{-b} & \overset{+}{1-b} & \overset{-}{-be} & \overset{+}{-W b_r^*} \end{pmatrix} \begin{pmatrix} dM \\ dB \\ dF \\ dr^* \end{pmatrix}$$

The determinant of D is $(W m_r b F - W b_r m F) < 0$.

The solutions of the system are easier to interpret when we clarify first the meaning of "asset substitutability" in this model.
The following relationships will also be of some importance in the theoretical analysis over the next chapters.

In all portfolio models with given demand functions for the various assets the interest rate elasticity of asset demands can be interpreted as a measure of the degree of substitutability between these

---

1) This result can be made intuitive by the following example. An increase in r lowers the demand for foreign assets and increases the demand for domestic bonds. Both demand changes must be set off by a decline in the exchange rate. This decline, however, lowers the domestic-currency value of foreign assets equiproportionally whereas the demand for bonds B is reduced only indirectly by the impact of a lower level of overall wealth. Hence, equilibrium in the domestic bond market requires a greater fall in the exchange rate than equilibrium in the market for foreign bonds.

assets.[1] Consider, for example, an increase in the domestic interest rate r in Branson's model. The rise in r leads to a demand shift from domestic money M and foreign bonds F to domestic bonds B. If asset holders regard domestic money and domestic bonds as good substitutes there will be a strong shift of demand from M to B. In other words, the interest elasticity of domestic money demand E(m/r) will be higher (in absolute terms) the higher is the degree of substitutability between money and domestic bonds. In the extreme case of perfect substitutability $E(m/r) = -\infty$.

Likewise, if domestic and foreign bonds are considered as perfect substitutes, the rise in r will cause a complete shift of demand from F to B. Thus, the interest elasticity of the demand for foreign bonds E(f/r) defines the degree of substitutability between domestic and foreign bonds. E(f/r) may lie between the benchmarks of perfect substitutability and no substitutability as $-\infty \leq E(f/r) \leq 0$.
On the other hand, the interest elasticity of domestic bonds E(b/r) depends on the substitutability relations between M and B, and B and F. Hence, E(b/r) is not an unambiguous measure of a specific substitutability relation.

Consider now an increase in the foreign interest rate r^*. The rise in r^* induces a demand shift from domestic money and bonds to foreign bonds. By the same way of reasoning as above, we may say that if M and F are perfect substitutes $E(m/r^*) = -\infty$ so that the degree of substitutability between these assets is defined by the span between $-\infty \leq E(m/r^*) \leq 0$. The same relation holds for B and F. The degree of substitutability between domestic and foreign bonds is described by

---

1) Note that foreign assets are held uncovered in portfolios so that deviations from the IRP condition $r = r^*$ reflect the existence of a risk premium. It follows, of course, that the relation mentioned above cannot be applied to covered assets: on a covered basis B and F would be perfect substitutes. However, as it has been shown by Girton and Henderson (1977), the presence of a forward market does not alter the general results from portfolio balance models since forward markets do not affect the amount of open positions demanded. In the following, "interest elasticity" should be understood as the elasticity of asset demands with respect to expected net returns.

the values between $-\infty \leq E(b/r^*) \leq 0$.[1] As $E(f/r^*)$ depends both on the substitutability between M and F, and B and F, it may be interpreted as a measure of the composite substitutability between domestic and foreign assets.

Summarizing, we consider the following "substitutability chain" as an example.

$$E(f/r) > E(m/r) > E(m/r^*)$$

Elasticities are defined in absolute terms. From the left to the right this inequality relation means that domestic bonds are considered as better substitutes for foreign bonds than for domestic money, but domestic money is easier to substitute by domestic bonds than by foreign bonds.

We return to Branson's asset market model. The system described above in matrix notation can be solved for the response of the endogenous variables r and e to changes in the exogenous variables r^*, M, B, and F.

To explain the operation of the model, we consider the following examples.[2]

a. Increase in F due to a CA surplus.

Although the increase in wealth raises the demand for F, not all of the increased wealth is planned to be held in F: at the initial r-e combination domestic agents hold more foreign assets than desired. Therefore, they attempt to sell some of the increment in F in order to rebalance portfolios. The induced fall in the exchange rate (appreciation of the domestic currency) reduces wealth again.
In Branson's system the exchange rate falls instantaneously by the same proportion in which F increased so that wealth keeps unchanged at the initial level in the new equilibrium. Since wealth does not

---

1) The substitutability relation between B and F is thus described by $E(b/r^*)$ as well as by $E(f/r)$. This should imply $E(b/r^*) = E(f/r)$.

2) A complete description of the model results can be found in Branson (1976, 1979).

change, money and bond markets remain in equilibrium at the initial interest rate. A formal analysis yields:[1)]

$$E(e/F) = -1$$

$$dr/dF = 0$$

b. Increase in B due to a bond-financed government budget deficit

The rise in wealth increases the demand for domestic bonds according to the desired portfolio share b. Since assets are no perfect substitutes, not all of the increment in wealth will be desired to be held in B ($b < 1$). Thus, the supply increase exceeds the demand increase and produces a rise in the domestic interest rate as asset holders attempt to shift out of B and into M. The impact on the exchange rate, however, is ambiguous: the wealth increase raises demand for foreign assets (depreciation effect) but the higher domestic interest rate lowers the demand again (appreciation effect).

If domestic bonds and money are considered as good substitutes, a relatively small increase in r is sufficient to produce portfolio equilibrium between B and M.[2)] In this case, the wealth effect on the demand for F may exceed the interest rate effect and bring about a depreciation of the domestic currency.
On the other hand, if domestic and foreign bonds are considered as good substitutes, even a small increase in r induces a large switch out of F and into B. The interest rate effect on the demand for F exceeds the wealth effect and leads to an appreciation of the domestic currency. The formal solution of the system yields:

$$de/dB \lesseqgtr 0 \quad \text{as} \quad |E(f/r)| \gtreqless |E(m/r)|$$

$$dr/dB > 0$$

---

1) E(X/Y) is the elasticity of X with respect to Y.

2) In the case of perfect substitutability of B and M there is no demand shift from B to M since it does not matter in which of the two assets the increment in wealth is held. Hence, there is no change in the interest rate.

If domestic and foreign bonds are considered as better substitutes than domestic bonds and money, that is, if $E(f/r) > E(m/r)$ in absolute terms, an increase in B leads to an appreciation of the domestic currency.

c. Reduction in the stocks of B and F in exchange for money M due to open-market purchases by the central bank.

Contrary to the examples a. and b., these operations involve a mere exchange of assets between the private sector and the central bank at constant private wealth.
If the money supply is increased by purchases of domestic bonds, asset holders find themselves with an excess supply of M and an excess demand for B. The attempt to buy domestic bonds lowers the interest rate and thereby increases the demand for foreign bonds. As a result, the exchange rate rises and the new equilibrium is established with a higher domestic interest rate and a devaluated domestic currency.
The exchange rate effect is stronger if the open-market operation is done with foreign assets. In this case, the excess demand for foreign assets, which raises the exchange rate, results both from a falling domestic interest rate and from the direct reduction in private foreign asset stocks. Branson's model yields:[1)]

$$^{M}/_{e}\ ^{de}/_{dM}\Big|_{dM=-dB} = -\ ^{M}/_{eF}\left[\frac{f_r/b_r}{b\ (m_r/b_r) - m}\right]$$

$$^{M}/_{e}\ ^{de}/_{dM}\Big|_{dM=-edF} = -\ ^{M}/_{eF}\left[\frac{-\ 1}{b\ (m_r/b_r) - m}\right]$$

Effects of various changes in exogenous variables on the equilibrium exchange rate and the equilibrium interest rate are summarized in the following table.

---

1) In a completely symetric system with $M = eF = B$ and thus $m_r = f_r = - 0{,}5\ b_r$, the first elasticity is -1 and the second is -2.

Effects on	Effects of Accumulation of Stocks			Effects of Open-Market Operations	
	dM	dB	dF	-dB=dM	-edF=dM
r	-	+	0	-	-
e	+	?	-	+	+

So far we considered only the instantaneous impact of various disturbances on the short run equilibrium values of the exchange rate and interest rate. As result of this analysis, the following reduced form equation for the exchange rate can be defined.

$$e = e\ (F,\ M,\ B,\ r^*) \quad \text{with} \quad e_F < 0$$

In the next step, we connect the short run asset market equilibrium with the long run stationary state in which both stock and flow markets must be in equilibrium. The dynamic link between the short and the long run is established by the following balance of payments equation.

$$(5) \qquad \dot{F} = X\ (e/P) + r^* F \qquad \text{with} \quad {}^{dX}/_{d(e/P)} > 0$$

X (e/P) denotes the trade account defined as net domestic exports expressed in foreign currency units. The trade account is a function of the relative price of domestic and foreign goods e/P.[1)] An increase in the relative price of domestic goods - a decline in e/P - reduces net domestic exports or, in other words, deteriorates the trade account. Although Branson does not give a precise description

---

1) The foreign price level P^* is assumed to be constant and normalized to 1.

of the goods sector, this assumption implies that the law of one price does not hold and the exchange rate gains influence on the terms of trade.[1] The service account is defined by the net receipts of interest payments on foreign bonds r^*F.
In the absence of official interventions, the CA must always equal the capital account defined as the increase in private net stocks of foreign assets $\dot{F}$. In the long run equilibrium the CA must be balanced and, accordingly, the change in F must be zero.

The dynamic interaction between asset stocks and balance of payments flows can now be described as follows.
At every point in time asset stocks M, B, and F as well as the domestic and foreign price level are given. Consider the case in which the initial portfolio equilibrium exchange rate is combined with a CA surplus. With $X(e/P) + r^*F > 0$ the stock of foreign assets increases and brings about an appreciation of the domestic currency. The declining exchange rate deteriorates the trade account while the increase in F leads to a rise in interest receipts on foreign bonds. Stability of the system requires that the relative price effect on the trade account predominates the improvement in the service account so that the CA surplus is gradually reduced. Given stability, the adjustment period is characterized by a steady rise in the exchange rate and an increase in F until in the long run stock-flow equilibrium the trade account deficit equals the service account surplus and hence $\dot{F} = 0$.[2]

---

1) This relationship is one of the important differences to the foregoing models. In Branson's model the exchange rate feeds back to the real sector through changes in the terms of trade and not through wealth effects on domestic consumption and absorbtion.

2) Stability of the dynamic adjustment to the long run equilibrium state with a balanced CA is guaranteed if the exchange rate effect on the trade account exceeds the investment income effect.
The conditions for stability can be derived from eq. (5):

$\dot{F} = X[e(F)/P] + r^*F$. Stability requires $d\dot{F}/dF = [dX/d(e/P)]\,e_F + r^* < 0$.

Since $e_F < 0$ is given, the Marshall-Lerner condition $dX/d(e/P) > 0$ is necessary to make sure that $[dX/d(e/P)]\,e_F < 0$.
In addition to that, stability is warranted only if $[-dX/d(e/P)] > r^*$ is fulfilled. It is remarkable that in Branson's model the Marshall-Lerner condition is necessary not only for a "normal" behaviour of the CA but for the dynamic stability of the system as a whole.

Since foreign assets have been accumulated during the adjustment process, the equilibrium investment income r^*F has risen and, hence, the equilibrium trade account deficit has increased.
This means that the new equilibrium exchange rate necessary to produce a balanced CA must be lower than the value that would have produced a balanced CA in the initial situation. Therefore, the long run equilibrium value of the exchange rate is partly determined by the adjustment process itself. A stylized overview of the causality relations is shown in the following figure.[1)]

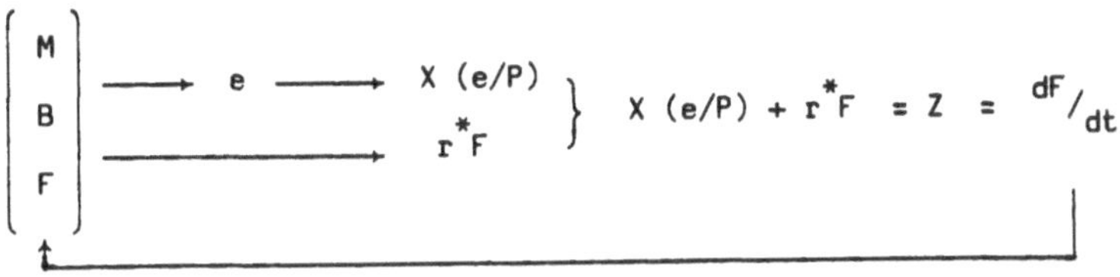

At every point in time the asset stocks M, B, and F determine the exchange rate e. Given the price level P, the exchange rate alters the relative price of domestic and foreign goods and hence affects the trade account. The value of the service account depends on the stock of foreign assets. The sum of net exports and investment income yields the CA balance Z which indicates the change in net foreign asset stocks. Thus, any imbalance in the CA feeds back to F and starts the dynamic adjustment process once again.

This framework can now be used to analyse dynamic effects of an open-market purchase of domestic bonds $-dB = dM$ (figure 2.).

Initially, the system is in stationary equilibrium with a balanced CA $-X(e/P) = r^*F$ and portfolio equilibrium.[2)] The initial effect of the open-market operation on the exchange rate is determined by adjustments in the asset sector. As described above, the open-market purchase of domestic bonds in exchange for money causes an immediate

---

1) A more elaborated version of this figure is included in Branson and Buiter (1981).

2) The initial equilibrium values $\bar{e}$, $\bar{P}$ are normalized to one.

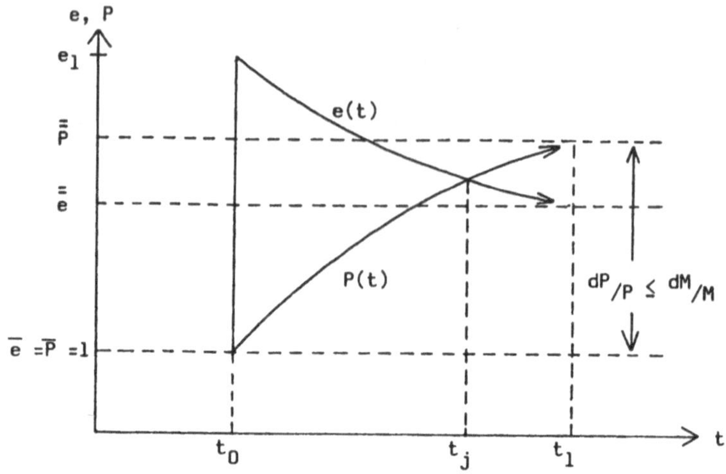

Figure 2.

jump of the exchange rate from $\bar{e}$ to e_1 at t_0.[1)]

During the adjustment process we have to take into account that the increase in the money supply will lead to a rise in the domestic price level. For that purpose, Branson introduces a simple price adjustment equation:[2)]

$$P = P\ (M) \quad \text{where} \quad 0 < E(P/M) \leq 1$$

He assumes a gradual adjustment of P which ends in t_1 when the price level has increased proportionally to the increase in the money supply and P has reached its new equilibrium value $\bar{\bar{P}}$.

---

1) Although it is assumed in the figure that the impact increase in e exceeds the long run increase in P (which in turn is assumed to be roughly the same as the rise in the money supply), this cannot be concluded from the model. As shown above, overshooting with respect to the increase in M depends on the initial proportions of assets in portfolios and on the degree of substitutability of assets. If the open-market operation is done with foreign assets, that is $-edF = dM$, then the instantaneous jump of the exchange rate would probably be higher but the dynamic adjustment remains the same.

2) A slightly different price adjustment equation is used in Branson (1981).

The immediate jump in the exchange rate at t_0 raises the price ratio to $(e_1/\overline{P}) > (\overline{e}/\overline{P})$. The sharp decline in the relative price of domestic goods induces an increase in net exports and hence leads to a CA surplus. The stock of foreign assets starts to rise and e appreciates along the e(t) path, gradually reducing the CA surplus.
Price path P(t) and exchange rate path e(t) cross at t_j.[1] At this time the price ratio e/P is equal to the initial price ratio $\overline{e}/\overline{P} = 1$ and, accordingly, net exports in t_j are equal to the initial net exports. But since the stock of foreign assets has increased between t_0 and t_j investment income r^*F has risen and the CA is in surplus at t_j. Thus, F is still accumulating and the exchange rate falls further. The appreciation lasts until $-X\ (e/P) = r^*F$. Since r^*F is higher in the new equilibrium than initially, X (e/P) has to be lower than in the beginning. A higher trade account deficit in the new equilibrium implies a higher relative price of domestic goods. Thus, the new long run equilibrium with $\overline{\overline{P}}$ is reached when the exchange rate has settled at $\overline{\overline{e}}$, such that $(\overline{\overline{e}}/\overline{\overline{P}}) < (\overline{e}/\overline{P})$.

This result stands in clear contradiction to the long run neutrality postulate of the PPP theory and the monetary approach. In Branson's model a purely monetary disturbance causes a change in equilibrium relative prices. The long run equilibrium depreciation following a monetary expansion must fall short of the price increase to achieve a higher deficit in the trade account which is necessary to balance the increased investment income. Hence, it follows $\overline{\overline{e}} < \overline{\overline{P}}$.

The dynamic section of Branson's model shows that the existence of outstanding interest-bearing assets and international interest payments may lead to non-neutrality results for monetary measures even in the long run.

---

1) In some earlier articles Branson (1976, 1979) analysed the case in which the exchange rate adjusts faster to its new equilibrium level than the price level. He concluded that in this case the exchange rate path exhibits a reversal so that the adjustment process is non-monotonic. By a formal analysis of the dynamic stability of the system, however, it can be proven that the adjustment must be monotonic. This has been shown in Branson (1981). The "super Marshall-Lerner condition" $[dX/d(e/P)]\ e_F + r^* < 0$ is a sufficient condition for stability and ensures a monotonic adjustment of the exchange rate.

3.4. Extension: Relative Price Adjustment with Traded and Nontraded Goods

The foregoing exposition provided a more detailed description of portfolio equilibrium yet treated the real sector and goods price determination in a very rudimentary way. Nonetheless, this analysis suggested that the interaction of financial and commodity markets play an important part in the dynamic adjustment of the exchange rate. The following extension focuses in particular on this aspect of exchange rate determination. In order to analyse movements in relative prices during the adjustment period we lay out a model which includes an explicit description of the goods sector.[1)]
The link between short run portfolio equilibrium and the long run stationary state is established by private savings which are seen as a function of the desired wealth position. Hence, over the dynamic adjustment period not only the composition of portfolios is endogenous but also the portfolio size.

The financial sector is described essentially in the same way as in Branson's model. Only the assumption of fixed-price assets is released. The foreign interest rate r^* is, as before, assumed to be given.

(1)	$M = m(r, r^*)\,W$	money market
(2)	$1/r\ B = b(r, r^*)\,W$	domestic bond market
(3)	$e/r^*\ F = f(r, r^*)\,W$	foreign bond market
(4)	$W = M + B/r + eF/r^*$	nominal wealth of the private sector

The real sector of the considered small country is built-up by the following relations.

1) In the following we refer to a model developed by Genberg and Kierzkowski (1975) in a substantially revised version presented in Genberg and Kierzkowski (1979). A good description of the 1975' model can be found in Schadler (1977).

The home country produces and consumes traded and nontraded goods. With perfect competition and free movement of resources, full employment in both goods sectors is always guaranteed by adjustments in relative prices. In the traded-goods sector the law of one price is always fulfilled. Because of the infinetely elastic demand, the traded-goods sector is always in equilibrium.

$$(5) \qquad P_T = e\,P_T^*$$

Equilibrium in the nontraded-goods sector is defined by the equality of real supply and real demand for nontraded goods.

$$(6) \qquad P_N\, S^N\,(P_N/P_T) = g\,(P_T/P_N)\,[\,Y^d + v\,(a - \bar{a})]$$

P_N : Price level of nontraded goods.

$S^N\,(P_N/P_T)$: Real supply of nontraded goods as a function of the relative price of nontraded goods.

$g\,(P_T/P_N)$: Fraction of total aggregate demand that falls to nontraded goods as a positive function of the internal price ratio (P_T/P_N).

Total aggregate demand consists of the disposable income Y^d and dissavings v.

$$Y^d = P_N\,S^N + P_T\,S^T + eF$$

Disposable income is equal to the sum of factor income and income from holdings of foreign assets.[1)]

---

1) Interest payments on domestic bonds are assumed to be financed by lump sum taxes and, therefore, the return on B/r is excluded from the definition of disposable income. Note that interest paid on foreign bonds is paid on the real value F/r^*. An increase in interest income due to a rise in r^* is exactly matched by a lower price of foreign assets so that the net income remains constant. This can be seen when we write the income from foreign investments as $eF = r^*\,(eF/r^*)$.

Savings are described by the expression $v\ (a - \bar{a})$. They are assumed to be a function of the gap between desired and actual wealth.[1)]

$a = W/P$	: Actual real value of wealth.[2)]
$\bar{a}$	: Desired real wealth, assumed as constant.
v	: Adjustment coefficient.

If 'a' exceeds $\bar{a}$, the excess of wealth will be spent and aggregate demand exceeds disposable income. Substituting the expression for the disposable income Y^d and dissavings $v\ (a - \bar{a})$ in eq. (6) yields for the equilibrium condition of the nontraded-goods sector:

$$(7) \qquad P_N\ S^N\ (P_N/P_T) = g\ (P_T/P_N)\ [P_N\ S^N + P_T\ S^T + eF + v\ (W/P - \bar{a})]$$

For given values of 'a', W/P, and eF, equilibrium in the nontraded-goods market can now be defined as a function of the internal price ratio P_T/P_N.[3)] This relationship is shown by the NN curve in figure 1. A rise in $e = P_T$ increases demand for nontraded goods by means of the relative-price substitution effect. To maintain equilibrium, P_N has to rise. It is an essential of the NN curve that the required increase in P_N must fall short of the rise in the exchange rate: an equiproportional movement of P_N and e keeps the internal price ratio constant but reduces the real value of disposable income and hence leads to an excess supply of nontraded goods.[4)]

---

1) This type of savings function was invented by Metzler (1951); see also Niehans (1978) for a discussion of the underlying rationale. For further applications in portfolio balance models see Dornbusch (1976c), Myhrmann (1976).

2) The price level P is a weighted average of P_N and P_T: $P = P_N^{\alpha}\ P_T^{1-\alpha}$ with $0 < \alpha < 1$.

3) P_T^* is assumed to be given and normalized to one so that $e = P_T$

4) This result follows from the assumption of a constant eF along the NN curve. If both 'a' and eF are included in the NN curve no change in relative prices is required if real wealth is not influenced by the depreciation. This point will be discussed later.

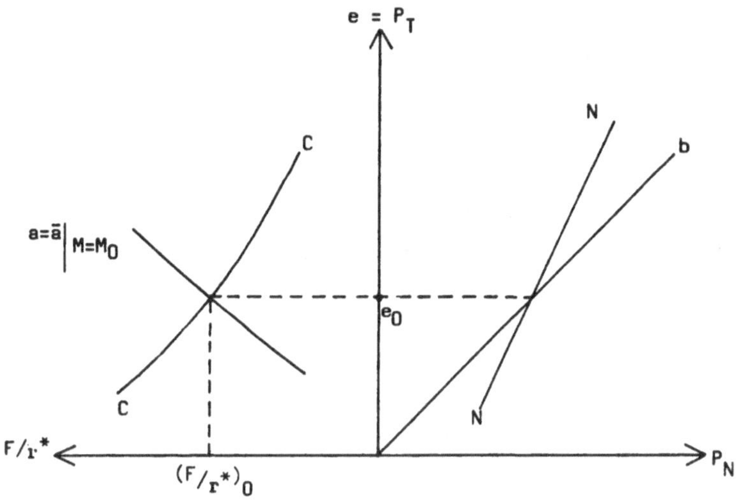

Figure 1.

An increase in real wealth 'a' reduces planned savings and raises demand for non-traded goods. The same is true for an increase in interest payments on foreign bonds. Therefore, an increase in 'a' and eF shifts NN to the right.

The reference line b indicates a constant internal price ratio P_T/P_N.

In the left-hand panel portfolio equilibrium is described by the CC curve. CC shows all combinations of the stock of domestically held foreign assets (F/r^*) and the exchange rate which yield, at given M, portfolio equilibrium. The CC schedule is derived from the following considerations. The domestic interest rate r is determined in domestic asset markets and has to adjust continuously to maintain equality between the desired and the actual money/bond ratio M/B. This portfolio equilibrium interest rate implies a certain desired value of foreign assets (eF/r^*) which has to be brought about - as F/r^* is fixed in the short run - by an exchange rate adjustment.[1)]

1) It is obvious that Genberg and Kierzkowski assume separate markets for domestic and foreign assets. An increase in F/r^* (a movement downwards along the CC curve) has no influence on the domestic interest rate.

An increase in M caused by an open-market operation (dM = -dB) reduces the domestic interest rate and leads to a higher demand for foreign bonds. The demand for F/r^* rises because of the interest rate induced substitution effect (a desired shift of asset shares in the given portfolio), but also because of the increased portfolio size (a decline in the interest rate r raises the value of the remaining stock of domestic bonds). Hence, an increase in M shifts CC to the left. The effect on the exchange rate is given by the following expression, derived from eqs. (1) to (4). Note that at every point in time $\hat{F} = 0$.

$$\hat{e} = -\hat{F} + 1 - \left[\frac{E(f/r) - E(m/r)}{1 + E(b/r) - E(m/r)} \right] \hat{M}$$

If the domestic interest elasticity of the demand for foreign bonds is greater, in absolute value, than the domestic interest elasticity of the demand for money, that is, if domestic and foreign bonds are closer substitutes than domestic bonds and money, the percentage change in the exchange rate is higher than the percentage change in the money stock: the coefficient on $\hat{M}$ is positive and greater than one.[1)] Thus, overshooting depends - as in Branson's model - on the substitutability of assets in the portfolio.

Genberg and Kierzkowski assume that asset and goods markets clear immediately, so that the economy is always on the CC and the NN curve. The impact effect of an asset market disturbance on the exchange rate is given by portfolio equilibrium conditions, but asset and goods markets are closely linked since the exchange rate influences at the same time the domestic price of traded goods and the domestic currency value of the stocks of foreign assets.

---

1) If B and F are closer substitutes, an increase in M leads to a desired portfolio shift in favour of foreign bonds. Therefore, a large part of the adjustment falls to the exchange rate. If there is no substitutability between domestic and foreign assets, E(f/r) = 0, the whole burden of the adjustment lies on the interest rate and the exchange rate remains unchanged.

The long run stationary state requires savings of zero. Thus, in long run equilibrium desired real wealth equals actual real wealth, income equals expenditure, and the current account is balanced. Long run equilibrium is illustrated by the $a = \bar{a}$ curve, drawn for given values of M and P_T. It is assumed that the slope of the $a = \bar{a}$ curve is positive so that an increase in the exchange rate requires a higher stock of foreign assets in the long run equilibrium.[1)] An increase in M or a decrease in P_T shifts $a = \bar{a}$ upwards.

The dynamic adjustment is, once more, governed by the CA which determines the change in F.

$$(8) \qquad (e/r^*)\ (dF/dt) = P_T\ (S^T - C^T) + eF$$

According to eq. (8), the CA consists of the trade account and the service account which includes only interest income from holdings of foreign bonds. The net export quantity is determined by the difference between domestic production S^T and consumption C^T of traded goods. On the other hand, the CA must be equal to net domestic savings. Hence, long run equilibrium with a balanced CA requires savings of zero.[2)]

To show the interaction of goods and asset markets and in order to describe the dynamic adjustment mechanism in some detail, we assume an open-market purchase of domestic bonds by domestic monetary authorities (dM = -dB). Figure 2. illustrates the different effects.

---

1) A formal derivation of the $a = \bar{a}$ locus, using the definition of real wealth, substituting the expression for the domestic interest rate from eqs. (1) and (2) and P_N from the equilibrium condition in the nontraded goods market eq. (5), shows that the slope of $a = \bar{a}$ may be positive or negative, steeper or less steep, than CC, depending in a fairly complicated way on demand and supply elasticities in goods markets and on asset shares in the portfolio. This, however, has no consequences for the stability of the system. Stability is guaranteed if a rise (decline) in the exchange rate leads to a fall (rise) in the real value of wealth. Since a movement in e is always combined with an increase in P this condition is always fulfilled.

2) Using eq. (5) and the definition of disposable income, eq. (8) can be written $(e/r^*)\ (dF/dt) = v\ (\bar{a} - a)$.

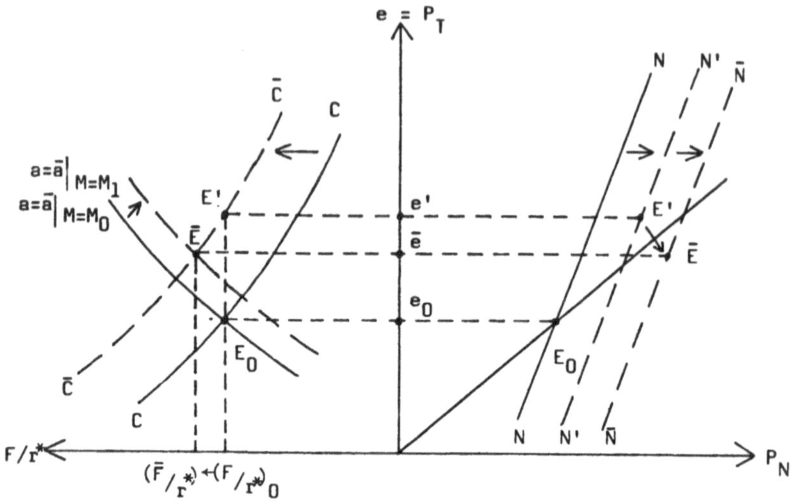

Figure 2.

As explained above, the impact effect on the financial sector consists in a decline in the interest rate and a rise in the exchange rate which exceeds, given sufficient elasticity conditions, the increase in M. The CC curve shifts leftwards to $\bar{C}\bar{C}$ and the asset market remains in equilibrium at the higher exchange rate e'.

The impact effect on the real sector can be split up into three single effects which actually work at the same time.

a. Substitution effect. According to the law of one price, the devaluation leads to an equiproportional increase in the internal price ratio. Demand switches to nontraded goods and P_N begins to rise. This effect can be illustrated by a movemant along the NN curve to a point corresponding to e'.

b. Income effect. The increase in e raises disposable income through the induced increase in interest receipts on foreign bonds. Part of this increase falls on the demand for nontraded goods and P_N has to rise further to preserve goods market equilibrium. This effect shifts NN to the right.

_c_. Wealth effect. The lower domestic interest rate rises the value of domestic bonds and the devaluation rises the value of foreign bonds; hence, nominal wealth increases. On the other hand, the higher overall price level lowers the real value of wealth and thereby diminishes expenditure. If real wealth declines, the rightwards shift of the NN curve will be reduced.

Unless the wealth effect is very strong, NN shifts to N'N' and short run equilibrium in the market for nontraded goods occurs in E' with a higher internal price ratio than in E_0 (E' is to the left of the b-ray). The change in the internal price ratio is due to the wealth effect of the depreciation.

In E' the lower stock of real wealth induces savings and the CA moves to a surplus. The accumulation of foreign assets during the adjustment to the long run equilibrium reduces savings gradually, the demand for domestic goods increases and so does P_N.

On the financial side, the increase in F/r^* leads to a decrease in e which in turn reduces the domestic price of traded goods P_T, so that during the adjustment P_T/P_N declines. The economy moves along the $\overline{CC}$ curve and on a continuously rightwards shifting N'N' curve to the long run equilibrium in $\overline{E}$ where $a = \overline{a}$.

In the new equilibrium the internal price ratio has declined, that is $(P_T/P_N)_{\overline{E}} < (P_T/P_N)_{E_0}$, and absolute goods prices have increased more than the money stock. This is due to the increased stock of foreign assets which leads - as in Branson's model - to higher interest receipts. With an unchanged relative price, the supply of nontraded goods would be unchanged but since disposable income has increased there would be an excess demand for nontraded goods. Therefore, $\overline{E}$ must be to the right of the constant-relative-price ray b.

It is interesting to point out the behaviour of the CA during the adjustment period (see figure 3.).

The service account improves in t_0, when the open-market operation takes place, equiproportionally to the depreciation but stays constant afterwards since the economy moves along $\overline{CC}$ which implies a constant value of foreign asset stocks.

The trade account moves in t_0 to a surplus since, with an increase in P_T/P_N, resources move into the traded-goods sector and increase production. This improvement in the trade account at continuous equilibrium in goods markets is possible because the reduction in real wealth increases savings and reduces the demand for domestic goods. The following gradually deterioration of the trade account is due to the decline in savings caused by the accumulation of foreign assets.

Similar to Branson's model, the long run deterioration of the trade account is possible because of higher interest receipts which keep the CA balanced. But unlike Branson's treatment of the trade account, it is not the direct terms of trade effect that determines trade flows; exchange rate changes alter successively the internal price ratio, the overall price level, the value of real wealth, savings behaviour, and, finally, the trade account.

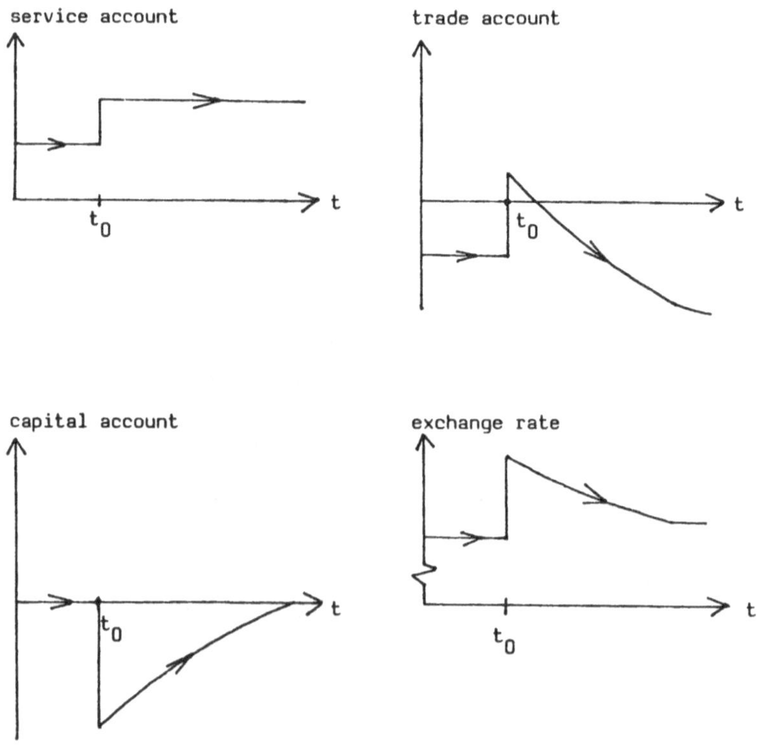

Figure 3.

3.5. Summary and Further Problems

Over the last four sections the discussion focused on the significance of the CA as a medium of international wealth shifts in the process of exchange rate determination. The models which have been presented suggest that the CA plays different parts in exchange rate determination depending on the time horizon under consideration.

In asset market models the exchange rate is determined at every instant by the relative demand for and supply of different types of financial assets. Within this short run equilibrium setting the CA gains direct influence on the exchange rate through its effect on relative asset supplies. CA imbalances cause immediate changes in the stock of net foreign assets and, hence, the CA position has to be taken into account even within short run exchange rate analysis. Since the portfolio balance effect constitutes the direct link between the CA and the exchange rate it is the most important argument in favour of the CA as an exchange rate determinant. Point-in-time analysis, however, is not necessarily restricted to the short run. As long as we consider the CA as exogenous to the asset markets any time period can be interpreted as a sequence of points in time and, hence, portfolio balance analysis can be applied to longer periods too. The portfolio balance effect of CA imbalances will be discussed later on in more detail.
It is interesting that the results for the exchange rate impact of CA imbalances which have been derived over the last sections conform to the results of traditional flow analysis: in all models the exchange rate appreciates whenever the CA is in surplus and depreciates whenever the CA is in deficit.

For the medium run it was shown above that the adjustment path of the exchange rate towards the long run equilibrium depends crucially on the behaviour of the CA. The CA establishes the connection between the real and the financial sector. The interaction of real and financial variables can be summarized in the following figure.

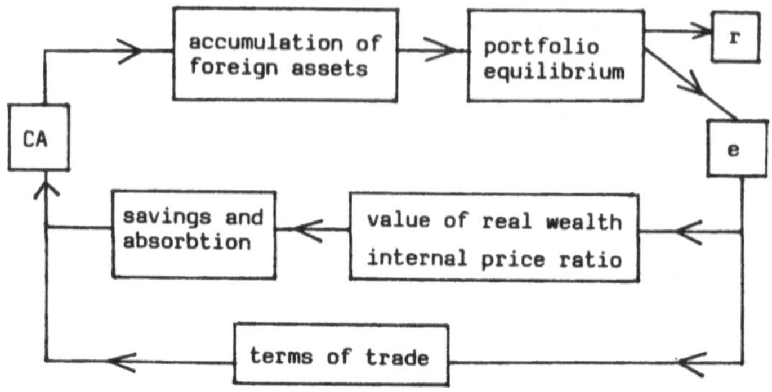

Figure 1.

The first line of figure 1. describes the portfolio balance effect of the CA, the second line below illustrates possible feedbacks of exchange rate changes to the CA. From fig. 1. it can be seen that wealth effects occur in both causality directions, either as CA induced wealth changes in financial portfolios or as exchange rate induced wealth changes in consumption and savings functions.
The interaction between the financial and the real sector depends essentially on the strength of these wealth effects.

Stability problems in the dynamic adjustment occur first of all in the second line leading from the exchange rate to the CA: if a depreciation worsens the CA in the first instant and thus leads to a decline in the stock of foreign assets and further depreciations, the economy may enter a vicious circle. This problem is of particular relevance in Branson's model which relies entirely on the Marshall-Lerner condition with respect to stability. A "J-curve" effect which causes a temporary "non-normal" behaviour of the CA may give rise to large and protracted exchange rate fluctuations.[1)] In Kouri's model and the model of Genberg and Kierzkowski this problem is

1) This problem is investigated in Bhandari (1982). He develops a Dornbusch-type exchange rate model which distinguishes between short and long run demand elasticities and gives special attention to the lags involved in the adjustment of the CA to a given change in the terms of trade. Bhandari concludes that exchange rate over-adjustments are more likely the consequence of real expenditure disturbances than the result of monetary disturbances.

largely rendered safe, since, with a continuously fulfilled law of one price, critical terms of trade effects are ruled out; a depreciation is always followed by a reduction in real wealth and, since real wealth is considered an important determinant of goods demand, brings about a reduction in domestic absorbtion that corresponds to an improvement in the CA. All models, however, indicate that the dynamic stability of the exchange rate is closely related to the reaction of the CA to exchange rate changes.

It was also shown above that an international wealth redistribution may cause different effects in goods markets of different countries. Thus, two-country stock-flow models which take care of differences in savigs behaviour and expenditure patterns may lead to other results with respect to the dynamic adjustment process and the long run equilibrium than the widely used small-country approach.

In section 3.4. it was suggested that even pure monetary disturbances may lead to systematic variations in the internal price ratio between traded and nontraded goods if wealth effects on consumption and savings are taken into account.

In the long run stationary state the CA must be balanced and savings cease because the desired level of wealth has been reached. The outcome of the foregoing analysis with respect to the long run stock-flow equilibrium stands in clear contradiction to PPP theory: the inclusion of international interest payments leads to non-neutrality results for monetary policy. Monetary disturbances alter the long run equilibrium internal price ratio and the equilibrium trade account balance.

So far the analysis has been conducted for the case of stationary expectations. Thus, the influence of changing expectations and the potential role of the CA in the process of expectation formation has been neglected. This omission may qualify the preceding theoretical results. But before we turn to this important feature in exchange rate determination it is necessary to point out some other problems involved in the represented models.

All of the foregoing models presume that the domestic country is "small" in international asset markets so that domestic assets are not internationally traded. The only internationally accepted financial instrument, which has to be used for CA financing, is a foreign-currency denominated asset. As a result, CA imbalances correspond to changes in the stock of this foreign asset and, likewise, the only way to change the stock of foreign assets is by running an imbalanced CA. The advantage of this assumption is that it permits a clear and unambiguous connection between the CA and the currency composition in portfolios. Furthermore, by virtue of the small country assumption it is admissible to neglect feedbacks from portfolio adjustments abroad. Nevertheless, for many industrialized countries like Germany, the United Kingdom or Japan, whose assets are also held in foreign portfolios, this assumption is rather unrealistic. For example, given that the DM is an internationally attractive currency and hence is held also in portfolios abroad, German CA imbalances can be financed both with foreign and/or domestic-currency denominated assets. It is important, however, to reckognize the theoretical background of the small-country assumption. The assumption of only one internationally traded asset constitutes the simplest way to establish an asymmetry in international portfolio preferences. Differences in portfolio preferences are necessary for CA induced wealth shifts to gain influence on the exchange rate. This point becomes clear when we assume a two-country two-asset model in which residents of both countries hold domestic and foreign assets. It is well established in the literature that a mere shift of wealth between these two countries has no influence on the relative price of the assets - the exchange rate - if residents of both countries have exactly the same portfolio preferences.[1)] All that matters in this case is the total net supply of both kinds of assets, not the international asset distribution. The equality of portfolio preferences follows from the assumption that residents of both countries consume the same basket of goods. This may be considered as unrealistic, too, but we will come back to this problem in chapter 5. [2)]

---

1) See, for example, Dooley and Isard (1982), Gaab (1982), Tobin (1982), Frankel (1983).

2) "Uniform portfolio preference" models can be found in Dornbusch (1980c), Frankel (1983).

Nevertheless, the theoretical possibility of uniform preferences challenges the former analysis which emphasized exchange rate effects caused by CA induced wealth shifts.

Our theoretical treatment of the wealth transfer problem assuming only one internationally traded asset may therefore be subject to two important objections. First, it is unrealistic for many countries which are not "small" in international asset markets and, second, it conceals problems arising from international portfolio diversification and portfolio preferences. Questions related to these issues, however, can only be dealt with in a two-country portfolio model in which residents of both countries hold assets denominated in the other country's currency. Such a model will be set out in chapter 5. after we have discussed possible influences of the CA on exchange rate expectations.

4. Exchange Rate Expectations and the Current Account

4.1. The Current Account in a Simple Rational-Expectations Portfolio Balance Model

In the preceding discussion our argument was based on the assumption of stationary expectations and hence, effects of expectations on portfolio equilibrium and the exchange rate were suppressed. Since expectations about future exchange rate developments can safely be considered as an important determinant of asset demands, this omission renders any short or medium run exchange rate analysis incomplete.

In a formal sense, there seems to be no difficulty in augmenting portfolio equilibrium conditions with exchange rate expectations. Expected exchange rate movements constitute an important determinant of expected net returns on assets; thus they may enter asset demand functions, e.g. in Branson's model, in the following way:

$$M = m(r, r^*, \pi)\, W \qquad m_\pi < 0$$
$$B = b(r, r^*, \pi)\, W \qquad b_\pi < 0$$
$$e\,F = f(r, r^*, \pi)\, W \qquad f_\pi > 0$$

where $\pi = \tilde{e}/e$ represents market expectations about the rate of depreciation of the home currency. The signs of the partial derivatives reflect the plausible assumption that an increase in π causes a decline in the demand for domestic assets and an increase in the demand for foreign assets. With specific assumptions about the determinants of π the system can be closed and solved in the same way as shown above.[1)]

The central problem in this context, however, consists in finding a reasonable approximation for the unobservable expected exchange rate and the therefrom deduced expected rate of depreciation π.

---

1) See, for example, Branson (1976, 1979).

Numerous hypotheses about the structural form of aggregated expectation equations can be found in the literature.[1] The mechanisms used to generate π in theoretical models may be roughly divided into adaptive mechanisms and in rational mechanisms.

Adaptive expectations are based on current and past actual exchange rates and derive therefrom, with specific assumptions about expectation elasticities, the expected future exchange rate.[2]

Contrary to the backward orientated adaptive mechanisms, rational expectations, in the sense of Muth, are derived from conditional forecasts based on the structure of the underlying model. Therefore, they provide an endogenous definition of the expected exchange rate.[3]

Empirical investigations give only rough clues for a judgement on the actual relevance of the various expectation hypotheses. Nevertheless, tests on market efficiency in foreign exchange markets supply only little support for a purely adaptive mechanism. The assumption of rational expectations, as a market result, seems to be closer to reality.[4] It seems fair to note, however, that perfect foresight, the deterministic equivalent of stochastic rational expectations, is hardly appropriate to reality since no allowance is made for forecasting errors and uncertainty. Furthermore, since the rational expectation mechanism includes only variables which are contained in the

---

1) It should be stressed that any aggregated expectation equation does not at all provide information about the actual process of expectation formation and the functioning of competitive speculative markets as clearing institutions for divergent expectations. Formal descriptions of expectations in this thesis (and in general) are merely approximations to the result of an (unknown) market clearing process which is reflected in observable prices. Hence, any assumption about the adequate form of such an equation remains, in absence of a sound microeconomic foundation of expectation formation, a "grin without a cat", Streit (1982, p. 24).

2) See, among many others, Argy and Porter (1972), Dornbusch (1976a).

3) On this concept see Muth (1961), Sargent and Wallace (1973), Shiller (1978).

4) As we have already attempted to show in section 2.3., it is not possible to interpret market efficiency tests as strict tests on expectation formation. The outcome of such tests can be interpreted in terms of "substitutability" or in terms of "rationality". Hence, there is always a personal judgement involved. See on this point also Stein (1980, p. 580).

in the model itself one should be careful in drawing conclusions from rational model-expectations to rational behaviour in reality. If the structure of two models differ, rationality within one model means nonrationality within the other.[1] This can be demonstrated by a comparison of rational expectations in the monetary approach described above and rational expectations in portfolio balance models. In the following we discuss some implications of the rational expectation assumption in a simple small-country portfolio model.[2]

The model includes a domestic asset D, denominated in domestic currency, and a foreign asset F, denominated in foreign currency. The change in the domestic stock of F is determined by the CA of the "small" home country. E denotes the exchange rate and $\tilde{E}$ denotes the expected future exchange rate. Consider the following condition for domestic portfolio equilibrium:

$$(1) \qquad {}^{EF}/_{D} = ({}^{\tilde{E}}/_{E})^{\alpha}$$

In eq. (1) we assume that the demand for foreign assets relative to domestic assets is a function of the expected change in the exchange rate. An increase (decrease) in the expected rate of depreciation of the home currency raises (lowers) the demand for foreign assets. α denotes the elasticity of the relative demand for foreign assets with respect to the expected rate of depreciation. Thus, α is a measure of the degree of substitutability between domestic and foreign assets ($0 \leq \alpha \leq \infty$).

---

1) Sharp critizism on rational expectations, in Muth's sense, was raised for similar reasons by Artus (1976, p. 317): "Being rational has often been shamelessly defined in the recent studies as accepting the simplified view of the world depicted by a given theoretical model. This may close the circle and insure the internal consistency of the model in question. It does nothing as far as determining how investors will actually behave under floating."

2) The following model is a straightforward application of the monetarist equilibrium rational expectations approach which has been described in section 2.2. We only substitute the underlying exchange rate model: instead of money market equilibrium conditions we use a simple version of portfolio equilibrium. The monetarist rational expectations approach is discussed, for example, in Bilson (1979a). Our model is similar to the model of Porter (1979). See also Rodrîguez (1980).

In terms of logarithms, eq. (1) can be solved for the exchange rate:

$$(2) \qquad e = (1/_{1+\alpha})\,(d - f) + (\alpha/_{1+\alpha})\,\tilde{e}$$

The change in the exchange rate can now be described as a function of the rates of change in the expected exchange rate $\hat{\tilde{e}}$, in the supply of domestic assets $\hat{d}$, and in the supply of foreign assets $\hat{f}$.

$$(3) \qquad de = (1/_{1+\alpha})\,(\hat{d} - \hat{f}) + (\alpha/_{1+\alpha})\,\hat{\tilde{e}}$$

Eq. (3) illustrates that the change in the exchange rate depends on the degree of substitutability between D and F. If there is no substitution ($\alpha = 0$), eq. (3) becomes $de = \hat{d} - \hat{f}$ and the exchange rate depends only on the relative supply of both assets. A change in the stocks of D and F leads to an equiproportional change in the exchange rate. Exchange rate expectations have no influence on e.

In the opposite case with perfect substitutability ($\alpha \to \infty$), actual asset stocks play no role in exchange rate determination. Eq. (3) becomes $de = \hat{\tilde{e}}$ and the exchange rate is a function only of the expected exchange rate. Expectations of a depreciation of the home currency cause an equiproportional rise in the actual exchange rate.

In order to introduce rational expectations in this model we specify eq. (2) as:

$$(2') \qquad e_t = (1/_{1+\alpha})\,(d - f)_t + (\alpha/_{1+\alpha})\,E_t\, e_{t+1}$$

where $E_t\, e_{t+1}$ denotes expectations in t about the exchange rate in t+1. With rational expectations, the expected value of the exchange rate in any further period t+j is determined by the actual exchange rate equation.

$$(4) \qquad E_t\, e_{t+j} = (1/_{1+\alpha})\,E_t\,(d - f)_{t+j} + (\alpha/_{1+\alpha})\,E_t\, e_{t+j+1}$$

Successive substitution of eq. (4) into eq. (2') yields for a finite time period:

$$(5) \qquad e_t = ({}^{1}/_{1+\alpha})(d-f)_t + [{}^{\alpha}/_{(1+\alpha)^2}]\, E_t\, (d-f)_{t+1} + [{}^{\alpha^2}/_{(1+\alpha)^3}]\, E_t\, (d-f)_{t+2} + \ldots + [{}^{\alpha^n}/_{(1+\alpha)^{n+1}}]\, E_t\, (d-f)_{t+n} + [{}^{\alpha^n}/_{(1+\alpha)^n}]\, E_t\, e_{t+n+1}$$

If t+n+1 coincides with the long run equilibrium, $E_t\, e_{t+n+1}$ equals the expected long run equilibrium rate.

When we substitute eq. (4) into eq. (2') for all values of t+j, that is for an infinite time period, the following reduced form equation for the exchange rate can be derived:

$$(5') \qquad e_t = {}^{1}/_{1+\alpha} \sum_{j=0}^{\infty} ({}^{\alpha}/_{1+\alpha})^j\, E_t\, (d-f)_{t+j}$$

Eq. (5') illustrates that the actual exchange rate in t depends on the actual and expected values of the exogenous asset stocks. Thus, expectations of future CA positions which will alter the stock of foreign assets in t+j are already taken into account in time t and influence the current exchange rate. Future changes in the supply of D and F will be discounted into the current spot rate. The discount factor ($\alpha/1+\alpha$) is related directly to the degree of substitution between domestic and foreign assets.

Eq. (5) and (5') permit an illustration of three possible relationships between CA expectations and the exchange rate.

a. Both equations show that the influence of future values of the CA on the current exchange rate diminishes with an increasing time horizon according to the degree of substitutability between domestic and foreign assets.

If both assets are considered as good substitutes ($\alpha \rightarrow \infty$), the discount factor from eq. (5) $\alpha^{n-1}/(1-\alpha)^n$ is relatively low so that future developments in the CA achieve a high significance for the current exchange rate. In the extreme case, the actual values of D and F will be negligible relative to their anticipated future values. Changes in expectations will be the prime cause of fluctuations in the exchange rate. Since the information which alters expectations must be new, the exchange rate will be moved exclusively by news related to the future asset stocks D and F.

On the other hand, a low degree of substitutability ($\alpha \rightarrow 0$) increases the discount factor for expected changes in asset stocks. In this case, the actual stocks will be more important to the exchange rate than expected future changes in D and F. This result suggests that even with rational expectations anticipated future changes in asset stocks may have very little influence on the current exchange rate if the degree of substitutability is low. Anticipated changes in asset stocks will have their maximum impact on the exchange rate at the time when they actually take place.[1)]

The important conclusion from this consideration can now be summarized. The exchange rate impact of "news" relative to the exchange rate impact of (anticipated) actual changes in the exogenous variables depends crucially on the degree of substitutability between domestic and foreign assets. The conclusion that in rational expectations models only unanticipated disturbances move the exchange rate presumes a high degree of substitutability. Likewise, it is possible to attribute an important role to actual disturbances if we combine the rational expectations assumption with the assumption of a low degree of substitutability between domestic and foreign assets.

b. In eqs. (5) and (5') asset stocks and thus the CA have been regarded as exogenous. It seems realistic, however, to assume that agents do not consider the CA as purely exogenous but form a view about the underlying determinants of the evolution of the CA. If the CA is endogenous with respect to these variables, expectations about the

---

1) This point is discussed and illustrated by a quantitative example in Porter (1979, pp. 17).

future values of F can be interpreted as expectations about the dynamic response of the CA to exogenous disturbances. Accordingly, the exchange rate depends on the dynamic adjustment path of the CA which links the different expected values of F in eqs. (5) and (5') over a longer time period.

Assume now that the CA can be split up in a structural component and in an endogenous component which depends on wealth, income, relative prices etc.[1)] An exogenous change in the structural component, say a deterioration of the terms of trade due to a sudden and lasting change in the prices of imports or a shift in the domestic absorbtion function, leads to an imbalanced CA. Given enough time and stability of the system, the endogenous components of the CA will adjust so as to restore flow equilibrium. But since this adjustment will take some time, a shift in the structural component will be followed by a period of CA imbalances. Therefore, in the case of an unanticipated CA deficit, asset holders will expect further declines in the stock of foreign assets and hence further depreciations. Thus, the demand for domestic assets declines and the demand for foreign assets rises immediately at the time of the initial disturbance. This shift in asset preferences coincides with the actual decrease in the supply of foreign assets and hence brings about a stronger depreciation than would have been in the absence of the expectational effect. If the depreciation tends to reduce the CA deficit, the induced shift in asset demands shortens the time period of flow disequilibrium and, therefore, may be considered as stabilizing in this sense. On the other hand, if the depreciation results merely in price increases with little or no effect towards a restoration of CA balance expectations will enforce the disequilibrium situation. The stabilizing or destabilizing effect of expectations based on the expected CA situtaion depends on the structure of the economy, that is, on the efficiency of the endogenous components in restoring flow equilibrium. Since the response of the CA to a depreciation is of crucial importance for further exchange rate movements,

---

1) For a similar approach see Rodríguez (1980).

asset holders will make an assessment about this dynamic relationship when forming their expectations. If the CA is expected to react very slowly to alterations in the endogenous components, this will result in a relatively stronger exchange rate depreciation at the time of the change in the structural component; expectations of a smoothly and quickly reacting CA will bring about a relatively moderate increase in the depreciation.

c. Another way in which the CA may gain influence on the exchange rate may consist in its influence on the expected long run equilibrium exchange rate in eq. (5). This line of argument may draw, for example, on our discussion of the long run equilibrium state in the models of Branson and Genberg/Kierzkowski.

Suppose that an exogenous disturbance causes a CA surplus which leads to an appreciation of the domestic currency. As explained above, the length of the subsequent surplus period depends on structural parameters which determine the adjustment speed at which the CA returns to its equilibrium level of zero. A long surplus period is associated with a strong increase in the stock of foreign assets and hence causes (given the foreign interest rate) a strong rise in capital inflows from foreign interest payments. Since the CA must be zero in the long run, a high level of foreign interest payments must be matched in equilibrium by a high trade account deficit. This in turn requires a long run appreciation which must be sufficient to produce this relatively high trade account deficit.

This consideration suggests that expectations of a slow return of the CA to its equilibrium level may lead to a substantial change in the expected long run equilibrium exchange rate. On the other hand, if the CA is expected to return quickly to its equilibrium level, the change in the expected long run equilibrium exchange rate may be smaller.

The discussion of points a. to c. illustrates that equilibrium in asset stock markets is not independent of equilibrium in flow markets. The rational expectations assumption constitutes a link between short run portfolio equilibrium at given asset stocks and long run flow equilibrim in goods markets and the CA.[1)]

Finally, we want to indicate another empirically important implication of the rational expectations assumption. The analysis above suggests that expectations about the future course of the exogenous variables constitute a major determinant of the exchange rate. We develope this idea further by introducing a specific time series process that generates the composite exogenous variable (d - f) = z into the general exchange rate equation (5').

A simple example with an interesting empirical background can be formed when we assume that the level of z follows a first-order autoregressive process.[2)]

$$(6) \qquad z_{t+1} = \rho z_t + u_{t+1}$$

where ρ denotes the first-order autoregressive parameter and u_{t+1} is an independently distributed random error with an expected value of zero. Eq. (6) can be used to specify rational exchange rate forecasts for period t+1.

$$(7) \qquad E_t e_{t+1} = (^1/_{1+\alpha}) (\rho z_t + u_{t+1}) + (^\alpha/_{1+\alpha}) E_t e_{t+2}$$

Substituting eq. (7) into the initial exchange rate equation (2') for all future values of the composite exogenous variable z yields equation (8).

---

1) A good description of this relationship is given by Dornbusch and Krugman (1976, p. 555): "with ... rational expectations, the current equilibrium level of exchange rates is a function of the entire subsequent path of the economy, including developments in income, prices and wealth. Although these variables may be predetermined at a point in time, their subsequent evolution affects the current equilibrium level of the exchange rate and thus restores the general-equilibrium determination of exchange rates ....".

2) For an example in which the change in z is generated by a first-order autoregressive process see Bilson (1979a).

$$(8) \qquad e_t = {}^{1}/_{1+\alpha} \; z_t \sum_{j=0}^{\infty} ({}^{\alpha}/_{1+\alpha})^j \rho^j$$

If the composite exogenous variable z follows a random walk ($\rho = 1$), the exchange rate e_t in eq. (8) depends only on the current values of the exogenous variables and on the degree of substitution between domestic and foreign assets. In this case, expectations about the future exchange rate focus exclusively on the current values of the exogenous variables. Thus, eq. (8) demonstrates that a combination of the rational expectations hypothesis and our specific random walk assumption leads to an exchange rate equation which includes only the current values of the exogenous variables: if the exogenous variables follow a random walk, their current values represent the best prediction for the future and hence, rational agents should take the current values of these variables as the best possible forecast.

Our specific random walk assumption, however, might appear to be a very restrictive special case. Accordingly, a theory which is formulated only in terms of actual values of the exogenous variables may be accused to be unduly simplified.[1)] Nevertheless, there is some empirical support for the random walk assumption. Gaab (1982) finds that relative money supply levels and real income levels of the US and Germany followed approximately a random walk process over the period from 1974.10 to 1981.5. Branson (1981) reports similar results for money stocks and current account balances of the US, Germany, and the United Kingdom. His calculations cover the period from late 1973 to late 1980.

---

1) See, for example, Frankel (1983, p. 88-89).

4.2. Current Account News in a Model of Real and Nominal Exchange Rate Determination

In the last section we attempted to show that the combination of rational expectations with a high degree of substitution between domestic and foreign assets may lead to a situation in which the current exchange rate is largely determined by expectations about the future course of the exogenous variables. The foreign exchange market responds immediately to all anticipated future disturbances. At the time when the disturbance actually occurs there is no reaction in the exchange rate if the market has been correct in its expectations: the disturbance has been discounted in advance. In this case, changes in the exchange rate predominantly reflect revisions in expectations in response to surprising new information.[1)]

Within the rational expectations model presented in the last section, actual and expected CA positions affected the exchange rate through their influence on actual and expected relative asset supplies. This consideration referred essentially to the wealth redistribution effect of the CA. In this section now we choose another approach in order to take the news-argument into account. We decompose expectations about the nominal exchange rate into a real component and a price level term. Our considerations are based on two assumptions. First, we assume that agents do not expect CA imbalances to cumulate infinetely; second, we assume that the real exchange rate, defined as the nominal rate deflated by relative price levels, is regarded by agents as the stabilizing force which equilibrates the CA in the long run. Thus, the expected real exchange rate is conceived as a function of the expected CA: expectations concerning the real exchange rate that is required to balance the CA in the long run (the expected equilibrium real exchange rate) are revised continuously in response to new information about the observed actual CA.

The operation of this expectation mechanism can be illustrated in an extended version of a Dornbusch-Frankel type interest rate parity model.[2)]

---

1) The news-argument is emphasized, for example, in Mussa (1979), Frenkel (1981a) and Dornbusch (1980b, 1982a).

2) Similar models can be found in Hooper and Morton (1980), Isard (1980), Frankel (1983), Edison (1983). The following exposition is a condensed version of Groß (1983).

Consider the following modified uncovered IRP equation:

(1) $$E_t \, \mathrm{dln}\, e_{t,T} = r_t^* - r_t + \varphi_t$$

$E_t \, \mathrm{dln}\, e_{t,T}$	: Expected change in the exchange rate between t and T. This term is equivalent to the expected rate of appreciation of the domestic currency.
$r_t^* - r_t$	: Interest rate differential at time t. Both interest rates refer to the same period as $E_t \, \mathrm{dln}\, e_{t,T}$.[1)]
φ_t	: Risk premium at time t.

φ is defined by the difference between the interest rate differential and the expected rate of appreciation of the domestic currency which must prevail in equilibrium if asset holders are to hold willingly the existing asset stocks. φ_t reflects the assumption of imperfect substitutability between domestic and foreign assets: the expected net returns of domestic and foreign interest-bearing assets may differ in portfolio equilibrium. A precise specification of the risk premium can be obtained by solving a conventional two-country portfolio model, holding the expected rates of return constant.[2)] The so determined risk premium depends mainly on two variables:

a. on the relative supply of outstanding assets denominated in domestic and foreign currency, respectively (net supplies of domestic and foreign bonds).

b. on the international distribution of net wealth as it results from actual CA balances.

Exchange rate effects of changes in φ_t are identical to the portfolio balance effect of changes in relative asset supplies and CA imbalances. Since this relationship has already been discussed in chapter 3. (and will be discussed further in chapter 5.), we leave it aside here and

---

1) Strictly speaking, the interest rate differential is defined in logarithms as $\ln [(1 + r_t^*)/(1 + r_t)]$. For normal values of interest rates, however, this expression is numerically very close to the interest rate differential given above.

2) The risk premium is explicitly derived from a simplified portfolio balance model in Dooley and Isard (1979, 1982).

concentrate on the specification of exchange rate expectations. Over the following discussion it should be remembered, however, that changes in φ_t may occur as the result of a wealth redistribution due to actual CA imbalances. This mechanism works beside the expectations effect.

We define the expected change in the exchange rate according to Frankel (1979a) as a function of the gap between the expected (long run) equilibrium rate $E_t \ln \bar{e}$ and the current "spot" exchange rate $\ln e_t$ plus the expected change in the equilibrium exchange rate $E_t \, d\ln \bar{e}$.

$$(2) \qquad E_t \, d\ln e_{t,T} = \Theta \, [\, E_t \ln \bar{e} \; - \; \ln e_t] \; + \; E_t \, d\ln \bar{e}$$

The adjustment speed parameter Θ is assumed to be a constant positive number $0 < \Theta \leq \infty$. Note that a deviation between the actual exchange rate and the expected equilibrium exchange rate following a monetary shock is possible only because of the assumption of sticky prices in the short run.[1)] Postulating a belief in long run relative PPP, we determine the expected change in the equilibrium exchange rate, similar to Frankel, by the currently expected long run inflation differential between the domestic and the foreign country.

$$(3) \qquad E_t \, d\ln \bar{e} \; = \; E_t \, \bar{\psi} \; - \; E_t \, \bar{\psi}^*$$

Taking eq. (3) into account, eq. (2) says that in the short run the exchange rate is expected to return to its equilibrium value at a rate which is proportional to the current gap, and that in the long run, when $e = \bar{e}$, the exchange rate is expected to change at the long run inflation differential.

Assuming that in the long run real interest rates are equal, the long run nominal interest rate differential must reflect the long run inflation differential (long run Fisher-parity). Therefore, we may

---

1) Frankel (1979a) relates Θ in a rational expectations framework through a price adjustment equation to the speed of adjustment in the goods markets.

substitute $E_t \overline{\psi} - E_t \overline{\psi}^*$ by the current differential between long-term nominal interest rates $LR_t - LR_t^*$. Using this approximation and substituting eq. (2) and eq. (3) into eq. (1) yields the following exchange rate equation:

$$(4) \quad \ln e_t = E_t \ln \overline{e} + 1/\Theta \; [(r^* - LR^*)_t - (r - LR)_t] + 1/\Theta \; \varphi_t$$

Eq. (4) states that the gap between the actual exchange rate and the expected equilibrium rate is proportional to Frankel's real interest differential (reflecting a slow adjustment of goods prices) and the risk premium.[1)]

Next we turn to the expected nominal and real exchange rate.

The equilibrium nominal exchange rate in eq. (4) can be divided into a relative price level term and into a real component. This can be seen when we define the real exchange rate q as the nominal rate deflated by relative price levels:

$$q = e \, (P^*/P)$$

where P and P^* denote domestic and foreign price levels, respectively. The nominal exchange rate can thus be expressed as the real exchange rate q times the price level term:

$$e = q \, (P/P^*)$$

We apply this relationship to the expected equilibrium exchange rate as it occurs in eq. (4):

$$(5) \quad E_t \ln \overline{e} = E_t \ln (\overline{P}/\overline{P}^*) + E_t \ln \overline{q}$$

---

1) Although nominal interest rates are short-term while the expected inflation differential is long-term, it can be shown by introducing a price adjustment equation that the term in brackets equals the short-term real interest differential; see Frankel (1979a), Appendix A.

In eq. (5) expectations about the equilibrium exchange rate are decomposed in expectations about the equilibrium price levels and expectations about the equilibrium real exchange rate.

Following the monetarist approach, equilibrium relative price levels are determined by relative money market equilibrium conditions. Agents are supposed to form their expectations accordingly. Using two Cagan-type demand functions, assuming equal interest and income elasticities in both countries, and bearing in mind that the nominal interest differential equals the inflation differential in the long run equilibrium, we state the following expectations equation:[1)]

$$(6') \qquad E_t \ln(\overline{P}/\overline{P}^*) = k + E_t \ln(\overline{M}/\overline{M}^*) - \eta E_t \ln(\overline{Y}/\overline{Y}^*) + \varepsilon (LR - LR^*)_t$$

where $\overline{M}$, $\overline{M}^*$ denote the equilibrium values of the domestic and foreign money supply, and $\overline{Y}$, $\overline{Y}^*$ denote the equilibrium values of domestic and foreign income levels.

If we assume that the expected equilibrium money supplies and incomes are given by their current actual levels, eq. (6') can be written:[2)]

$$(6) \qquad E_t \ln(\overline{P}/\overline{P}^*) = k + \ln(M/M^*)_t - \eta \ln(Y/Y^*)_t + \varepsilon (LR - LR^*)_t$$

Now we turn to the determination of the expected equilibrium real exchange rate. We assume that agents form their expectations on the basis of the following two relationships.

a. The real exchange rate has a major influence on the CA: an increase in the long run real exchange rate (a real depreciation of the domestic currency) increases the long run surplus (reduces the long run deficit) in the home country's CA. An analogous relation is assumed to hold in the case of a decrease in the long run real rate.

---

1) For a detailed derivation see Frankel (1976) or Bilson (1978, 1979a). The assumption of equal interest and income elasticities can easily be relaxed. As above, $E_t \overline{\Psi} - E_t \overline{\Psi}^*$ has been substituted by the nominal long-term interest differential $LR - LR^*$.

2) On this assumption see also Frankel (1979a, 1983) and Gaab (1982). The underlying rationale of this assumption has been discussed in the last section, see pp. 92.

b. The development of the real exchange rate is bound to prevent CA imbalances from cumulating infinetly. The real exchange rate is the stabilizing force with respect to the CA.

Thus $E_t \bar{q}$ is taken as the real exchange rate that is expected to equilibrate the CA in the long run.[1] This assumed relationship between $E_t \bar{q}$ and the CA is described by eq. (7).

(7) $$E_t \overline{CAS} = f(E_t \bar{q}, E_t \bar{X})$$

$E_t \overline{CAS}$ = Expected equilibrium CA surplus; set to zero in this model.[2]

$E_t \bar{X}$: Vector of expected equilibrium values of all variables others than the real exchange rate relevant to the CA.

With $E_t \overline{CAS}$ set zero (the CA is expected to balance in the long run), a change in $E_t \bar{X}$ requires a change in $E_t \bar{q}$ to maintain the given $E_t \overline{CAS}$. In a dynamic framework, every $E_t \bar{X}$ and $E_t \bar{q}$ consistent with $E_t \overline{CAS} = 0$ is linked to an expected path of CA imbalances and expectations about the reaction of the CA to changes in q while q is converging to $\bar{q}$. Therefore, a previously expected change in $\bar{X}$ which results in an expected CA situation has no influence on the expected $\bar{q}$. On the other hand, an unexpected change in $\bar{X}$ which produces an unexpected change in the CA leads to revisions in $E_t \bar{q}$. Hence, it may be assumed that agents infer expectations about $\bar{q}$ directly from actually observed CA imbalances: if the actual CA imbalance deviates from the expected CA imbalance, that is, from the expected time path of the CA linked to a certain $\bar{q}$, agents revise their expectations about $\bar{q}$.

---

1) Isard (1980, p. 13) puts it in the following way: "... if real exchange rates did not adjust to prevent a permanent unidirectional shift in the expected path of the current account, the associated expected shift in the cumulative current account would converge towards an infinite shift in wealth form one country to another, which is implausible.Thus it is rational to revise expectations about future real exchange rates in response to new information that would otherwise suggest a permanent unidirectional shift in current-account flows."

2) Since the equilibrium CA balance can be seen as determined by the desired rate of net accumulation of wealth in the long run, $E_t \overline{CAS} = 0$ is not compulsory but just a convenient simplification. For a different treatment see Hooper and Morton (1980).

Accordingly, we assume that market expectations about the real exchange rate which is necessary to achieve a balanced CA in the long run are revised in response to CA "news" - that is, in response to deviations between actual and expected CA surpluses.
For example, an unexpectedly high surplus in the home country's CA leads to a reduction ("appreciation") of the expected $\bar{q}$, and an unexpectedly high surplus in the foreign CA induces an increase ("depreciation") of the expected equilibrium real exchange rate.
In a two-country model, however, the CA surplus of the home country equals the CA deficit of the foreign country. Hence one CA is sufficient as point of reference. When the domestic CA is chosen as basis, one can formalize the considerations above as follows: [1)]

$$(8) \qquad E_t \ln \bar{q} = E_{t-1} \ln \bar{q} - \gamma \, (CAS_{t-1,t} - E_{t-1}\, CAS_{t-1,t})$$

γ is taken as positive constant. The term in parenthesis denotes the forecasting error (CA news),recognized at time t, with respect to the actual domestic CA surplus in period t-1,t. Thus, in eq. (8) the expected long run equilibrium real exchange rate $E_t \ln \bar{q}$ is defined by two variables. First, by the prediction made at the beginning of the foregoing period $E_{t-1} \ln \bar{q}$, and, second, by corrections due to forecasting errors which show up at time t on grounds of new statistical information on the actual development of the domestic CA within the period t-1,t.

Eq. (8), referring to two specific points in time, can be extended by subsequent substitution to a multi-period relationship:

$$(9) \qquad E_t \ln \bar{q} = E_{i-1} \ln \bar{q} - \gamma \sum_{i=1}^{t} (CAS_{i-1,i} - E_{i-1}\, CAS_{i-1,i})$$

According to eq. (9), the expected equilibrium real exchange rate at time t is determined by a base period initial-value $E_{i-1} \ln \bar{q} = E_0 \ln \bar{q}$ and the cumulative sum of current and past deviations of expected CA surpluses from their later actual values.

---

1) For an empirical model which links expectations both to the domestic and the foreign CA see Groß (1983).

In an empirical application of eq. (9) we would have to specify expectations about the future CA surplus. One could consider, for example, the following two assumptions.

$$(10) \qquad E_{i-1}\, CAS_{i-1,i} = CAS_{i-2,i-1} + \lambda\,(\overline{CAS} - CAS_{i-2,i-1})$$

$$= (1-\lambda)\, CAS_{i-2,i-1}$$

The expected CA surplus is taken as a positive fraction λ of the gap between the actual and the equilibrium CA surplus ($\overline{CAS} = 0$) that is expected to be eliminated in the next period.[1)]

$$(11) \qquad E_{i-1}\, CAS_{i-1,i} = w\, \underbrace{CAS_{i-2,i-1}}_{\text{stationarity assumption}} + (1-w)\, \underbrace{CAS_{i-1,i}}_{\text{perfect foresight}}$$

In eq. (11), the CA surplus expected for period i-1,i at time i-1 is derived from a weighted average of perfect foresight and stationarity.
Eqs. (10) or (11) can be substituted into eq. (9) to express $E_t \ln \overline{q}$ in observable values.

Before we join together the various components of the model, it is necessary to point out shortcomings in the assumed link between CA news and exchange rate expectations. The specification of expectations with regard to the real exchange rate, as depicted by eqs (8) and (9), represents certainly an oversimplification. Both equations do not distinguish permanent and transitory shifts in the CA - a distinction which might be crucial to reactions of real exchange rate expectations: if, for example, an unexpected CA imbalance is considered to be transitory (not resulting from permanent changes in underlying factors) there may be no or just a minor adjustment in the expected equilibrium real exchange rate. In the framework presented here we implicitly

---

1) This is the assumption used by Hooper and Morton (1980).

assume that every unexpeted CA imbalance is conceived to be permanent.[1]

Moreover, errors in CA expectations may not only be due to wrong forecasts about fundamental factors but also to wrong assessments of the influence of the real exchange rate on the CA. If this is recognized by agents, an unexpected CA imbalance may rationally lead to corrections in the expected time path of the CA without influencing the long run equilibrium real exchange rate.

Nevertheless, the foregoing description may serve as a simple illustration of the potential role of CA news in exchange rate determination.

The final exchange rate equation can now be obtained by substituting eqs. (6) and (9) into eq. (4).

$$(12) \qquad \ln e_t = a_t + \ln ({}^{M}/_{M^*})_t - \eta \ln ({}^{Y}/_{Y^*})_t + \varepsilon (LR - LR^*)_t - \gamma \sum_{i=1}^{t} (CAS_{i-1,i} - E_{i-1}\, CAS_{i-1,i}) + {}^{1}/_{\Theta} [(r^* - LR^*) - (r - LR)]_t + {}^{1}/_{\Theta}\, \varphi_t$$

with $a_t = k + E_0 \ln \bar{q}$

Eq. (12) defines the exchange rate at time t as dependent on:

a. expected equilibrium relative price levels, specified as functions of expected equilibrium money stocks and real incomes (proxied by their actual current values) and the long run inflation differential (proxied by the current differential in long-term interest rates);

b. the expected equilibrium real exchange rate, determined by a base period value (included in the constant a_t) and the cumulative sum of "unexpected" changes in the domestic CA since the base period;

---

1) Hooper and Morton (1980) assume that transitory changes in the CA can be expressed as a constant fraction of the deviation of the CA from its expected level (defined similar to eq. 10 above). This assumption too is certainly not very realistic.

c. the real interest differential, assumed to reflect the part of the deviation of the spot rate from its equilibrium value which is due to the slow adjustment of prices to monetary disturbances;

d. the risk premium, reflecting imperfect substitutability between domestic and foreign-currency denominated assets. As mentioned above, the risk premium can be specified further as a function of the net supplies of domestic and foreign bonds and as a function of the actual net wealth distribution between both countries given by the sum of past and current bilateral CA balances.

4.3. Anticipated Disturbances and Current Account Dynamics

Having discussed consequences of rational expectations and CA news for the exchange rate in portfolio balance models, we close our theoretical exposition by considering effects of an anticipated disturbance in a model which includes both a financial and a real sector. As an illustrative example we focus on impacts of a current announcement of a future increase in the nominal money supply on the dynamic evolution of the CA and the exchange rate. The following representation refers to the model of Dornbusch and Fischer (1980).[1)]

The Dornbusch/Fischer model starts from the usual small-country full-employment assumptions: the foreign interest rate r^* and the foreign price level P^* are given; domestic output is fixed at the full employment level. The domestic price level P is assumed to be perfectly flexible at every point in time. Deviations from PPP are possible since the home country produces a differentiated product whose world price is endogenous.[2)] Therefore, a change in the exchange rate alters the terms of trade. At a given stock of foreign assets the endogenous variables adjust immediately so as to preserve continuous equilibrium in asset and goods markets.

Domestic residents hold domestic money and foreign interest-earning bonds. Foreign bonds are the only internationally traded asset. They are defined as real bonds promissing to pay a unit of foreign output indefinitely.[3)] The price per one real bond 'a' corresponds to the reciprocal of the given foreign interest rate $1/r^*$.

The structure of the model is made up of the following equations:

$$(1) \qquad M = k(r^* + \pi) \; [Py + eP^*a] \; ; \quad k' < 0 \qquad \text{domestic money market}$$

$$(1') \qquad m = M/P = k(\pi) \; [y + \lambda a]$$

---

1) Similar examples have been analyzed by Dornbusch (1980a, b), Wilson (1979), Kouri (1980, 1983).

2) Import prices are given in foreign currency but there is some scope for an independent price determination of the domestically produced and consumed good so that the overall price level may deviate from PPP.

3) The definition of foreign assets as real bonds is crucial for the results of the model.

(2) $y = D(\lambda, W/P) + X(\lambda)$ domestic goods market

$$D_\lambda, X_\lambda > 0; \; D_{(W/P)} > 0$$

---

(3) $W/P = m + \lambda (a/r^*)$ real wealth

(4) $\lambda = eP^*/P$ terms of trade

(5) $S = S(W/P); \; S_{(W/P)} < 0$ domestic savings

(6) $\dot{a}/r^* = S(W/P) / \lambda$ current account surplus

where

- y : real output
- D : domestic demand for domestic output
- X : foreign demand for domestic goods
- π : expected rate of depreciation of the home currency
- a : number of income streams each yielding one unit of foreign output indefinitely.

In eq. (1) the demand for domestic money is assumed to be a function of the opportunity costs of holding money, represented by r^* and π, and nominal income. The income term in brackets consists of income from production Py and returns from foreign bonds eP^*a measured in terms of domestic currency. Accordingly, the real money demand depends on real output y and on income from foreign bonds measured in units of domestic goods λa. The equality of real balances and money demand is preserved by immediate adjustments of the price level P.

The goods market equilibrium condition eq. (2) determines the terms of trade at every point in time as a function of the existing stock of external assets 'a'. For given stocks of foreign assets and given exchange rate expectations π, the price level and the terms of trade adjust immediately to maintain simultaneous equilibrium in goods and asset markets.

The dynamic evolution of the system is governed by the CA, described in eq. (6). A surplus in the domestic CA is associated with an increase in real net stocks of foreign assets. According to the absorbtion approach, a surplus in the CA corresponds to savings S. S is defined as a decreasing function of real wealth. A CA surplus raises the stock of foreign assets and thus increases real wealth. The following increase in income from foreign assets induces a rise in the real money demand. At given nominal money supply, the price level must decline to satisfy the excess demand by an increase in real balances. In the goods market, the rise in external assets increases real wealth directly and via the induced change in real balances. To keep the increased demand for domestic goods in line with the fixed output the terms of trade must improve - the relative price of imports must decline.

Dornbusch and Fischer analyse this system with stationary expectations for various shocks. They derive the following comparative-static results.

a. An increase in the world demand for domestic goods (a structural export increase) leads to a higher stock of foreign assets and an improvement in the terms of trade which corresponds to an appreciated exchange rate.

b. A rise in the stock of money brings about an equiproportional and instantaneous depreciation with an unchanged stock of external assets.[1)]

c. A higher expected rate of depreciation induces an actual depreciation and a deterioration in the terms of trade.

Since the economic rationale behind the adjustment mechanism of the model is quite similar to the mechanisms described in chapter 3., we concentrate now on effects of an anticipated disturbance.

Assuming rational expectations, which means here that the anticipated rate of depreciation is set equal to the actual rate, the reaction of the economy to a current announcement of a future increase in the nominal quantity of money can be described in the following figure.

---

1) The long run neutrality property of the model is due to the flexible-price assumption and the definition of foreign bonds as real bonds.

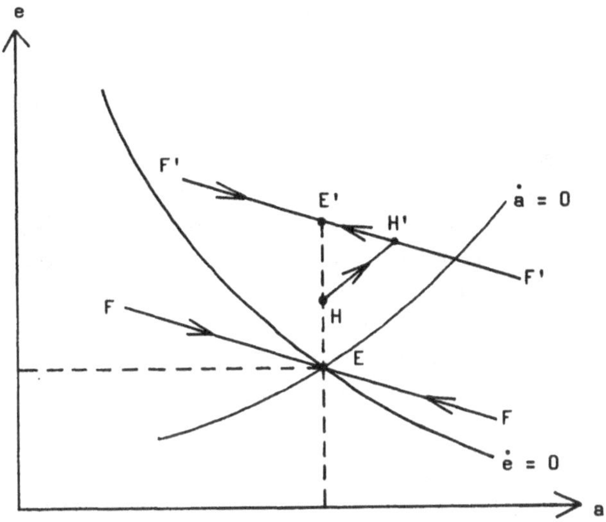

The e = 0 curve indicates all combinations of 'a' and e for which the exchange rate keeps unchanged. The reason for the negative slope is intuitively comprehensible: an increase in external assets (a CA surplus) must lead to an appreciation to keep the system in short run equilibrium.[1)]

Along the a = 0 curve the CA is balanced. An increase in 'a' implies a rise in wealth, higher spendings and thus a tendency towards a CA deficit. To restore external balance the exchange rate must depreciate. Points above $\dot{a} = 0$ are associated with a CA surplus, points below with a deficit.[2)]

---

1) The formal expression for e = 0 can be derived from the reduced forms of eqs. (1') and (2):

$\lambda = \lambda\ (a, \pi) \qquad \lambda_a < 0, \lambda_\pi > 0$
$m = m\ (a, \pi) \qquad m_a > 0, m_\pi < 0$

Combining these equations with the definition of the exchange rate $e = \lambda P/P^*$ yields, after some transformations and implementing the rational expectation assumption $\pi = \hat{e}$:

$e = \Theta(a, e/_{M/P^*})$ with $\Theta_1 > 0, \Theta_2 > 0$.

2) next page.

FF and F'F', respectively, are perfect foresight paths of the economy.[1)]

The initial equilibrium is situated in point E. The comparative-statics show that the new long run equilibrium following the increase in the money supply will be at point E' with an unchanged stock of foreign assets and an equiproportionally depreciated exchange rate. At the time of the announcement, the anticipated increase in the money stock causes an anticipated depreciation and hence the exchange rate jumps immediately to a point such as H. The actual depreciation reduces - at a still constant nominal stock of money - the demand for money. The price level increases and reduces real balances. With a lower stock of real wealth savings rise, the CA moves to a surplus and the stock of external assets increases.

This process continues during the transition period in which the economy moves from H to H'. The time between the announcement and the actual increase in the money supply is characterized by a depreciating exchange rate and a CA surplus.

The economy reaches H' exactly at the time the money supply increases. Since money demand already reacted to the higher nominal money supply at the time of the announcement, the actual increase rises real balances, wealth and domestic absorbtion and hence leads to a deficit in the CA. Over the following adjustment from H' to E' the economy moves along the new convergent perfect foresight path F'F': the exchange rate continues to depreciate and the CA deficit leads to decumulations of foreign assets.

(footnote 2. last page) The dynamic equation follows from eq. (6):

$$\dot{a}/r^* = (1/\lambda)\, S\, [m\,(a,\,\pi) + \lambda\,(a,\pi)\,(a/r^*)] \quad ;\ \text{in reduced form}$$

$$\dot{a} = \psi\,(a,\, e/_{M/P}{}^*) \quad \text{with} \quad \psi_1 < 0,\ \ \psi_2 > 0.$$

A formal derivation shows that $\psi_1 < 0$ (the total effect of an increase in external assets on the CA is negative) is not compulsory but has to be assumed.

1) The system exhibits saddle-point stability. It is not clear from Dornbusch and Fischer why the economy would choose the convergent perfect foresight path.

The following two interesting conclusions can be drawn from this analysis.

a. The exchange rate effect of an exogenous shock will, in general, differ according to whether the disturbance has been anticipated. An anticipated CA imbalance may produce exchange rate effects even before the imbalance occurs. This, in turn, may alter the later influence of an actual CA imbalance on the exchange rate.

b. Taking into account anticipations, the conventional conclusion from a CA deficit (surplus) to a depreciating (appreciating) exchange rate is not mandatory for the whole adjustment path. An anticipated increase in exports, for example, causes in the Dornbusch/Fischer model an immediate appreciation which continues (with different rates) over the entire adjustment path to the long run equilibrium; but during the transition period between anticipation and actual occurance of the export increase the CA is in deficit.

Considering the rather restrictive presuppositions of this model, as, for example, the structure of the asset sector, the assumption of short run price flexibility, and perfect foresight, we may close with a conclusion drawn by Wilson (1979, p. 646) from a similar analysis: "It is important to recognize, however, that this conclusion, as well as some of the other properties of the adjustment process, may be sensitive to the particular specification of the model. The announcement of an expansionary policy can generally be expected to have an impact, but the direction or extent of the impact may be different for different specifications."[1)]

---

1) This point is illustrated in a model of Greenwood (1983). Greenwood excludes real balances in his definition of real wealth upon which housholds base their consumption and savings decisions. As a result, an anticipated increase in the money stock leads to an exchange rate depreciation which coincides with a slight deterioration in the CA. This result contrasts with the Dornbusch/Fischer analysis where an anticipated increase in the money stock leads to a CA surplus in the first instance.

4.4. Summary and some Remarks on the Empirical Relevance of Current Account News

Over the last three sections we attempted to provide an overview of possible connections between the CA and exchange rate expectations. Our considerations suggest that the distinction between anticipated disturbances on the one hand, and unanticipated disturbances on the other is crucial for the exchange rate influence of CA balances. If a future CA position has been anticipated, then it is not the actual CA that moves the exchange rate but only the unanticipated part of the actual CA: the current exchange rate reacts to CA news and not to the actual CA. This relationship challenges the analysis in chapter 3. where the exchange rate was seen as a function of actual CA imbalances.

Although there is no lack of theoretical arguments in favour of the news-approach in the literature, one should also bear in mind its limitations. In section 4.1. it was shown that rational expectations imply a discounting process with regard to anticipated future events. The effect of a CA imbalance which has been anticipated in the past on the current exchange rate is not necessarily zero. Its influence on the exchange rate depends on the time span between anticipation and realization and on the discount factor which reflects the degree of substitutability between domestic and foreign assets.
With a view to an empirical investigation, this argument has two important consequences. First, while very short-term exchange rates may be largely influenced by news, the same must not apply to longer-term exchange rates. In general, the significance of news relative to (anticipated) actual disturbances can be expected to decline with an increase in the time span between the single exchange rate observations. Second, the relative importance of news declines also with decreasing substitutability between domestic and foreign assets.

In the exposition above, the imperfect substitutability assumption appeared in a twofold way: as determinant of the discount factor for anticipated future events and, in section 4.2., as justification for the existence of a risk premium. This risk premium has been defined independently of exchange rate expectations as a function of the actual supply of assets. The risk premium model offers qualitatively the same conclusion as the rational expectations model: the importance of actual asset stocks relative to exchange rate expectations and news increases with a decrease in the degree of substitution between domestic and foreign assets.

The models represented above suggest that anticipated and unanticipated changes in asset stocks simultaneously affect the exchange rate; but the relative importance of both depends on the considered time horizon and the the degree of substitutability.

From an empirical point of view, the major problem in assessing the relative importance of anticipated and unanticipated disturbances consists in specifying "news" in reality. Since expectations are not observable, results from econometric investigations which employ "news" instead of actual values depend crucially on the assumptions about expectation formation. The necessary ad hoc classification of disturbances in anticipated and unanticipated introduces a high degree of arbitrariness in empirical studies on the relevance of news: actual changes in asset stocks are observable (at least in principle) while news are not.

Empirical studies which include the CA as an exchange rate determinant can be divided into three groups. The first group concentrates on actual asset stocks, the second regards only news as relevant to the exchange rate, and the third group attempts to include both effects into the investigation.

The test results of the first group do not yield a homogeneous picture of the empirical relevance of changes in actual asset stocks for the exchange rate. The empirical verdict on portfolio models depends to a large extent on the investigated exchange rate, the specification of the econometric model and the underlying data set. Nevertheless, the majority of these tests lend some support to portfolio models which are formulated in terms of actual values.

Branson, Halttunen, and Masson (1977, 1979) and Murphy and Van Duyne (1980) estimate simple portfolio balance models for the DM/US dollar rate over the period from about 1973 to 1979. Both find a significant influence of the German and the US CA on the DM/dollar rate. This result is supported by Porter (1979) for the SDR-exchange rate of Germany, Japan, Australia and Switzerland. Dooley and Isard (1982) estimate a rational expectations portfolio balance model for the DM/US dollar rate from early 1973 to late 1977. They find that the forecasts generated by this model perform somewhat better than forward rates in predicting monthly changes in the spot rate. Martin and Masson's (1979) results for the Canadian dollar, the Japanese yen, and a weighted average of West European currencies against the US dollar for the time from early 1973 to early 1978, however, are not favourable to the simple portfolio model. Frankel's (1983) estimation of the DM/US dollar rate from January 1974 to October 1978 likewise produced rather poor results for the portfolio model. Meese and Rogoff (1981) and Edison (1983) find that exchange rate forecasts obtained from the portfolio model are inferior to forecasts from univariate time series models. In a more recent empirical study, Gaab (1982) employs a rational expectations model extended by an adjustment equation for goods price. His test of the DM/US dollar rate from late 1974 to mid-1981 supports the portfolio balance model against models with perfect asset substitutability.

The second group of tests attempts to estimate the influence of CA "news" on the exchange rate. Dornbusch (1980b) uses official forecast errors of the OECD Economic Outlook as measure for unanticipated CA imbalances. These CA "news" are employed to explain unanticipated exchange rate movements, defined as the difference between actual depreciations and interest rate differentials. Dornbusch tests this model on the nominal effective US dollar exchange rate with five major industrial countries and on the DM/US dollar and the Yen/US dollar rates for the period from mid-1973 to mid-1979. For the effective dollar exchange rate and the Yen/US dollar rate he finds that unanticipated CA surpluses

had a significant appreciation effect on the domestic currency. In the case of the DM/US dollar rate, however, this effect is not significant.
Branson (1981, 1982) uses a vector autoregression method for studying the relationship between innovations in money, the CA balance, relative price levels and the exchange rate. Each variable of the system is regressed against the lagged values of all variables (including itself) in the system. The residuals from these autoregressions are regarded as the innovations, e.g., the unanticipated movements in the variables. This method is applied to the average effective exchange rates of the US, the United Kingdom, Germany, and Japan for the period from end-1973 to end-1980. Branson's (1981) results support the hypothesis that unanticipated movements in the exogenous variables have a significant effect on the exchange rate. This result is clearest for the effects of CA innovations on exchange rates.

A final group of estimations attempts to include both the news-effect and the effect of actual disturbances in a comprehensive model. Hooper and Morton (1980) estimate an exchange rate equation similar to the one which has been derived in section 4.2. for the DM/US dollar rate over the period from mid-1976 to late 1978. Actual CA imbalances enter this model through the risk premium whereas CA news affect the exchange rate by altering the expectations about the long run equilibrium real exchange rate. The expected CA balance is defined as a specific fraction of the gap between the actual and the long run equilibrium CA surplus. Hooper and Morton (1980, p. 18-19) conclude from their test results "...that the CA influences the exchange rate primarily through its impact on long-run portfolio balance (expectations) considerations rather than operating through short-run rebalancing (risk premium)." In a similar test, Isard (1980) finds that both actual changes in the asset stocks and CA news are empirically significant for the exchagne rate. He performs his test on the DM/US dollar rate for the time from April 1973 through September 1979. The risk premium model of section 4.2. has also been tested by Groß (1983). The test refers to the DM/US dollar rate from early 1973 to mid-1982. Here the expected CA is derived from a weighted average of perfect foresight and stationarity. The results support the view that the DM/US dollar rate is influenced by actual imbalances in the US and German CA. The hypothesis that CA news affect the exchange rate is rejected for the German CA but supported in the case of the US CA. Artus (1981, 1982) estimates a multi-equation model which is composed of three blocks of equations: a price block, an output block, and an exchange rate block. The estimation period in Artus (1981) extends from late 1964 to late 1979, in Artus (1982) the period is updated through mid-1981. Similar to the studies above, the relative CA position of Germany and the US appears also in his DM/US dollar exchange rate model in a twofold way. First, the actual level of the CA is assumed to influence the short run equilibrium risk premium and second, the change in the CA is assumed to contain new information about future exchange rate developments. "An attempt was made in Artus (1981) to differentiate between these two effects of the current balance by introducing the change in the current balance in the exchange rate equation. This change was viewed as a proxy for unanticipated current balance developments on the grounds that quarterly changes in the current balance are difficult to forecast. The level of the current balance was then assumed to identify the effect of the limited asset substitutability. However, in the empirical analysis, the coefficient of the change in the current balance was found to be small and not significantly different from zero at the 5 per cent significance level, while the coefficient of the level of the current balance was found to be large and significant. This result could be interpreted as suggesting that either the limited-substitutability effect was the important one, or that even the level of the current balance was difficult to anticipate and came often as a 'surprise'. In the present study, the effect of the change in the current balance was again found to be not significant, and this variable was dropped from the exchange rate equation." Artus (1982, p. 36-37, footnote 8).

Two general conclusions seem to arise from these empirical studies.

First, the econometric results suggest that an empirical judgement on the importance of unanticipated disturbances depends to a crucial extent on the precise specification of what is considered as "news". Several assumptions can be introduced to distinguish anticipated and unanticipated disturbances, all more or less plausible. Consequently, the empirical verdict on the news-hypothesis depends on these arbitrary distinctions. Although the news-approach seems to be convincing in theory, a conclusive empirical test always suffers from the fact that expectations are not observable.

Second, based on the results reported above we cannot, in general, reject the hypothesis that the actual values of the exogenous portfolio variables have a significant influence on the exchange rate. Since the division of an actual disturbance into an expected and an unexpected part is a doubtful matter, it seems reasonable to formulate empirical tests in terms of actual values of the exogenous variables.

5. Diversified Current Account Financing in Portfolio Balance Models

5.1. Introduction

In this last chapter of the theoretical part we come back to a problem which has already been mentioned at the end of our discussion on the wealth redistribution effect of the CA. The vast majority of portfolio balance models which investigate this channel of influence proceed from the assumption that the domestic country is small in international asset markets: assets denominated in the currency of the home country are not internationally traded. The only financial instrument which is accepted as a medium for international payments is a foreign-currency denominated asset.[1)]

This assumption has three important implications. First, the net stock of foreign assets held by residents of the small domestic country can only be changed by an unbalanced CA. Since there is no trade in assets denominated in different currencies there is no possibility of swapping domestic assets for foreign assets and hence, changes in the currency composition of portfolios can only occur through CA imbalances. Second, any CA imbalance has to be financed by transferring foreign-currency denominated assets. Thus, there is no choice of the invoicing currency in international CA transactions. Third, the exchange rate is determind exclusively by the domestic portfolio equilibrium. In small country models, portfolio adjustments abroad have no impact on the relative price of domestic and foreign assets - the exchange rate - since domestic assets play no role in foreign portfolio equilibrium.

This small country assumption may be an appropriate simplification if applied to currencies which are unsuitable for economic, institutional or political reasons as medium for international financial investments. For the currencies of most industrialized countries, however, this assumption stands in apparent contradiction to reality.

---

1) In addition to the models of chapter 3., this assumption is made, for example, in Porter (1979), Martin and Masson (1979), Kouri (1980), Rodríguez (1980), Turnovsky (1981).

Another objection against the assumption of only one internationally traded asset refers to a more theoretical problem: it conceals the importance of differences in international asset preferences for the exchange rate impact of international wealth transfers due to CA imbalances. If domestic assets are assumed not to be held abroad, one introduces from the beginning an asymmetry in international portfolio preferences. Thus, an important objection against the exchange rate influence of CA imbalances is easily by-passed: "if all regions had identical portfolio preferences it would follow that market-clearing expected yields - and hence the expected rate of change in the exchange rate - would be completely independent of the global distribution of private wealth and therefore unaffected by any shifts in wealth through current account imbalances." [1)]

In the following we take these problems into account; we drop the assumption of only one internationally traded asset and analyse the more realistic case with bilaterally diversified portfolios.
The analysis is extended to two countries whose resident hold domestic and foreign interest-bearing assets. Therefore, CA transactions can be financed with domestic and/or foreign assets (diversified CA financing). The subsequent models allow us to address the following issues.

a. We attempt to clarify whether different ways of CA financing produce different effects on the exchange rate. Does a CA imbalance financed with domestic-currency denominated assets produce the same exchange rate effect as an imbalance which is financed by foreign currency assets? This question arises from our discussion in chapter 3. There it was shown that exchange rate effects of open-market operations differ according to the financial instrument used: foreign or domestic bonds.

b. We discuss implications of different assumptions about international asset preferences and the form of asset demand functions for the exchange rate impact of CA imbalances.

---

1) Dooley and Isard (1982, p. 258).

c. The two-country model may also serve as theoretical foundation for the discussion of a special exchange rate stability problem: negative net asset positions in foreign-currency denominated assets may lead to instabilities in flexible exchange rate regimes.[1)]

The analysis will be conducted in two steps.

First, we lay out a small-country framework, almost identical to Branson's (1976) model. But different to Branson we assume that foreign residents hold domestic-currency denominated assets and thus we allow for diversified CA financing.

The next section deals with a two-country model which is characterized by the existence of world markets for both countries' interest-bearing assets. The portfolio structure is familiar from the literature introduced by Tobin (1969) and McKinnon (1969). Our model resembles the two-country extension of this approach by Girton and Henderson (1977) and the multi-country model of Martin and Masson (1979).[2)]

The analysis is subject to the following limitations.

The models presented in this chapter are designed to investigate financial asset markets in a short run partial-equilibrium context. We take the real sector as exogenous. Consequently, we are not dealing with dynamic interactions between the real and the financial sector. As it has been already discussed above, a pure financial stock-equilibrium approach to short run exchange rate determination may be justified by a higher adjustment speed in asset markets than in goods markets: with sticky prices and quantities in goods markets and well-developed financial markets with a high degree of capital mobility, asset stock-equilibrium is reached much faster than flow equilibrium in the markets of goods. Hence it may be reasonable to ignore the real sector while analyzing the short run determination of exchange rates.

---

1) This problem is discussed in detail in chapter 11.

2) Girton and Henderson (1977) focus on central bank operations in foreign and domestic assets. In their model there is no CA. Martin and Masson (1979) include only one internationally traded asset. Some of the problems we are dealing with are also discussed in Dooley and Isard (1979, 1981, 1982) and in Henderson and Rogoff (1982). The structure of asset market equilibrium conditions in these models is different from the specific form we use. We refer to these models in the course of the discussion.

In the following we assume stationary expectations. As a result, we neglect the influence of changes in expectations on the relative net returns of financial assets and thus on relative asset demands. This is not a general shortcoming of the approach used but merely a simplification to allow for a clearer exposition of the arguments developed in this chapter.

The following definitions will be used throughout the chapter.

As above, the exchange rate is defined as the domestic currency price of one unit of foreign currency. At some places we draw as an illustration on the Deutsche mark (DM) price of US dollars ($). So too, for illustration purposes we label the domestic country as Germany and the foreign country as the United States.

The term "domestic (foreign) asset" is synonymously used for "domestic-(foreign-) currency denominated asset".

Mathematical details and stability analyses of the models, as well as the precise derivations of the results which are discussed in the textual part are largely banished to the enclosed appendices in order to improve the legibility of the text.

5.2. Basic Relations

We start our investigation with a description of the general relationship between CA financing and changes in the various asset stocks involved. As an accounting identity, the balance of the CA is equal to the change in the net foreign asset position of a country (CA = ΔNFP). We split up this identity according to the financial instruments involved in CA financing. From this general fromework we deduce a straightforward, model-tractable interpretation of diversified CA financing. At the same time we lay out some assumptions underlying the subsequent model analysis.

A country's CA transactions may be connected on the financial side with changes in the following stocks of assets.[1)]

FCDCs	=	foreign-currency denominated claims	=	$F_{\$}$
FCDLs	=	foreign-currency denominated liabilities	=	$B_{\$}^{*}$
DCDCs	=	domestic-currency denominated claims	=	F_{DM}
DCDLs	=	domestic-currency denominated liabilities	=	B_{DM}^{*}

All claims and liabilities are in relation to the foreign sector.

$B_{\$}^{*}$, B_{DM}^{*} : fiancial assets issued domestically in foreign ($) and domestic (DM) currency, respectively, and held abroad. The sum of both asset stocks represents overall domestic liabilities to the foreign sector.

$F_{\$}$, F_{DM} : financial assets issued abroad in foreign and domestic currency, respectively, and held in domestic portfolios. The sum of both asset stocks represents overall domestic claims on the foreign sector.

---

1) For a similar distinction see McGregor (1981).

Using this distinction we can write:

$$\Delta NFP = CA = (\Delta FCDCs - \Delta FCDLs) - (\Delta DCDLs - \Delta DCDCs)$$

$$= (\Delta F_{\$} - \Delta B^{*}_{\$}) - (\Delta B^{*}_{DM} - \Delta F_{DM})$$

In the following we abstract from political and default risk inherent in assets issued in different countries. We assume that there is only one respect in which domestic and foreign assets differ: in the currency of denomination. Hence, assets denominated in the same currency are considered as perfect substitutes, no matter where issued, and we can aggregate:

$F_{\$} - B^{*}_{\$} = F$ net claims on the foreign country denominated in foreign currency.

$B^{*}_{DM} - F_{DM} = B^{*}$ net liabilities to the foreign country denominated in domestic currency.

The net stocks of both assets F and B^{*} may be positive or negative: the domestic country may be a net debtor in foreign currency ($F < 0$) and a net creditor in domestic currency ($B^{*} < 0$) to the foreign sector. in the following we concentrate on the case in which both net asset stocks are positive: the domestic country is assumed to be a net creditor in foreign currency ($F > 0$) and a net debtor in domestic currency ($B^{*} > 0$). Problems arising from negative net foreign asset positions will be discussed in chapter 11.

We also maintain the conventional assumption that domestic and foreign residents hold only their own national money. Thus, domestic money M and foreign money N are taken as nontraded assets. Hence, F and B^{*} can be understood as stocks of (abstract) interest-bearing assets, furtheron called "bonds".

If we neglect for the moment central bank holdings of domestic and foreign assets,then the total net stock of domestic and foreign bonds ($\overline{B}$ and $\overline{F}$, respectively) falls either to private domestic residents or to private foreign residents.

$$\overline{B} = PB + PB^*$$

$$\overline{F} = PF + PF^*$$

The total supply of outstanding interest- bearing assets $\overline{B}$ and $\overline{F}$, respectively, is essentially given by the cumulated deficits in both countries' government budgets. Private wealth in both countries (in respective currencies) can be defined as follows:[1)]

$$W = M + PB + ePF$$

$$W^* = N + 1/e\ PB^* + PF^*$$

M	:	domestic (German) money supply, held only by domestic residents.
N	:	foreign (US) money supply, held only by foreign residents.
PB, PB^*	:	private net stocks of domestic-currency (DM) denominated interest-bearing assets.
PF, PF^*	:	private net stocks of foreign-currency ($) denominated interest-bearing assets.

The CA balance of the home country, expressed in domestic currency units, takes now the following form:

$$CA = e\ \Delta PF - \Delta PB^*$$

1) Hence, total net wealth of this two-country world is given by $W + W^* = M + N + \overline{B} + \overline{F}$.

A CA surplus of the home country may lead to an increase in the domestic stock of foreign assets PF (an increase in private net claims on the foreign country in foreign currency) and/or to a decrease in the foreign stock of domestic assets PB^* (a decrease in private net liabilities to the foreign country in domestic currency).

In a two-country world the CA of the foreign country is just the mirror-image of the home country's CA. The foreign CA, expressed in foreign currency, is thus given by:

$$CA = - CA^* = - \Delta PF^* + 1/e \, \Delta PB$$

Thus, an increase in PF corresponds to a decrease in PF^* and a decrease in PB^* corresponds to an increase in PB: a CA imbalance leads to a redistribution of financial wealth between domestic and foreign residents which accrues in the form of alterations in the respective stocks of domestic and/or foreign bonds; the net supply of domestic and foreign bonds, however, remains unaffected of CA imbalances.

5.3. A Small-Country Model

In this section a simple extension of the standard portfolio model will be presented which allows to investigate effects of CA financing with assets denominated in domestic and foreign currency.
The structure of the model is identical to Branson's (1976) model that has been described in section 3.3. We concentrate on implications of diversified CA financing. For convenience we repeat the asset market equilibrium conditions.

$$M = m(r, r^*)\,W \qquad \text{money market}$$

$$PB = \overline{B} - PB^* = b(r, r^*)\,W \qquad \text{domestic bond market}$$

$$e\,PF = f(r, r^*)\,W \qquad \text{foreign bond market}$$

$$W = M + PB + e\,PF \qquad \text{private domestic wealth (balance sheet constraint)}$$

The equilibrium conditions for the domestic money market and the market for foreign assets correspond to Branson's formulation. P denotes private asset holdings - a specification which becomes important when we introduce central bank asset holdings. The only structural change appears in the market clearing condition for domestic bonds.

As explained in the last section, the overall stock of domestic bonds corresponds to the sum of domestic private holdings and foreign holdings of DM bonds:

$$\overline{B} = PB + PB^*$$

Accordingly, the supply of DM bonds available to domestic residents depends on $\overline{B}$ and on the level of foreign DM bond stocks PB^*. PB^* is taken as exogenous in this section.

Applying this relationship, the domestic bond market equilibrium condition can be defined as given above:

$$PB = \overline{B} - PB^{*} = b\,(r, r^{*})\,W$$

The formulation of this market clearing condition is based on some rather restrictive assumptions: the foreign sector enters only on the supply side but not on the demand side. PB^{*} is taken as an outside asset for the domestic private sector. We assume that foreign residents hold domestic bonds but, nevertheless, do not have a demand which depends on interest rates but on some other determinants taken as exogenous. The following situations might justify this assumption.

a. DM bonds are not held by foreign private agents but by the foreign central bank. These stocks are made available to foreign private residents only for purposes of CA financing.

b. Foreign exchange controls abroad: foreign residents are not allowed to trade in DM bonds. DM bonds can only be used for financing international CA transactions.

c. DM bonds are held as pure transaction instruments for trade financing. A change in the domestic interest rate r or in the exchange rate has no influence on foreign demand for domestic bonds.[1)]

If PB^{*} is exogenous and changes only together with the CA (or as a result of exogenous shifts in portfolio preferences abroad) and the total net stock $\overline{B}$ is exogenous too, then the stock of domestic bonds PB held by the domestic private sector is given at every point in time. Since PB and M are given at every point in time also PF is given. Alterations in PB^{*} and PF occur only through CA transactions and some other exogenous events which will not be considered here.

The domestic CA has been defined as $CA = e\ dPF - dPB^{*}$.

---

1) This argument suggests that a change in the volume of the CA or a change in invoicing practices might imply a change in the desired portfolio structure. Through this channel the CA could enter the demand functions of both bonds. We are not pursuing this idea further.

The solution of the system for a net increase in domestic stocks of foreign assets (a CA surplus completely financed by F) yields as in Branson's model: [1)]

$$E\,(e/PF) = -1$$

The result for a CA surplus completely financed by DM bonds (a decrease in PB^* which equals the increase in PB) is:

$$de/-dPB^* \lesseqgtr 0 \quad \text{as} \quad |E(f/r)| \gtreqless |E(m/r)|$$

A decrease in PB^* leads to an appreciation of the domestic currency if the domestic interest elasticity of the demand for foreign bonds exceeds, in absolute terms, the interest elasticity of the money demand.

A comparison between both effects shows that even if a DM bond financed CA surplus brings about an appreciation of the DM, the induced fall in the exchange rate will be smaller than the fall caused by a CA surplus financed with foreign bonds.
The economic rationale behind these different effects is straightforward from our discussion of the Branson model in section 3.3. With an increase in PF agents attempt to rebalance their portfolios by selling some of the increment in PF on the foreign exchange market. In Branson's system the exchange rate falls instantaneously by the same proportion that PF increased so that wealth keeps unchanged at the initial level in the new equilibrium. Since wealth does not change, money and bond markets remain in equilibrium at the initial interest rate.

On the other hand, an increase in PB leads to a rise in the domestic interest rate as asset holders attempt to shift out of B and into M. The impact on the exchange rate is ambiguous but in any case smaller than the effect of an increase in PF: the wealth increase raises demand for foreign assets (depreciation effect) but the higher domestic interest rate lowers the demand again (appreciation effect).

---

1) E(X/Y) is the elasticity of X with respect to Y

The exchange rate effect of a balanced CA ($edPF = dPB^*$) is given by:

$$de/dPF\Big|_{dPF = dPB^*} = 1/|A| \, [-Wm_r] < 0$$

If a balanced CA is connected with an increase in PF which is equal to an increase in PB^* (decrease in PB), the net effect will be an appreciation of the domestic currency: asset holders try to rebalance their portfolios by increasing their demand for PB and decreasing their demand for PF. This drives the interest rate up and the exchange rate down. Such a situtation might occur if the foreign sector finances its import purchases with foreign bonds and the domestic sector with domestic bonds.

A balanced CA which is related to a decrease in PF that equals the decrease in PB^* (increase in PB) causes a depreciation of the domestic currency: the induced excess demand for foreign assets and the excess supply of domestic bonds lowers the interest rate and rises the exchange rate. This case may occur if the domestic sector finances its import purchases with foreign assets and the foreign sector with domestic bonds.

If only one asset, F or B, is used for CA financing, there is no exchange rate effect of a balanced CA.

Summarizing it can be concluded that under the given model assumptions diversified financing of the CA produces net effects on the exchange rate even in the case of a balanced CA. The strength of this impact depends on the relative importance of domestic and foreign assets as financing instruments.

Extended to the case of an imbalanced CA we can derive the following expression for the reaction of the exchange rate to CA imbalances:

$$de/CA \lesseqgtr 0 \qquad \text{as} \qquad \gamma/f \gtreqless 1 - \frac{E(f/r)}{E(m/r)}$$

$\gamma = dPF/CA$ is defined as the (given) ratio of the change in domestic holdings of foreign assets to the total net change of asset stocks $dPF - dPB^*$ due to the CA position ($-\infty \leq \gamma \leq +\infty$).

The expression purpots that a given CA situation may lead to a depreciation or an appreciation of the domestic currency depending on the substitutability of domestic and foreign assets and the sign and the size of the change in PF (γ).

We illustrate the condition for a "normal" reaction of the exchange rate ($de/CA < 0$) for the case of a domestic CA surplus.

$\gamma = 0$ if CA transactions are completely financed with domestic bonds. The condition for an appreciation reduces to $|E(f/r)| > |E(m/r)|$. This is the condition for $de/-dPB^* < 0$ already given above.

$\gamma = 1$ if the CA is completely financed with foreign bonds. The normality condition takes the form $(1-f)/f > -E(f/r) / E(m/r)$ and is always fulfilled. From the result given above we see that a CA surplus leads to an equiproportional appreciation $E(e/CA) = -1$.

$\gamma > 0$ if the CA surplus leads at least partly to an increase in PF. The result for $0 < \gamma < 1$ still depends on the relative interest elasticities of the demand for PF and M but in a less restricitive form than for $\gamma = 0$; $|E(f/r)| > |E(m/r)| (1 - \gamma/f)$ where $(1 - \gamma/f) < 1$. As long as $\gamma < 1$, a CA surplus may lead to a depreciation.

$\gamma < 0$ if a CA surplus is combined with a decrease in PF which is smaller than the decrease in PB^* (increase in PB). Since the depreciation effect of the decrease in PF is stronger than the (possible) appreciation effect of the increase in PB, one may expect a strong tendency towards a depreciation of the domestic currency. The condition for a normal reaction becomes $|E(f/r)| > |E(m/r)| (1 - \gamma/f)$ where $(1 - \gamma/f) > 1$.

The following conclusions may be drawn from the model.

The impact of a CA imbalance on the exchange rate increases with an increase in the ratio of the change in the net stock of foreign assets to the absolute amount of the imbalance.
If foreign assets play a predominant role in CA financing, CA imbalances will produce relative strong effects on the exchange rate. Even a small imbalance in the CA may obtain considerable influence on the exchange rate if it is connected with a large change in net foreign assets held domestically. The exchange rate impact of an unbalanced CA does not depend on the magnitude of the imbalance but on the magnitude of the absolute change of asset stocks behind this imbalance. Thus, it is not only the CA balance that matters but also the overall volume of CA transactions. A given CA situation may lead to different exchange rate effects depending on financial instruments used for CA financing.

In the case of a positive γ (a CA surplus is connected with an increase in PF and a deficit with a decrease in PF) the appreciation (depreciation) tendency of a given CA surplus (deficit) increase with an increase in γ.

In the case of a negative γ (a CA surplus is connected with a decrease in PF and a deficit with an increase in PF) there is a stronger tendency towards an "anomalous" reaction of the exchange rate than in the case of a positive γ. A CA surplus may lead to a depreciation and a CA deficit may cause an appreciation of the domestic currency.

The exchange rate effect of a balanced CA is zero only if $dPF = 0$ and $dPB^* = 0$. In all other cases a balanced CA may lead to an appreciation or depreciation of the domestic currency depending on the involved change in PF.

5.4. A Two-Country Model

The analysis of diversified CA financing in the small-country context yields rather unconventional result. Because of the restrictive assumptions underlying this analysis these results might, however, be regarded as very special cases which are of very limited relevance to reality. In order to generalize the discussion, we drop now the small-country assumption and extend the investigation to a two-country world. We assume that private agents in both countries hold and demand domestic and foreign-currency denominated interest-bearing assets. There are no restricitions on international capital movements and hence both bonds B and F are traded on free world markets. On these markets the total demand from residents of both countries meets the total supply of B and F. The world net supply of both assets is exogenously given. Since we include the central banks of both countries in the model, the supply available to the private sectors of both countries depends also on central bank actions. To facilitate the analysis we maintain the assumption that national moneys are held only in their respective countries: money is taken as a nontraded asset.

We define the net stocks of both interest-bearing assets B and F:

$$(1) \qquad \overline{B} = (CB + CB^*) + (PB + PB^*)$$

$$(2) \qquad \overline{F} = (CF + CF^*) + (PF + PF^*)$$

The given net supplies of both assets ($\overline{B}$, $\overline{F}$) are either held privately (P) or by central banks (C) of both countries. Central bank stockholding is treated as exogenous so that at every point in time the overall private asset stocks $\overline{PB}$ and $\overline{PF}$ are given for the world market.

Eqs. (3) and (4) describe the equilibrium conditions for both bond markets.

$$(3) \qquad \overline{PB} = PB + PB^* = b\,(r, r^*)\,W + eb^*\,(r, r^*)\,W^*$$

$$(4) \qquad \overline{PF} = PF + PF^* = (1/e)\,f\,(r, r^*)\,W + f^*\,(r, r^*)\,W^*$$

Nominal private wealth in both countries, expressed in respective currencies, is given by eq. (5) and (6).

$$(5) \qquad W = M + PB + ePF \qquad \text{domestic financial wealth}$$

$$(6) \qquad W^* = N + (1/e)\,PB^* + PF^* \qquad \text{foreign financial wealth}$$

The equilibrium conditions for both bond markets are simple extensions of the small-country case. Demand functions for both countries and both assets may differ, at given interest rates, in the desired wealth shares. All functions are assumed as linear homogeneous in the respective wealth. Since the world market for $\overline{PB}$ is defined in terms of domestic currency units (DM) and the world market for $\overline{PF}$ in foreign currency units ($), the exchange rate appears in eq. (3) and (4) as conversion factor for asset demands initially formed in other currency units.[1)]

Domestic and foreign money market equilibrium is defined by eqs. (7) and (8).

$$(7) \qquad M = CB + \bar{e}\,CF = m\,(r, r^*)\,W$$

$$(8) \qquad N = (1/\bar{e})\,CB^* + CF^* = n\,(r, r^*)\,W^*$$

The money supply in both countries depends on central bank holdings of domestic bonds and on official foreign exchange reserves held in foreign bonds. The central banks use a fixed exchange rate $\bar{e}$ to value their foreign exchange reserves so that capital gains or losses are not reflected in the money supply.[2)]

---

1) The denomination of world asset market equilibrium in either domestic or foreign currency units has no influence on the outcome ot the analysis.

2) For analytical simplicity $\bar{e}$ is arbitrarily set at 1, as is the initial value of e.

Equations (3), (4), (7), and (8) describe the portfolio equilibrium conditions for the four assets. Because of the wealth constraints eqs. (5) and (6), only three equations out of this system are independent and can be used to determine three endogenous variables, namely r, r^*, and e.

In our definition of the portfolio structure, wealth appears in the demand functions of all assets. In both countries overall private wealth is distributed to domestic money, domestic and foreign bonds according to the given portfolio preferences. Changes in wealth induce adjustments in all asset demand functions.
This specification differs from the portfolio structure underlying the models of Gaab (1982) and Frankel (1983). They assume money demands as independent of wealth. This assumption has important implications for the exchange rate effect of CA imbalances.
Dooley and Isard (1979, 1982) assume that the allocation of wealth between money and bonds is independent of the expected yield differential between domestic and foreign bonds. The demand for money is regarded as independent of the foreign interest rate. A change in the international yield differential affects only the partitioning of non-monetary wealth into DM and dollar bonds but not the division of overall wealth in money and non-monetary assets.
Both specifications can be understood as special cases in our model.

Before we discuss the solutions of the system, a brief look at the market clearing conditions for the bond markets is useful to understand the operation of the model.

The reaction of the world demand for DM bonds to a change in the exchange rate is given by:

$$dPB^d/de \;=\; b\ PF + b^*\ W^* - b^*\ PB^* \;=\; b\ PF + PB^*\ (1 - b^*) > 0$$

A depreciation of the DM increases the world demand for DM bonds.

An increase in e raises German wealth equiproportionally to the existing stock of foreign assets PF. Part of this wealth increase produces a higher demand for DM bonds in Germany (b PF).

Abroad we have two opposite effects: as a result of the depreciation, the dollar value of US wealth decreases equiproportionally to the existing US stocks of DM bonds ($b^* PB^*$). This leads to a reduction in the demand for DM bonds according to the (given) share of DM bonds in US portfolios b^*. On the other hand, the rise in e produces an equiproportional increase in the DM value of the desired stock of PB^* (US stock demand for DM bonds).

The overall effect is positive since the increase in the DM value of the US demand for DM bonds ($b^* W^*$) exceeds the reduction in the US demand due to the decrease in US wealth ($b^* PB^*$).

To keep the DM bond market in equilibrium the resulting excess demand for DM bonds has to be reduced by a fall in the domestic interest rate r (at given r^*).

We find an analogous result for the reaction of the world demand for dollar bonds to exchange rate changes: a depreciation of the DM decreases the world demand for dollar bonds.

$$dPF^d/de = f\,PF - f\,W - f^*\,PB^* = -f^*\,PB^* - PF\,(1 - f) < 0$$

The reduction in the dollar value of the German demand for US bonds exceeds the increase in German demand due to the wealth effect.
In the US, the wealth effect works in the opposite direction and decreases the US demand for dollar bonds. Since a rise in the exchange rate leads to an excess supply of dollar bonds, the foreign interest rate r^* has to rise to preserve equilibrium in the dollar bond market (at given r).

Similar wealth effects influence money demands:

$$dm/de = m\,PF > 0$$

$$dn/de = -n\,PB^* < 0$$

We choose the market clearing conditions for $\overline{PB}$, M and N (equations 3, 7, and 8) and solve the system for the equilibrium value of the exchange rate by applying Cramer's Rule. In deriving the comparative-static results we assume $m_r n_r* > n_r m_r*$ and, as condition for this to be true, $m_r < m_r*$ and $n_r* < n_r$: the response of money demands to changes in the respective domestic interest rate (m_r, n_r*) is, in absolute terms, greater than the response to a change in the respective foreign interest rate (m_r*, n_r); that is, we assume that domestic money is a better substitute for domestic bonds than for foreign bonds (for both countries). The solution of the model yields the following results.

A surplus (deficit) in the German CA, privately financed with dollar or DM bonds brings about an appreciation (depreciation) of the DM.[1] The exchange rate impact is exactly the same for both assets: the exchange rate effect of a given CA imbalance is independent of the used financial instrument. A balanced CA has no effect on the exchange rate.

$$de/dPF\Big|_{dPF = -dPF^*} = de/dPB\Big|_{dPB = -dPB^*} < 0$$

The formal solution reported in the appendix shows furthermore that the appreciation effect of a CA surplus increases with an increase in $(b - b^*)$: the higher the wealth share of DM bonds in German portfolios and the smaller their share in US portfolios, the stronger is the exchange rate reaction. Using the wealth constraints we can write:

$$(b - b^*) = (f^* - f) + (n - m)$$

The more the residents of both countries hold bonds denominated in their own currency, the stronger will be the ("normal") reaction of the exchange rate to CA imbalances.

1) We neglect here a special case; for the precise derivation see the appendix.

To illustrate these formal results we describe the main mechanisms of the model with two examples.[1)]

a. A surplus in the German CA, exclusively financed by a shift of DM denominated claims from foreign wealth holders to domestic wealth holders ($dPB = - dPB^*$).

The rise in the stock of DM bonds increases German wealth W by dPB. Portfolio holders plan to invest only part of this wealth increase in DM bonds (b dPB). The higher the desired increase in DM bond holdings, the smaller is the induced shift out of PB into money and dollar bonds. Since the desired ratio of DM bonds in German portfolios is smaller than one ($b < 1$), wealth holders switch out of PB and increase their demand for domestic money (m dPB). This raises the domestic interest rate r, hence increases domestic and foreign demand for DM bonds and decreases domestic and foreign demand for dollar bonds. This effect tends to appreciate the domestic currency. On the other hand leads the increase in W to a rise in the German demand for PF. Part of the wealth increase brings about a demand increase for dollar bonds (f dPB) and tends to depreciate the DM. The smaller f, the smaller is the rise in the demand for dollar bonds and therefore the depreciation tendency.
The net effect of the rise in PB is not unequivocally determined by the model but tends to be an appreciation of the domestic currency.

The decrease in DM bond stocks abroad corresponds to a fall in US wealth W^* and thereby reduces the overall US asset demand. Since this decrease accrues completely in the form of PB^*, asset holders lower their demand for dollar bonds and money but increase their demand for DM bonds to rebalance portfolios on a lower wealth level.
If the share of wealth which is desired to be held in DM bonds (b^*) is small, that is, if US agents have a preference for dollar assets (PF^* and N), the reduction in wealth reduces the demand for DM bonds proportionallyless than the demand for PF^* and N. As asset holders attempt to buy DM bonds the DM appreciates.
Since the decreasing money demand tends to reduce the foreign interest rate whereas the demand fall for dollar bonds tends to increase r^* the net effect on r^* is insecure.

---

1) A good description of a similar adjustment process can be found in Truman and Shafer (1982).

Compared with the initial situation, the world demand for DM bonds has increased and the DM appreciates against the dollar.
The appreciation reduces German wealth and establishes the stabilizing mechanism: the reduction in W accrues in the form of a reduced DM value of dollar bond holdings, hence increases demand for dollar bonds, decreases demand for DM bonds and money and diminishes the appreciation tendency for the DM.
The increase in W^* accrues in the form of an increase in the dollar value of DM bond holdings, hence decreases demand for DM bonds and raises demand for dollar assets. This effect too slows down the appreciation of the DM.

b. A surplus in the German CA, entirely financed by dollar bonds ($dPF = - dPF^*$).

The rise in dollar stocks increases German wealth and thus the desired holdings of dollar bonds according to f dPF. The higher f, the smaller is the planned shift from PF to other assets or, to put it the other way round, the smaller f, the more of the increased dollar bond stock will be sold and hence, the stronger is the appreciation tendency for the DM. Part of the wealth increase is planned to be invested in DM bonds and money. The rising money demand tends to increase the domestic interest rate r whereas the higher DM bond demand has the opposite effect. Therefore, the net effect on the domestic interest rate remains indetermined.

The reduction in dollar bond stocks abroad lowers the demand for dollar bonds according to $f^* dPF^*$; but since the decrease in wealth accrued completely as a reduction in PF^*, foreign asset holders try to buy dollar bonds to rebalance their portfolios on a lower level. The higher f^*, the smaller is the fall in the demand for other assets, that is, the demand-reducing effect of the wealth decrease falls more to dollar bonds than to other assets if f^* is high. Unless $f^* = 1$ there is a net increase in US demand for dollar bonds at the expense of reduced money and DM bond holdings. The foreign interest rate r^* declines. This in turn cuts down the demand for dollar bonds, increases demand for DM bonds and thereby induces an appreciation tendency for the DM. On the other hand, there is a reduction in foreign demand for DM bonds because of the wealth decrease ($b^* dPF^*$). The smaller b^*, the smaller is the fall in DM bond demand and hence, the depreciation tendency for the DM. Unless this wealth effect is very strong, the net result is an appreciation of the DM.

The stabilizing mechanism is analogous to the mechanism described above: the appreciation reduces German wealth again by reducing ePF and thus decreases sellings of dollar bonds and lowers the demand for PB and M. The exchange rate induced increase in US wealth too decreases demand for DM bonds and increases demand for dollar bonds and money N.

This description shows that CA imbalances give rise to a multitude of adjustments in asset markets which all work at the same time. The complexity of this adjustment process easily conceals the key role played by asset preferences. To clarify the fundamental importance of differences in international asset preferences we discuss the implications of alternative assumptions which can be made on asset preferences.

First, we consider the case of home asset preference or "preferred local habitat" with respect to interest-bearing assets.[1] These terms describe a situation in which the domestic preference for holding domestic bonds is greater than the foreign preference: at given interest rates, German asset holders wish to hold a greater proportion of their wealth in DM bonds than US asset holders, and US asset holders in turn prefer dollar bonds to DM bonds. In our model this assumption can be formalized as $(b - b^*) > 0$ and $(f^* - f) > 0$. It is well known from the literature that a wealth transfer from the foreign country to the domestic country under the condition of "preferred local habitat" leads to an appreciation of the domestic currency. A shift of wealth from the US to Germany due to a German CA surplus causes at given interest rates and exchange

---

1) The term "preferred local habitat" has been introduced by Frankel (1983); Tobin (1982) describes the same assumption as "home currency preference". Economic reasons which justify this assumption are discussed in Frankel (1983) and Tobin (1982).

rate an excess demand for DM bonds and an excess supply of dollar bonds. To equilibrate world bond markets the DM has to appreciate against the US dollar. This result holds irrespectively of the currency of denomination of the wealth shift.

Consider now the case of identical preferences with respect to domestic and foreign interest-bearing assets. This assumption can be formalized in the model by ($b = b^*$) and ($f = f^*$). From the formal solution of the model it can be seen that CA imbalances produce even in this case "normal" exchange rate effects. The assumption of identical preferences for domestic and foreign bonds does not lead to qualitatively different conclusions about the exchange rate impact of the CA.

This result is somewhat surprising since the assumption of identical preferences implies in other models that CA imbalances are irrelevant to the exchange rate.[1)]

With $b = b^*$ and $f^* = f$, a shift of wealth from the US to Germany does in fact not lead to an excess supply or demand in world bond markets. At initial interest rates and exchange rate the increase in the German demand for dollar and DM bonds is exactly balanced by the decrease in the US demand for these bonds. Hence equilibrium in world bond markets does not require a change in the exchange rate.

In our model, however, money is treated as a nontraded asset in both countries. Thus, the "preferred local habitat" assumption enters through the money market equilibrium conditions. Although the transfer of wealth from US residents to German resident does not cause disequilibrium in the bond markets, it causes an excess demand for German money and an excess supply of US money. The wealth effect on both money demands increases the German interest rate relative to the US rate and hence shifts demand towards DM bonds. As a result, the DM appreciates vis-á-vis the dollar.

With identical preferences for bonds, the wealth effect of an imbalanced CA induces via money market equilibrium in both countries a change in the yield differential between domestic and foreign bonds and thus causes a change in the exchange rate.

---

1) For example, see Henderson and Rogoff (1982).

This result is of course due to the fact that money is considered as nontraded asset in both countries. Portfolio preferences may be identical with respect to domestic and foreign bonds but they differ by definition with respect to money. The CA had no influence on the exchange rate if all asset would be traded and if preferences for all assets would be the same internationally.

Finally, we mention the theoretical possibility of reversed preferences with respect to bonds.[1)] If German residents prefer dollar bonds to DM bond and US residents prefer DM bonds to dollar bonds, CA imbalances may produce perverse effects on the exchange rate. This result becomes intuitive when we consider that "foreign asset preference" ($b < b^*$) and ($f > f^*$) implies that the roles of home and foreign residents are reversed; a transfer of wealth to home residents is like transferring wealth to foreign residents in the case of home asset preference. But also in this "perverse" case the effect of the wealth transfer on money demands tends to preserve the "normal" reaction of the exchange rate to CA imbalances.

We turn now to the results for the significance of diversified CA financing.

Formally it can be proven that DM bond financing and dollar bond financing of CA imbalances produce exactly the same effect on the exchange rate in our model specification. The basic reason for this outcome has already been indicated in our discussion on asset preferences. A wealth transfer from the US to Germany increases the German demand and decreases the US demand for all assets according to the given portfolio preferences. These demand effects are independent of the specific asset in which the change in wealth is embodied. Hence exchange rate effects of CA imbalances depend on asset preferences in both countries but not on the financial instrument used for CA financing. We come back to this point in section 5.5.

---

1) Enders (1977) and Masson (1980) discuss stability problems arising from this assumption.

Effects of diversified CA financing on the exchange rate can be investigated further when we divide the overall wealth transfer $dPF = - dPF^*$ and $dPB = - dPB^*$ in single components.

$$|de/dPF < 0| \quad > \quad |de/dPB \gtrless 0|$$

An increase in German private stocks of dollar bonds has a stronger appreciation effect on the DM than an increase in the German stock of DM bonds. The term on the left hand side of the inequality shows also the exchange rate effect of a (US) budget deficit financed by issuing dollar bonds to German residents. The second term (de/dPB) can also be understood as the impact of a deficit in the (German) government budget that is financed by issuing DM bonds to German residents. The economic rationale for these differences in the impacts lies in the different influences of both asset changes on the German interest rate.[1)]

$$|de/dPF^* \gtrless 0| \quad < \quad |de/dPB^* > 0|$$

A decrease in the stock of DM bonds held by US residents results in a stronger appreciation of the DM than a decrease in the US stock of dollar bonds. Similar as above, de/dPF^* can be interpreted as the exchange rate effect of an (US) budget deficit financed by issuing dollar bonds to US residents, and de/dPB^* gives the effect of a (German) budget deficit financed by issuing DM bonds to US residents.

The partial multipliers indicate that a change in the stock of the respective domestic bond produces a "weak" effect on the exchange rate and a change in the stock of the respective foreign bond a "strong" effect. Since either asset is a "foreign asset" for one country and a "domestic asset" for the other country, CA financing with dollar or DM bonds yields a net effect on the exchange rate; but the net effects are equal for both financing alternatives.

---

1) For a more detailed explanation see pp. 62 and pp. 126.

We close this section with a summary of the main results.

a. In the case of "preferred local habitat", the exchange rate reacts normally to CA imbalances: a domestic CA surplus causes an appreciation of the domestic currency and a deficit leads to a depreciation. The strength of this exchange rate effect increases with an increase in the preferences for the respective domestic asset.

b. In the case of identical preferences for domestic and foreign bonds we have to distinguish two situations.

If money demands in both countries depend on wealth and domestic money is more attractive to domestic residents than foreign money (home asset preference with respect to money) CA imbalances produce normal exchange rate effects.

If money demands do not depend on wealth, or if money is internationally traded and residents of both countries have identical money preferences, then the CA has no influence on the exchange rate.
The assumption that money demands are linear-homogeneous in wealth of degree zero leads to a Frankel-Gaab type of model in which differences in bond preferences determine the exchange rate effect of CA imbalances.

c. In all of the specifications above the financial instrument used for CA financing (domestic or foreign bonds) is irrelevant to the exchange rate impact of CA imbalances.

Central Bank Interventions

In order to complete our discussion on CA financing we have to allow for the possibility that an imbalanced CA is not entirely financed out of private portfolios but also out of official funds. Central banks of both countries may intervene in the foreign exchange market and absorb part of the wealth transfer. In the next step we consider therefore the exchange rate impact of various central bank operations. Afterwards we combine these results with the exchange rate effect of a CA imbalance and determine the net effect of such a mixed financing of the CA.

The results for the different central bank interventions confirm the findings of earlier studies.[1)]

A purchase of dollar bonds by the German central bank produces in all cases a depreciation of the DM. If this operation is conducted with German residents by switching domestic money for dollar bonds ($-\ dPF = dM$) the depreciation is stronger than in the case of a switch between dollar bonds and DM bonds conducted with residents of either country ($-\ dPF^* = dPB^*$, $-\ dPF = dPB$).
An increase in the domestic money supply in combination with a decrease in German private holdings of dollar bonds produces a higher excess demand for dollar bonds and hence a greater pressure on the DM than the increase in private holdings of DM bonds produces an excess supply of DM bonds.[2)]

If the German central bank neutralizes the money supply effect by selling DM bonds to German residents, both intervention operations produce identical exchange rate effects. This result is familiar from the literature on sterilized intervention.

The same relationships hold for interventions of the US central bank.

---

1) See, for example, Girton and Henderson (1977), Isard (1978), Truman and Shafer (1982).

2) If we compare the single exchange rate effects, we get in the case $-dPF = dM$ two "strong" depreciation effects whereas, in the case $-dPF^* = dPB^*$ only de/dPB^* is "strong" and de/dPF^* is "weak".

A purchase of DM bonds from US residents in exchange for US money ($- dPB^* = dN$) brings about a stronger depreciation of the dollar than a purchase of DM bonds from residents of either country in exchange for dollar bonds ($dPF = - dPB$, $dPF^* = - dPB^*$).
If the central bank neutralizes the money supply effect by selling dollar bonds to US residents, both intervention strategies yield the same result.

Moreover, if one abstracts from money supply effects and assumes perfect neutralization, the exchange rate effects of all interventions are identical regardless of whether the operation is conducted by the domestic or the foreign central bank, with domestic or foreign residents.

Current Account Imbalances and Central Bank Interventions

The results above allow us to combine exchange rate effects of CA imbalances with effects of different central bank interventions. The net effects apply to situations in which CA imbalances are partly financed out of official funds. We assume that either the US or the German central bank absorbs the CA induced wealth transfer by open-market interventions in domestic or foreign assets.
As example we consider a surplus in the German CA. Since CA financing with DM or dollar bonds yields exactly the same impact on the exchange rate, we neglect the currency of denomination of the initial wealth transfer.

a. The German central bank absorbs an increase in PF by purchases of dollar bonds in exchange for German money ($- dPF = dM$).
The net effect consists of an increase in the German money supply which tends to depreciate the DM and in a decrease in foreign private stocks of dollar bonds which tends to appreciate the DM ($dM = - dPF^*$). Although the net effect on the exchange rate is not clear, we may expect it to be different from zero. The central bank intervention does, in general, not neutralize the influence of the CA on the exchange rate.

<u>b</u>. The German central bank intervenes by selling DM bonds in exchange for dollar bonds ($dPB^* = - dPF^*$). The net effect is an increase in the German stock of PB and a decrease in the US stock of PF^* ($- dPF^* = dPB$). Both the increase in PB and the decrease in PF^* tends to appreciate the DM (under certain conditions which are described in the appendix). But the potential appreciation of the DM is smaller than it would be the case without intervening. Compared with policy a., there is a stronger net tendency towards an appreciation of the DM since the downward pressure on the exchange rate due to the rise in the domestic money supply does not take place.

<u>c</u>. If The German central bank pursues policy a. and neutralizes the money supply effect, a. and b. yield the same result: a net tendency towards an appreciation of the DM which is smaller than the pure effect of the CA surplus.

The model yields similar results for interventions of the US central bank.

If the US central bank attempts to counteract the depreciation tendency for the dollar due to a deficit in the US CA by sales of DM bonds in exchange for US money ($- dN = dPB^*$), this yields a better result than dollar bond purchases in exchange for DM bonds ($- dPF =$ $= dPB$). The reason is, once more, that the appreciation tendency triggered off by the decrease in the US money stock is omitted if the central bank action is done with domestic and foreign interest-bearing assets.

The net effect of a purchase of dollar bonds in exchange for DM bonds ($- dPF^* = dPB$) tends to be negative but has a smaller depreciation influence on the dollar than the CA deficit alone. The result of this policy is identical to the result of policy b. of the German central bank.

Both cases are identical in their influence on the exchange rate if the US central bank neutralizes the money supply effect by selling dollar bonds in exchange for US money.

As results we summarize:

By absorbing the inflow or financing the outflow of assets any of the central bank policies described above can reduce the exchange rate influence of a CA imbalance. But, in general, they cannot neutralize the exchange rate effect. This is because central banks cannot neutralize the wealth shift related to CA imbalances. Central bank interventions merely transform this wealth shift so that the change in private net wealth accrues in the form of other assets than initially used for CA financing. These "transformations" affect private portfolio dispositions and thus produce exchange rate effects which may counteract the effects of a pure CA imbalance.

Central bank interventions are most efficient, in the sense of reducing the exchange rate influence of CA imbalances, if the central bank operates with the money supply.

The results of the model are summarized in table 1.

(footnotes to table 1) The results have been derived with the following assumptions:

<u>a</u>. $PF > 0$, $PB^* > 0$; private net positions in foreign-currency denominated assets are positive in both countries.

<u>b</u>. $b \geq b^*$; "preferred local habitat" or identical preferences with respect to interest-bearing assets denominated in DM and dollar.

<u>c</u>. $m_r n_r^* > m_r^* n_r$; response of money demands to changes in the respective domestic interest rate is stronger than the response to changes in the respective foreign interest rate (for both countries). Sufficient but not necessary for c. to be fulfilled.

1) negative if, but not only if, DM and dollar bonds are better substitutes in German portfolios than DM bonds and German money.

2) positive if, but not only if, DM and dollar bonds are better substitutes in US portfolios than dollar bonds and US money.

<u>Table 1</u>: Effects of Some Exogenous Disturbances on the DM/US Dollar Rate [a)]

Disturbance	Exchange Rate Effect (- : appreciation of the DM vis-à-vis the $)
1. Surplus in the bilateral German CA with the US	
1.1. financed with $ bonds	- both effects are identical
1.2. financed with DM bonds	-
2. Government budget deficit financed by	
2.1. issuing DM bonds to German residents	? [1)] tends to appreciate the DM
2.2. issuing $ bonds to German residents	-
2.3. issuing DM bonds to US residents	+
2.4. issuing $ bonds to US residents	? [2)] tends to appreciate the $
3. Increase in the German money supply through	
3.1. open-market purchases of DM bonds	+
3.2. open-market purchases of $ bonds	+ stronger than 3.1.
4. Increase in the US money supply through	
4.1. open-market purchases of $ bonds	-
4.2. open-market purchases of DM bonds	- stronger than 4.1.
5. Central bank purchases of $ bonds from German or US residents in exchange for DM bonds (Intervention purchases of $ bonds in the world foreign exchange market)	+ smaller than 3.2. and 4.2.
6. Sterilized interventions	
6.1. policy 3.2. + open-market purchases of German money in exchange for DM bonds	+ identical to 5.
6.2. policy 4.2. + open-market purchases of US money in exchange for $ bonds	- identical to 5.
7. Surplus in the bilateral German CA with the US	
7.1. absorbed by the German central bank by purchases of $ bonds (from German residents) in exchagne for money	?
7.2. absorbed by the US central bank by sales of DM bonds (to US residents) in exchange for money	?
7.3. absorbed by central bank purchases of $ bonds in exchange for DM bonds	? stronger appreciation tendency for the DM than under 7.1. and 7.2.
7.4. policy 7.1. with neutralization of the increase in the German money supply	? equal to 7.3.
7.5. policy 7.2. with neutralization of the increase in the US money supply	? equal to 7.3.

For footnotes see page 145

5.5. A Qualification: The Role of Wealth in Asset Demand Functions

The two models exposed in the last sections yield opposite results for the exchange rate influence of diversified CA financing.
In the small-country case (model 1),the distinction between domestic and foreign assets is essential for the exchange rate impact of CA induced wealth transfers. In the two-country case (model 2), the exchange rate effect of CA imbalances is independent of the specific asset in which the wealth transfer is embodied. These contradictory results are not due to the fact that interest rate repercussion-effects are cut off in model 1 and taken into consideration in model 2.[1] The crucial difference between both models lies in the specification of the equilibrium condition for the DM bond market.

Model 1 is based on an asymmetry: the foreign sector holds domestic bonds but seems not to demand these bonds. In fact, what we have implicitly assumed is that a change in the foreign DM bond stock alters the foreign demand for DM bonds exactly by the same amount, whereas a change in the foreign stock of dollar bonds has no influence on the demand for DM bonds. In this case, neither a change in PB^* nor a change in PF^* affects foreign DM bond portfolio equilibrium.
By this assumption we postulated a special type of demand function which is linear with a positive slope of one in the foreign stock of DM bonds and otherwise independent of the foreign stock of wealth. This assumption guarantees that the foreign demand for PB^* is always in line with the given foreign stock of DM bonds. This selective wealth effect is the reason for the different exchange rate effects of alternative forms of CA financing.

---

1) This is easy to see if one replaces the DM bond market equilibrium condition in model 2 by an expression which assumes the foreign demand for DM bonds as independent of the interest rate; for example $PB + PB^* = b\,(r,\, r^*)\, W \;+\; e\, b^*\,(\mu)\, W^*$ where μ denotes an optional exogenous variable. This reformulation does not alter the qualitative results of model 2 for diversified CA financing.

The structure of model 2 is symmetric: both countries hold and demand domestic and foreign interest-bearing assets and asset demands in both countries are assumed as linear homogeneous in wealth. A bilateral CA imbalance produces a "normal" effect on the exchange rate independent of the specific asset, DM bonds or dollar bonds, which has been used for financing the imbalance. The reason for this result lies, as above, in the assumption about the wealth dependency of asset demands. An "asymmetric" market clearing condition, e.g. for the DM bond market, would lead, as in model 1, to different exchange rate effects for CA financing with DM or dollar bonds.

To investigate these differences further, we reformulate model 2 by applying a very general definition of the wealth dependency of asset demands. We substitute overall private wealth as argument in the asset demand functions by the individual wealth components. In this formulation the equilibrium condition for the DM bond market, for example, becomes:[1)]

$$\overline{PB} = PB + PB^{*} = \beta(r, r^{*}, M, PB, ePF) + e\beta^{*}(r, r^{*}, N, 1/e\ PB^{*}, PF^{*})$$

The partial derivatives of this demand function with respect to the various wealth components describe the marginal change in the domestic and foreign demand for DM bonds due to changes in the different asset stocks.

An analysis of the complete system yields the following results for the exchange rate impact of diversified CA financing.

<u>a</u>. Diversified CA financing does not matter for the exchange rate effect of CA imbalances if asset demand functions in both countries depend on wealth in like manner for all wealth components. That is, for example, if $\beta_W = \beta_M = \beta_{PB} = \beta_{PF}$ and $\beta^{*}_{W^*} = \beta^{*}_{N} = \beta^{*}_{PB^*} = \beta^{*}_{PF^*}$.

---

1) For an exposition of the complete model see appendix C.

The CA affects the exchange rate through the wealth effect on asset demands. If asset demands in both countries depend on overall wealth, then it follows intuitively that equal wealth transfers must produce equal exchange rate changes irrespective of the specific form in which the wealth transfer accrues.

b. The financing of the CA with DM or dollar bonds yields different effects on the exchange rate if asset demands in both countries depend on wealth but this dependency differs within each country according to the individual wealth components. That is, using the DM bond market equilibrium as an example, $\beta_M \neq \beta_{PB} \neq \beta_{PF}$ or $\beta^*_N \neq \beta^*_{PB^*} \neq \beta^*_{PF^*}$.

In this case, a change in the private stocks of dollar bonds produces a different effect on the same asset demand functions than a change in private DM bond stocks. If, for example, an increase in German private dollar bond holdings causes a wealth effect on the German money demand which differs from the wealth effect of an increase in DM bond stocks, then the exchange rate impact of a dollar financed CA differs from the effect of a DM financed CA.

This is the general form of the assumption made in model 1. Here a change in private DM bond stocks abroad led to an equiproportional change in the foreign demand for DM bonds ($\beta^*_{PB^*} = 1$) but a change in the foreign stock of dollar bonds had no influence on the foreign demand for DM bonds ($\beta^*_{PF^*} = 0$).

In our discussion of the small-country model we already described some real situations which may imply this specific type of asset demand functions. The following two examples may serve as additional illustrations.

The first example depicts the general case of structural differences in asset preferences within one country. Assume that the residents of a country (Germany or the US) can be divided into two groups: CA transactions which are denominated in dollars are conducted by exporters and importers of the "dollar group". CA transactions denominated in DM are conducted by the "DM group". The dollar group

has a greater preference for dollar bonds relative to DM bonds than the DM group.
A CA surplus financed with dollar bonds leads to an increase in wealth of the dollar group. Because of the different portfolio preferences of both groups, this increase in wealth is connected with a world excess supply of dollar bonds which is smaller than the excess supply of dollar bonds resulting from an equal CA surplus financed with DM bonds. Hence a dollar financed surplus in the German CA leads to a smaller appreciation of the DM than a DM financed surplus.
This example can be generalized: if CA transactions denominated in domestic and foreign currency alter the net wealth of different groups of persons with different asset preferences within one country, then the exchange rate impact of the CA depends on the financial asset used for CA financing. This argument suggests furthermore that the exchange rate in general can be seen as a function of the net wealth distribution within one country.

A second example can be constructed when we assume that preferences for DM and dollar bonds depend on the usability of both assets as means of payments in international transactions.
An increase in the relative importance of DM assets in CA transactions may raise the demand for DM bonds relative to dollar bonds both internationally and within one country. Thus a CA induced increase in PB may lead to an increase in the marginal demand of German residents for DM bonds (β_{PB}), and an increase in PF may lead to a decrease in the marginal demand for DM bonds (β_{PF}). Hence β_{PF} may differ from β_{PB} according to which asset is predominantly used for CA financing.
This example illustrates the general case in which developments in the CA itself cause changes in the desired portfolio structure. These changes depend on the relative importance of domestic and foreign assets in financing the CA.

Our analysis shows that the importance of diversified CA financing depends crucially on the assumptions which are made on the role of wealth in asset demand functions. Since we have no information about the right specification of asset demands, it is not possible to decide whether case a. or case b. corresponds better to reality. In chapter 10. we will thus continue the discussion with an investigation on the empirical relevance of diversified CA financing for the US and for Germany.

A short taxonomy of the model results for case a. and case b. is given in table 2.

Table 2: Taxonomy of the Exchange Rate Influence of Diversified CA Financing in the Two-Country Case.

Home Country: Germany (DM); Foreign Country: United States ($).

	Case a. Asset demands depend on the general level of wealth	Case b. Asset demands depend on the wealth compone
	= A change in wealth induces a change in asset demands which is independent of the source of the wealth change.	= A change in wealth induces a change in asset demands which depends on (differs according to) the particular form of the wealth change.
Results for the relative exchange rate impact of the currency parts of the current account	CA financing with DM or $ assets has equal effects on the DM/$ rate.	CA financing with DM or $ assets has different effects on the DM/$ rate.
Results for the effect of CA imbalances on the exchange rate	The exchange rate reacts normally to CA imbalances if, but not only if: A1: The response of money demands to changes in the domestic interest rate is (in absolute terms) stronger than the response to changes in the foreign interest rate (for both countries). $\lvert m_r \rvert > \lvert m_{r^*} \rvert$ and $\lvert n_{r^*} \rvert > \lvert n_r \rvert$ Equivalent to the assumption that domestic money is a better substitute for domestic bonds than for foreign bonds (for both countries). A2: Preferred local habitat: the part of wealth (or the part of the change in wealth) which is desired to be held in domestic bonds is greater at home than abroad. Linear homogenity: $b > b^*$ General case : $\beta_W > \beta^*_{W^*}$ A3: Identical international preferences for domestic and foreign bonds. Linear homogenity: $b = b^*$ General case : $\beta_W = \beta^*_{W^*}$ If money demands depend on wealth, conditions A1 and A2 are sufficient for a normal exchange rate reaction. If money demands are independent of wealth $(n_{W^*} = \mu_W = 0)$, A1 and A2 are necessary and sufficient for a normal exchange rate reaction.	The exchange rate reacts normally to CA imbalances if, but not only if: A1: See case a. A2: Preferred local habitat: for DM financing: $\beta_{PB} > \beta^*_{PB^*}$ for $ financing: $\beta_{PF} > \beta^*_{PF^*}$ Since β_{PB} may differ from β_{PF} (and $\beta^*_{PB^*}$ from $\beta^*_{PF^*}$) a combination of a normal/anormal reactions of the exchange rate is possible. A3: Identical international (marginal) preferences for domestic and foreign bonds. for DM financing: $\beta_{PB} = \beta^*_{PB^*}$ for $ financing: $\beta_{PF} = \beta^*_{PF^*}$ Equal to case a. Equal to case a.

APPENDICES TO CHAPTER 5:

TECHNICAL DETAILS AND STABILITY ANALYSES

5A. The Formal Solution of the Small-Country Model [1)]

Market clearing conditions:

$M = m(r, r^*)W$	domestic money market
$PB = \bar{B} - PB^* = b(r, r^*)W$	market for domestic (DM) bonds
$e\,PF = f(r, r^*)W$	market for foreign ($) bonds
$W = M + PB + ePF$	domestic private wealth (balance sheet constraint)

Partial derivatives: $b_r,\ f_{r^*} > 0$

$b_{r^*},\ f_r,\ m_r,\ m_{r^*} < 0$

Definitions and assumptions:

endogenous: e, r

exogenous : r^*, M, PB, PF

$m + b + f = 1$ balance sheet constraint

$m_r + f_r = -b_r < 0$
$m_{r^*} + b_{r^*} = -f_{r^*} < 0$ } gross substitutability assumption

Total differentials (initial value of $e = 1$)

MM: money : $(1-m)dM - m\,d\bar{B} + m\,dPB^* - m\,dPF - W\,m_{r^*}\,dr^* =$
$= m\,PF\,de + W\,m_r\,dr$

BB: DM bonds : $-b\,dM + (1-b)d\bar{B} - (1-b)dPB^* - b\,dPF - W\,b_{r^*}\,dr^* =$
$= b\,PF\,de + W\,b_r\,dr$

FF: \$ bonds : $-f\,dM - f\,d\bar{B} + f\,dPB^* + (1-f)dPF - W\,f_{r^*}\,dr^* =$
$= -(1-f)PF\,de + W\,f_r\,dr$

1) The formal analysis of the small-country model is in many respects identical to the analysis of the Branson (1976) model. See also Branson (1977, 1979, 1981).

Equilibrium in each of the three markets can be defined in terms of specific combinations of the exchange rate and the domestic interest rate. The graphical exposition and the economic rationale for the slopes of the equilibrium curves is identical to the exposition of the Branson model in section 3.3.

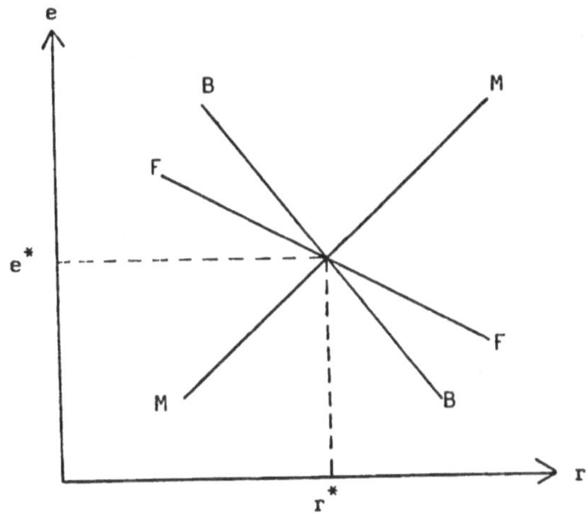

The MM curve is the equilibrium curve for the money market. The slope of the curve is positive:

$$de/dr = - W m_r / m_{PF} > 0$$

The BB curve describes the equilibrium in the DM bond market. The slope is negative:

$$de/dr = - W b_r / b_{PF} < 0$$

The FF curve illustrates equilibrium in the market for foreign bonds. The slope of FF is negative but in absolute terms smaller than the slope of the BB curve.

$$de/dr = W f_r / PF(1-f) < 0$$

FF is less steep than BB if $1-f > b$ and $b_r > -f_r$. These are also the conditions for local stability of the model which will be derived below. Because of the wealth constraint $1-f = m+b$ and according to the gross substitutability assumption $b_r = -f_r - m_r$ both conditions are fulfilled.

Because of the wealth constraint only two market clearing conditions are necessary to determine the short run equilibrium values of e and r. We choose the equilibrium conditions for the money and DM bond market. The total differential of this system yields in matrix form:

$$\underbrace{\begin{pmatrix} \overset{-}{Wm_r} & \overset{+}{mPF} \\ \overset{+}{Wb_r} & \overset{+}{bPF} \end{pmatrix}}_{A} \begin{pmatrix} dr \\ de \end{pmatrix} = \begin{pmatrix} 1-m & -m & m & -m & -Wm_{r^*} \\ -b & 1-b & -(1-b) & -b & -Wb_{r^*} \end{pmatrix} \begin{pmatrix} dM \\ d\bar{B} \\ dPB^* \\ dPF \\ dr^* \end{pmatrix}$$

The determinant of A is $|A| = W\,PF\,(m_r b - b_r m) < 0$

The solution of the system with respect to the change in the equilibrium exchange rate yields:

$$de = {}^{1}/_{|A|}\ \{ Wm_r [-b\,dM + (1-b)(d\bar{B} - dPB^*) - b\,dPF - W\,b_{r^*}\,dr^*] -$$

$$- Wb_r [(1-m)dM - m(d\bar{B} - dPB^*) - m\,dPF - W\,m_{r^*}\,dr^*]\}$$

Exchange rate effects of the current account

The domestic CA is defined as $CA = dPF - dPB^*$

a. Increase in PF (domestic CA surplus completely financed by dollar bonds)

$$de/dPF = 1/|A| \; (-Wm_r \, b + W \, b_r \, m) > 0$$

$$E(e/PF) = -1$$

b. Increase in PB due to a decrease in PB^* (domestic CA surplus completely financed by DM bonds)

$$de/dPB^* = 1/|A| \; [-Wm_r \, (1-b) - Wb_r m \,] \gtrless 0$$

The sign of the exchange rate effect is not unambiguously determined by the model. A "normal" reaction of the exchange rate to imbalances in the domestic CA requires $de/dPB^* > 0$.
In this case, an increase in PB^* (equal to the decrease in PB) due to a domestic CA deficit brings about a depreciation of the domestic currency. The condition for a "normal" reaction of the exchange rate in the case of DM financing is

$$b_r \, m > -m_r \, (1-b)$$

After introducing the gross substitutability assumption $m_r + f_r <$ $< -b_r$ this condition can be transformed to

$$|E(f/r)| > |E(m/r)|$$

A comparison of the exchange rate effects from a. and b. shows that

$$|de/dPF| > |de/dPB^*| \quad \text{if} \quad m_r < 0$$

The exchange rate effect of a dollar financed CA exceeds the exchange rate effect of a DM financed CA if the domestic money demand decreases in response to an increase in the domestic interest rate.

c. Since variations in PF and PB^* yield different effects on the exchange rate, an equiproportional change in both asset stocks (a diversified financed balanced CA) has a net effect on the exchange rate.

We define $\gamma = dPF/CA$ with $-\infty \leq \gamma \leq +\infty$ and write for the change in the equilibrium exchange rate (dM, dr^* are set at 0):

$$de = 1/|A| \; \{Wm_r \; [dPF - dPB^*(1-b) - bdPF - dPF] + \\ + Wb_r \; [m \; (dPF - dPB^*)]\}$$

Introducing γ yields:

$$de/CA = 1/|A| \; [Wm_r \; (1 - b - \gamma) + Wb_r \; m]$$

A "normal" reaction of the exchange rate to CA imbalances is defined as $de/CA < 0$. Applying gross substitutability assumptions one can derive from

$$de/CA \lesseqgtr 0 \quad \text{as} \quad m_r \; (1 - b - \gamma) + b_r m \gtreqless 0$$

the normality condition which is explained in the textual part:

$$de/CA \lesseqgtr 0 \quad \text{as} \quad \gamma/f \gtreqless 1 - \frac{E(f/r)}{E(m/r)}$$

<u>Short run stability</u>

The short run dynamic adjustment system for r and e is given by:

$$\dot{r} = -\lambda\ [\ b(r,\ r^*)\ W - PB\ ]$$

$$\dot{e} = \nu\ [\ f(r,\ r^*)\ W - ePF]$$

where λ and ν denote constant adjustment coefficients $0 < \lambda,\nu \leq 1$. According to the basic assumption of the portfolio balance approach, agents react instantaneously to changes in the exogenous variables. Hence, the values for λ and ν should be very close to 1.

The dynamic system is nonlinear and nonhomogeneous. We linearize the system around the equilibrium points r_o and e_o, and derive the following system of linear differential equations.

$$d(r-r_o)/dt = \dot{r} = -\lambda\ [\ Wb_r(r-r_o) + bPF(e-e_o)]$$

$$d(e-e_o)/dt = \dot{e} = \nu\ [\ Wf_r(r-r_o) - (1-f)\ PF\ (e-e_o)]$$

The adjustment system in matrix notation:

$$\begin{pmatrix} \dot{r} \\ \dot{e} \end{pmatrix} = \underbrace{\begin{pmatrix} -\lambda\ W\bar{b}_r & -\lambda\ \bar{b}PF \\ \nu\ W\bar{f}_r & -\nu\ P\bar{F}(1-f) \end{pmatrix}}_{S} \begin{pmatrix} r - r_o \\ e - e_o \end{pmatrix}$$

Local stability of this system in the neighbourhood of the equilibrium values requires that the trace (S) < 0 and that the determinant S > 0.

Trace condition: $(-\lambda W b_r) + [-\nu PF(1-f)] < 0$

The trace condition is fulfilled.

Determinant S: $\lambda\nu WPFb_r(1-f) + \lambda\nu Wf_r bPF =$

$$= \lambda\nu WPF\,[b_r(1-f) + f_r\, b] > 0$$

According to the gross substitutability assumption $b_r > -f_r$ and the balance sheet constraint $(1-f) > b$ the determinant is positive. Thus, the equilibrium is locally stable.

Global stability of the system requires, according to the theorem of Czeslaw and Olech, the following additional conditions.[1)]

$$(-\lambda\, Wb_r)\,[-\nu\, PF(1-f)] \neq 0$$

or, alternatively,

$$(-\lambda\, bPF)\,(\nu Wf_r) \neq 0$$

Both terms are different from zero so that the equilibrium system exhibits also global stability.

1) See Neumann (1973, p. 187).

5B. The Two-Country Model with Asset Demands Linear Homogeneous in Wealth

Market clearing conditions:

$\overline{PB} = PB + PB^*$	$= b(r, r^*)\,W$	$+\; e\, b^*(r, r^*)\,W^*$	DM bonds
$\overline{PF} = PF + PF^*$	$= (1/e)\, f(r, r^*)\,W$	$+\; f^*(r, r^*)\,W^*$	\$ bonds
$M = CB + \bar{e}\, CF$	$= m(r, r^*)\,W$		German money
$N = (1/\bar{e})\, CB^* + CF^*$	$= n(r, r^*)\,W^*$		US money

$W = M + PB + e\,PF$ — German private wealth

$W^* = N + (1/e)\,PB^* + PF^*$ — US private wealth

Partial derivatives: $b_r,\ b^*_r,\ f_{r^*},\ f^*_{r^*} > 0$

$b_{r^*},\ b^*_{r^*},\ f_r,\ f^*_r,\ m_r,\ m_{r^*},\ n_r,\ n_{r^*} < 0$

Definitions and assumptions:

endogenous: $r,\ r^*,\ e$

exogenous : $PB,\ PB^*,\ PF,\ PF^*,\ M,\ N$

$m + b + f = 1$
$n + b^* + f^* = 1$
} balance sheet constraints

$m_r + f_r = -b_r < 0$
$m_{r^*} + b_{r^*} = -f_{r^*} < 0$
$n_r + f^*_r = -b^*_r < 0$
$n_{r^*} + b^*_{r^*} = -f^*_{r^*} < 0$
} gross substitutability assumptions

Total differentials (initial value of e = 1, $\bar{e}$ = constant):

BB: DM bonds : $(1-b)dPB + (1-b^*)dPB^* - b\ dM - b\ dPF - b^*dN - b^*dPF^* =$

$$= (b_r W + b_r^* W^*)dr + (b_{r^*} W + b_{r^*}^* W^*)dr^* + \underbrace{(b\ PF + b^* W^* - b^* PB^*)}_{b\ PF\ +\ PB^*(1-b^*)}\ de$$

FF: $ bonds : $(1-f)dPF + (1-f^*)dPF^* - f\ dM - f\ dPB - f^*dN - f^*dPB^* =$

$$= (f_r W + f_r^* W^*)\ dr + (f_{r^*} W + f_{r^*}^* W^*)\ dr^* - \underbrace{(f^* PB^* + f\ W - f\ PF)}_{f^* PB^*\ +\ PF(1-f)}\ de$$

MM: German money: $dCB + dCF - m\ dM - m\ dPB - m\ dPF =$

$$= m_r W\ d_r + m_{r^*} W\ dr^* + mPF\ de$$

NN: US money : $dCB^* + dCF^* - n\ dN - n\ dPB^* - n\ dPF^* =$

$$= n_r W^*\ dr + n_{r^*} W^*\ dr^* - nPB^*\ de$$

The change in the equilibrium exchange rate in response to an increase in the domestic interest rate which is necessary to keep the respective asset markets in equilibrium is given by the following derivatives. They represent the slopes of the equilibrium curves in the e - r space (at given r^*).

$$\text{BB:} \quad de/dr = \frac{-(b_r W + b_r^* W^*)}{bPF + PB^*(1-b^*)} < 0$$

$$\text{FF :} \quad de/dr = \frac{f_r W + f_r^* W^*}{f^* PB^* + PF(1-f)} < 0$$

MM: $de/dr = \frac{-m_r W}{mPF} > 0$

NN: $de/dr = \frac{n_r W^*}{nPB^*} < 0$

From the assumptions made so far it is not possible to draw conclusions on the relative steepness of the BB and FF curve.[1)]
The negative slope of BB is, in absolute terms, greater than the negative slope of FF if:

$$\underbrace{(f_r W + f_r^* W^*)}_{1.}\ \underbrace{[bPF + PB^*(1-b^*)]}_{2.} + \underbrace{(b_r W + b_r^* W^*)}_{3.}\ \underbrace{[(1-f)PF + PB^* f^*]}_{4.} > 0$$

where 1. : interest response of the demand for dollar bonds in both countries.

2. : Wealth effect of a rising exchange rate on the demand for DM bonds.

3. : Interest response of the DM bond demand in both countries.

4. : Wealth effect of a falling exchange rate on the demand for dollar bonds.

As a sufficient but not necessary condition for this expression to become > 0 one can derive by introducing gross substitutability assumptions $n\ PB^* < m\ PF$. This condition is not guaranteed by the model assumptions. Since we cannot determine the relative slopes of the equilibrium curves in the e - r space we omit a graphical exposition.

---

1) On the whole, it is not possible to rank the three negative slopes of BB, FF, and NN.

It is interesting to note, however, that the slopes of the equilibrium curves in the $r - r^*$ space can be ranked by applying gross substitutability assumptions and the additional assumption:

$$n_{r^*} m_r > n_r m_{r^*} \quad \text{if} \quad n_{r^*} < n_r \quad \text{and} \quad m_r < m_{r^*}$$

In words: the response of the money demand in both countries is stronger with respect to the respective domestic interest rate than with respect to the respective foreign interest rate.

The slopes of the equilibrium curves in the $r - r^*$ space are (e = constant):

$$\text{BB:} \qquad dr/dr^* = \frac{-(b_{r^*}W + b^*_{r^*}W^*)}{b_r W + b^*_r W^*} > 0$$

$$\text{FF:} \qquad dr/dr^* = \frac{-(f_{r^*}W + f^*_{r^*}W^*)}{f_r W + f^*_r W^*} > 0$$

FF is steeper than BB since $f_{r^*} > -b_{r^*}$ (for both countries) and $b_r > -f_r$ (for both countries).

$$\text{MM:} \qquad dr/dr^* = -\frac{m_{r^*}}{m_r} < 0$$

$$\text{NN:} \qquad dr/dr^* = -\frac{n_{r^*}}{n_r} < 0$$

NN is steeper than MM if $n_{r^*} m_r > n_r m_{r^*}$.

A graphical exposition using the equilibrium curves in the $r - r^*$ space may be instructive for analyzing discretionary exchange rate changes in a fixed-rate system (see, e.g., Girton and Henderson 1977) but since the exchange rate is not visible such a diagram is of little value for illustrating a flexible-rate system.

Because of the wealth constraints only three market clearing conditions are necessary to solve the simultaneous system for the three endogenous variables r, r^*, and e. We choose the equilibrium conditions for BB, MM and NN and write the system in matrix notation:

$$\begin{pmatrix} \overset{+}{b_r W + b_r^* W^*} & \overset{-}{b_{r^*} W + b_{r^*}^* W^*} & bPF + \overset{+}{PB^*(1-b^*)} \\ \overset{-}{m_r W} & \overset{-}{m_{r^*} W} & \overset{+}{m\,PF} \\ \overset{-}{n_r W^*} & \overset{-}{n_{r^*} W^*} & \overset{-}{-n\,PB^*} \end{pmatrix} \begin{pmatrix} dr \\ dr^* \\ de \end{pmatrix} =$$

$$= \begin{pmatrix} -b & -b^* & (1-b) & (1-b^*) & -b & -b^* & 0 & 0 & 0 & 0 \\ -m & 0 & -m & 0 & -m & 0 & 1 & 0 & 1 & 0 \\ 0 & -n & 0 & -n & 0 & -n & 0 & 1 & 0 & 1 \end{pmatrix} \begin{pmatrix} dM \\ dN \\ dPB \\ dPB^* \\ dPF \\ dPF^* \\ dCB \\ dCB^* \\ dCF \\ dCF^* \end{pmatrix}$$

The determinant of the coefficient matrix is:

$$D = (\overset{+}{b_r W} + b_r^* W^*)(\overset{+}{-m_{r^*} W n PB^*} - \overset{+}{n_{r^*} W^* m PF}) - (b_{r^*} W + \overset{+}{b_{r^*}^* W^*})$$
$$(\overset{+}{-m_r W n PB^*} - \overset{+}{n_r W^* m PF}) + [bPF + \overset{+}{PB^*(1-b^*)}]\overset{+}{WW^*}(\overset{-}{m_r n_{r^*} - n_r m_{r^*}})$$

The following assumptions secure that $D > 0$

a. $m_r n_{r^*} > m_{r^*} n_{r^*}$ — domestic money is a better substitute for domestic bonds than for foreign bonds in both the US and Germany (sufficient but not necessary for a. to be fulfilled).

b. $PF, PB^* > 0$ — private net stocks of the respective foreign bonds are positive in both the US and Germany.

For our discussion of negative private net foreign asset positions in chapter 11. the following two cases are also important:

b1. if $PF < 0$, $PB^* > 0$ or $PF > 0$, $PB^* < 0$, the sign of D is ambiguous $D \gtrless 0$.

b2. if $PF < 0$, $PB^* < 0$ it follows $D < 0$.

Applying the Cramer rule, the system can be solved for changes in the equilibrium values of e, r, r^* in response to changes in the exogenous variables. In the following we concentrate on the change in the equilibrium exchange rate. The comparative-static results for both interest rates are given in table 1. at the end of the appendix.

$$
\begin{aligned}
de = (1/D) \{ & \Phi \, [m_{r^*} W \, (dCB^* + dCF^* - n \, dN - n \, dPB^* - n \, dPF^*) - \\
& - n_{r^*} W^* (dCB + dCF - m \, dM - m \, dPB - m \, dPF)] - \\
& - \rho [m_r W \, (dCB^* + dCF^* - n \, dN - n \, dPB^* - dPF^*) - \\
& - n_r W^* \, (dCB + dCF - m \, dM - m \, dPB - m \, dPF)] + \\
& + WW^* \, \psi \, [(1-b) dPB + (1-b^*) dPB^* - b \, dM - b \, dPF - \\
& - b^* \, dN - b^* \, dPF^*] \}
\end{aligned}
$$

where $\Phi = b_r W + b_r^* W^* > 0$

$\rho = b_{r^*} W + b_{r^*}^* W^* < 0$

$\psi = m_r n_{r^*} - m_{r^*} n_r > 0$

Domestic CA surplus equal to a foreign CA deficit

The model yields identical results for DM or dollar bond financing.

$$de/dPF \Big|_{dPF=-dPF^*} = de/dPB \Big|_{dPB=-dPB^*} =$$

$$= (1/D)\{ \overset{-}{\Phi(m_{r^*}Wn + n_{r^*}W^*m)} - \overset{-}{\rho\,(m_r Wn + n_r W^* m)} - \overset{?}{\psi(b-b^*)WW^*}\} < 0$$

From this expression we can deduce three cases:

a. "Preferred local habitat" ($b > b^*$)

If the part of wealth which is held in DM bonds is greater in Germany than in the US ($b>b^*$), a surplus in the German CA brings about an appreciation of the DM against the dollar.
The appreciation impact increases with an increase in b and a decrease in b^*. 1)

b. Identical preferences with respect to DM bonds ($b = b^*$).

The appreciation impact on the DM declines but the exchange rate still reacts normally to the CA surplus.

c. Reversed preferences with respect to DM bonds ($b < b^*$).

Even if $b < b^*$ it is unlikely that the sign of the overall effect becomes positive (perverse reaction of the exchange rate). To see this, we rewrite the right hand side of the equation and apply gross substitutability relations:

---

1) See next page.

$$= (1/D)\ WW^* \{n_{r^*}m\ [-m_r(1 + \frac{b-b^*}{m}) + b_r^*\ (W^*/W) - f_r] + m_{r^*}\ n$$

$$[-n_r\ (1 + \frac{b-b^*}{n}) + b_r\ (W/W^*) - f_r^*\ ] - m_r\ n\ [b_{r^*}\ (W/W^*) +$$

$$+ b_{r^*}^*] - n_r\ m\ [b_{r^*} + b_{r^*}^*\ (W^*/W)]\}$$

The only positive (depreciation) effect in this expression could come from $-m_r\ [1 + (b-b^*)/m]$ and $-n_r\ [1 + (b-b^*)/n]$. For this to occur it is necessary that $(b-b^*)/m < -1$ and $(b-b^*)/n < -1$. In addition to that, both depreciation effects must overwhelm all the other appreciation (negative) effects appearing in the equation.

Considering the wealth constraint $(b - b^*) = (f^* - f) + (n - m)$, the results from a. to c. apply not only to domestic and foreign DM bond holdings but in like manner to dollar bond holdings.

Asset accumulation: changes in the net stocks of $\overline{B}$ and $\overline{F}$

a. Deficit in the US government budget, financed by issuing dollar bonds to US residents (net increase in $\overline{F}$ which accrues as an increase in PF^*).

$$de/dPF^* = (1/D)\{\ \overset{+}{\Phi\ (-nm_{r^*}W)} - \overset{+}{\rho(-nm_rW)}\ \overset{-}{-\psi\ b^*WW^*} \gtrless 0$$

appreciation tendency for the dollar

This can be transformed into:

$$= (1/D)\ WW^*\ \{-m_{r^*}\ [-b^*n_r + nb_r^* + nb_r(W/W^*)] -$$

$$-m_r\ [\underbrace{b^*n_{r^*} - nb_{r^*}^*}_{a} - nb_{r^*}\ (W/W^*)]\} \gtrless 0$$

(Footnote 1. last page) Since b and b^* occur in D, the whole expression has to be differentiated with respect to b and b^*. Holding the other portfolio shares appearing in the expression (m and n) constant, the verbal statement given above proves to be right.

The only negative term in this expression is $b^* n_{r^*}$. As a sufficient but not necessary condition for the inequality to become positive, we can derive from 'a' (in absolute terms) $E(b^*/r^*) > E(n/r^*)$. Even in the case $E(b^*/r^*) < E(n/r^*)$ all other terms appearing in the inequality support the appreciation tendency.

<u>b</u>. Deficit in the German government budget, financed by issuing DM bonds to German residents (net increase in $\overline{B}$ which accrues as an increase in PB).

$$de/dPB = (1/D)\,[\overset{-}{\Phi(n_{r^*}W^*m)} - \overset{-}{\rho(n_r Wm)} + \overset{+}{\psi(1-b)WW^*}] \gtrless 0 \quad \text{appreciation tendency for the DM}$$

Rearranged:

$$= (1/D)\, WW^* \,\{n_{r^*}\,[\overbrace{m_r(1-b) + b_r m}^{a} + b^*_r m(W^*/W)] -$$

$$-n_r\,[m_{r^*}(1-b) + b^*_{r^*}m + b_{r^*}m(W/W^*)] \gtrless 0$$

Similar to above, we derive from 'a' $E(f/r) > E(m/r)$ as sufficient but not necessary condition for $de/dPB < 0$.

From a. and b. follows (for both countries): an increase in the respective domestic net bond stock tends to appreciate the domestic currency if, but not only if, the elasticity of the domestic demand for foreign bonds with respect to the domestic interest rate is higher than the interest elasticity of the domestic money demand.

<u>c</u>. Deficit in the US government budget, financed by issuing dollar bonds to German residents.

$$de/dPF = (1/D)\,[\overset{-}{\Phi(n_{r^*}Wm)} - \overset{-}{\rho(n_r Wm)} - \overset{-}{\psi bWW^*}] < 0$$

d. Deficit in the German budget, financed by issuing DM bonds to US residents.

$$de/dPB^* = (1/D)\,[\overset{+}{\phi(-nm_{r*}W)} - \overset{+}{\rho(-nm_rW)} + \overset{+}{\psi(1-b^*)}] \quad > 0$$

From c. and d. follows (for both countries): a domestic budget deficit, financed by domestic-currency denominated bonds tends to appreciate the domestic currency if the bonds are issued to domestic residents, but depreciates the domestic currency if the bonds are issued to foreign residents.

Central bank actions

A. German central bank

a. An expansionary open-market policy conducted with German residents leads to a depreciation of the DM (purchases of PB in exchange for M).[1)]

$$de/dCB\Big|_{dCB=-dPB=dM} = (1/D)\,[\overset{+}{\Phi(-n_{r*}W^*)} + \overset{+}{\rho(n_rW^*)} - \overset{-}{\psi WW^*}] \quad > 0$$

b. A Purchase of dollar bonds from domestic residents (PF) in exchange for money leads to a depreciation of the DM which is stronger than in case a.

$$de/dCF\Big|_{dCF=-dPF=dM} = (1/D)\,[\overset{+}{\Phi(-n_{r*}W^*)} + \overset{+}{\rho(n_rW^*)}] \quad > 0$$

---

1) By rearranging and introducing $b_r = -m_r - f_r$ it can be shown that $de/dCB > 0$ is always fulfilled.

c. Policy b. with neutralization of the money supply effect by sales of DM bonds to domestic residents leads to a depreciation of the DM which is smaller than in case b.

$$de/dCF\Big|_{\substack{dCF=-dPF=dM \\ \parallel \\ dCB=\ dPB=-dM}} = (1/D)\ (WW^{*}\psi) > 0$$

d. A purchase of dollar bonds from foreign residents (PF^*) in exchange for DM bonds (PB^*) leads to a depreciation of the DM which is equal to the depreciation in case c.

$$de/dCF\Big|_{\substack{dCF=-dPF^{*} \\ \parallel \\ -dCB=\ dPB^{*}}} = (1/D)\ (WW^{*}\psi) > 0$$

B. US central bank

a. An expansionary open-market policy conducted with US residents leads to a depreciation of the dollar (reduction in PF^* in exchange for N).

$$de/dCF^{*}\Big|_{dCF^{*}=-dPF^{*}=dN} = (1/D)\ [\Phi(\overset{-}{m}_{r}*W) - \rho(\overset{-}{m}_{r}W)] < 0$$

b. A purchase of DM bonds (PB^*) in exchange for money N depreciates the dollar. The depreciation effect is stronger than in case a.

$$de/dCB^{*}\Big|_{dCB^{*}=-dPB^{*}=dN} = (1/D)\ [\Phi(\overset{-}{m}_{r}*W) - \rho(\overset{-}{m}_{r}W) - \overset{-}{\psi}WW^{*} < 0$$

c. Policy b. with neutralization of the money supply effect by selling dollar bonds in exchange for money leads to a depreciation of the dollar which is smaller than without neutralization.

$$de/dCB^{*}\Big|_{\substack{dCB^{*}=-dPB^{*}=dN \\ \| \\ -dCF^{*}=dPF^{*}=-dN}} = (1/D)\,(-\psi WW^{*}) < 0$$

d. A purchase of DM bonds from German residents (PB) in exchange for dollar bonds (PF) leads to a depreciation of the dollar.

$$de/dCB^{*}\Big|_{\substack{dCB^{*}=-dPB \\ \| \\ -dCF^{*}=dPF}} = (1/D)\,(-\psi WW^{*}) < 0$$

Current account imbalances and central bank interventions

We assume a surplus in the German CA (deficit in the US CA) financed with DM or dollar bonds ($dPF = -dPF^{*}$ or $dPB = -dPB^{*}$).

A. German central bank

a. Absorbing an increase in PF by dollar bond purchases in exchange for M (policy b. above).

Policy : $dCF = -dPF = dM$

net effect : $dCF = -dPF^{*} = dM$ ambiguous

$$= (1/D)\{\Phi\,[m_{r^{*}}Wn - n_{r^{*}}W^{*}(1-m)] - \rho[m_{r}Wn - n_{r}W^{*}(1-m)] + (b^{*}-b)\,WW^{*}\psi\} \lessgtr 0$$

b. Sales of DM bonds to US residents in exchange for dollar bonds (policy d. above).

Policy : $-dCB = dPB^*$
$\| $
$dCF = -dPF^*$

net effect : $dCF = -dCB = dPB = -dPF^*$ appreciation tendency for the DM

$$= (1/D)\{\ \Phi[m_r{*}Wn + n_r{*}W^*m] - \rho[m_rWn + n_rW^*m] + + (1-b+b^*)\ WW^*\psi\} \lessgtr 0$$

The net effect is negative (appreciation of the DM) as $de/dPB < 0$ and $de/dPF^* > 0$. This is not secured by the model but depends on the conditions described above.

At any rate, the appreciation tendency under policy b. is stronger than under policy a.

c. The net effect of a. with neutralization of the money supply effect is equal to the net effect of b.

US central bank

a. Absorbing a decrease in PB^* by sales of DM bonds in exchange for N (policy b. above).

Policy : $-dCB^* = dPB^* = -dN$

net effect : $-dCB^* = dPB = -dN$ ambiguous

$$= (1/D)\{\ \Phi[n_r{*}W^*m - m_r{*}W(1-m)] - \rho\,[n_rW^*m - m_rW(1-m)] + (1-b+b^*)\ WW^*\psi\ \} \lessgtr 0$$

b. Purchases of dollar bonds from German residents in exchange for DM bonds.

Policy : $dCF^* = -dPF$
$\quad\quad\quad\;\; \| $
$-dCB^* = dPB$

net effect : $dCF^* = -dCB^* = -dPF^* = dPB$ depreciation tendency for the dollar

The net effect is equal to net effect of policy b. conducted by the German central bank.

c. The net effect of a. with neutralization of the money supply effect is equal to the net effect of b. and hence equal to the net effect of b. in the case of the German central bank.

A summary of the various comparative-static results including interest rate effects is given in table 1. at the end of the appendix.

Short run Stability [1)]

We define the dynamic adjustment of the endogenous variables by the following system of nonlinear, nonhomogeneous differential equations. The adjustment speeds are set at 1 in order to simplify the exposition.

$$\dot{r} = m\,(r,\, r^{*})\, W - M$$
$$\dot{r}^{*} = n\,(r,\, r^{*})\, W^{*} - N$$
$$\dot{e} = (1/e)\, f\,(r,\, r^{*})\, W + f^{*}(r,\, r^{*})\, W^{*} - \overline{PF}$$

The equilibrium of the system at $\dot{r} = \dot{r}^{*} = \dot{e} = 0$ represents the particular solution of the differential equation system $(r_o,\, r^{*}_o,\, e_o)$.

To analyse the local stability in the neighbourhood of the equilibrium we define $(r - r_o)$, $(r^{*} - r^{*}_o)$, $(e - e_o)$ and expand the equations in Taylor series at the equilibrium point, neglecting all terms of order higher than the first. This yields the following system of linear differential equations as an approximation to the nonlinear system above:

$$d(r-r_o)/dt = \dot{r} = m_r W\,(r-r_o) + m_{r^*} W\,(r^{*}-r^{*}_o) + mPF\,(e-e_o)$$
$$d(r^{*}-r^{*}_o)/dt = \dot{r}^{*} = n_r W^{*}\,(r-r_o) + n_{r^*} W^{*}(r^{*}-r^{*}_o) - nPB^{*}\,(e-e_o)$$
$$d(e-e_o)/dt = \dot{e} = (f_r W + f^{*}_r\, W^{*})\,(r-r_o) + (f_{r^*} W + f^{*}_{r^*} W^{*})\,(r^{*}-r^{*}_o) - [f^{*}PB^{*} + PF(1-f)]\,(e-e_o)$$

We try the following functions as general solutions to the system:

$$r(t) = C_1\, e^{\lambda t}\;;\quad r^{*}(t) = C_2\, e^{\lambda t}\;;\quad e(t) = C_3\, e^{\lambda t}$$

1) The mathematical background of the following stability analysis is discussed in Gandolfo (1971, pp. 254), Chiang (1974, pp. 466). See also Neumann (1973, pp. 308).

In matrix notation the system is given by:

$$\begin{pmatrix} \dot{r} \\ \dot{r}^* \\ \dot{e} \end{pmatrix} = \begin{pmatrix} \overset{-}{a_{11}} & \overset{-}{a_{12}} & \overset{+}{a_{13}} \\ m_r W & m_{r^*} W & mPF \\ \overset{-}{a_{21}} & \overset{-}{a_{22}} & \overset{-}{a_{23}} \\ n_r W^* & n_{r^*} W^* & -nPB^* \\ \overset{-}{a_{31}} & \overset{+}{a_{32}} & \overset{-}{a_{33}} \\ f_r W + f_r^* W^* & f_{r^*} W + f_{r^*}^* W^* & -[f^* PB^* + PF(1-f)] \end{pmatrix} \begin{pmatrix} r - r_o \\ r^* - r_o^* \\ e - e_o \end{pmatrix}$$

Substituting the general solutions r(t), $r^*(t)$, e(t) into the system of linear equations yields:

$$r: \quad \lambda C_1 e^{\lambda t} = m_r W C_1 e^{\lambda t} + m_{r^*} W C_2 e^{\lambda t} + mPFC_3 e^{\lambda t}$$

$$0 = -(m_r W - \lambda) C_1 e^{\lambda t} - m_{r^*} W C_2 e^{\lambda t} - mPFC_3 e^{\lambda t}$$

$$r^*: \quad \lambda C_2 e^{\lambda t} = n_r W^* C_1 e^{\lambda t} + n_{r^*} W^* C_2 e^{\lambda t} - nPBC_3 e^{\lambda t}$$

$$0 = -n_r W^* C_1 e^{\lambda t} - (n_{r^*} W^* - \lambda) C_2 e^{\lambda t} + nPBC_3 e^{\lambda t}$$

$$e: \quad \lambda C_3 e^{\lambda t} = (f_r W + f_r^* W*) C_1 e^{\lambda t} + (f_{r^*} W + f_{r^*}^* W^*) C_2 e^{\lambda t} -$$

$$- [f^* PB^* + PF(1-f)]\, C_3 e^{\lambda t}$$

$$0 = - \,.........\, -[\, - [f^* PB^* + PF(1-f) - \lambda]] C_3 e^{\lambda t}$$

We simplify for $e^{\lambda t}$ and derive for the characteristic equation:

$$\det(D - \lambda I) = \begin{vmatrix} -a_{11}+\lambda & -a_{12} & -a_{13} \\ -a_{21} & -a_{22}+\lambda & -a_{23} \\ -a_{31} & -a_{32} & -a_{33}+\lambda \end{vmatrix}$$

Local stability of the equilibrium is guaranteed if all Eigenvalues (characteristic roots) of this matrix are negative or have negative real parts.

We derive for the characteristic equation:

$$\det(D - \lambda I) = (-a_{11} + \lambda)\,[(-a_{22} + \lambda)(-a_{33} + \lambda) - a_{23}\,a_{32}] +$$

$$+ a_{12}\,[\,-a_{21}(-a_{33} + \lambda) - a_{23}\,a_{31}] -$$

$$- [a_{21}\,a_{32} + a_{31}(-a_{22} + \lambda)]$$

$$= \lambda^3 - [\overset{-}{a}_{33}+\overset{-}{a}_{11}+\overset{-}{a}_{22}]\,\lambda^2 + [\overset{-}{a}_{11}\overset{-}{a}_{33} + \overset{-}{a}_{22}\overset{-}{a}_{33} + \overset{-}{a}_{11}\overset{-}{a}_{22} -$$

$$- \overset{-}{a}_{23}\overset{+}{a}_{32} - \overset{-}{a}_{12}\overset{-}{a}_{21} - \overset{+}{a}_{13}\overset{-}{a}_{31}]\lambda - \overset{-}{a}_{11}\overset{-}{a}_{22}\overset{-}{a}_{33} +$$

$$+ \overset{-}{a}_{12}\overset{-}{a}_{21}\overset{-}{a}_{33} - \overset{-}{a}_{12}\overset{-}{a}_{23}\overset{-}{a}_{31} - \overset{+}{a}_{13}\overset{-}{a}_{21}\overset{+}{a}_{32} + \overset{+}{a}_{13}\overset{-}{a}_{31}\overset{-}{a}_{22} +$$

$$+ \overset{-}{a}_{11}\overset{-}{a}_{23}\overset{+}{a}_{33}$$

This third-degree polynomial equation possess negative real parts of all roots if the λ coefficients x_i ($i = 0, 1, 2, 3$) fulfill the Routh-Hurwitz conditions.

Routh-Hurwitz conditions:

1. $x_0 > 0$

2. $x_1 > 0$

3. $(x_1 x_2 - x_3) > 0$

4. $(x_1 x_2 - x_3) x_3 > 0$ fulfilled if $x_3 > 0$ and 3. is fulfilled

$\underline{x_0} = 1 > 0$

$\underline{x_1} = -(a_{33} + a_{11} + a_{22}) = -[\,-[\,f^* PB^* + PF(1-f)] + m_r W + n_{r^*} W^*] > 0$

$$\underline{x_3} = -a_{33}(a_{11}a_{22} - a_{12}a_{21}) + a_{32}(a_{11}a_{23} - a_{13}a_{21}) - $$
$$-a_{31}(a_{12}a_{23} - a_{13}a_{22}) > 0$$

$$= [f^* PB^* + PF(1-f)]\, WW^* (m_r n_{r^*} - m_{r^*} n_r) + \qquad > 0 \text{ if } \begin{cases} m_r < m_{r^*} \\ n_{r^*} < n_r \end{cases}$$

$$+ (f_{r^*} W + f_r^* W^*)(-m_r W n PB^* - n_r W^* m PF) - \qquad > 0$$

$$- (f_r W + f_r^* W^*)(-m_{r^*} W n PB^* - n_{r^*} W^* m PF) \qquad > 0$$

condition for $x_3 > 0$: $m_r n_{r^*} > m_{r^*} n_r$

fulfilled if $m_r < m_{r^*}$ and $n_{r^*} < n_r$ <u>cond. (1)</u>

An economic interpretation of this condition is given in the textual part.

$$
\begin{aligned}
\underline{x_1x_2 - x_3} = \; & -a_{11}a_{33}^2 - a_{22}a_{33}^2 - a_{11}a_{12}a_{33} + a_{23}a_{32}a_{33} + \\
& + a_{12}a_{21}a_{33} + a_{13}a_{31}a_{33} - a_{11}^2a_{33} - a_{22}a_{33}a_{11} - \\
& - a_{11}^2a_{22} + a_{23}a_{32}a_{11} + a_{12}a_{21}a_{11} + a_{13}a_{31}a_{11} - \\
& - a_{11}a_{33}a_{22} - a_{22}^2a_{33} - a_{11}a_{22}^2 + a_{23}a_{32}a_{22} + \\
& + a_{12}a_{21}a_{22} + a_{13}a_{31}a_{22} + a_{11}a_{22}a_{33} - a_{11}a_{23}a_{32} - \\
& - a_{12}a_{21}a_{33} + a_{12}a_{23}a_{31} + a_{13}a_{21}a_{32} - a_{13}a_{31}a_{22}
\end{aligned}
$$

$$
\begin{aligned}
= & -a_{33}^2(\overset{+}{a_{11}} + a_{22}) - \overset{+}{a_{11}}{}^2a_{33} - \overset{+}{a_{22}}{}^2a_{33} - \overset{+}{a_{11}}\underbrace{(a_{11}a_{22} - a_{12}a_{21})}_{1.} - \\
& - \overset{+}{a_{22}}\underbrace{(a_{11}a_{22} - a_{12}a_{21})}_{2.} + \underbrace{\overset{-}{a_{31}}(a_{12}a_{23} + a_{13}a_{11} + a_{13}a_{33})}_{3.} + \\
& + \underbrace{\overset{+}{a_{32}}(a_{13}a_{21} + a_{23}a_{22} + a_{23}a_{33})}_{4.} - \\
& - 2\,(\overset{+}{a_{22}}a_{11}a_{33})
\end{aligned}
$$

<u>1. and 2. > 0</u> if $m_r n_{r*} > m_{r*} n_r$

<u>3. > 0</u> if $a_{12}a_{23} + a_{13}a_{11} + a_{13}a_{33} < 0$

$$a_{12} > a_{11}(-a_{13}/a_{23}) - a_{33}a_{13}/a_{23}$$

$$a_{12} > (a_{11} + a_{33})(-a_{13}/a_{23})$$

$$a_{12} > \underbrace{a_{11}\,[1 + (a_{33}/a_{11})]\,(-a_{13}/a_{23})}$$

$$\frac{a_{33} + a_{11}}{a_{11}}(-a_{13}/a_{23}) = \underbrace{\frac{-a_{13}(a_{33} + a_{11})}{a_{11}a_{23}}}_{\Psi > 0}$$

<u>cond. (2)</u>: $-a_{12} < -a_{11}\,\Psi$

Condition (2) is fulfilled if $m_{r^*} > m_r$ and $\Psi > 1$.

The first part of this condition is in accordance with cond. (1). The value of Ψ depends on the amount of assets in the portfolios and cannot be determined conclusively by the model.
Even if $\Psi < 1$ and $m_r^* < m_r\,\Psi$, all the other effects appearing in $x_1x_2 - x_3$ exhibit a positive sign so that this potential negative effect is most likely to be overwhelmed.

If we neglect the special case $0 < \Psi < 1$ which might lead to $a_{12} < a_{11}\,\Psi$, condition (2) reduces to $m_{r^*} > m_r$.

<u>4. > 0</u> if $a_{13}a_{21} + a_{23}a_{22} + a_{23}a_{33} > 0$

$$a_{21} > (-a_{23}a_{22}/a_{13}) - (a_{23}a_{33}/a_{13})$$

$$a_{21} > (a_{22} + a_{33})\,(-a_{23}/a_{13})$$

$$a_{21} > a_{22}\,\underbrace{[1 + (a_{33}/a_{22})]\,(-a_{23}/a_{13})}$$

$$\frac{a_{33} + a_{22}}{a_{22}}(-a_{23}/a_{13}) = \underbrace{\frac{-a_{23}(a_{33} + a_{22})}{a_{13}a_{22}}}_{\Phi > 0}$$

<u>cond. (3)</u>: $-a_{21} < -a_{22}\,\Phi$

Condition (3) is fulfilled if $n_r > n_{r*} \Phi$.

If we once more neglect the special case in which $0 < \Phi < 1$ leads to $n_r < n_{r*} \Phi$ (with $n_r > n_{r*}$), the condition reduces to $n_r > n_{r*}$.

Conditions (2) and (3) are fulfilled if condition (1) is fulfilled. Thus, in general, local stability of the system is guaranteed if

$$m_r < m_{r*} \quad \text{and} \quad n_{r*} < n_r$$

These are the assumptions made in deriving the comparative-static results. The economic interpretation of these assumptions are given in the textual part.

Table 1: Comparative-Static Results of the Two-Country Model [a)]

Shock	de	dr	dr^*
1. Surplus in the bilateral German CA with the US		1.1 identical to 1.2	1.1 identical to 1.2
1.1. $dPF = -dPF^*$	< 0 } identical	? } if $b=b^*$ and $PB^*=PF$ { > 0	? } if $b=b^*$ and $PB^*=PF$ {
1.2. $dPB = -dPB^*$	< 0 } identical	? } if $b=b^*$ and $PB^*=PF$ { > 0	?
2. Government budget deficit			
2.1. $dPB > 0$	?; < 0 if $E(f/r) < E(m/r)$	> 0	?
2.2. $dPF > 0$	> 0	?	?
2.3. $dPB^* > 0$	< 0	?	?
2.4. $dPF^* > 0$	?; > 0 if $E(b^*/r^*) < E(n/r^*)$	?	> 0
3. Increase in the money supply through open-market operations			
3.1. $dM = -dPB$	> 0	< 0	? stronger tendency for > 0 than 3.2.
3.2. $dM = -dPF$	> 0 greater than 3.1.	< 0 in absolute terms smaller than 3.1.	?
3.3. $dN = -dPF^*$	< 0	?	< 0
3.4. $dN = -dPB^*$	< 0 in absolute terms greater than 3.3.	? stronger tendency for < 0 than 3.3.	< 0 in absolute terms smaller than 3.3.
4. Central bank purchases of $ bonds in exchange for DM bonds $(-dPF=dPB)=(-dPF^*=dPB^*)$	> 0 in absolute terms smaller than 3.2. and 3.4.	> 0 in absolute terms smaller than 3.1.	< 0 in absolute terms smaller than 3.3.
5. Sterilized interventions			
5.1. $dM=-dPF$, $-dM=dPB$; $-dPF=dPB$	> 0 identical to 4.	> 0 identical to 4.	< 0 identical to 4.
5.2. $dN=-dPB^*$, $-dN=dPF^*$; $-dPB^*=dPF^*$	< 0 in absolute terms identical to 4.	< 0 in absolute terms identical to 4.	> 0 in absolute terms identical to 4.
6. Surplus in the bilateral German CA with the US $dPF=-dPF^*$ or $dPB=-dPB^*$ combined with			
6.1. policy 3.2. net effect: $dM = -dPF^*$	?	?	?
6.2. policy 3.4. net effect: $-dN=dPB$	?	?	?
6.3. policy 4. net effect: $dPB=-dPF^*$	? stronger tendency for < 0 than 6.1. and 6.2.	?	?

a) The results have been derived assuming that (i) $PF > 0$, $PB^* > 0$ (ii) $b \geq b^*$ and (iii) $m_r n_{r^*} > m_{r^*} n_r$.

5C. The Two-Country Model with a General Specification of the Wealth Dependency of Asset Demands

We rewrite the system developed above with the general assumption that asset demands depend positively on wealth. This general specification includes a constant portfolio structure as a special case but allows also for nonproportional changes in asset demands in response to wealth changes.

$\overline{PB} =$	$PB + PB^*$	$= \beta(r, r^*, W) + e\,\beta^*(r, r^*, W^*)$	DM bonds
$\overline{PF} =$	$PF + PF^*$	$= (1/e)\,\varepsilon(r, r^*, W) + \varepsilon^*(r, r^*, W^*)$	\$ bonds
$M =$	$CB + \overline{e}\,CF$	$= \mu(r, r^*, W)$	German money
$N =$	$(1/\overline{e})\,CB^* + CF^*$	$= \eta(r, r^*, W^*)$	US money

$$W = M + PB + e\,PF$$

$$W^* = N + (1/e)\,PB^* + PF^*$$

Partial derivatives: $\beta_r, \beta^*_r, \varepsilon_{r^*}, \varepsilon^*_{r^*}, \beta_W, \beta^*_{W^*}, \varepsilon_W, \varepsilon^*_{W^*}, \mu_W, \eta_{W^*} > 0$

$\beta_{r^*}, \beta^*_{r^*}, \varepsilon_r, \varepsilon^*_r, \mu_r, \mu_{r^*}, \eta_r, \eta_{r^*} < 0$

Definitions and assumptions:

endogenous: r, r^*, e

exogenous : PB, PB^*, PF, PF^*, M, N

$\mu + \beta + \varepsilon = W$

$\eta + \beta^* + \varepsilon^* = W^*$

$\mu_W + \beta_W + \varepsilon_W = 1$ — balance sheet constraints

$\mu_x + \beta_x + \varepsilon_x = dW/dx$

for $x = M, PB, PF$

$\mu_r + \varepsilon_r = -\beta_r < 0$

$\mu_{r^*} + \beta_{r^*} = -\varepsilon_{r^*} < 0$ — gross substitutability assumptions (analogous for the US)

The system can be solved in the same way as shown in 5B.

Case a: A change in wealth induces a change in asset demands which is independent of the source of the wealth increase (for all demand functions); for example:

$$\beta_W = \beta_M = \beta_{PB} = \beta_{PF} > 0$$

The result for alternative ways of CA financing corresponds to the result derived in appendix 5B. The only modification is that the term "wealth share of the specific asset times total private wealth" is substituted by a term indicating the change in the demand of the specific asset in response to a change in wealth (and interest rates, respectively). For convenience:

$$de/dPF\Big|_{dPF=-dPF^*} = (1/Det)\ [(\beta_r + \beta_r^*)\ (\mu_{r^*}\eta_{W^*} + \eta_{r^*}\mu_W) - (\beta_{r^*} + \beta_{r^*}^*)(\mu_r\eta_{W^*} + \eta_r\mu_W) - (\beta_W - \beta_{W^*}^*)\ (\mu_r\eta_{r^*} - \eta_r\mu_{r^*})]$$

The result is identical for both ways of financing the CA even if one or more asset demands should be homogeneous of degree zero in the respective wealth. If all asset demands appearing in the equation are independent of wealth, then CA imbalances have no effect on the exchange rate.

$$de/dPF\Big|_{dPF=-dPF^*} = de/dPB\Big|_{dPB=-dPB^*}$$

Case b.: A change in wealth induces a change in asset demands which depends on (differs according to) the source of the wealth change (for all demand functions); for example:

$$\beta_M \neq \beta_{PB} \neq \beta_{PF}$$

We derive for a German CA surplus, financed with dollar bonds:

$$de/dPF\Big|_{dPF=-dPF^*} = (1/Det)\left[(\beta_r + \beta_r^*)(\mu_{r^*}\eta_{PF^*} + \eta_{r^*}\mu_{PF}) - (\beta_{r^*} + \beta_{r^*}^*)(\mu_r\eta_{PF^*} + \eta_r\mu_{PF}) - (\beta_{PF} - \beta_{PF^*}^*)(\mu_r\eta_{r^*} - \eta_r\mu_{r^*})\right]$$

The exchange rate impact in the case of DM bond financing is:

$$de/dPB\Big|_{dPB=-dPB^*} = (1/Det)\left[(\beta_r + \beta_r^*)(\mu_{r^*}\eta_{PB^*} + \eta_{r^*}\mu_{PB}) - (\beta_{r^*} + \beta_{r^*}^*)(\mu_r\eta_{PB^*} + \eta_r\mu_{PB}) - (\beta_{PB} - \beta_{PB^*}^*)(\mu_r\eta_{r^*} - \eta_r\mu_{r^*})\right]$$

As can be seen by a comparison of both results, the exchange rate effects of CA financing with DM and dollar bonds differ if:

$\eta_{PB^*} \neq \eta_{PF^*}$	response of the foreign money demand to a change in wealth differs according to the source of the wealth increase (PB* or PF*).
or $\mu_{PB} \neq \mu_{PF}$	(response of the German money demand to changes in PF and PB)
or $\beta_{PF^*}^* \neq \beta_{PB^*}^*$	(response of the foreign demand for DM bonds to changes in PF* and PB*)

or $\beta_{PF} \neq \beta_{PB}$ (response of the domestic demand for DM bonds to changes in PF and PB)

(unless the differences balance).

The implicit assumption made in the small-country model (5A.) can now be formalized:

$$\beta^{*}_{PB^*} = 1 \quad \text{and} \quad \beta^{*}_{PF^*} = 0$$

This assumption generates the result of the small-country model also in the two-country model: if all other wealth effects are identical for all sources of wealth and $\mu_r \eta_{r^*} - \eta_r \mu_{r^*} > 0$ (as assumed above) it follows:

$$de/dPF\Big|_{dPF=-dPF^*} > de/dPB\Big|_{dPB=-dPB^*}$$

A dollar bond financed CA surplus yields a stronger appreciation effect for the DM than a CA surplus financed with DM bonds.

PART II:

EMPIRICAL EVIDENCE

Testing Portfolio Balance Models of Exchange Rate Determination - Some Critical Remarks and Further Empirical Evidence

"A model that was able to explain more than 50 percent of quarter-to-quarter changes in exchange rates should either be rejected on the grounds that it is too good to be true or should be reported to the Vatican as a miracle justifying the canonization of a new saint."
Mussa (1979, p. 52)

6. Introduction and Outline

The first part of this thesis has been devoted to theoretical analysis of the foundations and results of the portfolio balance approach to short run exchange rate determination. Now we turn our attention to the empirical application of the portfolio theory. As in part I. so in the empirical second part, our main interest concerns the significance of the CA as an exchange rate determinant. The chapters following contain a critical review of econometric tests of standard asset market models. We try to evaluate the theoretical foundations as well as the empirical results of these studies in particular with respect to the CA variables. Subsequently, estimations for the standard model and for the model with diversified CA financing will be presented.

Chapters seven and eight deal with empirical estimations of models which we label as "standard" portfolio(asset market)models. These estimations are essentially based on the assumption of only one internationally traded asset or, in somewhat weaker versions, on the assumption that CA transactions are exclusively financed with foreign-currency denominated assets. As a consequence, any change in a country's net foreign asset position can be identified with a change in the net stock of one specific kind of asset.

The main part of the discussion will be restricted to model estimations which proceed from partial asset market equilibrium under the conditions of stationary expectations. This is the empirical approach, for example, of Branson, Halttunen, and Masson (1977, 1979), Martin and Masson (1979), Porter (1979), and Murphy and Van Duyne (1980).

In recent literature on empirical tests of asset market theories this basic model has frequently been extended and modified, for example, by incorporating rational expectations,[1] by attempts to model the sluggish price adjustment in the goods sector,[2] or by distinguishing between expected and unexpected disturbances.[3] All these sophistications, however, are possible only at the cost of additional (ad hoc) assumptions

---

1) See, e.g., Dooley and Isard (1979, 1982), Gaab (1982).

2) See, e.g., Gaab (1982), Frankel (1983), Hooper and Morton (1980), Edison (1983).

3) See, e.g., Dornbusch (1980), Isard (1980), Branson (1981, 1982).

which have to be introduced on the theoretical and empirical level to formalize the process of expectation formation, the adjustment structure in the goods sector etc.. Considering the difficulties already arising with the attempt to convert the most simple asset market model into a consistent empirical reduced form, we decided to neglect these refinements and to concentrate on the basic model.[1)]

In the course of the discussion we will argue that all investigated tests suffer from inconsistencies in the transformation of the respective underlying theoretical model into the empirically tested model. These inconsistencies are due mainly to the following two problems. First, assumptions made in deriving the theoretical results are often not maintained in or conclusively incorporated into the empirical test. Second, asset market models are formulated in terms of variables which have no reliably measurable counterparts in available real data sources. This is, of course, a fairly general problem in all empirical tests; but in portfolio theory this obstacle becomes particularly crucial since it applies to a high degree to one of the central variables of these models, namely to the CA variable: the stock of net foreign assets.

The analysis in chapters seven and eight provides the foundation of the empirical investigation in chapter nine. As in the empirical studies quoted in chapter seven and eight we estimate a "basic" portfolio balance model assuming stationary expectations and only one internationally traded asset. Thus, the exchange rate equation employed is best characterized as an equation of portfolio "fundamentals" rather than a complete equation of short run exchange rate determinants.

---

1) A more comprehensive empirical Dornbusch-Frankel type interest-rate-parity model is developed and estimated in Groß (1983, 1984). These papers deal explicitly with expectations of changes in the real and nominal exchange rate and with the formalization of "news". However, this attempt has led to the insight that the level of arbitrariness inherent in the sum of assumptions necessary to derive the final reduced form might exceed the level of plausibility. Thus, the interpretation of the estimation results from such extended models, in the sense of the theory, seems to be very problematic. Moreover, the fundamental problem of converting the basic portfolio model into an empirically testable form appears also in these more comprehensive models and constitutes also here a crucial point.

We apply the theory to three different exchange rates: the Deutsche mark/ US dollar (DM/$) rate, the Japanese yen/US dollar (¥/$) rate, and the pound sterling/US dollar (£/$) rate. We consider three different sample periods for our test. The first estimation period runs from April, 1973 to October, 1978. This is the period which has been investigated by most of the previous tests, and hence allows for a comparison of results. Based on the estimations for 1973.4 to 1978.10 we perform monthly exchange rate forecasts for the period from 1978.11 to 1982.8. Finally, we reestimate the exchange rate equation over the entire sample period (1973.4 - 1982.8) with monthly and quarterly data. The chapter is concluded with a short summary of the empirical findings.

In chapter ten we discuss the empirical application of the portfolio balance model to the case of diversified CA financing. Following the theoretical model laid out in part I. we drop the assumption of only one internationally traded asset and allow for bilateral trade in assets denominated in two different currencies.

The discussion centers on three issues. First, we discuss problems arising in translating the theoretical two-country model in a consistent empirical reduced form. Second, we investigate the empirical relevance of CA financing with assets denominated in different currencies for the US and for Germany. Finally, we make an attempt to estimate the relative exchange rate impact of diversified CA financing for the DM/$ rate. These estimations, however, are subject to such severe limitations that our results can only be regarded as tentative.

In chapter eleven we investigate the empirical relevance of negative net foreign asset positions. In some recent articles it has been suggested that negative holdings of foreign-currency denominated assets cause dynamic instability in flexible exchange rate regimes. In chapter eleven we discuss the theoretical and empirical importance of this argument to the countries to which the portfolio model has been applied over the last chapters. We report figures on net foreign asset positions for the United States, Germany, Japan, and the United Kingdom.

7. Testing the Basic Model: The Approach of Branson, Halttunen and Masson

The empirical study of Branson, Halttunen and Masson (BHM)[1] is based on Branson's (1976) small-country asset market model.[2] The theoretical model has been described and discussed in the first part of the thesis. Therefore, we concentrate in the following on BHM's empirical application to the \$/DM exchange rate.

BHM derive their empirical model for the \$/DM rate from the functional relationship given by eq.(1):[3]

$$\text{(1)} \quad e(\$/DM) = h\ (\overset{-}{M_G}, \overset{+}{M_u}, \overset{+}{F_G}, \overset{-}{F_u}, \overset{?}{B_G}, \overset{?}{B_u})$$

where M_G, M_u: German and US money supplies, respectively.

F_G, F_u: German and US stocks of net foreign assets, respectively.

B_G, B_u: German and US net stocks of domestic interest-bearing assets, respectively.

BHM explain the underlying rationale of their empirical two-country model as follows:

"When we move to a bilateral model for a particular rate -e.g. the \$/DM rate- the natural extension of the (one-country-the author) theory is a model that includes movements in both the U.S. and West German money stocks and net foreign assets. Changes in these variables have clear effects on the \$/DM rate..... Symmetrically, an increase in the U.S. money stock should raise the \$/DM rate and an increase in the German money stock should lower it;....the opposite should hold for the two F variables." BHM (1977, p. 310)

Since the exchange rate effect of a change in the stock of domestic bonds B is ambiguous in Branson's theoretical model, BHM exclude these asset variables for both countries from the test.

---

1) The following discussion draws on BHM (1977, 1979).

2) This model has been presented in Branson (1976, 1979, 1981, 1982).

3) BHM define the exchange rate as the \$/DM rate which is the inverse of the definition we used throughout the theoretical part of the thesis. Therefore, the expected signs for the exchange rate influence of the asset variables are exactly the opposite for our exchange rate definition.

Modifying eq.(1) by introducing privat net foreign asset stocks for both countries, BHM derive their final regression equation for the \$/DM rate:

$$(2) \quad e(\$/DM)_t = a_0 + a_1\, M1_G + a_2\, M1_u + a_3\, PF_G + a_4\, PF_u + u_t$$

where all asset stocks refer to time t and the expected sign pattern for the coefficients is given by:

$$a_1, a_4 < 0 \quad \text{and} \quad a_2, a_3 > 0$$

The empirical variables are defined as follows:[1]

$M1_G$, $M1_u$: German and US money stocks M1 in billions of respective domestic currencies, seasonally adjusted and converted from end-of-period values to period averages.

PF_G, PF_u : Private net foreign asset stocks of German and US residents in billions of \$. PFs are calculated as cumulated CA surpluses on benchmark figures minus central bank reserves defined as total central bank reserves minus gold minus cumulated SDR allocations.[2]

e(\$/DM) : \$/DM exchange rate index, 1970 = 100.

Before we turn to the results of the estimation it is important to note that the basic equation (1) is not a rigorously derived reduced form of the underlying theoretical model: BHM's test equation is deduced from ad hoc plausibility extensions of Branson's small-country model.
In our opinion, these extensions are partly inconsistent not only with the small-country model but also with the two-country model presented in the last chapter of the theoretical part of this thesis.
To substantiate this view we will discuss some basic problems arising with the attempt to convert Branson's theory into an empirically testable form. These problems originate mainly from the assumption of only one internationally traded asset, and from the neglect of third-country effects in the theoretical model.

---

1) Data sources and exact definitions are given in BHM (1977).

2) Monthly CA figures for the US are interpolated from monthly trade account figures. The empirical specification of the PF variables will be discussed in detail in chapters nine and eleven.

Branson's small-country model stipulates that only one asset - an interest-bearing asset issued by the large country and denominated in the large country's currency - can be used for international payments. Applied to the DM/$ case, Branson's model assumes that German residents hold their own domestic money, DM bonds, and dollar bonds whereas US residents hold only US money and dollar bonds. Only dollar bonds are internationally negotiable. This assumption implies that any imbalance in the German CA vis-à-vis the US must cause an equiproportional shift of dollar bonds between both countries. This, in turn, means that any change in the net foreign asset position (NFP) of both countries must accrue in the form of changes in the stock of dollar bonds. Applied to the regression equation (2) it follows that PF_G as well as PF_u should denote the change in the respective stocks of dollar bonds due to bilateral CA imbalances.

In a two-country world the CA surplus of one country must be equal to the CA deficit of the other country, implying $\Delta PF_G = -\Delta PF_u$. Thus, an empirical two-country model should include only <u>one</u> CA; that is, the NFP of only one country. Any CA imbalance of the small country is connected with a change in the stock of dollar bonds which must be equal to an opposite change in the stock of dollar bonds for the large country. Taking into account this relationship we derived in the two-country model in chapter five the appreciation impact for the DM due to a German CA surplus with the US, financed with dollar bonds:[1]

$$ {}^{de}/_{dPF} \Big|_{dPF=-dPF^*} < 0 $$

Clearly, the real world is not a two-country world. A surplus in the German CA may be at the expense of deficits in CAs of third-countries, and the same may hold true for the CA of the US. In fact, this seems to be the most relevant case in reality.[2] Thus, it appears reasonable to

---

1) Note that in chapter five the exchange rate has been defined as DM/$.

2) From the data it can be seen that from 1973.I to 1976.I and from 1981.II to 1982.II both countries increased their NFP. From 1978.III to 1980.III the NFP of the US kept rather constant whereas the NFP of Germany was sharply declining. Only between 1976.II and 1978.III we observe a decline in the US NFP which, however, exceeds by far the increase in the German NFP during the same period. For data sources see appendix. The NFPs are calculated as cumulated CA imbalances.

use both countries' total NFPs in an empirical investigation in order to take into account exchange rate effects of CA imbalances with third-countries. Seen from this point of view, the coefficient on PF_U should measure the effect of a change in the stock of net foreign assets of US private asset holders, due to imbalances in the overall CA of the US, on the $/DM rate. An analogous interpretation should be applied to the coefficient on PF_G. However, the problem with this interpretation is that neither Branson's small-country approach nor the two-country model in chapter five is sufficient to give clear predictions of the expected signs, in particular of the PF_U coefficient.

In Branson's model, US agents, as residents of the large country, do not hold assets denominated in foreign currency. Hence, US portfolio equilibrium is described by the market clearing conditions for US money and dollar bonds. Because of the wealth constraint only one of them is independent and determines the interest rate on dollar bonds. The exchange rate plays no role in US portfolio equilibrium.
Alternatively, we might try to infer effects of an imbalanced CA of the US on the $/DM rate from the viewpoint of the third-country: assume that the US run a CA surplus, for example, with Japan. The decrease in the dollar bond stocks in Japan should lead to an appreciation of the dollar vis-à-vis the yen. Now we might conclude that the existence of cross-rate arbitrage between ¥/$, ¥/DM, and $/DM should, ceteris paribus, bring about also an appreciation of the dollar vis-à-vis the DM. But this mechanism lies outside the scope of the portfolio balance model.

To apply the two-country model we have to assume that US residents hold assets denominated in foreign currency. We may do so while maintaining the assumption that CA transactions are exclusively financed with dollar bonds. If we furthermore neglect effects of changed stocks of dollar bonds in third-countries and consider only the impact on German and US portfolios, we may divide the multipliers for the two-country case in their components:

$de/dPF < 0$	for an increase in the German private net stock of dollar bonds;
$de/dPF^* \lesseqgtr 0$	for an increase in the US net stocks of privately held dollar bonds.

This - theoretically inadmissible - procedure yields a clear appreciation tendency for the DM in the case of a German CA surplus whereas the effect of an US CA surplus is unclear. [1)]

Before we discuss this problem further we quote BHM's justification for introducing two separate overall net foreign asset stocks in the test:

"Because of the symmetry, we should include only one (originally in italics) F for ($/DM), German net claims on U.S. Due to data limitations we use, however, both countries' total stocks of net foreign assets. This implicitly assumes that third-country assets are perfect substitutes for German assets for U.S. portfolio-holders, and vice versa." BHM (1977, p. 310, footnote 6).

This statement introduces special assumptions related to the portfolio composition of US asset holders and the substitutability of assets in BHM's empirical model.

First, BHM's justification implies that US residents are indeed assumed to hold assets denominated in currencies others than dollar and thus, contradicts the assumption of only one internationally traded asset underlying their theoretical model. The theoretical framework adequate to this empirical assumption should consequently cover problems arising from trade in assets denominated in different currencies and the possibility of diversified CA financing. An attempt in this direction has been made by Murphy and Van Duyne (MD) (1980). They try to justify BHM's regression equation by a two-country model in which residents of both countries hold bonds of the respective other country.[2)]

In their empirical test PF_G is defined as net private German holdings of dollar assets, proxied by the total private stock of net foreign assets in Germany. Likewise, PF_u is taken as net private US holdings of DM assets, proxied by the total private NFP of the US.[4)]

---

1) The formal analysis above showed that the sign of de/dPF^* depends essentially on the degree of substitutability among assets in the US, but tends to be positive.

2) Although MD lay out the structural form of this model they do not derive explicitly the solutions for exchange rate effects of changes in the exogenous variables. The reduced form stated by MD is identical to eq.(1) above.

3) The use of total private stocks of net foreign assets instead of a bilateral variable is justified by MD, as in BHM, by the assumption "that all assets denominated in foreign currencies are perfect substitutes in asset holders' portfolios." MD (1980, p. 643).

4) A similar assumption is made in Frankel (1983) in an empirical test of a synthesis model of the monetary and the portfolio balance approach.

Since PF_G and PF_u are calculated basically by cumulating CA surpluses of both countries, MD's definition is synonymous with the assumption that any surplus in the German CA accrues in the form of dollar bonds and any surplus in the US CA is completely financed with DM assets. Obviously, this assumption is impossible in a closed two-country model. There has to be a third country that takes the counter-position of these asset shifts. When we neglect exchange rate effects of changes in asset stocks in third-countries as above, we may repeat our theoretically doubtful procedure of dividing the exchange rate multipliers of the two-country model laid out in chapter five:

$^{de}/_{dPF}$	< 0	for an increase in German private net stocks of dollar bonds;
$^{de}/_{dPB^*}$	> 0	for an increase in US private net stocks of DM bonds.

An exogenous increase in private net stocks of dollar bonds in Germany brings about an appreciation of the DM relative to the dollar, and a rise in US private net stocks of DM bonds leads to an appreciation of the dollar vis-à-vis the DM. These partial multipliers allow for a clear prediction of the signs of the coefficients on PF_G and PF_u. Nevertheless, as regards the theoretical consistency with the underlying model, this procedure is simply wrong.[1)]

We close this part of the discussion by saying that, in our opinion, it is not possible to derive theoretically consistent statements for the coefficients on the PF variables neither from Branson's one-country model nor from a two-country model. If data constraints force the introduction of both countries' NFPs in the regression equation we implicitly include effects of CA imbalances with third-countries on the bilateral $/DM rate in the test. It is merely an ad hoc method to combine the results of two one-country models or of two two-country models to dermine the impact of PF_G and PF_u on the $/DM rate.

We are not saying that the hypothesised coefficients are implausible or cannot be justified in one way or the other. For example, one may use a two-country portfolio model for the US and the "rest of the world" to

---

1) The assumption that the German CA is, at least partly, financed by dollar assets may be considered as realistic. On the other hand, it is rather unrealistic to assume that US CA transactions are completely financed with DM assets. In fact, empirical data - to which we refer in chapter ten - suggests that US CA transactions are financed almost completely with dollar assets.

determine the exchange rate of the dollar to a weighted average of other currencies. In this interpretation it would be justified to use the total NFP of the US as a proxy for the PF_u variable, and PF_u would be the only CA variable appearing in the test. One may argue further that an appreciation of the dollar vis-à-vis this currency basket due to a surplus in the US CA is probably also connected with a rise in the DM/$ rate, for example, brought about by a cross-rate arbitrage mechanism. An analogous line of reasoning could be put forward to justify the appreciation impact of an increase in the German total NFP on the DM relative to the dollar. But this argument leaves the portfolio balance framework by introducing additional assumptions and exchange rate mechanisms. Thus, we end up with a test which is not really a test of the underlying portfolio model.

Next we turn to the particular substitutability assumption which has been put forward by BHM and MD to justify the use of total stocks of net foreign assets of the US and Germany separately in the test.

They assume that, from the point of view of US asset holders, assets denominated in DM and third-country currencies can be grouped together to a composite asset, and, from the point of view of German portfolio holders, dollar bonds and bonds denominated in other non-dollar currencies can also be grouped together to a composite asset.

Apart from being rather unrealistic,[1] there is a further theoretical problem involved in this assumption. Maintaining the assumption of stationary expectations, US portfolio equilibrium would require equality between interest rates on third-country assets and DM bonds. For the same reason German portfolio equilibrium requires equality between the interest rate on dollar bonds and the rate on third-country assets. Combining these two equilibrium conditions we end up with interest rate parity between dollar and DM bonds. Thus, the complete portfolio approach which is essentially based on the assumptions of imperfect substitutability between interest-bearing assets denominated in different currencies is called into question by BHM's and MD's particular substitutability assumption.

---

1) BHM's argument states, for example, that US asset holders view Argentinean or Brasilian bonds as perfect substitutes for German bonds, whereas German bonds are viewed as imperfect substitutes for US bonds. Considering the actual risk differences involved in holding these bonds uncovered, this assumption seems to be at least doubtful.

Alternatively, BHM's assumption could be combined with the presumption of imperfect capital mobility due, for example, to restricitions in capital transactions. In this case interest rates may differ from each other. But this presumption too would contradict the initial starting point of point-in-time portfolio equilibrium models.

Summing up, it may be said that a rigorous test of the portfolio theory, applied to a bilateral exchange rate, which employs the total NFP of both countries, requires at least a three-country model as a theoretical foundation in order to take third-country effects consistently into account. BHM's and MD's regression approach to the bilateral $/DM rate may give some rough empirical indications for the significance of US and German CA imbalances as exchange rate determinants, but it does not constitute a real test of the underlying theoretical model.

Nevertheless, in the next section we show that the theoretical foundation of the regressin equation (1) can be improved in a way which takes into account portfolio adjustments in third-countries. Martin and Masson's (1979) model, which will be discussed in chapter eight, demonstrates that there are good theoretical reasons - others than put forward by BHM and MD - to formulate an empirical test of the basic portfolio balance model according to BHM's and MD's proposal.

Having discussed some of the difficulties arising with the attempt to apply the portfolio balance model empirically to a particular bilateral exchange rate,we return to BHM's and MD's actual test procedure.

For convenience we repeat the exchange rate equation (2) used in these estimations.

$$(2) \qquad e(\$/DM)_t = a_0 + a_1 \, M1_G + a_2 \, M1_u + a_3 \, PF_G + a_4 \, PF_u + u_t$$

with a_1, $a_4 < 0$ and a_2, $a_3 > 0$.

The variables are defined as described above. These definitons as well as the used data sources are largely identical in both estimations.

Since data on the US CA is available only on a quarterly basis MD conduct their test with quarterly data. BHM interpolate monthly CA figures for the US from monthly trade account figures and estimate eq.(2) with monthly data. Their test covers the time period from 1971.8 to 1976.12.
In a later paper, BHM (1979), they extend the sample period to 1978.3.
MD use the time period from 1973.2 to 1978.2 as their reference period.

Both authors are very careful in specifying the exogenous test variables. This problem arises because eq.(2) might not represent a one-way causal relationship leading from money supplies and private net foreign asset stocks to the exchange rate. If the exchange rate feeds back on the M1 and PF variables a simple OLS estimation produces biased coefficients as the regressors are correlated with the error term in the equation. In this case it is important to estimate eq.(2) simultaneously with reaction functions for the money supplies and foreign asset stocks to obtain consistent estimates of the coefficients.

There are good reasons to suppose a causal chain running from the exchange rate to the right-hand variables of eq.(2).

First, authorities might use the domestic money supply as a measure of exchange rate policy and thus, react systematically to changes in the exchange rate by varying the monetary base.
Both authors test for the impact of changes in the exchange rate on central bank money and the money supply M1 in the case of Germany.

They did not find significant indications for effects running from the exchange rate to money over the sample period. Hence, both authors treat the M1 variables as exogenous to the $/DM exchange rate equation.

Second, one has to bear in mind that private stocks of net foreign assets are calculated from cumulated CA surpluses minus the increase in central bank reserves. To the extent that central banks' intervention behaviour is systematic with respect to the exchange rate a single equation estimation of eq.(2) will yield biased results. In order to take into account this possible endogenous policy response both authors introduce the following reaction function for official foreign exchange reserve holdings.

$$(3) \qquad R_t = b_0 + b_1 R_{t-1} + b_2 [(e_t - e_{t-1}) / e_{t-1}] + \nu_t$$

Equation (3) expresses the level of official reserves R_t as a function of official reserves lagged one period and the rate of change in the $/DM exchange rate over the foregoing period.[1] Applied to the German Bundesbank, b_1 and b_2 are expected to be positive, assuming that the Bundesbank attempts to smooth 'erratic' fluctuations in the $/DM rate.

Eq.(2) and eq.(3) constitute a two-equation simultaneous model for the $/DM rate and the Bundesbank's intervention policy [2] which can be estimated consistently by using 2SLS.

A summary of the results is given in table 1 and table 2.

---

1) BHM derive this intervention function from a quadratic objective function assuming that authorities act in order to minimise the cost of divergence from target values of the exchange rate and reserve stock. The derivation of the objective function subject to various policy constraints yields the reaction function eq.(3).

2) MD test also for the endogenity of US reserves by applying the same reaction function as described above. Their results, however, do not indicate a significant intervention response of the Federal Reserve with respect to the $/DM rate. BHM simply assume US reserves as exogenous.

Table 1: Consistent Estimates (2SLS) for e($/DM)[a),b)]

Independent Variables and Expected Signs of the Coefficients / Author / Time Period / Dep. Var.		BHM	BHM	MD
Time Period		71.8 - 76.12	71.8 - 78.3	73.II - 78.II
Dep. Var.		($/DM) index	($/DM) index	($/DM)cent p.DM
		Monthly	Monthly	Quarterly
Constant		-40,380 (-0,9)	1,960 (0,04)	28,00 (1,69)
$M1_G$ (billions of DM)	·/.	-0,4493 (-1,3)	-0,2425 (-0,9)	-0,068 (-0,58)
$M1_u$ (billions of $)	+	0,9933* (3,6)	0,7365* (2,8)	0,147 (1,45)
PF_G (BHM: billions of $) (MD : billions of DM)	+	0,1144 (0,2)	-0,0718 (-0,1)	0,093 (1,56)
PF_u (billions of $)	·/.	-0,5912* (-3,0)	-0,5828* (-3,4)	-0,231* (-3,18)
$\bar{R}^2$		0,943	0,961	0,755
DW		1,349	1,366	2,17
RHO		0,8314 (12,0)	0,8828 (16,7)	--

a) Definitions of the variables are given above. $\bar{R}^2$: squared coefficient of multiple determination, adjusted for degrees of freedom; DW: Durbin-Watson statistic; RHO: first order serial correlation coefficient; t-ratios are given in parantheses; * denotes significance at the 95% level.

The results of BHM are taken from BHM (1979); in this paper BHM correct some minor errors of the 1977 paper.

b) Note that BHM define e($/DM) as an exchange rate index (1970=100), whereas MD define e($/DM) as period average rate, expressed as US cents per DM.

Table 2: Consistent Estimates (2SLS) for the Reaction Function of German Foreign Exchange Reserves R [a)]

Author / Time Period / Dep.Var. — Independent Variables and Expected Signs of the Coefficients		BHM	BHM	MD
Time Period		71.8 - 76.12	71.8 - 78.3	73.II - 78.II
Dep.Var.		R_t	R_t	R_t
		Monthly	Monthly	Quarterly
Constant		2,636 (2,6)	1,894 (2,2)	-0,870 (-0,07)
R_{t-1} (BHM: billions of $) (MD : billions of DM)	+	0,9183* (27,7)	0,9431* (33,5)	1,012* (7,10)
$\Delta e(\$/DM)$ b)	+	0,0829* (4,4)	0,1801* (2,7)	2,015* (3,3)
$\bar{R}^2$		0,975	0,969	0,677
DW		1,613	1,784	2,41
RHO		--	0,2799 (2,6)	--

R_t: total German reserves minus gold minus cumulated SDR allocations; in BHM, R_t is denominated in billions of $; in MD, R_t is expressed in billions of DM. Definitions of the variables are given above. For further explanations see Table 1.

see footnote b) of Table 1.

The estimation results for the exchange rate equation in table 1 can be interpreted in support of the portfolio balance model in BHM's empirical version: all coefficients have the expected signs, except the insignificant coefficient on PF_G for the period 1971.8 to 1978.3. Nevertheless, only the US variables are significant at standard levels suggesting a stronger impact of the US money supply and stocks of net private foreign assets on the $/DM rate than the impact of German asset stocks. In particular, the coefficients and t-ratios for PF_u indicate a relatively high significance of the US private foreign asset stock, that is of imbalances in the US CA, for the $/DM rate.[1)]

So too, the results for the reaction function for Bundesbank interventions in table 2 confirm the theoretical predictions: all coefficients are significant with the expected sign. The positive sign on the Δe variable supports the view that the Bundesbank pursued an intervention policy of 'leaning-against-the-wind' by absorbing or at least mitigating 'erratic' movements in the $/DM rate.[2)]

In addition to this regression analysis both authors employ the estimated exchange rate equations to calculate ex-post forecasts for the $/DM rate.

BHM use the equation estimated for the period 1971.8 - 1976.12 (column 1, table 1) to predict the $/DM rate over the period 1977.1 - 1978.6. Forecasts for these 18 months are obtained by using the actual values of the asset stock variables for the forecast period.[3)] A comparison of actual and predicted values shows a consistent overvaluation of the dollar vis-à-vis the DM by BHM's exchange rate equation. Although the

---

1) Gaab (1982) draws a similar conclusion from his test of a more comprehensive version of the portfolio model for the time period from 1974.10 to 1981.5: "Die Einbeziehung von Portefolio-Überlegungen führt zu einer Erhöhung des Erklärungsbeitrages gegenüber dem Dornbusch-Modell, wenn die amerikanische Nettoforderungsposition gegenüber dem Ausland als erklärende Variable erscheint. Die Veränderung der deutschen Nettoforderungsposition bzw. der deutschen Portefeuille-Struktur hat keinen signifikanten Einfluß auf die Wechselkursentwicklung." Gaab (1982, p. 40).

2) This simple test is of course not sufficient for a qualified conclusion about the actual intervention behaviour of the Bundesbank.

3) Naturally, such a procedure does not yield forecasts for predicting the exchange rate ex-ante since it is assumed that the values for all exogenous variables are known. Ex-post(perfect foresight)forecasts abstract from wrongly anticipated changes in the exogenous variables. On this point see Meese and Rogoff (1981), Dooley and Isard (1979).

forecast errors are large,the ex-post forecasts do not move away progressively from actual values: starting in 1977.1, BHM's equation exhibits an increasing overprediction of the dollar up to 1977.9; from 1977.10 on, the forecast errors decline, and in 1978.3 the predicted value for the $/DM rate lies rather close to the actual value. Considering the fact that BHM's equation is formulated in terms of 'asset fundamentals' and hence, do not count for speculative influencies, it is interesting to note that calculations of the IMF suggests that March, 1978, values were indeed near long run equilibrium.[1)]

MD compute ex-post forecasts for the six quarters from 1978.III to 1979.IV using the exchange rate equation estimated for the period 1973.II to 1978.II (column 3, table 1).[2)] They find that the portfolio model generally captures the direction of the change in the $/DM rate but underpredicts the magnitude of the change. MD confront the forecasts from the portfolio balance model with forecasts obtained from a simple monetary model and from the purchasing-power-parity theory. A comparison of the respective root-mean-square-errors and inequality coefficients[3)] suggests that the portfolio model predicts more accurately the level and the change in the $/DM rate over the period 1978.III - 1979.IV than the alternative models.

Summarizing, it can be said that the results of BHM and MD lend some support to their empirical version of the portfolio approach. Equation (2) seems to provide a rough guideline for explaining movements in the $/DM rate over the period 1971.8 - 1979.12.

---

1) See BHM (1979).

2) The calculation methode applied by MD differs somewhat from BHM methode. Their forecasts are obtained by a dynamic simulation of the two-equation model in which solution values for the endogenous variables, lagged and current, are used instead of actual values to calculate the predicted values of the $/DM rate.

3) For a definiton of these error statistics see chapter 9.

8. Testing a Multi-Country Model: The Approach of Martin and Masson

In the last section we criticized the insufficient theoretical foundation of BHM's and MD's regression analyses. The discussion focused on two mainpoints.

First, both authors introduced US and German total private net stocks of foreign assets as two separate variables in the test equation for the bilateral $/DM rate. Thus, their estimations implicitly include effects on the $/DM rate due to imbalances in the German and US CA with third-countries. Neither Branson's small-country model, however, nor a more comprehensive two-country approach provide a consistent theoretical framework for conclusions about the effect of portfolio adjustments in third-countries on the $/DM rate.

Second, the assumption of only one internationally traded asset, underlying the Branson model, has not been observed in the empirical application. Both authors proceed in their empirical tests from the opposite assumption, namely that both countries, the US and Germany, hold assets denominated in currencies others than their own. Nevertheless, both authors do not give any special theoretical consideration to possible implications of this empirical assumption for the exchange rate impact of CA imbalances.

Martin and Masson (MM) (1979) take the first problem as starting point for their analysis. They attempt to account in a consistent way for effects of portfolio adjustments in many countries on a specific bilateral exchange rate.

Their theoretical multi-country framework is characterized by the following assumptions.

Only one country, the US, issues bonds which are held internationally; its money, however, is not traded. All other countries ($i = 2,\ldots,n$) issue nontraded money and bonds, denominated in their own currencies and held only by domestic residents. Thus the portfolio of these countries consists of their respective money, domestic bonds and dollar bonds, whereas US residents hold only US money and dollar bonds.[1)] The other assumptions are identical to the common assumptions of standard stationary-expectations portfolio analysis.

It is important to note that MM adhere in their theoretical model as well as in the empirical application to the assumption of only one internationally traded asset, namely dollar bonds. Hence, international CA imbalances lead to accumulations and decumulations of dollar bond stocks of the countries involved. This assumption allows us to analyse consistently effects on the \$/DM exchange rate caused by imbalances of Germany and/or the US with third-countries.[2)]

---

1) Using the same symbols as for the two-country model in the theoretical part of the thesis (see pp. 127), portfolio equilibrium in MM's model is described by the following conditions:

For the US (country 1)

$$M_1 = m_1\ (r_1)\ W_1$$
$$F_1 = f_1\ (r_1)\ W_1$$
$$\overline{W_1 = M_1 + F_1}$$

For country i ($i = 2,\ldots,n$)

$$M_i = m_i\ (r_1,\ r_i)\ W_i = CB_i + 1/\bar{e}_i\ CF_i$$
$$PB_i = b_i\ (r_1,\ r_i)\ W_i$$
$$PF_i = e_i\ f_i\ (r_1,\ r_i)\ W_i$$
$$\overline{W_i = M_i + PB_i + 1/e_i\ PF_i}$$

where e_i is the bilateral exchange rate expressed as dollar per unit of currency i, e.g., \$/DM.

Each country's i ($i = 2,\ldots,n$) holdings of dollar bonds are predetermined as sum of past current account surpluses CAS:

$F_i = PF_i + CF_i = \int_{-\infty}^{0} CAS_i\ (t)\ dt$; it follows for the change in F_i :

$dF_i = dPF_i + dCF_i = CAS_i$ and for the change in the net supply of dollar bonds by the US: $dF_1 = dF + CAS_1 = dF - \sum_2^n CAS_i$.

The system yields 2n market clearing conditions of which 2n - 1 are independent. Hence, the model determines r_1 to r_n interest rates and e_2 to e_n exchange rates.

2) See next page.

The following comparative-static solutions of MM's model deserve special emphasis. As points of reference we consider the case of a CA surplus and refer to the $/DM rate. The results apply analogously to CA deficits and any other bilateral exchange rate with the dollar.[1)]

a. A bilateral surplus in the German CA with the US leads to an appreciation of the DM vis-à-vis the dollar.

b. A bilateral CA surplus of a third-country, for example Japan, with the US depreciates the dollar relative to the DM. The rise in the $/DM rate, however, is smaller than in case a.

c. A bilateral CA surplus of Germany with a third-country causes an appreciation of the DM vis-à-vis the dollar.

d. A bilateral CA surplus of a third-country, for example Japan, with an other third-country, for example the United Kingdom, has no influence on the $/DM rate.

From a. and c. follows that any increase in net foreign asset stocks of German private asset holders brings about an appreciation of the DM against the dollar, no matter whether the increase in private net stocks of dollar bonds is due to a CA surplus with the US or a third-country.

(footnote 2. last page) The model is not unequivocally solvable if we allow for trade in assets denominated in currencies of the countries i (i = 2,...,n). The assumption of only one internationally traded asset is necessary for the solubility of the model.

1) The direction of the comparative-static results, however, crucially depends on the sign of the net private foreign asset position of Germany or, generally, of country i (PF_i, i = 2,...,n). If country i's private sector is a net debtor in dollar internationally ($PF_i < 0$), most of the comparative-static results change signs: the effect of a change in the exogenous variables on a specific exchange rate e_i is completely opposite depending on the sign of country i's private net stocks of dollar bonds. This result has major implications for results and stability of all stationary-expectations portfolio models, and, in fact, constitutes the main topic in MM's paper.
A more thorough discussion of this problem will be given in chapter eleven. For the time being we assume all relevant $PF_i > 0$.

From a. and b. follows that any increase in US net private foreign asset stocks leads, via portfolio adjustments in other countries, to a decline in the \$/DM rate, no matter whether this increase is caused by a CA surplus with Germany or a third-country.

In the empirical part, MM apply their multi-country model to monthly data on three exchange rates against the US dollar: the Canadian dollar, the Japanese yen, and a weighted average of West European currencies.[1)] The sample period for the estimations runs from 1973.4 to 1978.4.

The exchange rate of the home country (Canada, Japan, West Europe) is specified by the following function.

$$(1) \quad e \text{ (US \$/home currency)} = g\,(\overset{-}{M_H}, \overset{+}{M_u}, \overset{?}{B_H}, \overset{-}{B_u}, \overset{+}{F_{HU}})$$

Subscripts 'H' and 'u' denote home country and US, respectively. F_{HU} stands for the bilateral net foreign asset position of the home country with the US, denominated in US dollar.

The formulation of eq.(1) and the subsequent regression analysis departs from BHM and MD in several respects.

a. MM include variables for the stocks of net domestic bonds of both countries (B_H, B_u) in their exchange rate equation. Although the impact of a change in the home countries' bond stock on the exchange rate is - as in Branson's model - not clear, MM's model allows us to determine the exchange rate effect of a change in the net stocks of US dollar bonds: a bond financed budget deficit in the US leads to an increase in the US interest rate and thus attracts foreign investors. The resulting appreciation tendency can not be offset, as in the two-country model in the theoretical part of the thesis, by a wealth-induced increase in the US demand for foreign bonds since US agents hold only US dollar assets.

---

1) All exchange rates as indices (December 1971=1); the West European rate is calculated as a geometric average of exchange rate indices for France, Germany, Italy, the United Kingdom, Belgium, Netherlands, Sweden, and Switzerland. These exchange rates are weighted according to the relative size of the respective monetary base.

b. While BHM and MD use both countries' total net stocks of foreign assets in their estimation equation for the \$/DM rate, MM include only one net foreign asset variable in the test: the bilateral net foreign asset stock of the home country vis-à-vis the US (F_{HU}). This variable is defined in two different ways.[1)]

First, F_{HU} is taken as the cumulated overall CA of the home country net of direct foreign investment claims.
Second, F_{HU} is calculated as the cumulated bilateral CA of the home country vis-à-vis the US. Since bilateral CA data for the relevant countries vis-à-vis the US have not been available MM compute F_{HU} from bilateral trade balance figures and interpolated service account figures which are weighted according to the relative importance of the respective home country in the US service balance. The so calculated bilateral flows were cumulated from benchmark figures for end-1975 US net international investment positions vis-à-vis Canada, Japan, and West Europe.[2)]

c. MM do not use an aggregated variable for the private sectors' net foreign asset stock (PF_{HU}) in their regressions but estimate the exchange rate influence of changes in authorities' holdings of foreign exchange reserves and of changes in total national net claims on the US separately.

The final regression equation takes the following form.

$$(2) \quad e \text{ (US \$/home currency)} = a_0 + a_1 M_H + a_2 M_u + a_3 B_H + a_4 B_u + a_5 R_H + a_6 F + u_t$$

MM's model predicts[3)] $a_2, a_6 > 0$; $a_4, a_5 < 0$; $a_3 \lesseqgtr 0$.

M_H : domestic money stock, end-of-month, seasonally adjusted; for Canada and Japan in billions of local currency units, for West Europe converted in US dollar using a fixed exchange rate.

---

1) MM also use a F_{HU} variable defined as the cumulated bilateral CA excluding direct foreign investment claims. The introduction of this alternative variable, however, does not change the general results for the test of the portfolio model. Direct foreign investments are excluded in the definition of F_{HU} since MM suppose that "long-term direct investment flows are not related to the exchange rate in the same way as short-term financial flows." MM (1979, p. 19).

2) For details see MM (1979). Unrequited transfers are obviously not included in the CA definition.

3) Assuming that $PF_i > 0$ for i= Canada, Japan, and West Europe.

M_u : US money stock, end-of-month, seasonally adjusted, billions of US dollars.

B_H : Net domestic bond stock in billions of local currency units, proxied by central government debt at month-end. The West European aggregated bond stock is converted into US dollars by a fixed exchange rate.

B_u : Net supply of US dollar bonds in billions of US dollars, proxied by US central govenment debt at month-end.

R_H : Foreign exchange reserves of the respective home country, converted into US dollar using the SDR exchange rate, end-of-month.

F : Net foreign asset stock of the home country, denominated in US dollar. We report results for two different definitions of F:

F_{bil} : Bilateral CA of the home country and the US cumulated on benchmark figures for the bilateral net investment position at the end of 1975.

F_{total} : Overall CA of the home country net of direct investments cumulated on benchmark figures for the home countries' overall net investment position at the end of 1975.

To correct for a possible simultaneous equations bias MM estimate the exchange rate equation jointly with a reaction function for the change in the home countries' foreign exchange reserves. This intervention function incorporates three components:

a. a desire to smooth changes in the exchange rate;
b. an attempt to hit a target exchange rate level which depends on purchasing power parity and capacity output relative to actual output;
c. a target level of foreign exchange reserves the level of which is assumed to grow with nominal income.

Table 1 shows the results of MM's estimations of the two-equation simultaneous system.[1)]

---

1) MM give no empirical results for the reaction function. In the following we are only reporting on the 2SLS estimates and leave aside the OLS results.

Table 1: Consistent Estimates (2SLS) for e(US $/home currency), Monthly Data, Sample Period 1973.4 to 1978.4. a)

Country / Independent Variables and expected signs of coef. (Dep. Var.)		Canada		Japan		West Europe
		e(US $/Can $) index 1971=1		e(US $/Yen) index 1971=1		e(US $/currency basket) index 1971=1
Constant		1,054* (5,89)	1,006* (4,09)	1,218 (1,41)	1,475* (5,22)	0,966 (0,97)
M_H b)	·/.	0,005 (1,10)	0,008* (1,73)	-0,000004 (-0,72)	0,000005 (1,01)	0,0004 (0,65)
M_U b)	+	-0,002* (-2,67)	-0,0007 (-0,85)	-0,0004 (-0,15)	-0,002 (-1,16)	-0,00002 (-0,03)
B_H	?	-0,0003 (-0,26)	-0,0002 (-0,58)	0,0000002 (0,05)	0,000006* (1,70)	-0,001 (-0,87)
B_u	·/.	0,0001 (0,71)	0,0002 (0,58)	-0,0004 (-0,76)	-0,004 (-1,28)	0,00003 (0,39)
F_{bil}	+	-0,003 (-0,84)		0,006 (0,57)		0,001 (0,11)
F_{total} c)	+		0,007 (1,07)		0,013* (5,39)	
R_H	·/.	0,035* (6,27)	0,025* (4,95)	0,028* (3,44)	0,009* (2,15)	0,006* (2,30)
QUEDUM d)		-0,035* (-4,26)	-0,041* (-5,12)			
R^2		0,98	0,98	0,95	0,97	0,88
DW		1,58	1,63	2,02	1,86	1,45
RHO		0,882 (14,51)	0,952 (24,13)	0,771 (9,38)	0,389 3,27)	0,805 (10,51)

a) Definitions of the variables are given above. R^2= squared coefficient of multiple determination; DW: Durbin-Watson statistic; RHO: first order serial correlation coefficient; t-ratios are given in parantheses; * denotes significance at the 95% level; the variables are listed with their theoretically expected sign for the creditor case $PF_i > 0$.

b) For US/Canada and US/Japan both money stocks are M1; for US/West Europe M3.

c) According to MM not available for West Europe.

d) Dummy for the Quebec election in late 1976.

The first general impression of the test results is not very favourable to the portfolio model: very few coefficients have the expected signs and their t-ratios are rather low.

For Cananda almost all coefficients have signs opposite to those predicted by the theory. The negative coefficient of the US money stock is even significant at the 95% level indicating that an expansion of the US money supply appreciates the US dollar against the Canadian dollar. The positive and significant coefficient for Canandian foreign exchange reserves implies that a purchase of US dollars by the Canadian central bank produces a depreciation of the US dollar against the Canadian dollar. This conclusion, which contradicts all conventional hypotheses about the exchange rate effect of central bank interventions, might be due, however, to an oversimplified specification of the central bank reaction function; the intervention function may not have eliminated the simultaneity bias from exchange rate feedbacks on foreign exchange reserves entirely. Nevertheless, it is interesting that the same "perverse" exchange rate effect of changes in central bank reserves is confirmed by the results for all other sample countries in table 1.[1)]

MM's estimates for the influence of the Canadian CA on the US $/Can $ rate too provide no support for the theoretical model. The coefficient on the cumulated bilateral CA has a wrong negative sign but is insignificant; the coefficient for the cumulated overall CA, however, has the expected positive sign but is also insignificant on standard levels.

An interesting feature of MM's test results lies in the fact that the reported R^2s are fairly high over all equations but the t-ratios for the coefficients are, in general, rather low. This might indicate a strong interrelationship among the independent variables. Multicollinearity implies that the individual coefficients of the exogenous variables cannot be estimated precisely and "wrong" signs may be one of the results. Although we have no clear-cut evidence for multicollinearity in MM's data sample, our own empirical study suggests that there is some support for the conjecture of a strong linear relationship between money supplies and central government debt used as proxy for net bond stocks B.

---

1) This result appears also in the estimations of chapter nine. We return to this problem in chapter nine.

The presumption of multicollinearity is supported by the results for Japan: although R^2 is high, none of the coefficients in the first equation (column 3) is significant on standard levels - except for the wrong positive coefficient on Japan's foreign exchange reserves.
In the second equation MM replace the bilateral CA variable F_{bil} by the overall CA variable F_{total}. This brings about a considerable change in coefficients and t-ratios. Now the coefficient for the cumulated overall Japanese CA takes the predicted positive sign and becomes significant. This might suggest that the overall CA is of higher importance for the US $/¥ rate than just the bilateral CA between Japan and the US.

When F_{total} is introduced instead of F_{bil} first-order autocorrelation declines strongly. Autocorrelation in the residuals is often explained by the assumption that the residuals comprise a number of omitted variables which are themselves serially correlated. The sharp decline in RHO resulting from the change from F_{bil} to F_{total} suggests that one of these omitted variables could be the CA of Japan with third-countries.

The estimation results for the West European currency basket are likewise very disappointing. All coefficients have the wrong sign, except the insignificant coefficient for F_{bil}, and no coefficient is significant at the 95% level, except the wrong coefficient for Western Europe's foreign exchange reserves.

Summing up, it may be said that MM's empirical results can hardly be interpreted as support of the portfolio balance model. On the contrary, "the empirical verdict on the utility of the portfolio balance model, at least on this data set, must be judged unfavourable." 1)

---

1) Martin and Masson (1979, p. 33).

Before we now turn to our own empirical study, we close with some critical remarks on MM's test construction. The following comments may also be regarded as a first justification for the specific form of the empirical exchange rate equation which will be used in chapter nine.

One of the crucial differences between the empirical analysis of MM, on one hand, and BHM or MD, on the other hand, consists in the fact that MM use only one foreign asset variable: the bilateral net foreign asset stock of the home country vis-à-vis the US (F_{HU}). As proxy for this bilateral asset stock MM define F_{bil}, an artificial variable calculated basically from bilateral trade flows between the US and the home country, and F_{total}, the cumulated overall CA of the home country excluding direct investment flows. The latter measure, however, is essentially the same as the total net foreign asset position of the home country with the rest of the world and thus not a bilateral asset position between the US and the home country.[1)]

MM's test results for Cananda and Japan suggest that F_{total} performs better in explaining exchange rate movements than F_{bil} whose coefficient takes the wrong sign for Canada and is insignificant in all cases. And, in fact, we think there are good reasons to employ total NFP's in an empirical test instead of a bilateral measure of net foreign asset stocks. MM's multi-country model shows that a particular bilateral exchange rate, for example the $/DM rate, will be affected not only by bilateral CA imbalances between these two countries, US and Germany, but also by both countries' CA imbalances with third-countries: a surplus in the German CA with third-countries appreciates the DM against the dollar, and a surplus in the US CA with third-countries appreciates the dollar vis-à-vis the DM.

An empirical test which uses only a (true) bilateral definition of the CA variable cuts off effects from CA imbalances with third-countries and hence narrows the empirical content of the portfolio approach unnecessarily. Accordingly, it might be more appropriate to use the total CAs of both countries to account for third-country effects on the bilateral exchange rate.

---

1) MM claim that their empirical analysis represents an extension of BHM's approach as they calculate bilateral net foreign asset stocks. This claim is not rally justified in the case of F_{total}; in essence, MM simply drop the US net foreign asset stock in their analysis and label the total net foreign asset position of the home country as bilateral.

The main problem with this proposal is that the introduction of two overall NFPs may cause serious overlappings in the data. To be clear on this point we consider the following reduced form of MM's model, including a third country - the rest of the world (subscript R).

$$(3) \quad e\ (\$/\text{home}) = f\,(\overset{-}{M_H}, \overset{+}{M_U}, \overset{0}{M_R}, \overset{?}{B_H}, \overset{-}{B_U}, \overset{0}{B_R}, \overset{+}{F_{HR}}, \overset{-}{F_{UR}}, \overset{+}{F_{HU}})$$

The F variables denote bilateral net foreign asset positions according to the subscripts. All Fs are denominated in dollar since dollar bonds are the only internationally traded asset. The total net foreign asset positions of the three countries are defined by eq. (4) to eq. (6).

$$(4) \quad F_H = F_{HR} + F_{HU}$$

$$(5) \quad F_U = F_{UR} - F_{HU}$$

$$(6) \quad F_R = -F_{HR} - F_{UR}$$

The effect of a change in the rest-of-the-world's money supply M_R and in its bond stock B_R on the \$/home rate is, according to MM's model, zero. MM's model allows us to determine the exchange rate effects of changes in the three bilateral net foreign asset stocks. The signs for the comparative-statics are shown above the variables.

a. From eq. (3) and the identities (4) to (6) it is clear that F_H and F_U are perfectly independent of each other only if all CA imbalances of the home country and the US take place with the rest of the world ($F_{HU} = 0$, $F_H = F_{HR}$, $F_U = F_{UR}$). In this case, it would be justified to use both countries' total net foreign asset positions separately in an empirical test of the portfolio balance model.

b. If, on the other hand, all CA imbalances of the home country take place with the US, and vice versa, ($F_{HR} = F_{UR} = 0$) the total net foreign asset position of the home country is equal to the total net foreign asset position of the US with opposite sign ($F_H = -F_U = F_{HU}$).
A regression analysis using F_H and F_U separately would suffer from perfect collinearity between F_H and F_U.

For most countries the reality lies between these two cases.
Yet it is extremely difficult to make an empirical judgement about their relevance for a specific country because data on bilateral CAs vis-à-vis the US are generally unavailable.[1)]

To find a clue for our own empirical analysis we calculated simple correlation coefficients for the relationship between the CAs of Germany, Japan, and the United Kingdom and the CA of the US. If case b. is a good approximation to reality the correlation coefficient should lie close to -1.

Table 2: Correlation between the US and the home countries' CA [a)]

Home Country / Time Period	Germany	Japan	United Kingdom
	73.4 - 82.8	73.4 - 80.8	73.I - 82.II
	Monthly	Monthly	Quarterly
Correlation Coefficient for CA(home) / CA (US)	0,1927	-0,2950	0,0457

a) For data sources and definitions see data appendix

The results for Germany and the United Kingdom provide no support for the hypothesis $F_H = -F_U = F_{HU}$. The CAs of both countries are very weakly and positive correlated with the US CA.[2)] Japan's CA, however, is negatively correlated with the US CA but the correlation coefficient is also rather low.

---

1) MM's method to calculate F_{bil} from bilateral trade flows plus interpolated and weighted service account figures may be sufficient as a rough approximation but is certainly not a measure for the true bilateral CA.

2) This is not surprising; for instance, in 1980 only 7,5% of German exports and 6,1 % of German imports were related to the US.

These results indicate that we would probably lose important information about the actual exchange rate impact of CA imbalances if we conduct a test of the portfolio model using only a bilateral CA. Taking into account this empirical evidence, the theoretical considerations discussed above and the great difficulties involved in calculating "true" bilateral CAs it seems more appropriate to use overall CAs in an empirical test of the portfolio balance model.

9. The Standard Portfolio Model: Further Empirical Evidence

9.1. Test Design

9.1.1. General Remarks

Before reporting on the results of our empirical study we give an outline of the general test procedure, the applied econometric methods, the chosen sample periods, and of some problems involved in our empirical approach. The construction of our test is guided by the following two considerations.

First, we attempt to achieve as much comparability as possible amongst our own test results for the different countries and exchange rates. For that reason we apply the same test procedure and methods to all of the investigated exchange rates, and we choose identical sample periods for all regressions. For the same reason we take most of the data from the International Monetary Fund "International Financial Statistics" data tape. Contrary to data from national sources, IMF data are largely based on similar definitions for the variables of all countries.[1)]

Second, in order to allow for a comparison with previous empirical studies on the standard portfolio model we follow wherever possible and reasonable the tests of BHM (1977, 1979), MD (1980), and MM (1979). Since these studies are frequently quoted to illustrate the empirical relevance of the portfolio theory, they constitute an important point of reference for further empirical investigations. The following empirical analysis draws in several respects on these sources:

The regression equation used as starting point for our exchange rate estimations corresponds, despite some extensions and alterations, to the equation put forward by BHM and MD. The theoretical justification of this equation, however, is provided by MM's multi-country model assuming only one internationally traded asset, namely dollar bonds. We depart from MM's empirical specification of the portfolio model as we introduce total net stocks of foreign assets for both, the home

---

1) Most of the former empirical tests, in particular BHM and MD, used IMF data as well. This fact too influenced our decision.

country and the US in the test. This decision is not founded on BHM's and MD's reasoning but on results from the theoretical and empirical considerations discussed in chapter eight.

The sample period for which we run our first regressions covers roughly the time period underlying the test of BHM, MD, and MM.

Proxy variables for unavailable asset-stock variables are defined and calculated approximately in the same way as in the studies mentioned above.

Despite these similarities we depart from these previous empirical tests in many respects which will become clear over the next sections.

However, before we go into details, a general warning seems called for. Empirical tests like the following, and all other previous ones, suffer from a number of shortcomings and oversimplifications. In fact, it is one of the aims of this chapter to point out and discuss these problems. Consequently, we do not believe that the following estimations provide a safe basis for clear-cut conclusions on the empirical relevance of the portfolio theory. Since the data basis available is weak and the theoretical conception of the relevant portfolio wealth variables allows for a wide spectrum of alternative empirical interpretations, any such test is a questionable and refutable matter. Judged from the point of view of the factual testability of the theory it thus seems reasonable to refrain from an empirical test - all the more as applying sophisticated regression techniques feigns an accuracy and reliability of results which is by no means justified by the data basis and the theoretical conception of the test.
On the other hand, economics is an empirical discipline. Economic theory should have something to say about realtiy, or, at least should try to give some hints about the practical relevance of theoretical conceptions and ideas. The fact that empirical tests usually fall short of giving the one and only correct picture of reality should not be reason enough to avoid confronting a theory with reality.
The following empirical study was conducted not because we think the first line of argument is unreasonable; it was conducted because we think that one has to try and find a clue, however weak, to the empirical content of theoretical considerations.

9.1.2. Test Equations

9.1.2.1. Exchange Rate Equations

Based on the discussion in the last chapters, our empirical analysis proceeds from the following general form of the exchange rate equation.

(1) $e(\text{home}/\$) = a_0 + a_1 M_H + a_2 M_u + a_3 PF_H + a_4 PF_u + a_5 PB_H + a_6 PB_u + u$

all variables are measured at time t, the end of the period t-1 to t. The variables are defined as follows.[1)]

e : Exchange rate, defined as units of domestic currency per one US dollar; measured at the end of the period.

M : Money supply M1, seasonally adjusted, end-of-period value, denominated in billions of respective domestic currency units.[2)]

PF : Proxy for private net foreign asset stocks, defined as the difference between the total net foreign asset position F and net foreign assets held by the respective central bank R. PF is calculated according to the formula:

$$PF_t = F_t - R_t = \sum_{i=0}^{t} CAS_i - \sum_{i=0}^{t} (R_i - R_{i-1})$$

i = 0 denotes the beginning of the sample period.

The end-of-period value of F is obtained by cumulating CA surpluses over the sample period. The CA is defined as the sum of the trade account, the service account, and the balance of unrequited transfers.

The end-of-period value of the stock of foreign exchange reserves R is calculated as sum of the changes in R over the sample period.

---

1) For further details and data sources see data appendix.

2) We preferred M1 to other definitions of the money supply because M1 coincides best with the assumption of money as a noninterest-bearing asset underlying the portfolio model.

R is defined as total reserves minus gold minus SDR holdings minus the reserve position with the Monetary Fund.[1)]

Since we maintain the assumption of only one internationally traded asset, dollar bonds, all variables PF, F, and R are expressed in billions of US dollars.

Contrary to the empirical studies discussed above we do not cumulate CA surpluses on benchmark figures for the net foreign asset position of the respective country.[2)] Our cumulations start from the first observation of the sample period assuming $F_0 = 0$. Accordingly, we do not use the overall stock of R but rather the sum of changes in R over the sample period; that is, R_0 is set at zero as well. As a result, PF represents the private net stock of foreign assets as it accrues over the sample period, neglecting stocks accumulated in the past. Thus, our version of the PF variable implicitly assumes that the sign of the actual stock of PF, that is the actual creditor or debtor position of the domestic private sector with the foreign sector, is unimportant to the exchange rate effect of a change in PF. In this case, the initial levels of F, R, and accordingly, PF can be treated as constants absorbed in the intercept term of the regression equation.
We chose this method because an examination of the data showed that the conventional procedure for calculating the level of a country's net foreign asset position by cumulating CAs on benchmark figures yields a very poor approximation to the actual net foreign asset position.[3)]

---

1) This definition is equal to the IMF definition of "foreign exchange".

2) Apart from this deviation, our way of generating net foreign asset stocks is identical to the calculation method applied in BHM (1977, 1979) and in MD (1980). Hooper and Morton (1980), Meese and Rogoff (1981), Gaab (1982), Edison (1983), and Frankel (1983) define F in essentially the same way: that is, they give no consideration to the initial value of net foreign asset stocks at the beginning of the investigation period.

3) As mentioned earlier, the sign of the private net foreign asset position of the home country is important to the comparative-static results of MM's model. Our empirical analysis presumes $PF_i > 0$ for i = Germany, Japan, and the United Kingdom. Data on actual net foreign asset positions, on a yearly basis, can be found in special surveys included in national sources of the respective countries. Differences between these yearly figures and figures resulting from the common method of cumulating CAs will be discussed in chapter eleven.

PB : Proxy for private net stocks of domestic bonds, denominated in billions of domestic currency units and measured at the end of the period. PBs are created as central government debt minus central bank's net holdings of government debt.[1)]

We run regressions for the following four versions of eq. (1).

$$(1.1)\quad e(home/\$) = a_0 + a_1\, M1_H + a_2\, M1_u + a_3\, PF_H + a_4\, PF_u + u$$

This is the equation estimated by BHM and MD. Exchange rate effects of central bank interventions and imbalances in overall CAs are not considered separately; R and F are aggregated to PF.[2)] In the following eq. (1.1) will also be called "BHM's equation". The coefficients are hypothesised:

$$a_1,\, a_4 > 0 \quad \text{and} \quad a_2,\, a_3 < 0.$$

$$(1.2)\quad e(home/\$) = a_0 + a_1\, M1_H + a_2\, M1_u + a_3\, F_H + a_4\, R_H + a_5\, F_u + a_6\, R_u + u$$

In this equation we divide PF into its components, F and R, and estimate the exchange rate effect of changes in foreign exchange reserves and CA imbalances separately.[3)] In the following eq. (1.2) will also be called "PF divided". MM's portfolio model yields the following expected signs for the coefficients:

$$a_1,\, a_4,\, a_5 > 0 \quad \text{and} \quad a_2,\, a_3,\, a_6 < 0.$$

---

1) See critical on this commonly used definition of outstanding bond stocks Penati (1983, pp. 563), Tobin (1982, p. 122).

2) An aggregated PF variable is also used in Hooper and Morton (1980), Gaab (1982), and Frankel (1983).

3) See also Isard (1980), Meese and Rogoff (1981), and Edison (1983).

$$(1.3)\quad e(home/\$) = a_0 + a_1\, M1_H + a_2\, M1_u + a_3\, PF_H + a_4\, PF_u + a_5\, PB_H + a_6\, PB_u + u$$

Eq. (1.3) is equal to eq. (1.1) extended for private net stocks of domestic bonds of both countries. We expect the following signs of the coefficients:

$$a_1,\ a_4,\ a_6 > 0;\quad a_2,\ a_3 < 0;\quad a_5 \gtrless 0.$$

$$(1.4)\quad e(home/\$) = a_0 + a_1\, M1_H + a_2\, M1_u + a_3\, F_H + a_4\, R_H + a_5\, F_u + a_6\, R_u + a_7\, PB_H + a_8\, PB_u + u$$

Eq. (1.4) is equal to eq. (1.2) extended for private net stocks of domestic bonds of both countries. Accordingly, the hypothesised coefficients are:

$$a_1,\ a_4,\ a_5,\ a_8 > 0;\quad a_2,\ a_3,\ a_6 < 0;\quad a_7 \gtrless 0.$$

Regression results for eqs. (1.3) and (1.4) will not be discussed in detail in the textual part. Estimations of these equations, however, can be found in the appendix. We opt for this treatment for the following reasons. First, we do not want to overload the text with estimation results which are of minor importance to the empirical significance of the CA in short run exchange rate determination.[1)]
Second, in most cases the introduction of PB variables does not improve the empirical performance of the portfolio model relative to eq. (1.1) and eq. (1.2).[2)] On the contrary, for all exchange rate equations we found indications for a considerable increase in the degree of multi-

---

1) Moreover, we have no theoretical hypothesis about the sign of the PB_H coefficient.

2) In the estimations for the DM/$ rate the PB coefficients are hardly ever significant on standard levels; in some cases $\bar{R}^2$ even declines when PBs were introduced. In the case of the yen/$ rate the PB coefficients are significant but with the wrong sign for PB_U. Similar negative evidence for the exchange rate influence of outstanding bond stocks is discussed in Penati (1983), Frankel (1983).

collinearity due to the introduction of the PB variables.[1)]

Over all equations we assume all right-hand variables as exogenous, except for the home countries' foreign exchange reserves for which we include a reaction function in the estimation.[2)]

9.1.2.2. Central Bank Reaction Function

Following previous empirical studies, we test for a systematic influence of the exchange rate on the home country's foreign exchange reserves. As we have explained above, to the extent that R is endogenous with respect to the exchange rate OLS estimations will produce biased results. To take into account this potential bias in the coefficient estimates of the exchange rate equation we simultaneously estimate eq. (1.1) to eq. (1.4) with a reaction function for central bank's intervention behaviour.

Having tried several versions of central bank reaction functions ("intervention functions") we selected the following equation.[3)]

$$(2) \quad R_t = b_0 + b_1 R_{t-1} + b_2 \Delta e_t(\text{home/\$}) + b_3 \text{ TAR} + u$$

$$b_2 < 0; \quad b_1, b_3 > 0.$$

R : Net foreign exchange reserves of the domestic central bank at the end of the period, denominated in billions of dollar. R is defined in the same way as described above in connection with the PF variable.

---

1) Estimates of the coefficients and t-ratios changed by large magnitudes, with R^2 almost unchanged, in almost all estimations when PBs were included. In particular, there seems to be a substantial intercorrelation between money supplies and the PB proxies.

2) To test in a simple way for our exogeneity assumptions we run regressions for money supplies and CAs as functions of the respective nominal dollar exchange rate (current and lagged), and, alternatively, as functions of the rate of change in the dollar rate. For money supplies we did not find any significant dependencies. The same holds generally for the CAs. Here, however, we found a slightly significant positive response on the part of the German and the Japanese CA to the DM/$ and yen/$ rate, respectively, lagged two quarters.

3) Eq. (2) is equal to BHM's reaction function except for the TAR term.

Δe : $(e_t - e_{t-1})/e_{t-1}$; rate of devaluation of the domestic currency vis-à-vis the dollar between time t-1 and t.
According to official announcements of central banks and the rules for interventions released by the IMF we expect $b_2 < 0$; an increase in the rate of devaluation of the home currency should motivate the domestic central bank to "lean against the wind", that is, to sell dollar against domestic currency.

TAR : $[(P_H/P_u)\cdot 100]_t - e_{t-1}$. Part of the central bank interventions, reflected in changes in the stock of net foreign exchange reserves R, might be directed towards a specific exchange rate target. We define such a possible target exchange rate by a purchasing-power-parity measure as the ratio between domestic and US consumer prices. By introducing the TAR term we assume that the central bank responds to deviations of the actual exchange rate from the target exchange rate, occuring between t-1 and t, by intervening in the foreign exchange market. We expect $b_3 > 0$; an increase in the gap between the target and the actual exchange rate - a devaluation of the target rate relative to the actual rate - should lead to dollar purchases of the domestic central bank to narrow the gap again.

Finally, we want to stress that our aim in incorporating this reaction function into the analysis is not to provide a detailed and comprehensive explanation of the central bank's intervention behaviour.[1)]
We simply wish to account for a potential simultaneity bias in the estimations of the exchange rate equation. Nevertheless, our results for the intervention function might give some interesting indications as to whether intervention is aimed at achieving a certain exchange rate target or at just smoothing short run exchange rate fluctuations.

---

1) It may be doubted, for example, whether our definition of F, or any other definition based on total reserves, is sufficient to measure the actual extent of official interventions in the foreign exchange market. See, e.g., M.J.M. Neumann (1983).

9.1.3. Procedure and Methods

9.1.3.1. Countries and Currencies

We apply the empirical portfolio model to the exchange rates of three currencies against the US dollar: the German mark (DM/$ rate), the Japanese yen (¥/$ rate), and the pound sterling (£/$ rate).

Among these three exchange rates the DM/$ rate takes a special position. Firstly, because over the last years the DM/$ rate has become the probably most important exchange rate in international financial transactions, and, secondly, previous tests using the DM/$ rate as reference rate provide some support for the portfolio theory. It seems interesting, therefore, to confront the DM/$ case with results for other exchange rates. For this comparison we choose the ¥/$ and the £/$ rate.

As the DM, the yen and the sterling may be considered as major currencies which tend to fulfil the basic assumption underlying the portfolio model, namely highly developed and relatively unrestricted capital markets.[1)]

Movements in the ¥/$ and £/$ rate differed quite considerably from movements in the DM/$ rate over our sample period. Thus, a confrontation of the test results for these two exchange rates with results for the DM/$ rate may be of additional interest in an empirical assessment of the portfolio theory.

9.1.3.2. Sample Periods

The overall time period for estimation purposes runs from April, 1973, the beginning of the managed floating regime, to August, 1982, the time when data series for some variables stopped at the time of estimation.

---

1) Over the period from 1973 to 1982 measures were adopted to regulate capital flows in all of the investigated countries particularly, however, in the United Kingdom and Japan. See IMF, Annual Report on Exchange Restrictions, various issues. Thus, the assumption of perfectly free capital markets would certainly be unrealistic. Although capital restrictions may produce some undesired side-effects on our empirical results for the portfolio model, it is very difficult (considering the development of non-national asset markets) to assess the actual importance of capital restrictions to international portfolio investments. In our empirical study we proceed from the simplifying assumption that national regulations governing capital flows did not have a major impact on international portfolio dispositions. For a similar view see IMF Survey, July 16 (1984, p. 216).

Besides a comparison of the empirical performance of the portfolio theory for different exchange rates, we want to allow for an intertemporal comparison of test results for each exchange rate. Therefore, we divide the overall time period into sub-periods. This subdivision is conducted according to the following criteria.

a. The sub-periods should be the same for all exchange rates.

b. One of the chosen time periods should cover approximately the sample periods used in previous empirical studies to enable a comparison with earlier results.

c. The sub-periods should be large enough to provide a sufficient number of observations and small enough to justify a reestimation using the overall sample including observations of the sub-period.

d. It would be desirable to determine the sub-periods in such a way that exchange rate movements in each of the sub-periods differ from each other in order to judge the empirical content of the portfolio theory in different situations.

The following diagram (figure 1) shows the differences in movements of the three exchange rates over the period from 1973 to end-1982.

Starting in 1973, rather substantial fluctuations in the DM/$ rate can be observed. From autum 1975 on the DM appreciated strongly against the dollar. This trend lasted roughly until early 1980 and was reversed afterwards.

The yen depreciated slightly against the dollar until the end of 1975. Between 1976 and the end of 1978 the yen is characterized by a strong appreciation against the dollar. This was followed by an equally strong depreciation lasting until the first quarter of 1980.

Between 1973 and the end of 1976 sterling lost steadily in value against the dollar. Starting around early 1977 this trend was inverted and we observe an appreciation trend for sterling lasting until the end of 1980.

According to the criteria described above we divide this overall time period into the following sub-periods.

Figure 1: End-of-month Spot Exchange Rates for DM/$, ¥/$,and £/$

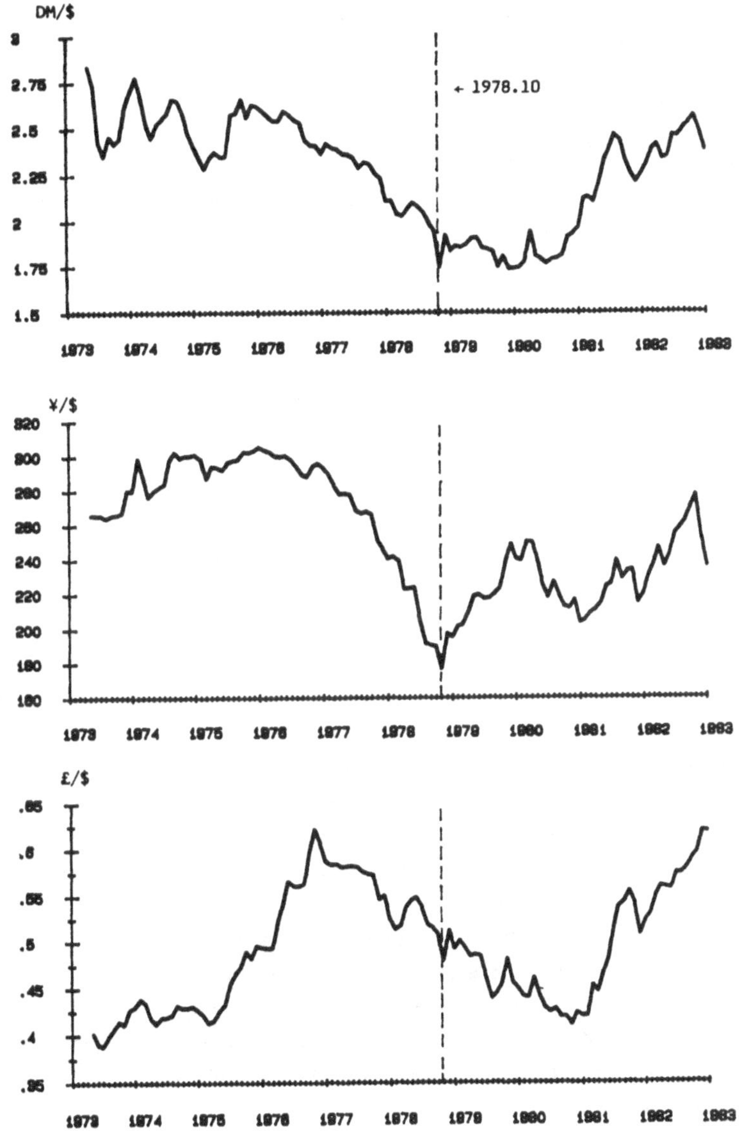

Source: IMF International Financial Statistics, data tape, line ae.

April, 1973 to October, 1978

This time period includes the strong appreciation of the yen between 1975 and the end of 1978 and most of the appreciation of the DM against the dollar which lasted until the end of 1979. The sharp rise in the £/$ rate too falls in this period.

The chosen sub-period covers most of the sample period underlying the empirical tests of BHM, MD, and MM. Thus, we may contrast our results with the conclusions of these authors. In particular, it is interesting to see whether the support for the portfolio model provided by the DM/$ case is also provided in the case of the ¥/$ and £/$ rate.

The DM/$ and ¥/$ rate are estimated with monthly data for 1973.4 to 1978.10. Since CA data for the United Kingdom are unavailable on a monthly basis, we use quarterly data from 1973.I to 1978.III in the case of the £/$ rate.[1)]

November, 1978 to August, 1982

The remaining observations of the complete sample have been used for forecasting purposes. Based on the exchange rate equations estimated for April, 1973 to October, 1978, we calculate ex-post exchange rate forecasts for the period from November, 1978 to August, 1982. These forecasts "predict" the values of the three exchange rates using actual values of the exogenous asset stocks.

The interesting point in these forecasts lies in the fact that the time series of all of the three exchange rates possess one or more turning-points within the forecast period. For the DM and sterling we observe a change in the general trend of an appreciation at the beginning of the forecast period to a persistent depreciation against the dollar starting around the end of 1980. Movements in the ¥/$ rate show even more turning-points. If the portfolio model is to be considered a reasonable explanation of movements in the three exchange rates these trend changes should be reflected in the exchange rate forecasts - the more as our ex-post calculations assume that agents have perfect foresight with respect to the exogenous variables.

---

1) Since monthly data for the CAs of Japan and Germany are directly available from national sources, we decided to interpolate the missing monthly series for the US CA from monthly trade account figures and to run the regressions with monthly data. The method used in this interpolation is described in the appendix.

April, 1973 to August, 1982

Finally, we reestimate all exchange rate equations for the complete sample period to allow for a direct comparison of test results for different time periods. Since the sample for which we conducted our first estimations is included in the overall time period, we may attribute changes in the estimates to developments within the period from November, 1978 to August, 1982. Changes in coefficients and t-ratios may indicate shifts in the relative importance of the exogenous variables in short run exchange rate determination.

For the DM and the yen we run regressions, as above, with monthly data.[1)] Additionally, all estimations are carried out with quarterly data as well. This is done for the following reasons:

The use of quarterly data avoids possible interpolation errors caused by the proxy variable for the unavailable monthly data series for the US CA.

As the exchange rate equations are stated in terms of portfolio "fundamentals", that is, they do not explicitly incorporate expectations, quarterly data might be more adequate than monthly data: contrary to monthly data series, quarterly series reduce the impact of short-term erratic exchange rate fluctuations and thereby influences of volatile expectations.

A comparison of test results produced with monthly and quarterly data may yield conclusions on the applicability of the portfolio theory to different time horizons.

For data reasons mentioned earlier, estimations of the £/$ rate have been conducted with quarterly data only.

---

1) For Japan the data series on central government debt, used in computing the proxy for Japan's stock of domestic bonds PB, stops in August, 1980. Therefore, we run the following regressions: JAPAN LONG for the period from 1973.4 to 1982.8, excluding PBs, and JAPAN SHORT for the period from 1973.4 to 1980.8, including PBs. Since we are not reporting within the textual part on test equations including domestic bond stocks, JAPAN SHORT will not be given special attention but is included in the appendix.

9.1.3.3. Estimation Methods

From a technical point of view the following estimations can be divided into two groups.

First, we run single-equation tests for all exchange rate equations and the central bank reaction function using the conventional ordinary-least-squares method (reported as OLS). Since most of the estimations, especially in the case of monthly data, show a rather high degree of first-order serial correlation among the residuals, we reestimate the single equations applying the Cochrane-Orcutt iteration technique (reported as CORC).[1)]

Second, we estimate the exchange rate equations simultaneously with the reaction function for the central bank of the home country (Germany, Japan, United Kingdom). To obtain consistent estimates of the coefficients we estimate all equations with an instrumental variable method (reported as 2SLS). Since we use all exogenous variables appearing in both equations as instruments, and no other variables, our instrumental variables estimates are the same as two-stage least squares estimates. In the case of first-order autocorrelation a correction method developed by Beach and MacKinnon (1978), which is based on the maximum-likelihood principle, is applied.[2)] Fair (1970) has shown that all lagged endogenous and exogenous variables must be in the instrument list to obtain consisten estimates from simultaneous equations models with first-order serially correlated errors. We adopt this method and report the results as FAIR.

The exchange rate forecasts for the period 1978.10 to 1982.8 are obtained by the following procedure. We use the results (constant and

---

1) By this method the original equation $y_t = \alpha + \beta x_t + u_t$ with the autocorrelated error $u_t = \rho u_{t-1} + \mu_t$ is transformed into its quasi-first-difference form $y_t - \rho y_{t-1} = \alpha(1 - \rho) + \beta(x_t - \rho x_{t-1}) + \mu_t$ with ρ denoting the serial correlation coefficient, RHO, and μ_t denoting the first-difference error term which is serially independent with a constant variance σ^2_e. The first estimate for ρ is taken from the OLS residuals and subsequently used in the quasi-first-difference equation. Iterations are stopped when successive values of ρ differed by less than 0,005.

2) This method treats the first observation in a special way, rather than dropping it like by CORC. The Cochrane-Orcutt procedure is asymptotically equivalent to this maximum-likelihood procedure, but estimates may differ in small samples.

coefficients) of the "best" exchange rate estimation for period 1973.4 to 1978.10 and compute prediction values for the exchange rate by using the right (perfect foresight) set of data for the exogenous variables over the period 1978.10 to 1982.8. The quality of these ex-post forecasts (out-of-sample forecasts) is judged on the basis of the difference between the actual values of the exchange rate and the so computed fitted values of the exchange rate.

In the case when estimates from CORC and FAIR are used to calculate fitted values, the procedure is somewhat more complicated. To obtain a "true dynamic forecast" we use the estimated values of RHO from the forecast equation and calculate fitted values for the exchange rate from the quasi-first-difference regression by using fitted values (not the actual ones) for the lagged dependent variables.

The estimations have been conducted on PRIME (European University Institute, Florence) and, to a smaller extent, on ICL (Commission of the European Communities, DG II, Brussels). In both cases TSP 3.5 and 3.5c, respectively, has been used.

9.1.3.4. A Note on Reported Results

Instead of giving a description of the regression statistics in connection with the estimation results we decided, considering the number of tables, to provide the relevant information on the statistical measures separately. The given definitions apply to tables appearing in the text as well as to tables reported in the appendices.

$\underline{R^2}$: In the case of OLS and 2SLS estimations we report $\bar{R}^2$, the squared coefficient of multiple determination, corrected for degrees of freedom. In the case of CORC and FAIR estimations $\hat{R}^2$ is claculated from the RHO-transformed variables and corrected for degrees of freedom.[1)]

<u>DW</u> : Durbin-Watson statistic for first-order serial correlation in the residuals.

<u>RHO</u> : Final, iterated value of the estimated first-order serial correlation coefficient.

---

1) Note that, opposite to R^2 in OLS and CORC estimations, R^2 in FAIR and 2SLS regressions can be negative and, in fact, is negative in some estimations.

Following the common practice we show t-ratios in parentheses below the estimated constants, coefficients and RHO-values.
An asterisk indicates that the estimated coefficient is significantly different from zero at the 95% probalbility level.
The independent variables are listed with their theoretically expected coefficient sign.

In exchange rate forecasts we report the following statistical measures.

RMSE : Root-mean-square error.

Let e_t be the actual value of the exchange rate in period t and $\tilde{e}_t$ the predicted value for the same period. The actual relative change then is $a_t = (e_t - e_{t-1})/e_{t-1}$, and the predicted relative change is given by $p_t = (\tilde{e}_t - e_{t-1})/e_{t-1}$. The mean-square error MSE is defined as

$$MSE = (1/n) \sum_{t=1}^{n} (p_t - a_t)^2 = (1/n) \sum_{t=1}^{n} \left(\frac{\tilde{e}_t - e_t}{e_{t-1}} \right)^2 \quad \text{or}$$

$$MSE = (\bar{p} - \bar{a})^2 + \sigma^2_{p-a}$$

This yields for the root-mean square error RMSE

$$\sqrt{MSE} = \sqrt{(\bar{p} - \bar{a})^2 + \sigma^2_{p-a}}$$

where $\bar{p}$, $\bar{a}$ are the means and σ_{p-a} denotes the variance of the prediction error. Now let 'r' denote the correlation coefficient between 'a' and 'p'; then we can write

$$MSE = (\bar{p} - \bar{a})^2 + (\sigma_p - r\,\sigma_a)^2 + (1 - r^2)\sigma^2_a$$

Thus, in terms of proportions we can divide MSE into the following components

U^M = bias proportion = $(\bar{p} - \bar{a})^2/MSE$

U^R = regression proportion = $[(\sigma_p - r\,\sigma_a)^2]$ /MSE

U^D = disturbance proportion = $[(1 - r^2)\sigma^2_a]$ /MSE

where $U^M + U^R + U^D = 1$. These measures can be interpreted in the following way.

$\underline{U^M}$: A large U^M means that the average predicted change in the exchange rate deviates substantially from the average actual change. Thus, the bias component indicates the extent to which MSE is the consequence of a tendency to estimate too high or too low a level of the exchange rate.

$\underline{U^R}$: To explain the meaning of U^R we consider the regression of the actual exchange rate on the predicted rate, that is, $e_t = \alpha + \beta\tilde{e}_t$.
It can be shown that U^M will be zero if $\hat{\alpha} = 0$, and U^R will be zero if $\hat{\beta} = 1$. The smaller U^R the better "explains" the change in the predicted exchange rate the actual change.
U^M and U^R measure "systematic" forecast errors. They tend to zero in optimal predictions.

$\underline{U^D}$: The disturbance proportion U^D indicates the extent to which MSE is due to the variance of the residuals obtained by regressing the actual relative changes of the exchange rate on predicted changes.

In addition to U^M, U^R, and U^D we report

<u>REG</u> : Regression coefficient of the actual on the predicted exchange rate.

<u>CORR</u> : Correlation coefficient between predicted and actual values of the exchange rate.

The estimation results reported and interpreted in the text are selected from the full set of estimations included in the appendix. As mentioned before, we do not explicitly consider test results for equations which include proxies for private net stocks of domestic bonds PB. Nevertheless, in some places we refer to these results, and a complete list of the estimations is included in the appendix.

Results for the forecasting procedure are given in the text only for equations (1.1) and (1.2) which produced the "best" result in the base period for the respective exchange rate. Since we run forecasts from all equations (1.1) and (1.2) we report the relevant statistical measures for these forecasts together with the regression results for the base period in the appendices.

The complete list of our estimation results for the respective central bank reaction function is also given in the appendices.

9.1.4. Limitations and Problems

Before we turn to the results of our estimations it seems appropriate to indicate some limits, problems and possible shortcomings of the following empirical investigation.

First of all, it is not the aim of our study to supply a full explanation of movements in the investigated exchange rates. We are not asking what particular circumstances are responsible for the behaviour of a certain exchange rate at a certain point in time. We attempt rather to find an answer to the question whether the portfolio theory, in our specific empirical interpretation, can be considered as a useful tool in explaining the overall time-series behaviour of the investigated exchange rates. Accordingly, we are not going into the particulars of certain situations and certain countries. Likewise we give no special consideration to socio-political or socio-economic events, like oil crises or political elections, which certainly influenced exchange rates. Therefore, we are not expecting the portfolio theory to give a complete explanation of past exchange rate fluctuations - a thing no exchange rate theory does. We would be satisfied if we could draw a conclusion on the usefulness of our empirical equations as rough guidelines for describing past exchange rate movements.

A second constraint relates to exchange rate expectations. Expectations on the future value of exchange rates are not explicitly incorporated in our test equations. The implicit role of expectations in our test can be understood in two ways. First, we may simply say that our

equations are based on the assumption of stationary expectations. This is the assumption underlying the model of MM which constitutes the theoretical foundation of this test. Second, we might say that we assume that at time t the current values of all exogenous variables represent best forecasts for the future values of these variables at time t+1. In fact, if the exogenous variables follow a random walk, rational agents should take the current value of these variables as the best predictors for the future.[1)]
Clearly, one may introduce other assumptions on the way expectations are formed and hence reach different results in testing the portfolio theory. Besides the fact that all assumptions on expectation formation on a macro-level are in like manner arbitrary, we preferred the stationarity assumption for two reasons. All prior tests of the basic portfolio model have been conducted under this assumption. Since we want to relate our results derived for different time periods and different exchange rates to these former tests, it seems appropriate to use as far as possible the same theoretical background.
The assumption of stationary expectations allows us to formulate the test equations exclusively in terms of portfolio "fundamentals". It might be more interesting to get an impression of the influence of these fundamental factors on the exchange rate, rather than to explain exchange rate behaviour by an arbitrary expectations term.

Nevertheless, we do not deny the great importance of expectations to exchange rate movements, and we are quite aware that our test might leave out one of the most important factors in short run exchange rate determination.

A further set of problems relates to the fact that our test equations are based on the comparative-statics of a point-in-time model. Since the sample period of our test covers almost ten years, some of the assumptions underlying our estimations may be rather unrealistic or even inadequate. What actually is estimated could be considered as the "exchange rate block" of a more comprehensive model which should also

---

1) See pp. 92 for a theoretical discussion of this assumption. For further theoretical discussion and empirical evidence on the random walk hypothesis with respect to the exogenous variables used in monetary and portfolio balance models see Branson (1981), Gaab (1982), Frankel (1983). The empirical evidence suggests that, in general, the random walk assumption, applied to these exogenous variables, is in most cases not unrealistic.

include the real sector with price and output specifications. Thus, we neglect dynamic stock-flow interactions in our partial-equilibrium test - a fact which is reflected in the exogeneity assumptions. As an alternative, we could have estimated the reduced or structural form of a fully specified model.[1] Such models are, however, confronted with additional problems in determining prices, output flows or the specification of the dynamic behaviour of the CA. Since we did not want to expand the portfolio approach to a general equilibrium model at the cost of further simplifying ad hoc assumptions we have to take into account shortcomings resulting from a partial-equilibrium test.

The following simplifications may further reduce the reliability of our results.

- We do not consider the existence of real capital and hence we ignore long or medium run substitution between real and financial assets.

- We neglect the possibility of structural changes in the desired portfolio (currency-) composition. Shifts in asset preferences could have had quite an important influence on exchange rate movements over our sample period of almost ten years.

- Considering the insufficient data basis we have to accept errors created by employing proxy variables.

- The assumption of only one internationally traded asset, US dollar bonds, may certainly be regarded as unrealistic.

- With respect to changes in relative price levels and, in particular, with respect to their influence on the real value of asset stocks and wealth, we are in a somewhat better position: specifying asset demand functions as linear homogeneous in wealth eliminates the price level from asset market equilibrium conditions and hence from our test equations. Yet, we have no empirical support for this simplifying assumption.

---

1) See, e.g., Artus (1982), Gaab (1982).

9.2. Results for the Deutsche Mark/US Dollar Rate

9.2.1. Estimations for 1973.4 to 1978.10

Table 1 shows the results of our estimations for the time period from 1973.4 to 1978.10. The first four columns contain the estimated coefficients of the variables included in BHM's equation, our equation (1.1). A first examination yields the impression that eq. (1.1) performs rather well in explaining the variance of the DM/$ rate over the investigated period: when estimated with OLS, 2SLS, and FAIR, all coefficients take the theoretically predicted signs; R^2s are significant and rather high. When we correct for a possible simultaneity bias by estimating eq. (1.1) jointly with the intervention function for the Bundesbank the coefficients on PF_G and PF_U increase in absolute terms and their standard errors decline. Examining the t-ratios of the estimated coefficients we see, however, that only $M1_U$ and PF_U have a significant influence, at the 95% level, on the DM/$ rate. This might indicate that the impact of the US money supply and the US CA on the exchange rate was stronger over the sample period than the impact of the German money supply and the German CA.[1)]

Summing up, our results for the period 1973.4 to 1978.10 are quite in line with earlier empirical tests. They support the portfolio model for the DM/$ exchange rate.

In the next step we divide the PF variables into their components - cumulated CA surpluses and central bank reserves - and reestimate the equation over the same sample period.
A comparison of eq. (1.2) with BHM's equation shows a strong increase in R^2s and F-statistics together with a slight reduction in autoregression. From this we might, prima facie, conclude that the single components of PF explain the variance of the DM/$ rate much better than the aggregated PF variables. Now it is interesting to compare the estimates for the PF variables from eq. (1.1) with the estimates for their components F and R from eq. (1.2).

---

1) The same conclusion can also be drawn from BHM's test and the estimations of Gaab (1982).

Table 1: Estimates for the DM/$ Exchange Rate, Sample Period 1973.4 - 1978.10, Monthly Data. a) next page

		BHM's Equation (Eq. 1.1)				PF Divided (Eq. 1.2)			
		OLS	CORC	2SLS	FAIR	OLS	CORC	2SLS	FAIR
C		465,62 (10,44)	522,84 (7,14)	447,22 (9,80)	425,67 (5,45)	325,24 (7,92)	322,59 (5,23)	327,44 (7,49)	337,61 (5,11)
$M1_G$	+	0,3370 (0,8632)	0,0880 (0,1807)	0,4724 (1,1847)	0,3169 (0,5953)	0,5902* (1,7263)	0,2845 (0,6147)	0,5936* (1,7319)	0,4954 (1,1294)
$M1_u$	·/.	-0,9718* (-2,8050)	-1,0573* (-2,2271)	-0,9826* (-2,7887)	-0,8323 (-1,6447)	-0,2995 (-0,9808)	-0,1900 (-0,4603)	-0,3154 (-0,9737)	-0,3506 (-0,8278)
PF_G	·/.	-0,1820 (-0,3636	2,4984* (3,1782)	-0,9119 (-1,6672)	-1,1461 (-1,0031)				
F_G	·/.					-1,8145* (-3,6221)	-1,1531 (-1,3476)	-1,8150* (-3,6224)	-1,5649* (-1,7317)
R_G	+					-4,2417* (-5,4323)	-3,9112* (-5,3205)	-4,1211* (-3,6456)	-3,5095* (-2,5545)
PF_u	+	0,8129* (3,5960)	0,2406 (0,5466)	1,0543* (4,4074)	1,2930* (2,4943)				
F_u	+					-0,1637 (-0,6414)	0,0822 (0,2644)	-0,1321 (-0,3964)	0,1449 (0,3169)
R_u	·/.					11,7683* (2,3849)	6,1460 (1,2287)	11,4200* (2,0872)	4,6637 (0,8860)
$\bar{R}^2$		0,7785		0,7709		0,8672		0,8672	
$\hat{R}^2$			0,3993		0,8158		0,6792		0,8952
F		59,00	11,61	52,16	68,64	72,86	21,91	65,30	85,46
DW		0,6248	1,4498	0,6574	1,4180	0,7107	1,5291	0,7071	1,5955
RHO			0,7821 (10,1959)		0,6835 (6,9565)		0,6441 (6,8411)		0,6778 (6,9646)

The coefficients for the cumulated German CA surpluses, F_G, are considerably higher for all estimation methods than the coefficients of PF_G. Moreover, the estimated appreciation (depreciation) effect of an increase (decrease) in F_G is significant in all equations, except CORC. The negative coefficients on PF_G, on the other hand, are alway insignificant.[1)] The reason why F_G improves so considerably over PF_G in explaining movements in the DM/$ rate may be found in the reserve component R_G which is included in PF_G:

According to the theory, a purchase of dollar assets by the Bundesbank which leads to an increase in German reserves should have a depreciation impact on the DM. Thus, we should expect a positive sign of the coefficient on R_G. Our results, however, suggest quite the opposite effect; the sign of the R_G coefficient is always negative and significant which seems to indicate that increasing German foreign exchange reserves cause an appreciation of the DM.[2)] This result remains true even when we estimate eq. (1.2) simultaneously with the reaction function for the Bundesbank to take into account feedbacks of the DM/$ rate on R_G. By looking at the time series for DM/$ and R_G we observe that an appreciation of the DM is generally combined with an increase in R_G indicating an attempt of the Bundesbank to smooth exchange rate fluctuations.[3)] This surmise is supported by the estimation results for the Bundesbank's intervention function. If all the other variables included in eq. (1.2) are unable to provide a complete explanation of the underlying movement in the DM/$ rate, it is likely that the strong effect running from the exchange rate to the reserve stock dominates the impact of reserve changes ("interventions") on the exchange rate and, hence, brings about the negative sign on the R_G coefficient.

---

a) To avoid too many digits after the decimal point we multiplied the DM/$ rate by 100 in the regressions. Subscripts G and u denote "Germany" and "US", respectively. For further explanations see chapter 9.1.3.4.

1) When estimated with CORC, PF_G is significant with the theoretically wrong sign. When we divide PF_G in its components, F_G takes the predicted sign and is significant at the 90% level.

2) The problem of a "wrong" and significant coefficient sign for the reserve variable R arises in almost all our estiamtions, irrespective of the tested exchange rate and time period. That is why we discuss this problem in more detail here.

3) Time series plots of net private foreign asset stock variables are included in the appendix.

Equally well we may presume that our reaction function is oversimplified and may not have served to eliminate entirely the simultaneity bias.[1] Recent empirical evidence, however, shows that "perverse" exchange rate effects of central bank interventions are not uncommon in econometric tests of exchange rate models - even when a central bank reaction function is included in the test.[2] It proves to be extremely difficult to find empirical support for the theoretically expected impact of reserve changes on the exchange rate.[3] Leaning-against-the-wind effects running from the exchange rate to the reserve stock seem to be much stronger than the influence of reserve changes on the exchange rate.[4]

Taking into account the "wrong" negative sign of the coefficient on R_G it seems problematic to run a test of the portfolio model by using the artificial PF variable: we aggregate two variables, F and R, of which one, R, cannot be estimated in accordance with the underlying theory. For this reason it seems more meaningful to use the CA directly as proxy for the relevant initial change in the stock of net foreign assets.

When we now contrast the estimated coefficients for PF_u with the coefficients for the PF_u components, F_u and R_u, we come to very similar conclusions. The influence of F_u on the DM/$ rate changes direction when estimated with different methods and is never significantly different from zero. The positive coefficient of R_u runs against the predicition of the underlying theory.

---

1) MM (1979) too found "perverse" effects of central bank foreign exchange market interventions in their empirical test. The intervention function employed by MM, however, is far more comprehensive than our version (see chapter eight).

2) See, e.g., Martin and Masson (1979), Suss (1980), Genberg (1981), Hacche and Townend (1982).

3) On this point see Obstfeld (1982), Henderson and Sampson (1983). Genberg, consequently, provides a different intervention theory: "...intervention systematically gives information about future monetary policy, so that a purchase of foreign exchange for domestic currency is interpreted as a temporary (originally in italics) easing of monetary conditions and hence generates expectations of future contraction. The expected future contraction then leads to an immediate appreciation of the home currency." Genberg (1981, p. 463). See also Suss (1980) for a further explanation.

4) As mentioned above, it may be doubted, of course, whether our definition of R, or any other definition based on total reserves, is adequate to measure the actual extent of official interventions.

The results for eq. (1.2) demonstrate that although the influence of PF_u can be estimated according to the theory, the results for its components do not support the theory (F_u) and may even contradict the theory (R_u).

Summing up, we may draw the following conclusions from the test.

If we look at the results for the PF variables, we might get a wrong impression of the influence of both countries' CAs on the DM/$ rate: the impact of the German CA will be underestimated and the impact of the US CA will be overestimated. Our estimations suggest a significant influence of the German CA on the DM/$ rate which is comparatively stronger than the influence of the US CA.

The same conclusion holds, to a smaller extent, for the influence of both countries' money supplies: in eq. (1.1) $M1_u$ has a significant influence on the DM/$ rate whereas the impact of $M1_G$ is always insignificant. In eq. (1.2) this result turns around; $M1_u$ becomes insignificant and $M1_G$ becomes significant when estimated with OLS and 2SLS. In both equations (1.1) and (1.2), however, the money stock variables are estimated with the theoretically expected signs by all methods.

In general, our estimates support the portfolio model for the period from 1973.4 to 1978.10.

9.2.2. Exchange Rate Forecasts for 1978.11 to 1982.8

Out of the set of estimations for 1973.4 to 1978.10 (table 1) we choose for each equation (1.1) and (1.2) the regression which corresponds best to the theory. For both empirical versions of the portfolio model the FAIR estimates yielded the "best" results.[1)] Based on these equations we calculate ex-post forecasts for the DM/$ rate using the actual values of all exogenous variables over the period from 1978.11 to 1982.8.

---

1) The ranking was conducted according to the following criteria: a. Equality of the signs of the estimated coefficients with the theoretical predictions. b. Relative values of R^2s, F-statistics, and RHOs. In addition to forecasts from these two equations, we calculated forecasts from all equations listed in table 1. It turned out that the forecasts computed from the two selected equations were indeed superior in terms of root-mean-square errors to predictions from the other equations of the same group.

The following diagram (figure 1) illustrates the results of the forecasting procedure. From figure 1 it is easy to see that BHM's equation fails almost completely in predicting the actual movement of the DM/$ rate over the forecasting period. Neither the appreciation of the DM between mid-1979 and the beginning of 1980 nor the substantial depreciation of the DM starting in June, 1980 is predicted by the forecast. Moreover, from 1980.6 on, the equation moves progressively away from the actual track, predicting an appreciation of the DM through most of the period. It is interesting to note, however, that from the point of view of BHM's fundamentals equation, the DM was constantly and, from June, 1980 on, even increasingly undervalued against the dollar.

The weak forecasting capacity of eq. (1.1) does not necessarily mean that BHM's asset fundamentals were meaningless for the actual development of the DM/$ rate over the period 1978.11 to 1982.8. A change in the relative importance among these asset variables, occuring after 1978.10, may have seriously distorted the forecasting quality.
In fact, our estimations for the total time period suggest that both countries' money supply variables were subject to a considerable change in significance for movements in the DM/$ rate over the forecast period.[1)]

In contrast to BHM's equation, eq. (1.2) predicts both the level and the rate of change in the DM/$ rate rather well. Thus, if taken by face value, eq. (1.2) seems to be superior to BHM's equation as a forecasting instrument. The good fit of the forecast from eq. (1.2), however, is mainly the merit of the "wrong" signs of the coefficients for both countries' foreign exchange reserves: eq. (1.2) predicts an increase in the DM/$ rate whenever German reserves decrease and US reserves increase. For instance, the strong depreciation of the DM against the dollar, starting in June, 1980, was connected with massive dollar sellings of the Bundesbank and the Federal Reserve. The attempt to smooth the ongoing rise in the DM/$ rate, constituting a reaction to the actual exchange rate movement, keeps eq. (1.2) close to the actual track.

---

1) A prediction based only on developments in both countries' net stocks of foreign assets would have captured the depreciation trend of the DM: the period between 1980.6 and 1981.9 is characterized by large deficits in the German CA which led to decreasing values of F_G and PF_G. During the same period F_U and PF_U showed a tendency to increase. Both developments would have correctly suggested a depreciation of the DM against the dollar. See the appendix for time series plots of the F variables.

Figure 1: Actual and Predicted Values of the DM/$ Exchange Rate.

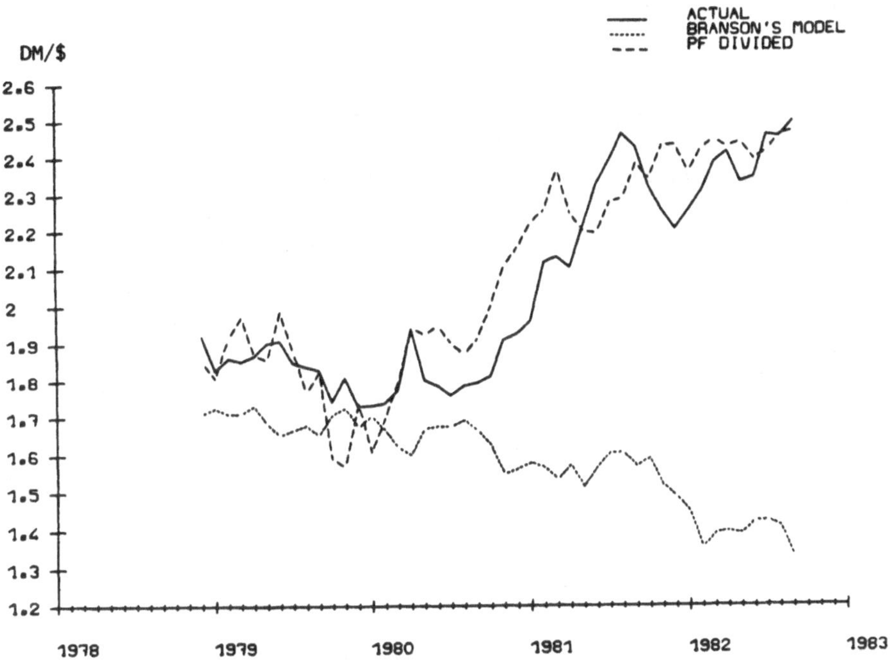

Table 2: Error Statistics for the Ex-Post Forecasts of the DM/$ Rate over the Period 1978.11 to 1982.8; Monthly Data. [a)]

Forecasting Model	RMSE	U^M	U^R	U^D	REG	CORR
BHM's equation (1.1)	0,58	0,6199	0,3167	0,0634	-1,89	-0,83
PF Divided (1.2)	0,12	0,1153	0,1067	0,7780	0,85	0,91

a) For definitions and explanations see section 9.1.3.4.

9.2.3. Estimations for 1973.4 to 1982.8

Table 3 contains the estimates for the total investigation period. Changes in the coefficients relative to the results for the first period (1973.4 - 1978.10), reported in table 1, can be assigned to changes in the importance of the respective asset variables which occured during the time from 1978.11 to 1982.8. The poor forecasting results, in particular with respect to the strong depreciation of the DM starting in June, 1980, suggest that such changes indeed have taken place. We comment first on the regression results for BHM's equation.

In general, our estimates can hardly be interpreted as support for BHM's empirical version of the portfolio model. The high degree of autocorrelation indicates that BHM's fundamental factors are capable of explaining only a very small fraction of the actual change in the DM/$ rate.[1)] When we correct for autocorrelation and estimate eq. (1.1) simultaneously with the intervention function for the Bundesbank (FAIR), we find nothing significant except for an autocorrelation coefficient very close to one. A comparison of RHO's and $\hat{R}^2$s with the results in table 1 suggests that the empirical relevance of the portfolio model in BHM's version declined drastically during the period from 1978.11 to 1982.8. Besides this general impression it is interesting to note that signs and values of the money supply coefficients take frequently wrong signs which are even significant in some cases. This may indicate that the strong depreciation of the DM from 1980.6 on was not due to portfolio effects of changes in both countries' money supplies.

A comparison of the estimates of eq. (1.2) and BHM's equation yields a picture very similar to that for the shorter sample period. When we divide the PF variables into their components, R^2 and F values increase considerably, in particular when we correct for autocorrelation. So too, the degree of autocorrelation declines drastically. This effect is even stronger for the longer test period than for the short period from 1973.4 to 1978.10.

The relationship between the coefficients of PF and its components, F and R, is quite similar to the relationship described for the shorter test period. As before, the coefficients on R_G and R_u are significant

---

1) In the CORC estimation only 6% of the variance in the DM/$ rate can be ascribed to changes in asset stocks. See also Gaab (1982).

Table 3: Estimates for the DM/$ Exchange Rate, Sample Period 1973.4 - 1982.8, Monthly Data. a) see table 1.

		BHM's Equation (Eq.1.1)				PF Divided (Eq. 1.2)			
		OLS	CORC	2SLS	FAIR	OLS	CORC	2SLS	FAIR
C		251,74 (20,73)	7,93 (0,0840)	261,84 (20,71)	-958,12 (-1,8654)	314,81 (24,65)	288,46 (13,98)	315,10 (24,63)	296,54 (13,37)
$M1_G$	+	-1,5052* (-7,0576)	0,2274 (0,6167)	-1,2859* (-5,6920)	0,1894 (0,4282)	-0,1181 (-0,4963)	-0,0917 (-0,3130)	-0,1002 (-0,4161)	-0,0012 (-0,0038)
$M1_u$	·/.	0,7484* (5,0534)	0,4240* (1,7012)	0,5942* (3,7834)	0,2852 (0,8307)	-0,0203 (-0,1447)	0,0341 (0,1889)	-0,0240 (-0,1708)	-0,0249 (-0,1326)
PF_G	·/.	-0,4259 (1,3843)	1,2551* (2,8942)	-0,7837* (-2,3726)	-0,1798 (-0,2304)				
F_G	·/.					-1,1617* (-4,0448)	-1,2739* (-3,2193)	-1,1431* (-3,9434)	-1,4472* (-3,4180)
R_G	+					-2,4593* (-6,2414)	-2,1504* (-5,1912)	-2,6020* (-5,3144)	-2,1788* (-2,7170)
PF_u	+	1,3891* (9,0896)	0,6032 (1,1441)	1,5018* (9,5052)	0,3530 (0,5671)				
F_u	+					0,5093* (3,2398)	0,7245* (3,0843)	0,4637* (2,5394)	0,6398* (1,9663)
R_u	·/.					2,7594* (3,8401)	1,6171* (1,7771)	2,8773* (3,7958)	1,5293 (1,5590)
$\bar{R}^2$		0,8329		0,8308		0,9052		0,9051	
$\hat{R}^2$			0,0642		-0,2715		0,6665		0,8311
F		140,55	2,8227	132,57		179,33	36,88	168,54	88,59
DW		0,5465	1,7289	0,5476	1,7542	0,6143	1,7278	0,6190	1,7724
RHO			0,9599 (36,24)		0,9994 (1686,54)		0,6809 (9,8395)		0,7242 (10;29)

but with signs which contradict the prediction of the theory. Nevertheless, the coefficients of PF_G and PF_u take in all regressions the theoretically predicted signs.[1] However, neither PF_G nor PF_u are significant with the expected signs when we correct for autocorrelation.

Splitting up PF reveals that the exchange rate influence of the German CA might be underestimated if it is incorporated in the PF-concept: the estimates for F_G are in absolute terms considerably higher than the coefficients of PF_G. The influence of F_G is always significant and keeps quite stable over all testings, no matter if estimated together with domestic bond stocks, with quarterly or monthly data, for the short or the long period.
The estimates for F_u suggest a significant exchange rate impact also for the US CA. Contrary to the results for the short period, F_u takes always the predicted positive sign and is significant at the 95% level. However, t-ratios and the absolute values of the F_u coefficients are always lower than for F_G.

From these results we may tentatively draw two conclusions. First, the importance of the US CA to the DM/$ rate will probably be overestimated in comparison to the importance of the German CA if PF variables are employed. Second, the contribution of both countries' CAs in explaining movements in the DM/$ exchange rate increased over the period 1978.11 to 1982.8. Our estimations support the view that the substantial devaluation of the DM against the dollar from 1980.6 on was at least partly caused by imbalances in the German and the US CA.[2]

Finally, we turn to the coefficients of the money supply variables. The separation of the reserve variables R_G and R_u in eq. (1.2) has a rather strong impact on the estimates for $M1_G$ and $M1_u$. The $M1_G$ coefficient takes always a wrong negative sign in eq. (1.2) but is never significantly different from zero. On the other hand, the coefficient of $M1_u$ changes in the right direction in eq. (1.2) but is likewise never significant.[3]

---

1) Except for PF_G in the CORC estimation.

2) For a similar conclusion see Artus (1982, pp. 21).

3) The inclusion of both countries' net stocks of domestic bonds PB affects the money supply coefficients in a similar way.

The strong change in money supply coefficients might indicate a substantial degree of multicollinearity between money supplies and central bank reserves.[1)]

Table 4 contains the estimations of eq. (1.1) and eq. (1.2) with quarterly data series from 1973.I to 1982.II. Since the RHO values obtained by CORC and FAIR proved to be low and insignificant, we report only on OLS and 2SLS regressions.

Above all, we realize from table 4 a considerable improvement in the empirical performance of BHM's version of the portfolio model when tested with quarterly data. All 2SLS coefficient estimates of eq. (1.1) have the theoretically expected sign; the absolute value of the coefficients and t-ratios increase compared to the values in the monthly estimation. Even the coefficients of $M1_G$ and $M1_u$, though still insignificant, are now estimated with signs according to the theory.
The exchange rate influence of PF_G and PF_u is significant in the right direction for all estimation methods.

It is remarkable that we would have to reject BHM's equation for the overall time period from 1973.4 to 1982.8 on the basis of the monthly estimates, whereas the quarterly results support the theory.
A possible explanation for this change in the empirical evidence has already been given above in section 9.1.3.2.: the use of quarterly data might surpress volatile speculative influences on the exchange rate which may have concealed the significance of BHM's fundamental asset factors in the monthly estimations.[2)]

Our estimations of eq. (1.2) once more produce theoretically incorrect signs for the coefficients of the reserve variables R_G and R_u. When estimated with 2SLS, however, they are not significantly different from zero at the 95% level.

The coefficients of both countries' cumulated CAs have the expected signs but only F_G is significant. It is interesting that the quarterly

---

1) This is not surprising as foreign exchange reserves are part of the monetary base and thus constitute a fundamental source of the money creating process. Regressions of both countries' M1s on the respective central bank reserves, however, did not reveal significant dependencies. Moreover, additional estimations showed that R_G reacts strongly to exchange rate changes whereas changes in the German M1 could not be related significantly to changes in the DM/$ rate.

2) This is also indicated by the sharp decline in autocorrelation in the quarterly estimates.

Table 4: Estimates for the DM/$ Exchange Rate, Sample Period 1973.I - 1982.II, Quarterly Data. a)

		BHM's Equation (Eq.1.1)		PF Divided (Eq. 1.2)	
		OLS	2SLS	OLS	2SLS
C		287,69 (11,32)	320,58 (11,24)	372,42 (14,50)	372,68 (13,40)
$M1_G$	+	-0,6600 (-1,2610)	0,2355 (0,3841)	0,6692 (1,5548)	0,6700 (1,5531)
$M1_U$	·/.	0,1397 (0,3778)	-0,4967 (-1,1456)	-0,5004* (-1,8498)	-0,4988* (-1,7927)
PF_G	·/.	-1,4637* (-2,4751)	-2,6099* (-3,6713)		
F_G	·/.			-1,7343* (-3,7010)	-1,7256* (-2,9295)
R_G	+			-2,6748* (-3,5012)	-2,7130 (-1,5528)
PF_U	+	1,6238* (5,0088)	2,0283* (5,5935)		
F_U	+			0,3778 (1,2692)	0,3658 (0,6322)
R_U	·/.			2,8920* (2,1149)	2,9255 (1,5061)
$\bar{R}^2$		0,7664	0,7398	0,8922	0,8923
F		31,35	23,46	52,07	42,79
DW		1,4562	1,4350	1,5201	1,5208

a) See footnote a. table 1.

results for F_G confirm the monthly estimates. This is not the case for F_u: contrary to the test results obtained with monthly data, F_u is never significant in the quarterly estimations.[1] Furthermore, a comparison of coefficients and t-ratios for PF_u and F_u once more indicates that PF_u probably overestimates the actual influence of the US CA on the DM/$ rate.

We conclude with some short remarks on the results for the Bundesbank's reaction function.[2] In all estiamtions, no matter if conducted with quarterly or monthly data, we find a significant dependence of the Bundesbank's foreign exchange reserves on the rate of change in the DM/$ rate and on the target exchange rate variable TAR. All coefficients have the predicted sign: an increase (decrease) in the rate of depreciation of the DM causes a decrease (increase) in German official reserves. A devaluation of the PPP-target rate against the actual exchange rate leads to an increase in R_G.[3]

Our estimations support the view that the Bundesbank pursued an intervention policy of "leaning-against-the-wind" over the time period from 1973.4 to 1982.8. On the other hand, interventions seemed to be directed to purchasing-power-parity considerations as well.

9.2.4. Summary

The test results we presented over the last sections do not yield a homogeneous picture of the empirical relevance of the portfolio balance model for the DM/$ rate. Support or rejection depends on the sample period, the precise test specification, and on the periodicity of data used for the estimations.

Over the period from 1973.4 to 1978.10 BHM's empirical version of the portfolio model performed rather well in explaining monthly movements in the DM/$ rate. Our results, as those of BHM and MD, lend some support to BHM's theory. On the other hand, BHM's exchange rate equa-

---

1) This result is of particular importance since original data on the US CA is not available more frequently than quarterly. Thus, our monthly estimates for F_U might be distorted due to interpolation errors in calculating monthly proxies for F_U.

2) Estimation results are given in the appendix.

3) In the quarterly 2SLS estimation together with eq. (1.2) the TAR variable is significant only at the 90% level.

tion fails drastically in predicting ex-post developments of the DM/$ rate over the period from 1978.11 to 1982.8.

When we extended the data sample to the overall time period from 1973.4 to 1982.8, we found that monthly movements in the DM/$ exchange rate are indeed hardly explained by changes in BHM's asset stock variables. Surprisingly, however, if tested with quarterly data, our results support BHM's version of the portfolio model. These contradictory outcomes might indicate that changes in actual asset stocks lost influence on short run exchange rate movements over the period from 1978.11 to 1982.8. Monthly fluctuations in the DM/$ rate are likely to be dominated over the last years by volatile expectations and structural changes in asset demands. The importance of asset supply fundamentals become visible only in a longer (quarterly) time perspective. In particular, the coefficients for both countries' M1 money stocks became very unstable and took frequently signs opposite to those predicted by the theory when we extended the monthly estimations for the period 1978.11 to 1982.8. By way of contrast, the estimates for BHM's CA variables PF_G and PF_U behaved comparatively stable and had the predicted sign in almost all our estimations.

When we divided BHM's PF variables into their components, official foreign exchange reserves R and total net foreign asset stocks F, we observed an increase in R^2s and F-statistics and a decrease in autocorrelation, the latter especially for the long estimation period. These statistical improvements, however, may be partly due to strong feedbacks of the exchange rate on the reserve variables: R_G and R_U were always estimated with theoretically wrong signs although we included a reaction function for the Bundesbank's foreign exchange reserves in the test. Nevertheless, the estimates from eq. (1.2) are interesting with respect to the exchange rate influence of the US and German CA.

F_G, the cumulated German CA, took always the predicted negative sign for all periods and all data sets and was almost always significant at the 95% level.[1)] Thus our test supports the view that the German CA had a significant impact on the DM/$ exchange rate over the period from 1973.4 to 1982.8.

---

1) Except for the CORC estimation in table 1 where F_G is significant only at the 90% level.

On the other hand, the influence of the US CA was not significant in the earlier sample period from 1973.4 to 1982.8. However, when we included the time from 1978.11 to 1982.8 in the data sample, the coefficient of F_u took always the expected positive sign and was always significant in the monthly estimations. This result might indicate a growing importance of the US CA to the DM/$ rate over the last years up to 1982.8.

9.3. Results for the Japanese Yen/US Dollar Rate

9.3.1. Estimations for 1973.4 to 1978.10

The regression results for the ¥/$ exchange rate, estimated over the first sub-period from 1973.4 to 1978.10, are set out in table 1. The estimates for BHM's version of the portfolio model yield a rather contradictory picture.

The coefficients for the Japanese money supply $M1_J$ take a theoretically wrong negative sign in all regressions. When estimated jointly with the reaction function for Japan's foreign exchange reserves, the negative coefficients become even significant. $M1_U$ has the expected negative coefficient in the single equation estimations OLS and CORC but takes a positive sign in the 2SLS and FAIR regressions. Thus, the estimation results for the exchange rate influence of both countries' money stocks M1 run essentially against the theoretical predictions.

Our estimates for the PF variables, however, support BHM's theory. The private net foreign asset stock of Japan, PF_J, always has the expected negative coefficient (except for CORC) and is significant at the 95% level. The coefficient on PF_U has the predicted positive sign and is likewise significant in all cases.

A comparison with our estimates from eq. (1.2) tends to confirm the results from BHM's equation. $M1_J$ is still estimated with a negative coefficient but now the standard errors increase slightly. The coefficients of $M1_U$ take positive signs in all estimations and, moreover, the t-ratios of these positive coefficients increase considerably in comparison with eq.(1.1). Thus, our results suggest, in contrast to the theory, that an increase in the Japanese money supply M1 and a decrease in the US M1 tend to appreciate the yen against the dollar.

The coefficients on the CA variables F_J and F_U, however, have the theoretically expected signs in all estimations. F_J is significant at the 95% level in all cases indicating that the Japanese CA had a marked impact on the ¥/$ rate over the investigated period: a surplus in Japan's CA tends to appreciate the yen against the dollar.[1)]

---

1) This is not surprising since the strong appreciation of the yen against the dollar between 1976 and 1979 coincides with large surpluses in the Japanese CA.

Table 1: Estimates for the Yen/$ Exchange Rate, Sample Period 1973.4 - 1978.10, Monthly Data. a) next page

		BHM's Equation (Eq. 1.1)				PF Divided (Eq. 1.2)			
		OLS	CORC	2SLS	FAIR	OLS	CORC	2SLS	FAIR
C		421,86 (9,47)	532,54 (8,86)	378,27 (8,03)	350,68 (5,66)	185,17 (4,03)	199,64 (3,52)	206,29 (4,25)	271,17 (4,23)
$M1_J$	+	-0,0020 (-1,5371)	-0,0017 (-1,3879)	-0,0027* (-1,9991)	-0,0032* (-2,0081)	-0,0013 (-1,2472)	-0,0010 (-0,9472)	-0,0016 (-1,4627)	-0,0020 (-1,4994)
$M1_u$	·/.	-0,1660 (-0,4634)	-0,6729* (-1,8226)	0,1311 (0,3486)	0,3163 (0,6845)	0,6026* (1,9218)	0,4879 (1,4709)	0,5768* (1,7977)	0,4088 (1,1215)
PF_J	·/.	-3,0535* (-5,0886)	0,3414 (0,4274)	-4,2756* (-6,2820)	-4,8380* (-4,0056)				
F_J	·/.					-3,6066* (-8,9817)	-3,1909* (-5,3508)	-3,9110* (-8,7485)	-4,1705* (-4,8510)
R_J	+					-1,7682* (-2,7237)	-2,2524* (-2,7199)	-0,6982 (-0,7675)	1,3306 (0,6811)
PF_u	+	1,5659* (7,4914)	2,0299* (5,2900)	1,3479* (6,0811)	1,2594* (3,4573)				
F_u	+					0,0006 (0,0026)	0,1680 (0,5182)	0,1554 (0,6404)	0,6436 (1,5689)
R_u	·/.					7,4170* (1,9625)	3,6668 (0,9340)	6,0069 (1,5207)	0,6503 (0,1386)
$\bar{R}^2$		0,9291		0,9244		0,9700		0,9686	
$\hat{R}^2$			0,6091		0,8606		0,9237		0,9282
F		217,24	25,89	189,43	95,70	356,77	120,89	308,98	129,21
DW		0,7115	1,9888	0,7940	1,7676	1,1076	1,7274	1,1124	1,7199
RHO			0,8263 (11,9200)		0,5914 (5,7482)		0,4973 (4,6466)		0,4970 (4,4920)

In contrast to this, the exchange rate influence of F_u is never significantly different from zero. As in the case of the DM/$ rate, this result indicates that BHM's PF_u variable might overestimate the influence of the US CA on the ¥/$ rate.

The intervention variables R_u and R_J have coefficients with theoretically wrong signs in all our estimations, except for R_J in FAIR: when we correct for autocorrelation in the simultaneous-equation estimation, R_J takes the expected positive coefficient and the t-ratio as well as the absolute value of the positive coefficient on R_u declines sharply.

Recapitulating the results, we may say that our test provides no support for the portfolio model with respect to the exchange rate effect of changes in both countrie' money supplies but it confirms the theoretical hypotheses, at least for Japan, on the exchange rate influence of CA imbalances. The estimates in table 1 confirm the empirical findings of MM's test for the ¥/$ rate.

9.3.2. Exchange Rate Forecasts for 1978.11 to 1982.8

Our ex-post forecasts of the ¥/$ rate are calculated for both versions of the portfolio model on the basis of the FAIR estimations in table 1. It is important to note that these predictions are not really predictions in the sense of the underlying theory: the signs of the estimated coefficients for $M1_J$ and $M1_u$ stand in both equations in contradiction to the theory.[1] Nevertheless, a comparison of actual and predicted values of the ¥/$ exchange rate suggests some interesting conclusions, in particular with regard to the significance of the Japanese CA to movements in the ¥/$ rate. A closer examination of the computed forecasts gives the impression that the predictions produced by eq. (1.1)

---

1) In our estimations of eq. (1.2) the coefficients on $M1_J$ and $M1_u$ have always the wrong sign, no matter whether we include domestic bond stocks or not. For eq. (1.1) we could have selected the OLS regression where at least the influence of $M1_u$ is estimated in accordance with the theory. However, a comparison of the forecasts produced by OLS and FAIR regressions showed that the latter performed better on all measures.

2) Subscripts J and u denote "Japan" and "US", respectively. For further explanations see section 9.1.3.4.

Figure 1: Actual and Predicted Values of the ¥/$ Exchange Rate

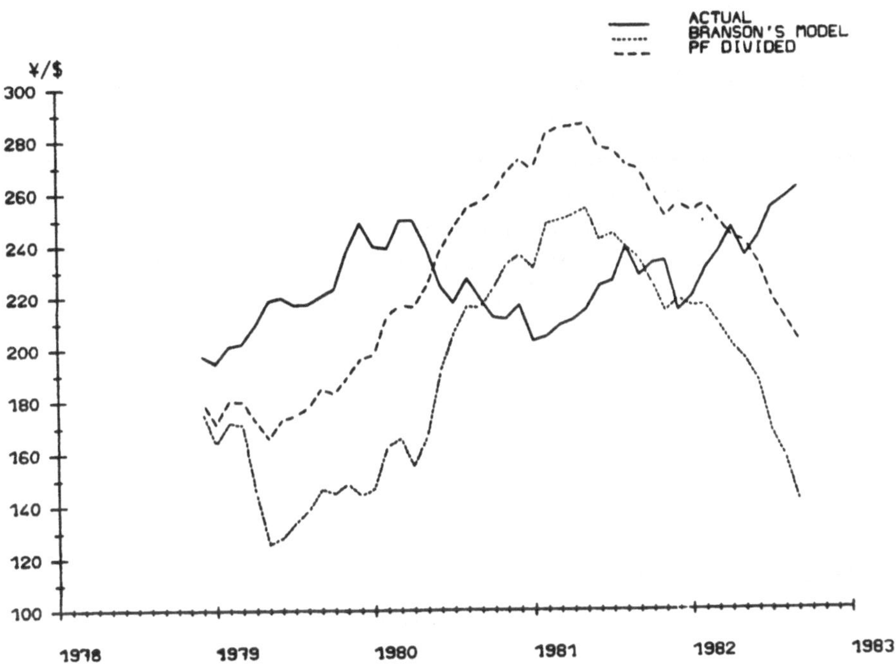

Table 2: Error Statistics for the Ex-Post Forecasts of the ¥/$ Exchange Rate over the Period 1978.11 to 1982.8, Monthly Data. a)

Forecasting Model	RMSE	U^M	U^R	U^D	REG	CORR
BHM's Equation (1.1)	57,83	0,3508	0,5736	0,0757	-0,1108	-0,2648
PF Divided (1.2)	42,36	0,0096	0,8388	0,1515	-0,0082	-0,0190

a) For definitions and explanations see section 9.1.3.4.

and eq. (1.2) are dominated by developments in Japan's net stock of foreign assets. This will become clear when we discuss the results in more detail.[1)]

The forecasts from eq. (1.1) and eq. (1.2) differ mainly with respect to the level of the exchange rate. The predicted direction of change in the ¥/$ rate is roughly the same in both equations.[2)]

Between May, 1979 and May, 1981, Japan ran large CA deficits which brought about a fall in Japan's total net stocks of foreign assets of about 20 billions US dollar. Taking into account changes in Japan's official foreign exchange reserves, the calculated decline in PF_J was even stronger (ca. 23 bill. dollar). Accordingly, both equations (1.1) and (1.2) predict an extreme depreciation of the yen for this period. The predicted decline in the value of the yen vis-à-vis the dollar amounts to about 70% for eq. (1.2) and 100% for eq. (1.1).

Starting in June, 1981, the trend turned around and the Japanese CA moved to a surplus position. Between June, 1981 and August, 1982, F_J increased again by approximately 20 bill. dollar and PF_J rose by ca. 24 bill. dollar. Based on this development both equations predict an appreciation of the yen from June, 1981 on.

When we now contrast actual and predicted movements in the ¥/$ rate, we see that our forecasts capture the direction of the change in the exchange rate only in two cases, namely for the depreciation periods between April, 1979 and February, 1980, and between December, 1980 and April, 1981. For all other periods our forecasts predict movements in

---

1) A look at the forecasting equations in table 1 reveals that the coefficients on PF_J, F_J, and R_J have, in absolute terms, higher values than the coefficients on PF_U, F_U, and R_U. The data set underlying our forecast calculations shows furthermore that changes in the Japanese CA and in Japan's foreign exchange reserves exceeded, in absolute terms, by far changes in the corresponding US variables throughout the period from 1978.11 to 1982.8.

2) The deviation in the level of the forecasts is essentially due to the wrong prediciton of a fall in the ¥/$ rate in March and April, 1979 by BHM's equation. Over these two months F_J actually declined, which tends to rise the predicted rate in eq. (1.2), but R_J declined as well causing a fall in the predicted ¥/$ rate. Since the decline in R_J exceeded the decline in F_J, BHM's PF_J variable indicates an increase in the private net stocks of foreign assets and hence eq. (1.1) predicts a relatively stronger appreciation of the yen than eq. (1.2).

the ¥/$ rate opposite to the actual direction. Thus, taking into account the above remarks, we may conclude that the general development of the ¥/$ rate from early 1980 on can certainly not be explained by portfolio effects of Japanese CA imbalances.

9.3.3. Estimations for 1973.4 to 1982.8

In table 3 we set out the results for the monthly estimations of the ¥/$ rate over the period from 1973.4 to 1982.8. This extended sample period includes the forecasting period of the last section.

The estimates for eq. (1.1) provide little support for BHM's empirical portfolio model. R^2s and F-statistics decrease relative to the results in table 1. As in the case of the DM/$ rate, autocorrelation increases strongly in eq. (1.1) when we include the time from 1978.11 to 1982.8 in the sample. Both results indicate that during this period the ¥/$ rate has been considerably affected by factors not included in BHM's equation.

On the whole, the estimates for the Japanese and US money supply confirm the poor results of table 1 for the shorter investigation period. In eq. (1.1), as well as in eq. (1.2), the coefficients of $M1_J$ always take negative signs - contrary to the theoretical prediction. When we correct for autocorrelation, none of the coefficients is significantly different from zero. In BHM's equation $M1_U$ takes a positive and significant coefficient in the 2SLS and OLS estimations. When we correct for autocorrelation the coefficients take the expected negative sign but they are not significant. In eq. (1.2) the estimated coefficient for $M1_U$ contradicts the theoretical hypothesis in all estimations. Thus, the teoretical predictions of the stationary-expectations portfolio model have to be rejected with regard to the exchange rate influence of money supplies.

Next we turn to effects of Japanese and US CA imbalances on the ¥/$ rate. These effects are of particular interest to our study and, in fact, the results seem to be more productive here than in the case of the M1 money stocks.

Table 3: Estimates for the Yen/$ Exchange Rate, Sample Period 1973.4 - 1982.8, Monthly Data. a) see table 1.

		BHM's Equation (Eq. 1.1)				PF Divided (Eq. 1.2)			
		OLS	CORC	2SLS	FAIR	OLS	CORC	2SLS	FAIR
C		277,78 (16,69)	241,48 (2,5219)	280,86 (16,75)	305,68 (4,9220)	269,67 (15,66)	266,66 (7,11)	267,61 (15,43)	274,73 (8,28)
$M1_J$	+	-0,0047* (-5,7883)	-0,00002 (-0,0326)	-0,0045* (-5,4770)	-0,00014 (-0,1935)	-0,0019* (-3,3396)	-0,0002 (-0,3246)	-0,0018* (-3,3797)	-0,0003 (-0,5120)
$M1_U$	·/.	0,6731* (4,1775)	-0,0067 (-0,0275)	0,6359* (3,9030)	-0,1021 (-0,5243)	0,2454* (2,1076)	0,0323 (0,2110)	0,2546* (2,1798)	0,0299 (0,2005)
PF_J	·/.	0,5407 (1,2610)	1,0189* (2,0121)	0,3895 (0,8863)	-0,3158 (-0,4912)				
F_J	·/.					0,4171 (1,4903)	-0,4477 (-0,9206)	0,4686 (1,6654)	-0,3946 (-0,8361)
R_J	+					-4,7033* (-11,8603)	-3,4070* (-5,3279)	-4,8549* (-11,5415)	-3,5746* (-3,4126)
PF_U	+	1,9367* (8,2352)	0,9707* (1,8753)	1,8861* (7,9423)	0,9567* (1,8790)				
F_U	+					1,4107* (8,6113)	0,8882* (2,1794)	1,4181* (8,6430)	0,8458* (2,2890)
R_U	·/.					0,8539 (1,0875)	0,1666 (0,1538)	0,8590 (1,0931)	0,2402 (0,2402)
$\bar{R}^2$		0,7390		0,7387		0,9061		0,9060	
$\hat{R}^2$			0,0365 b)		0,6869		0,3627		0,7290
F		80,29	1,9948	76,34	59,22	181,14	11,20	170,23	47,51
DW		0,2448	2,0786	0,2395	1,9152	0,4661	2,0817	0,4716	2,0590
RHO			0,9674 (40,42)		0,9488 (35,16)		0,8681 (18,51)		0,8503 (16,33)

b) insignificant

First, we note from table 3 that the coefficient on PF_J, the Japanese net private foreign asset stock, is estimated by all methods (except FAIR) with the theoretically wrong positive sign. The negative coefficient in the FAIR estimation does correspond to the theory but is not significant at standard levels. A comparison with the estimates for PF_J in table 1 suggests that the significant appreciation (depreciation) effect of surpluses (deficits) in the Japanese CA during the period from 1973.4 to 1978.10 diminishes strongly when we extend the investigation period to 1982.8. Considering the discussion of the forecast results in the previous section, this result is not surprising.

The presumption of a strong decline in the significance of the Japanese CA for the ¥/$ exchange rate over the period 1978.11 to 1982.8 is supported by the estimation results for the F_J variable in eq. (1.2). Although the coefficient of F_J takes the expected negative sign when we correct for autocorrelation, it is not significant at the 95% level. Hence, the estimates for F_J and PF_J indicate that the general movement in the ¥/$ rate after 1978.11 can be hardly explained by developments in the Japanese CA.[1)]

Turning to the US CA we see from table 3 that the coefficient on PF_U has the expected positive sign and is significant in all estimations. Coefficients and t-ratios are relatively stable over all three test periods.[2)] Our estimations for F_U in eq. (1.2) show a considerable increase in coefficients and t-ratios relative to the results in table 1. Contrary to the F_U estimates for the period from 1973.4 to 1978.10, the coefficients of F_U are now significant with the expected positive sign. Thus, our results support the view that the US CA had a significant influence in the theoretically expected direction on the ¥/$ rate

---

1) In our estimations for the period 1973.4 to 1980.8 the coefficient of PF_J always has the predicted negative sign, except for CORC, but is insignificant when we correct for autocorrelation. The coefficient of F_J has the expected negative sign and is significant in all cases. However, in comparison with the estimates for the period from 1973.4 to 1978.10, coefficients and t-ratios for both variables decline in absolute terms quite strongly. These results support the presumption of a continuous decline in the importance of the Japanese CA to ¥/$ rate movements over the period from 1978.11 to 1982.8.

2) In our estimations for the period 1973.4 to 1980.8 the coefficient of F_U is also significant with the expected positive sign in all cases. When we include both countries' stocks of domestic bonds, coefficients and t-ratios increase strongly.

over the whole investigation period. Furthermore, a comparison with the results given in table 1 suggests that the US CA gained markedly in influence against the Japanese CA over the period from 1978.11 to 1982.8.

Summing up, our monthly estimations for the overall time period from 1973.4 to 1982.8 provide support for the portfolio model only with respect to the exchange rate influence of the US CA.

Table 4 shows the estimation results with quarterly data for the period from 1973.I to 1982.II.

The results for eq. (1.1) indicate no radical change in the empirical evidence of BHM's version of the portfolio model in comparison to the monthly estimations. The strong changes in coefficients and RHO values which characterized the difference between monthly and quarterly estmations of the DM/$ rate cannot be observed in the ¥/$ case.[1)]

The coefficient of $M1_J$ still has the theoretically wrong negative sign which, however, is insignificant in the 2SLS and FAIR estimations. The coefficient of $M1_u$ takes the expected negative sign when eq. (1.1) is estimated together with the reaction function for Japan's central bank but is insignificant as well.

PF_J has the predicted negative coefficient when estimated with 2SLS and FAIR but is also not significant at the 95% level. The absolute value and the t-ratio of the PF_J coefficient declines considerably in the quarterly FAIR estimation. Only the coefficient of PF_u has the expected positive sign in all estimations and is significant at the 95% standard level.[2)] A comparison of the quarterly and the monthly FAIR estimates shows a higher value and a lower standard error of the quarterly coefficient of PF_u.

Thus, on the whole, our quarterly estimations of BHM's equation, in particular the FAIR regressions, confirm the monthly results. They support the portfolio model only with respect to the exchange rate influence of the US CA, represented by the PF_u variable.

---

1) In particular, the drastic decrease in autocorrelation in the quarterly regressions for the DM/$ rate does not occur for the ¥/$ exchange rate.

2) Except for the 2SLS regression where PF_u is significant only at the 90% level.

Table 4: Estimates for the Yen/$ Exchange Rate, Sample Period 1973.I - 1982.II, Quarterly Data. a) see table 1.

		BHM's Equation (Eq. 1.1)				PF Divided (Eq. 1.2)			
		OLS	CORC	2SLS	FAIR	OLS	CORC	2SLS	FAIR
C		279,96 (7,00)	174,69 (1,310)	337,64 (6,96)	292,91 (5,20)	372,83 (10,76)	315,41 (7,41)	374,52 (10,53)	335,73 (9,06)
$M1_J$	+	-0,0040* (-1,9351)	0,0003 (0,1587)	-0,0004 (-0,1601)	-0,0002 (-0,1073)	0,0012 (0,8156)	0,0015 (1,1301)	0,0031 (0,8382)	0,0011 (0,8697)
$M1_u$	./.	0,5698 (1,3176)	0,1071 (0,3408)	-0,1602 (-0,2928)	-0,0947 (-0,3194)	-0,3631 (-1,1946)	-0,2424 (-0,9794)	-0,3896 (-1,1873)	-0,2379 (-0,9514)
PF_J	./.	0,1637 (0,1558)	1,0129 (1,3854)	-2,0121 (-1,4127)	-0,0563 (-0,0605)				
F_J	./.					-0,9831 (-1,3883)	-1,0502 (-1,4985)	-1,0936 (-1,2500)	-1,0490 (-1,4015)
R_J	+					-3,4684* (-4,4118)	-3,2915* (-4,0574)	-3,2759* (-2,7520)	-2,9690* (-2,3501)
PF_u	+	1,8640* (3,3527)	1,8785* (2,8053)	0,9620 (1,3833)	1,5770* (2,5508)				
F_u	+					0,7338* (1,7902)	0,8228 (1,6488)	0,6999 (1,5929)	0,7092 (1,4616)
R_u	./.					1,6124 (1,1901)	0,0615 (0,0452)	1,5988 (1,1776)	0,2048 (0,1514)
$\bar{R}^2$		0,7127		0,6754		0,8904		0,8902	
$\hat{R}^2$			0,1342 b)		0,6745		0,6176		0,8410
F		23,95	2,395	17,17	17,10	51,10	10,69	41,88	27,33
DW		0,5079	1,7992	0,5351	1,7051	0,7726	1,9990	0,7668	1,9441
RHO			0,9230 (14,593)		0,8509 (10,443)		0,6950 (5,879)		0,6899 (5,089)

b) insignificant

Contrary to the results for BHM's equation, our quarterly estimates of eq. (1.2) do differ considerably from the corresponding monthly estimates. First of all, all coefficients - except for the intervention variables R_J and R_U - have the predicted sign.[1)] Most surprisingly perhaps, the coefficients of both countries' money supply variables $M1_J$ and $M1_U$ change their signs in the theoretically expected direction in all estimations. Nevertheless, none of them is significant at the 90% or 95% level.[2)]

So too, the coefficient of F_J, the cumulated Japanese CA, has the expected negative sign in all quarterly estimations. When we correct for autocorrelation, F_J is significant at the 90% level but not at the 95% standard level. In comparison to the monthly estimates we observe an increase in the absolute value of the F_J coefficient and a decrease in its standard error. Just the opposite is the case for the quarterly estimates of F_U: although the coefficient on F_U has the predicted positive sign and is significant at the 90% level in all estimations, its value decreases slightly and its standard error increases rather strongly compared to the monthly estimates.[3)]

Despite the fact that all money supply and CA coefficients have the predicted sign, it seems problematic to interpret the quarterly estimations of eq. (1.2) as support for the portfolio model. None of the M1 and F coefficients is significant at the 95% level and R_J as well as R_U have coefficients which are inconsistent with the theory.
A comparison of quarterly and monthly estimations and of the results for eq. (1.1) and eq. (1.2) demonstrates that support or rejection of the theory essentially depends on the exact specification of the test equation and on the periodicity of the data sample.

---

1) Although R_J is significant with the "wrong" negative sign also in the quarterly regressions, the absolute value of its coefficient declines slightly and the standard error increases in comparison with the monthly test.

2) The large change in the money supply coefficients suggests, as in the case of Germany, a high degree of collinearity between M1 and foreign exchange reserves. Regressions of the Japanese M1 on central bank reserves R_J, however, did not show a significant dependence when we corrected for autocorrelation.

3) The estimates for F_U changed in similar manner in the quarterly estimations of the DM/$ rate. These results might possibly indicate that interpolation errors in the monthly data series of F_U lead to an overestimation of the exchange rate influence of the US CA in the monthly estimations.

Finally, we turn briefly to the estimations of the reaction function for Japan's foreign exchange reserves. As in the case of the German Bundesbank, our regressions confirm the theoretical expectations. All coefficients are estimated with the predicted signs for all data sets: an increase (decrease) in the rate of depreciation of the yen against the dollar causes a decrease (increase) in Japan's foreign exchange reserves,[1)] and a devaluation of the PPP-target exchange rate against the actual ¥/$ rate - an increase in TAR - leads to an increase in R_J.

9.3.4. Summary

By and large, the empirical results for the portfolio model were very mediocre for the ¥/$ exchange rate.

In all monthly estimations of eq. (1.1) and eq. (1.2) the coefficient on the Japanese money stock $M1_J$ was estimated with a negative sign - opposite to the prediction of the model. So too, the coefficient of $M1_U$ took in all estimations of eq. (1.2) a "wrong" positive sign. In the few cases in which the US money stock M1 was estimated with the expected negative sign in eq. (1.1), the coefficient proved to be insignificant at standard levels. Furthermore, both money supply coefficients showed a very instable behaviour in all estimations. They reacted very sensitive to the estimation method, the specification of the test equation, and to the periodicity of the data. On the whole, our results for the exchange rate influence of changes in the Japanese and US money stock M1 do not support the portfolio model for neither investigation period.[2)]

The same conclusion applies to both countries' foreign exchange reserves. Our results suggest that central bank interventions in the foreign exchange market produce "perverse" exchange rate effects. The negative coefficients of R_J were even significant in all monthly and quarterly tests when we included the time period from 1978.11 to 1982.8 in the data sample. The positive coefficients on R_U, however,

---

1) However, the negative coefficient on $\Delta e(¥/\$)$ is not significantly different from zero in the monthly FAIR estimations for the complete sample period 1973.4 to 1982.8.

2) With the possible exception of the quarterly estimations of eq. (1.2) for the complete sample period 1973.I to 1982.II where $M1_U$ and $M1_J$ took the predicted signs but were insignificant, though.

were never significantly different from zero.
The results for the exchange rate effects of imbalances in the Japanese and the US CA are more favorable to the portfolio model. Our monthly estimations for the period from 1973.4 to 1978.10 support the view that movements in the ¥/$ rate were significantly influenced by the development in the Japanese CA. The coefficients of Japan's private net foreign asset stock, PF_J, as well as the coefficient of Japan's overall net foreign asset stock, F_J, had the predicted sign and they were significant in all tests.[1] The same holds for PF_u, However, when we divided the PF variables into their components and estimated the impact of the cumulated CAs separately, the US CA, represented by F_u, were no longer significant. This result suggests, as in the case of the DM/$ rate, that BHM's PF_u variable tends to overestimated the exchange rate influence of imbalances in the US CA.

When we included the forecasting period from 1978.11 to 1982.8 in the test, the picture changed drastically. The coefficients of PF_J and F_J frequently took signs opposite to those predicted by the theory.
When we corrected for autocorrelation in the monthly and quarterly simultaneous-equation estimations, both CA variables had the expected negative coefficient, they were however not significant at the 95% level. On the other hand, the coefficients of PF_u kept rather stable with significant positive signs. Moreover, the extension of the sample period brought about a strong increase in the value and in the t-ratio of the coefficient of F_u. Now the influence of F_u proved to be significant in the theoretically expected direction.[2] These changes in the estimates for the US and the Japanese CA suggest the following conclusion: from 1973.4 to 1978.10, movements in the ¥/$ exchange rate were dominated by developments in the Japanese CA. Afterwards, up to 1982.8, the significance of the Japanese CA for the ¥/$ rate declined strongly in comparison to the significance of the US CA.

---

1) Except for the PF_J estimate in the CORC regression.

2) At the 95% level in the monthly estimations, and at the 90% level in the quarterly regressions.

9.4. Results for the Pound Sterling/US Dollar Rate

9.4.1. Estimations for 1973.I to 1978.III

Table 1 shows the regression results for the £/$ exchange rate. The sample period runs from 1973, first quarter, to 1978, third quarter. We conduct all estimations with quarterly data series since data on the CA of the United Kingdom (UK) are not available on a monthly basis.

The results for BHM's equation are rather disappointing. Only the estimates for the UK money supply and the US private net stock of foreign assets correspond to the theoretical hypotheses: the coefficients on $M1_K$ always have the expected positive sign but they are never significant at standard levels. Merely the coefficients of PF_u are significant in all estimations with the predicted positive sign. The estimates for the US money supply $M1_u$ and the UK private net stock of foreign assets PF_K have signs opposite to those postulated by the theory in all cases. None of them, however, is significantly different from zero. Thus, our empirical results provide very little support for BHM's version of the portfolio model.

The empirical performance is not much better when the theory is tested in the form of eq. (1.2). The $M1_K$ coefficients still take the expected positive sign when we correct for autocorrelation but values and t-ratios of the coefficients decline in comparison to the results produced by eq. (1.1). The theoretically wrong positive coefficients of $M1_u$ increase in value and significance. On the other hand, our estimates for the cumulated CA of the UK, F_K, correspond better to the theory that the estimates for PF_K in eq. (1.1): when we correct for autocorrelation, F_K takes the predicted negative coefficient which, however, is not significant. On the whole, our estimations do not establish a theoretically consistent and significant impact of imbalances in the UK CA on the £/$ exchange rate.
The cumulated CA of the US, F_u, has the expected positive coefficient in all regressions but t-ratios are considerably lower than the t-ratios for the PF_u variable.

Table 1: Estimates for the £/$ Exchange Rate, Sample Period 1973.I - 1978.III, Quarterly Data. a) next page

		BHM's Equation (Eq. 1.1)				PF Divided (Eq. 1.2)			
		OLS	CORC	2SLS	FAIR	OLS	CORC	2SLS	FAIR
C		-5,4139 (-0,1831)	6,3810 (0,2071)	-2,8413 (-0,0914)	22,451 (0,7379)	-23,68 (-0,8270)	9,675 (0,3151)	-16,846 (-0,5484)	18,11 (0,6129)
$M1_K$	+	0,4656 (0,4711)	0,6157 (0,5559)	0,4689 (0,4739)	0,7219 (0,6488)	-0,4318 (-0,4165)	0,1463 (0,1278)	-0,7183 (-0,6424)	0,4023 (0,3552)
$M1_u$	./.	0,1579 (0,9909)	0,1015 (0,6055)	0,1474 (0,8980)	0,0358 (0,2164)	0,2822* (1,7690)	0,1215 (0,7294)	0,2706 (1,6040)	0,0850 (0,5220)
PF_K	./.	0,2834 (1,6129)	0,1617 (0,8023)	0,2505 (1,1727)	0,0265 (0,1123)				
F_K	./.					0,5711* (2,0370)	-0,3814 (-0,8385)	0,5273* (1,7692)	-0,2597 (-0,6133)
R_K	+					-0,0012 (-0,0058)	-0,2251 (-0,9280)	0,2801 (0,8953)	-0,3213 (-1,2618)
PF_u	+	0,3853* (7,8892)	0,3993* (5,6299)	0,3851* (7,8754)	0,3694* (4,9118)				
F_u	+					0,4539* (4,5275)	0,2234 (1,6591)	0,4872* (4,4661)	0,1921 (1,4046)
R_u	./.					2,5841 (1,2942)	2,7985 (1,5609)	3,5203 (1,5747)	2,6155 (1,4640)
$\bar{R}^2$		0,8974		0,8972		0,9117		0,9016	
$\hat{R}^2$			0,7544		0,7562		0,4856		0,7393
F		49,09	16,12	61,07	13,96	38,88	3,445	24,44	7,56
DW		1,1273	1,8752	1,1106	1,8721	1,5763	1,9059	1,6118	1,8802
RHO			0,4340 (2,2598)		0,5083 (2,5866)		0,6915 (4,4905)		0,7196 (4,5468)

Finally, the signs of the coefficients on both countries' official foreign exchange reserves, R_K and R_u, are in contradiction to the prediction of the theory.[1]

All in all, we may say that the empirical results for the £/$ rate are not favorable to the simple version of the portfolio model. Solely for the CA of the US we were able to establish a significant and theoretically consistent influence on the £/$ exchange rate.

9.4.2. Estimations for 1973.I to 1982.II

Because of the poor performance of the portfolio model over the period from 1973.I to 1978.III we did not calculate ex-post forecasts. Instead we move directly to our estimations for the extended investigation period from 1973.I to 1982.II (see table 2).

A first comparison of the estimates from table 1 with those reported in table 2 shows substantial changes. When we include the time from 1978.IV to 1982.II in the estimations, the coefficients on both countries' money supplies M1 take the theoretically expected signs in all regressions. The coefficients of $M1_K$ are significantly positive in eq. (1.1) as well as in eq. (1.2). Their values and t-ratios increase drastically in comparison to the results reported in table 1. $M1_u$, the US money stock, has the expected negative coefficient in all estimations but is not always significant at the 95% level.[2]

The large changes in the estimates for $M1_u$ and $M1_K$ suggest that movements in the £/$ rate over the period from 1978.IV to 1982.II were strongly influenced by monetary factors in both the UK and the US. In particular, our results support the view that the monetary policy of the UK government had a considerable impact, in the theoretically expected direction, on the £/$ exchange rate.

The results for the US CA too are quite favorable to the portfolio theory. The coefficient of PF_u has the expected positive sign and is

---

a) The £/$ rate is defined as pence per one US dollar, that is (£/$)·100 Subscripts K and u denote "United Kingdom" and "US", respectively. For further explanations see section 9.1.3.4.

1) Except for the coefficient of R_K in the 2SLS estimation.

2) $M1_u$ is significant at the 90% level in all estimations.

significant at the 95% level in all cases. In comparison with the PF_u results given in table 1, the values of the coefficients increase only slightly but standard errors decline considerably.
The same positive results hold for the F_u variable. The cumulated CA of the US is always significant with the expected sign when we include the time from 1978.IV to 1982.II in the sample. Compared with the first investigation period we observe a sharp increase in the significance of the US CA to movements in the £/$ rate.

While our estimates for the US CA support the portfolio model, the results for the CA of the UK contradict the theory almost completely. As for the shorter period, PF_K is estimated also for the complete sample period with a positive coefficient by all methods. The values of the coefficients, however, decrease in comparison to those shown in table 1, and none of the coefficients is significant at the 95% level. On the other hand, the coefficient on the cumulated overall CA of the UK is significant with a "wrong" positive sign in all equations (except CORC) suggesting a perverse exchange rate effect of UK CA imbalances: a surplus (deficit) in the UK CA causes a depreciation (appreciation) of sterling against the dollar. It is interesting, however, that PF_K and F_K tend to have the predicted negative coefficient when we include both countries' net stocks of domestic bonds PB in the regression.[1) 2)]

Finally, we mention another notable outcome of our test. When we extend the investigation period, the coefficients on official foreign exchange reserves of both countries, R_K and R_u, have the predicted signs in almost all estimations.[3)] When estimated with 2SLS they are significant at the 95% level. These estimates suggest that foreign exchange interventions of the Federal Reserve and the Bank of England had the theoretically expected and significant impact on the £/$ exchange rate over the period from 1978.IV to 1982.II. Conversely, our estimations of the reaction function for foreign exchange interventions by UK authorities indicate significant repercussions of changes in the £/$ rate on the stock of foreign exchange reserves.[4)]

---

1) These negative coefficients are, however, never significant at standard levels;in fact, t-ratios are close to zero.

2) It is furthermore interesting that PB_U always has the expected positive coefficient and is significant at the 95% level. Contrary to this, PB_K frequently changes sign and is never significant.

3) and 4) See next page.

Table 2: Estimates for the £/$ Exchange Rate, Sample Period 1973.I - 1982.II, Quarterly Data. a) see table 1.

		BHM's Equation (Eq. 1.1)				PF Divided (Eq.1.2)			
		OLS	CORC	2SLS	FAIR	OLS	CORC	2SLS	FAIR
C		61,29 (6,852)	46,49 (3,978)	61,28 (6,847)	48,38 (4,381)	55,35 (4,386)	37,90 (2,399)	62,42 (4,542)	54,40 (3,953)
$M1_K$	+	2,0550* (5,1440)	1,3490* (2,7879)	2,0516* (5,1317)	1,3713* (2,8641)	1,8442* (4,2490)	0,9679* (1,8041)	1,7904* (3,8743)	1,5320* (3,1071)
$M1_u$	·/.	-0,1802* (-3,3757)	-0,0877 (-1,3301)	-0,1804* (-3,3761)	-0,0952 (-1,4740)	-0,1496* (-2,2190)	-0,0281 (-0,2940)	-0,1781* (-2,4508)	-0,1325* (-1,7967)
PF_K	·/.	0,0647 (1,5938)	0,0645 (0,9674)	0,0559 (1,3625)	0,0476 (0,7352)				
F_K	·/.					0,1909* (1,8971)	-0,0889 (-0,4114)	0,3213* (2,6767)	0,2719* (1,9276)
R_K	+					0,0913 (0,5078)	-0,5176* (-2,1345)	0,4531* (1,8604)	0,3340 (1,2198)
PF_u	+	0,4652* (11,2760)	0,4656* (6,3980)	0,4642* (11,2402)	0,4502* (6,9256)				
F_u	+					0,5062* (7,8849)	0,2460* (1,8611)	0,6004* (7,6216)	0,5610* (6,1564)
R_u	·/.					-0,7569* (-2,3347)	-0,4053 (-1,1869)	-0,6202* (-1,7746)	-0,6910* (-1,9529)
$\bar{R}^2$		0,8478		0,8476		0,8481		0,8282	
$\hat{R}^2$			0,6119		0,6760		0,2476		0,7311
F		52,53	15,19	45,88	17,21	35,42	2,969	24,90	14,05
DW		1,2621	2,0511	1,2618	2,0734	1,4174	2,1190	1,5666	1,9217
RHO			0,4912 (3,4299)		0,4874 (3,2988)		0,7827 (7,6489)		0,2623b) (1,5348)

b) insignificant

Recapitulating our results, it is surprising that the extension of the investigation period to 1982.II brought about such a considerable change in results in favour of the portfolio model. All asset variables - except for the net foreign asset stock of the UK - were estimated with the theoretically expected coefficients and, in most cases, also as significantly different from zero.
Our estimations suggest that during the period from 1978.IV to 1982.II movements in the £/$ rate were strongly influenced by changes in the US and UK money supplies and by imbalances in the US CA. On the other hand, it is astonishing that we cannot confirm the frequently advanced opinion about the high importance of the UK CA to the £/$ rate.

9.4.3. Summary

The most remarkable feature of our test for the £/$ exchange rate consists in the substantial change in estimation results when we included the period from 1978.IV to 1982.II in the sample.

For the shorter period from 1973.I to 1978.III we found very little support for the portfolio model. On the contrary, our estimations provide good reasons to reject the simple portfolio model for the £/$ exchange rate. According to our regressions, only the US CA had a significant and theoretically consistent impact on the £/$ rate.

However, when we reestimated the test equations for the complete sample period from 1973.I to 1982.II, all variables took the predicted signs and were significant in almost all cases - with one important exception: the two variables representing net foreign asset stocks of the UK, PF_K and F_K, had coefficients opposite to those predicted by the theory.

Our results suggest that over the time from 1978.IV to 1982.II changes in asset stocks others than PF_K and F_K had a strong effect, in the theoretically expected direction, on the £/$ rate. In particular, it seems that over this period monetary policy played a pivotal role for the £/$ rate.

(footnote 3. p. 270) The only exception is the coefficient of R_K when estimated with CORC.

(footnote 4. p. 270) In our regressions of the UK reaction function all variables have the expected coefficients at the 95% significance level. The results are given in the appendix.

Our test once more demonstrates that support or rejection of the portfolio theory depends crucially on the respective sample period. A relatively small variation in the sample may lead to totally different results for the complete investigation period.

9.5. Summary and Conclusions

Having estimated different versions of the standard portfolio model for three different exchange rates and different time periods one certainly feels the need for a summary in order to get a condensed impression about the empirical validity of the theory. Unfortunately, the diversity of our results does not allow for general conclusions. Except for one conclusion, perhaps: the standard portfolio balance model is certainly not capable of providing an universal guideline for explaining movements in floating exchange rates.
Support or rejection of the portfolio model depends not only on the investigated exchange rate but in like manner on the sample period, the precise test specification, and on the periodicity of the data used in the estimations. Nevertheless, it might be useful to summarize some of our results and to indicate possible implications for the significance of the various asset variables in short run exchange rate determination.

The first estimation period ran from early 1973 to late 1978. Our regressions for the DM/$ rate provided some support for the portfolio model. All asset variables, except for US and German foreign exchange reserves, tended to have the expected coefficients. Thus, our study confirms the results of BHM's and MD's analyses.

In our estimations of the ¥/$ rate the empirical verdict on the theory was not so favorable. The coefficients on the US and Japan's money and reserve stocks had mostly signs opposite to those predicted by the theory. On the other hand, our regressions indicated a significant and theoretically consistent influence of the Japanese CA on the ¥/$ rate. All in all, our results confirm the previous findings of Martin and Masson's empirical study.

Applied to the £/$ exchange rate, the portfolio model proved to be a rather unsatisfactory instrument for explaining exchange rate movements. According to our estimations, merely the US CA had a theoretically consistent and significant impact on the £/$ rate.

With respect to the empirical performance of single asset variables we consider the following two results as particularly interesting. First, in the case of Japan and Germany we were able to establish a significant exchange rate impact of domestic CA imbalances. Sencond, in all FAIR estimations changes in the domestic and the US money stock never had a significant exchange rate effect for none of the three investigated exchange rates.

Our attempts to forecast the DM/$ and the ¥/$ rate for the period from 1978.11 to 1982.8 on the basis of the exchange rate equations estimated for the foregoing period from 1973.4 to 1978.10 failed almost completely. The large deviations of the predicted exchange rates from their actual values indicated a substantial change in the relative importance of the underlying exchange rate determinants. This conjecture was confirmed by the regression results for the extended sample period from early 1973 to late 1982.

In the monthly estimations for the ¥/$ rate the significant impact of the Japanese CA vanished and most of the other variables were estimated with coefficients which contradicted the theory.

In the case of the DM/$ rate, only the German and the US CA variables were estimated in accordance with the theory and as significant at the 95% level.

For both the DM/$ and the ¥/$ rate we found that the money supply variables frequently took coefficients with "wrong" signs. On the other hand, our estimations suggest an increase in the relative importance of the US CA for both exchange rates.

In general, we may say that the inclusion of the time from 1978.11 to 1982.8 affected the empirical performance of the portfolio model negatively in the case of the DM/$ and ¥/$ exchange rate.

The quarterly estimations for the complete investigation period brought about an improvement in the performance of the theory in comparison with the monthly results. The portfolio model generally worked better on a quarterly basis. A possible explanation for this improvement in results was already given above: the use of quarterly data might suppress volatile speculation influences on the exchange rates which, in the case of monthly data, could conceal the significance of fundamental asset factors.

Contrary to the Japanese and German case, we observed a considerable change in the estimation results in favour of the portfolio model for the UK when we extended the data sample. For the period from 1973.I to 1982.III all asset variables, except for the UK CA, were estimated in accordance with the theory.

Regarding our results for the single asset variables we are in a similar difficult position as with the asset market model as a whole: our estimations do not allow for general and clear-cut conclusions on the relative importance of the various asset variables in exchange rate determination.

The estimated exchange rate influence of changes in domestic and foreign money stocks contradicted the theoretical prediction in the case of the ¥/$ rate for the whole investigation period.

Our results for the money stock variables were likewise disappointing for the DM/$ rate when we included the period from 1978.11 to 1982.8 in the sample, and for the £/$ rate over the period from 1973.I to 1978.III. Thus, our tests lend little support to the hypothesis of a central role of relative money supplies in exchange rate determination.

The theoretical presumptions about the importance of imbalances in the domestic CA were supported for the DM/$ rate for all CA-measures and for all test periods.

In the case of the ¥/$ rate the CA-hypothesis was supported for the time from early 1973 to late 1978. However, when we extended the investigation period to late 1982, the significance of the Japanese CA variables diminished strongly.

Our estimates for the influence of the UK CA on the £/$ rate, on the other hand, contradicted the theory almost completely for all test periods.

The coefficients on the US CA variables tended to have the predicted positive sign in almost all cases. Thus, our test supports the view that imbalances in the US CA had the theoretically expected impact on all three exchange rates during all investigation periods.

Finally, the coefficients on the domestic and foreign official foreign exchange reserves had signs opposite to those predicted by the theory in almost all cases. The only exception was the estimation for the £/$ rate when the period from 1978.IV to 1982.II was included in the sample. Hence, the conventional opinion concerning the exchange rate impact of official foreign exchange market interventions is not supported by our tests.

10. Diversified Current-Account Financing: Some Empirical Signs of Its Significance in the Deutsche Mark/US Dollar Case

10.1. An Outline of the Problem

The empirical analysis in chapter nine has been conducted under the assumption that all international claims and liabilities are denominated in US dollar. By virtue of this assumption it was possible to relate any CA imbalance to changes in net stocks of dollar bonds ($CAS = \Delta NFP = \Delta F$). For major industrial countries, however, it is rather unrealistic to consider dollar denominated assets as the only internationally negotiable financial instruments. Therefore we dropped this assumption in the theoretical part of the thesis and presented in chapter five a two-country-four-asset model in which bonds denominated in domestic and foreign currency have both been regarded as tradeable. This extension has strong implications for CA financing: when we allow for two internationally accepted assets, any CA imbalance and thus any change in a country's net foreign asset position may accrue in the form of changed stocks of domestic and/or foreign assets ($CAS = \Delta NFP = e\,\Delta F + \Delta B$). The exchange rate effect of CA imbalances may be different for domestic and foreign bond CA financing depending on the specific way in which the respective wealth components affect asset demands. The short taxonomy of the theoretical results derived in chapter five is repeated in table 1.[1)]

Since we have no information about the actual form of asset demand functions, it is not possible to give a clear-cut theoretical answer to the question whether diversified CA financing really matters for the exchange rate impact of CA imbalances.

In this chapter now we attempt to approach this question from the empirical side. For the subsequent analysis we choose the DM/$ rate on a quarterly basis as reference exchange rate.[2)]

---

1) The symbols used in table 1 refer to the two-country model in chapter five.

2) This choice is dictated by the availability of data necessary for dividing the CAs into a domestic-currency and a foreign-currency denominated part.

Table 1: Taxonomy of the Exchange Rate Influence of Diversified CA Financing in the Two-Country Case.

Home Country: Germany (DM); Foreign Country: United States ($).

	Case a. Asset demands depend on the general level of wealth	Case b. Asset demands depend on the wealth components
	≡ A change in wealth induces a change in asset demands which is independent of the source of the wealth change.	≡ A change in wealth induces a change in asset demands which depends on (differs according to) the particular form of the wealth change.
Results for the relative exchange rate impact of the currency parts of the current account	CA financing with DM or $ assets has <u>equal</u> effects on the DM/$ rate.	CA financing with DM or $ assets has <u>different</u> effects on the DM/$ rate.
Results for the effect of CA imbalances on the exchange rate	The exchange rate reacts <u>normally</u> to CA imbalances if, but not only if:	The exchange rate reacts <u>normally</u> to CA imbalances if, but not only if:
	A1: The response of money demands to changes in the domestic interest rate is (in absolute terms) stronger than the response to changes in the foreign interest rate (for both countries). $\lvert m_r \rvert > \lvert m_{r^*} \rvert$ and $\lvert n_{r^*} \rvert > \lvert n_r \rvert$ Equivalent to the assumption that domestic money is a better substitute for domestic bonds than for foreign bonds (for both countries).	A1: See case a.
	A2: Preferred local habitat: the part of wealth (or the part of the change in wealth) which is desired to be held in domestic bonds is greater at home than abroad. Linear homogenity: $b > b^*$ General case : $\beta_W > \beta^*_{W^*}$	A2: Preferred local habitat: for DM financing: $\beta_{PB} > \beta^*_{PB^*}$ for $ financing: $\beta_{PF} > \beta^*_{PF^*}$ Since β_{PB} may differ from β_{PF} (and $\beta^*_{PB^*}$ from $\beta^*_{PF^*}$) a combination of a normal/anormal reaction of the exchange rate is possible.
	A3: Identical international preferences for domestic and foreign bonds. Linear homogenity: $b = b^*$ General case : $\beta_W = \beta^*_{W^*}$	A3: Identical international (marginal) preferences for domestic and foreign bonds. for DM financing: $\beta_{PB} = \beta^*_{PB^*}$ for $ financing: $\beta_{PF} = \beta^*_{PF^*}$
	If money demands depend on wealth, conditions A1 and A3 are sufficient for a normal exchange rate reaction.	Equal to case a.
	If money demands are independent of wealth ($\eta_{W^*} = \mu_W = 0$), A1 and A2 are necessary and sufficient for a normal exchange rate reaction.	Equal to case a.

In a first step we lay down a simple theoretical framework for the division of the CA into two currency parts:

a. The domestic-currency denominated CA, including all CA transactions which are invoiced in domestic currency. Surpluses and deficits in this part of the overall CA can be identified with shifts of domestic-currency denominated claims and liabilities ("domestic bonds") between the domestic and the foreign sector.

b. The foreign-currency denominated CA, including all CA transactions which are invoiced in foreign currency. Imbalances in this second part of the CA cause shifts in foreign-currency denominated asset stocks ("foreign bonds").

This framework then will be applied to the US and German CA reality. We report evidence for the actual currency composition of both countries' CAs which may give a clue to the importance of diversified CA financing in the US/German case.

Finally, we make an attempt to estimate the relative exchange rate impact of both currency parts of the CA on the DM/$ exchange rate. This test, however, suffers from inconsistencies and shortcomings which necessarily arise when a two-country model is put to an empirical test in a multi-country world. We discuss these problems first and conclude with a report on our tentative estimation results.

10.2. The Real and the Financial Side of Current Account Transactions

Building on the theoretical foundation already presented in section 5.2. we develop in the following a theoretical model for the analysis of the link between actual CA transactions (the "real side") and international shifts in asset stocks denominated in different currencies (the "financial side").

In section 5.2. we distinguished between two internationally traded assets: domestic-currency (DM) and foreign-currency (dollar) denominated bonds. We denoted the stock of net foreign assets held by private domestic (German) residents as PF and the stock of net domestic assets held by private foreign (US) residents as PB^*. As a result of our considerations we wrote the CA surplus of the home country (Germany), expressed in domestic currency units (DM), as:[1)]

$$CAS = e\,\Delta PF - \Delta PB^*$$

A surplus in the home country's CA corresponds to an increase in the domestic stock of foreign assets PF and/or to a decrease in the foreign stock of domestic assets PB^*.

$e\,\Delta PF$ denotes the part of the domestic CA which is financed with foreign bonds and hence represents the "foreign-currency denominated CA" (expressed in domestic currency).

ΔPB^* denotes the remaining part of the domestic CA, financed with domestic bonds and thus describes the "domestic-currency denominated CA.

As an accounting identity the financial side of the CA must be equal to the real side:

$$(1') \quad CAS = e\,\Delta PF - \Delta PB^* = X - Im$$

---

1) For the sake of continuity, we abstract here, as in section 5.2. from changes in central bank holdings of domestic and foreign assets. Accordingly, a change in the overall net foreign asset position implies a change in the private net foreign asset position, and, thus, any CA imbalance leads to an equiproportional change in private asset stocks.

where X and Im are expressed in domestic currency and are defined as:

X : total positive entries in the CA ("exports"), comprising total exports of goods and services plus total claims from unrequited transfers.

Im : total negative entries in the CA ("imports"), comprising total imports of goods and services plus total liabilities from unrequited transfers.

A direct empirical application of eq. (1'), however, is impeded by two problems. Firstly, no direct data are available on the currency composition of the financial side of the CA. And, secondly, it is not possible to attach exports and imports to changes in one specific asset stock: a change in PF may be due to export and/or import transactions, and the same applies to changes in PB^*.

To solve this problem we define ΔPF_x as the change in the stock of foreign assets which is due to export transactions and ΔPF_{im} as the change in PF due to imports. ΔPF then can be written

$$(2) \qquad e\ \Delta PF = e\ (\Delta PF_x + \Delta PF_{im})$$

An analogous relationsship holds for the change in the stock of domestic-currency denominated liabilities to the foreign sector:

$$(3) \qquad -\ \Delta PB^* = -\ (\Delta PB^*_x + \Delta PB^*_{im})$$

Now we introduce the following ratios:

$\alpha^x = (e\ \Delta PF_x/X)$: share of exports which is associated with a change in PF. α^x can be approximated by the share of exports which is denominated (invoiced) in foreign currency.

$\alpha^{im} = (e\ \Delta PF_{im}/Im)$: share of imports which causes changes in the stock of foreign assests. α^{im} can also be approximated by the share of imports which is invoiced in foreign currency units.

The application of these ratios allows us to rewrite eqs. (2) and (3) in terms of export and import values:

$$(4) \qquad e\ \Delta PF = \alpha^{x}\ X \ - \ \alpha^{im}\ Im$$

$$(5) \qquad -\ \Delta PB^{*} = (1 - \alpha^{x})\ X \ - \ (1 - \alpha^{im})\ Im$$

Both eqs. (4) and (5) can be introduced in eq. (1') to arrive at the desired result:

$$(1) \qquad CAS = \underbrace{[\alpha^{x}\ X - \alpha^{im}\ Im]}_{e\ \Delta PF} + \underbrace{[(1 - \alpha^{x})\ X - (1 - \alpha^{im})\ Im]}_{-\ \Delta PB^{*}} = X - Im$$

Eq. (1) shows that the CA can be divided into a foreign-currency and a domestic-currency part on the basis of data on gross exports and imports provided that we have information on the actual values of α^{x} and α^{im}. Given the data sources available, however, these ratios can only be determined approximately.

The empirical application of eq. (1) to the US and German CA is furthermore aggravated by another problem. The theoretical two-country identity between domestic CA surpluses and foreign CA deficits does not hold for the US and Germany. The vast major y of CA transactions of both countries relates to exports and imports with third-countries. That means that the theoretical correspondence between changes in asset stocks $\Delta PF = -\ \Delta PF^{*}$ and $\Delta PB = -\ \Delta PB^{*}$ can not be maintained for the US/German CA reality. Thus, when we divide both countries' CAs into their currency parts we have to determine α^{x} and α^{im} separately for the US and for Germany. Apart from doubling the calculation work, this non-correspondence does not constitute a serious problem for the currency classification of both CAs; but it does have major consequences for the empirical test in the next section.

Table 2 shows our first estimates for the α-ratios. The most important simplifying assumption underlying these α-estimates consists in the supposition that the currency composition of overall CA transactions is approximately reflected in the currency composition of claims and liabilities from commercial transactions.[1] Taking this for granted, table 2 allows for some interesting conclusions.

On average over the period from 1974 to 1982 around 76% of German claims from CA transactions were denominated in DM,[2] and only the remaining minor part of 24% in foreign currency. For the import side of the German CA the average DM-share amounts to 64% and thus is somewhat lower than the DM-share of the export side. Our results suggest that the DM plays a major role in both German export and import transactions. Imbalances in the German CA seem to lead to a large extent to changes in DM denominated claims and liabilities, that is, in terms of the portfolio theory, to changes in the stock of DM bonds.

Not surprisingly, the dominant use of domestic-currency denominated financial instruments in CA transactions is even more pronounced for the US. From 1978 to 1982 an average value of about 96% of US claims and about 91% of US liabilities from CA transactions were denominated in dollar. Foreign-currency assets appear to be of very low significance for the financial side of US CA transactions.

For both countries we find, so too not unexpected, that foreign currencies are relatively more used in import transactions than in export transactions.

Table 3 confronts our α-estimates with previous results reported in the literature on the choice of invoicing currency in merchandise trade.

---

1) There are some other inaccuracies incorporated in the data, e.g., in the case of Germany commercial claims and liabilities must be reported to the Bundesbank only if the sum of financial and commercial claims and liabilities exceeds the amount of 100.000 DM (from August 1982 on 500.000 DM).

2) With a slight but continuous trend downwards.

Table 2: Estimates of Foreign-Currency Shares in German and US Claims and Liabilities from Current Account Transactions.[a)]

	1974	1975	1976	1977	1978	1979	1980	1981	1982
α_G^x	0,19	0,23	0,22	0,24	0,25	0,26	0,27	0,29	0,28
α_G^{im}	0,36	0,36	0,35	0,34	0,34	0,35	0,39	0,38	0,36
α_u^x	--	--	--	--	0,032	0,035	0,032	0,035	0,046
α_u^{im}	--	--	--	--	0,107	0,081	0,087	0,102	0,072

a) Subscripts G and u denote Germany and the US, respectively.

α^x = share of 'exports' which are denominated in foreign currency in total 'exports' (positive entries in the CA).

α^{im}= share of 'imports' which are denominated in foreign currency in total 'imports' (negative entries in the CA).

α-ratios for Germany are calculated on the basis of Bundesbank data on "Forderungen und Verbindlichkeiten inländischer Unternehmen gegenüber dem Ausland aus Zahlungszielen und Anzahlungen im Waren- und Dienstleistungsverkehr"; claims and liabilities are measured at the end of the year; source: Statistische Beihefte zu den Monatsberichten der Deutschen Bundesbank, Reihe 3: Zahlungsbilanzstatistik, Table 9d; data series start in 1974.

α-ratios for the US are based on data on "claims and liabilities to unaffiliated foreigners from trade, advanced receipts and payments, and other commercial claims an liabilities reported by nonbanking business enterprises in the US"; end-of-year data; source: Federal Reserve Bulletin, A64, tables 3.22 (line 7, 10, 11) and 3.23 (line 11, 14, 15); data series start in 1978.

Table 3: Different Estimates for the Foreign-Currency Share in German and US Current Account Transactions [a)]

	1	2	3
	ø (1972 - 1976)	1980	ø from table 2
α_G^x	0,13	0,18	0,24
α_G^{im}	0,56	0,57	0,36
α_u^x	--	0,02	0,04
α_u^{im}	--	0,15	0,09

a) column 1: average foreign-currency shares in merchandise exports and imports, respectively, over the period 1972 through 1976; single values: α_G^x (1972 = 0,16; 1973 = 0,14; 1974 = 0,12; 1975 = 0,11; 1976 = 0,13), source: Page (1977), Scharrer and others (1978); α_G^{im} (1972 = 0,50; 1973 = missing; 1974 = 0,58; 1975 = 0,57; 1976 = 0,58), source: Scharrer and others (1978).

column 2: foreign-currency shares in merchandise exports and imports, respectively, in 1980; source: Page (1981).

column 3: average foreign-currency shares in claims and liabilities, respectively, from commercial CA transactions over the period 1974 through 1982 (Germany) and 1978 through 1982 (US); source: see table 2.

Table 3 shows rather pronounced differences between our α-estimations, calculated from table 2 and shown in column 3 and those reported by Page (1977, 1981) and Scharrer and others (1978). This holds true no matter if we compare average α-values calculated, however, for different time periods, or single α-values for each year.In particular, the results for the German α^{im}-ratio differ considerably: whereas our estimations yield an average DM share in German liabilities from CA transactions of 64% the estimations of Page and Scharrer of 43% and 44%, respectively, suggest a much lower share for the DM.

These deviations can be explained by the different data sets and definitions underlying the calculations. Our α-ratios in table 2 and in column 3 of table 3 are based on the currency composition of claims and liabilities from trade and service account transactions reported by business enterprises. Hence, the estimated foreign-currency shares relate to the stock of claims and liabilities. The estimates of Page and Scharrer (table 3, colums 1 and 2) cover only merchandise trade. Furthermore, the estimated foreign-currency share in German merchandise exports is based on statements of German exporters in the customs declaration[1)] while the α-ratio for German merchandise imports is calculated from data on the currency used in payments. Basically, the currency shares in columns 1 and 2 refer to increases and decreases in asset stocks due to merchandise trade and thus, they are flow ratios.[2)]

Nevertheless, the general tendency in the estimations confirms our above conclusions:

a. Domestic-currency invoicing dominates in both countries' CA transactions. In all estimations the foreign-currency share in German "exports" exceeds never 30%. For the import side the foreign-currency share varies between 34% and 58%. In the case of the US, the foreign-currency share in "exports" is with 2% - 4% almost negligible and still very low for the import side (7% - 15%).

b. The foreign-currency share is for both countries higher on the import side than on the export side.

With regard to our initial question about the relevance of diversified CA financing in the case of Germany and the US we are now in the posi-

---

1) Since 1975 export claims are reported only if they exceed 50.000 DM in every single case. According to Scharrer and others (1978, p.139) this led to a decline in the ratio of currency-wise registered export claims to total German exports from 92% in 1972/1974 to 61,5% in 1975 and 63,1% in 1976.

2) Differences arising from the use of stock and flow data are crucial only if the maturity of claims and liabilities from CA transactions exceeds one year. This, however, applies only to a minor part of German CA claims and liabilities; see Scharrer and others (1978).

tion to draw the following conclusions.[1] A strict correspondence between CA imbalances and changes in the stock of foreign-currency denominated assets, implied by the assumption of only one internationally traded asset, does certainly not hold true for the German CA.[2] To the contrary, imbalances in the German CA can be expected to cause primarily changes in the stock of DM claims and liabilities and only to a minor extent changes in foreign-currency asset stocks. Thus, diversified CA financing is highly significant in the German case. For the US an almost complete domestic-currency (dollar) financing seems to be the rule.

Proceeding from our estimations of the α-ratios, in a next step we divide the German and the US CA into their domestic and foreign-currency parts by applying eq. (1). As above, X and Im are defined as total positive and negative CA entries, respectively, on a quarterly basis.[3] The α-ratios from table 2 are assumed to be constant within each year. Calculations have been conducted for three different time periods under alternative assumptions on the α-ratios.

a. 1978.II to 1982.II. α-ratios for this period are available for both countries from table 2. However, the time-span from 1978.II to 1982.II includes only 17 observations. Such a small number of observations might introduce instabilities in the subsequent exchange rate estimations.

---

1) The application and interpretation of the above results is guided by the final aim of the analysis, namely the examination of the significance of diversified CA financing for exchange rate effects of imbalanced CAs. Besides that, the currency composition of exports and imports has major implications for the existence and the strength of J-curve effects. A discussion of this problem, however, is outside of the question we are dealing with here. On this point see Magee (1973), Page (1977, 1981), Magee and Rao (1980).

2) Nor does it for other industrial countries. The "Grassman-Rule" (Grassman 1973), which appears to hold for most of these countries, provides a rough yardstick for the currency composition of CA transactions. According to this rule, two-thirds of trade is denominated in the exporter's currency and one-fourth is denominated in the importer's currency. More detailed empirical evidence is contained in Page (1977, 1981), Scharrer and others (1978), Carse and Wood (1979), Magee and Rao (1980), Bilson (1983).

3) Since we have no information on the currency composition of unrequited transfers, they have been attached to the import side. Assuming equal foreign-currency shares in import transactions and in unrequited transfers is certainly an oversimplification.

b. 1974.II to 1982.II. To extend the sample period beyond the point from which on estimations for US α-ratios can be obtained (1978) we substitute the missing US values for the period from 1974 to 1977 by average α-ratios calculated over the period from 1978 to 1982 ($\alpha_U^x = 0{,}036$ and $\alpha_U^{im} = 0{,}090$ for 1974 to 1977).

c. 1973.I to 1982.II. For the third period we attempt to take into account possible over- and underestimations of the actual α-ratios by our estimations given in table 2. In particular, our results for the foreign-currency share in German imports lie considerably below the values indicated by the other estimations in table 3. As an alternative to the estimations from table 2 we use the following "corrected average values" of the α-ratios: $\alpha_G^x = 0{,}2$; $\alpha_G^{im} = 0{,}55$; $\alpha_U^x = 0{,}03$; $\alpha_U^{im} = 0{,}12$. These ratios are taken as constant over the complete sample period.

Despite different α-ratios and time periods, the qualitative results of our computations prove to be identical in all calculations a. to c. The foreign-currency denominated part of the US CA and the German CA shows constantly deficits over all time periods. In other words, the (quarterly) balance between foreign-currency denominated claims and liabilities from CA transactions is permanently negative for both countries. This result is insofar not surprising as the foreign-currency share in imports (liabilities from import transactions) exceeds for both countries the foreign-currency share in exports (claims from export transactions). On the other hand, the domestic-currency denominated part of both countries' CAs is almost continuously in surplus over all investigation periods.[1)]

Our results indicate that the development of both countries' total CAs over the period from 1973.I to 1982.II was connected with a continuous decline in both countries' stocks of foreign-currency denominated assets and with a continuous increase[2)] in both countries' stocks of domestic-currency denominated assets.

---

1) There are some exceptions for the dollar-part of the US CA. Our calculations yield deficits for the quarterly US dollar-CA in 1974.III, 1977.III and 1977.IV, 1978.I and 1978.III (calculation method b.), and in 1977.III, 1978.I and 1978.III (calculation method c.).

2) With the exceptions mentioned in footnote 1.

10.3. Testing the Portfolio Balance Model with Diversified Current Account Financing

10.3.1. Theoretical Implications of Diversified Current Account Financing for the DM/$ Exchange Rate Equation

Having divided the US and German CA into a domestic-currency and a foreign-currency part, we now have to introduce these parts into the empirical reduced form of the portfolio balance model.

In converting the theoretical exchange rate model for diversified CA financing into an empirically testable form we face the same problem that has already been discussed above: the model results have been derived for a closed two-country world in which the CA surplus of one country is the exact mirror image of the CA deficit of the other country. In such a world one CA, divided into its currency parts, completely reflects the asset transfer involved in CA imbalances. An empirical investigation, however, is confronted with a multi-country world. By far the largest part of US and German CA transactions is done with third-countries and not with each other. Consequently, the counterpart of CA induced changes in German and US asset stocks is to be found mainly in third-country portfolios. Our theoretical model, however, does not consider impacts from asset shifts with third-countries on the bilateral DM/$ rate. As long as we assumed that only one asset is internationally negotiable (dollar bonds), the multi-country model of Martin and Masson provided a consistent theoretical foundation for determining third-country effects on the bilateral exchange rate. In the case of two internationally traded assets (dollar and DM bonds) we have no consistent theoretical model-background for precise predictions on third-country influences.

As a way out of the problem we could consider using only a bilateral measure of US and German CA transactions in the empirical test.
The disadvantages of this approach have already been discussed in chapter eight:

a. We have no data on bilateral CA transactions between the US and Germany. Calculating artificial proxy-time-series or reducing the CA to bilateral trade flows, for which data are available, would introduce further inconsistencies and data errors into the estimations.

b. If we take the German CA as basis in calculating bilateral US/German CA flows and if we use bilateral US/German trade flows as proxy for bilateral CA flows, we would exclude more than 90% of all German CA transactions. That is, we would have to assume that more than 90% of the German CA, and even a larger part of the US CA, have no impact at all on the DM/$ rate. A three-country model incorporating two internationally traded assets may yield no clear-cut conclusions on the DM/$ exchange rate impact of German and US CA imbalances with third-countries but a general zero-effect will certainly be only a very special case.[1)]

Mainly for these two reasons[2)] we decided to use both the US and the German overall CA, divided into their respective currency parts, in the regressions. This, however, means that our estimation results for DM/$ exchange rate effects of imbalances in the German and US CA include effects of CA imbalances with third-countries for which we have no theoretical model predictions.

A second empirical problem ensues from the specification of the term "foreign currency" in determining the foreign-currency denominated part of the US and the German CA. In the subsequent empirical estimations

---

1) There are no fundamental difficulties in developing such a model along the lines laid out in the first part of the thesis. Nevertheless, when we attempted to calculate an extended general model (with asset demands linear homogeneous in wealth) the solution proved to be very messy. The signs of the comparative-static multipliers depend on the relative amounts of assets initially held in portfolios and on the relative desired asset shares in each country and on the degree of substitutability of assets in each country reflected in the respective interest elasticities. The list of assumptions necessary to determine unambigious signs of the multipliers would be extensive and completely ad hoc. This outcome suggests that even slight extensions in scope can easily push portfolio models of the general form employed here to the limits for giving clear and intuitive theoretical answers. Another example supporting this conclusion in the case of an extended two-country model is given by Tobin and Macedo (1980).

2) A further obstacle, for instance, consists in determining bilateral α-ratios. The available data cover only merchandise trade and only very few years.

the dollar is taken as the foreign currency in the case of Germany, and the DM represents the foreign currency for the US. That is, we assume that all CA transactions, if not denominated in the respective domestic currency, are denominated in dollar for Germany and in DM for the US. As a result, we abstract from the use of currencies others than DM and dollar also in the case of CA imbalances with third-countries. This assumption, though in line with the theoretical model, constitutes of course an unrealistic simplification in an empirical application.[1)]

The regression equation used in the following estimations is an extended version of the equation already used in chapter ten. The essential difference consists in the division of both countries' CA variables into a domestic-currency and a foreign-currency part.

$$e\ (DM/\$) = a_0 + a_1\ M1_G + a_2\ M1_u + a_3\ FD_G + a_4\ FM_G + a_5\ R_G + \\ + a_6\ FD_u + a_7\ FM_u + a_8\ R_u + a_9\ PB_G + a_{10}\ PB_u + u$$

All variables are measured at time t (end-of-quarter). The subscripts G and u denote Germany and US, respectively.

Money supplies $M1_G$, $M1_u$, and bond supplies PB_G, PB_u are defined as in chapter ten. The stocks of foreign exchange reserves held by the German and the US central bank, R_G and R_u, are also defined as above with the only exception that R_u is now expressed in DM.

FD_G, FM_u : Net stocks of foreign-currency denominated assets resulting from imbalances in the foreign-currency denominated CA.[2)] FD_G and FM_u have been calculated by cumulating imbalances in the foreign-currency part of the CA:

---

1) The following figures may illustrate the relative importance of the DM and the dollar as "foreign currencies" in US and German exports and imports. In 1980 the share of US merchandise exports denominated in DM amounted to 1% (α_u^x = 2%) and the corresponding DM share in US merchandise imports was 4,1% (α_u^{im} = 15%). For Germany the share in merchandise exports denominated in dollar came to 7,2% (α_G^x = 18%) and in merchandise imports 33,1% (α_G^{im} = 57%). A comparison with the corresponding shares for other "foreign currencies" shows that the DM and the dollar, respectively, can indeed be considered as the most important foreign currencies in export and import transactions of both countries. All figures are taken from Page (1981).

2) See next page.

$$FD_G = \sum_{i=0}^{t} (\alpha^x X_i - \alpha^{im} Im_i)_G$$ expressed in billions of dollar, end-of-quarter

$$FM_u = \sum_{i=0}^{t} (\alpha^x X_i - \alpha^{im} Im_i)_u$$ expressed in billions of DM, end-of-quarter

i = 0 denotes the beginning of the respective sample period.

FD_u, FM_G : Net stocks of domestic-currency denominated assets resulting from imbalances in the domestic-currency denominated CA.[1)] FD_u and FM_G have been calculated by cumulating imbalances in the domestic-currency part of the respective CA.

$$FD_u = \sum_{i=0}^{t} [(1 - \alpha^x)X_i - (1 - \alpha^{im})Im_i]_u$$ billions of dollar, end-of-quarter

$$FM_G = \sum_{i=0}^{t} [(1 - \alpha^x)X_i - (1 - \alpha^{im})Im_i]_G$$ billions of DM, end-of quarter

We determine the theoretically expected signs of the regression coefficients as follows.

(footnote 2. last page) Note that, unlike than in chapter ten, these F variables do not describe the net stocks of respective foreign-currency assets actually held by residents of both countries. The assumption of two internationally traded assets (DM and dollar bonds) allows for changes in the currency composition of a given net foreign asset position (NFP = ΣCAS). Residents of one country may change their net stocks of foreign-currency assets by buying or selling domestic-currency denominated bonds to the foreign sector. Such changes in the currency composition of a given NFP, however, can be interpreted as endogenous reactions to exogenous changes on the asset supply side. The F variables, on the other hand, denote the sum of exogenous changes in the supply of foreign-currency assets to the US and German private sector.

1) Although FD_u and FM_G consist of exactly the same types of assets as PB_u and PB_G, namely dollar and DM bonds, the exchange rate effects of changes in FD_u and FM_G differ from effects of changes in PB_u and PB_G in the theoretical model. A change in FD_u or FM_G involves an asset shift and hence induces portfolio adjustments in two-countries. An increase in PB describes an increase in the total net supply of bonds which, firstly, triggers off portfolio adjustments in one country (provided that deficits in the governments budget are financed by issuing bonds to domestic residents only).

The coefficients on the money supplies $M1_G$, $M1_u$ and on central bank foreign exchange reserves R_G, R_u can be determined unambiguously in the two-country model exposed in chapter five.[1)] We expect

$a_1 > 0$; $a_2 < 0$; $a_5 > 0$; $a_8 < 0$.

To derive unambiguous predictions of the signs of the coefficients on net bond stocks additional assumptions have to be introduced.

$a_9 < 0$ provided that increases in private net stocks of DM bonds are brought about by issuing DM bonds to German residents and if, but not only if, $E(f/r) > E(m/r)$.

$a_{10} > 0$ provided that increases in private net stocks of dollar bonds are brought about by issuing dollar bonds to US residents and if, but not only if, $E(b^*/r^*) > E(n/r^*)$.

As discussed above, it is not possible to determine consistently the remaining coefficients for the CA variables by applying the results of the two-country model presented in chapter five. In the case of a true two-country test we could expect the following coefficient restrictions to hold.[2)]

a_3, $a_4 < 0$ (or, alternatively a_6, $a_7 > 0$) "normal" reaction of the DM/$ exchange rate to imbalances in the CA between US and Germany.

$a_3 = a_4$ (or, alternatively $a_6 = a_7$) if wealth shifts caused by CA imbalances induce adjustments in asset demands which are independent of the specific wealth parts, i.e. financial assets, in which wealth shifts are embodied (case a. in the taxonomy given in table 1).

---

1) Assuming that changes in R_G reflect changes in German dollar reserves and changes in R_U reflect changes in US DM reserves.

2) A true two-country test would have to employ either the German or the US CA. In a true two-country world the inclusion of both countries' CAs would result in perfect collinearity.

$a_3 \neq a_4$ (or, alternatively $a_6 \neq a_7$) if asset demands react differently to changes in different wealth components, i.e. financial assets (case b. in the taxonomy given in table 1 above).[1)]

Our test specification, however, bears with regard to the CA variables much more the character of a multi-country test than of a two-country test. The empirical evidence quoted above indicates that both countries' CAs and hence, also the CA-dependent asset stocks reflect primarily trade relations with third-countries. This is also a reason for the fact that the basket of currencies actually used in US and German CA transactions is not only composed of dollar and DM assets.

Considering the cleavage between theoretical model presumptions and actual conditions under which we put the theory to the test, our estimations can hardly be regarded as a consistent examination of the model. Hence it would be misleading to draw conclusions from these estimations to the specific form of asset demand functions.

Nevertheless, the estimation results might be of interest with respect to some other, more general questions; for instance: "is there an empirically significant difference between exchange rate effects of imbalances in the foreign-currency part of the CA and imbalances in the domestic-currency part of the CA? Do these results allow us to maintain the empirical conclusions of section nine about the exchange rate effect of imbalances in the overall CAs of both countries?"

---

1) Note that the equality-restriction $a_3 = a_4$ (or $a_6 = a_7$) has been derived within a nominal portfolio equilibrium model. Only if asset demands are specified as linear homogeneous in wealth can the price level be eliminated from the asset market equilibrium conditions and equilibrium in real terms is equivalent to equilibrium in nominal terms. Thus, an empirical test which employs nominal asset variables presupposes that asset demands are linear homogeneous in wealth. If asset demands are non-linear homogeneous in wealth, the condition $a_3 = a_4$, which still may be valid as case a. does not depend on the degree of homogeneity, should be tested with asset stocks expressed in real values.

10.3.2. Estimation Results

According to our calculations of the currency partition in the US and the German CA in section 10.2., we conduct estimations for three different time periods. The results are shown in table 4 (1978.II - 1982.II), table 5 (1974.II - 1982.II), and in table 6 (1973.I - 1982.II). It is important to note that differences in the results of these estimations can not be attributed only to different sample periods. For each period we made different assumptions on the α-ratios when we divided the CAs into their currency parts. This was necessary to obtain a sufficiently large number of observations for our estimations.
As in chapter nine, we estimate different versions of the basic regression equation as can be gathered from the structure of tables 4 to 6. So, for example, we run two series of regressions: one which includes the variables for the net supply of DM and dollar bonds, PB_G and PB_U, and a second one which excludes these variables. This procedure has been chosen for reasons which will become clear in the following.

We start with the results for the net supplies of dollar and DM bonds. The incorporation of net bond supplies does not lead to an improvement in the general estimation results: compared with the equations where PB_G and PB_U are excluded, there is almost no increase in R^2s and the values of the F-statistics decline. The single results for PB_G and PB_U are disappointing too. The coefficient of the net supply of DM bonds, PB_G, takes a theoretically wrong positive sign in all estimation periods[1)] but is never significant. The coefficient of PB_U is estimated for the first two periods (table 4 and 5) with the expected positive sign which, however, is significant only in eq. 5-4 and becomes negative in the third period (table 6) where the CAs are calculated with different α-ratios. Thus our estimations provide very little support for the theoretical hypotheses about the exchange rate effect of changes in DM and dollar net bond stocks.[2)] The results for PB_G and PB_U, however, point to a general problem in our estimations: the independent asset variables seem to exhibit a strong interrelation among

---

1) With the exception of eq. 6-4.

2) See also the remarks on pp. 224. A similar conclusion is drawn in Penati (1983, pp. 563).

Table 4: Estimates for the DM/$ Exchange Rate in the Case of Diversified CA Financing.[a)] next page
Sample Period 1978.II - 1982.II, Quarterly Data.

		4-1	4-2	4-3	4-4	4-5	4-6	4-7	4-8
		OLS	CORC	OLS	2SLS	OLS	CORC	OLS	2SLS
C		518,66 (1,6822)	829,07 (3,6664)	-560,26 (-1,3288)	-422,22 (-0,8823)	265,57 (0,8059)	362,66 (0,6858)	-562,62 (-1,2817)	-396,89 (-0,7806)
$M1_G$	+	0,4919 (-0,3810)	-1,7693 (-1,7293)	3,3543* (2,0848)	2,8783 (1,6064)	-0,1030 (-0,0827)	-0,6272 (-0,4072)	3,1912* (1,8558)	2,5398 (1,2742)
$M1_u$	·/.	-0,5872 (-1,2581)	-0,6843 (-1,7192)	0,2625 (0,5943)	0,1456 (0,3013)	-0,6660 (-1,4892)	-0,7109 (-1,6445)	0,1266 (0,2585)	-0,0512 (-0,0909)
FD_G	·/.	-0,0260 (-0,0331)	-0,3102 (-0,5908)	1,0557 (1,5488)	0,9049 (1,2402)	0,0805 (0,1079)	-0,0141 (-0,0223)	1,0349 (1,4255)	0,8191 (1,0162)
FM_G	·/.	-0,3998 (-0,4805)	0,4626 (0,7519)	-2,4893* (-2,6969)	-2,2206* (-2,1663)	-0,6845 (-0,8338)	-0,3969 (-0,3545)	-2,3656* (-2,4412)	-2,0234* (-1,8274)
R_G	+			-2,7476* (-2,9694)	-2,3181* (-2,0108)			-2,5200* (-2,2551)	-1,8773 (-1,2809)
FM_u	+	0,7879 (0,9650)	1,8936* (2,5562)	-0,3643 (-0,4889)	-0,1702 (-0,2092)	0,9718 (1,0984)	1,2623 (1,0646)	0,0743 (0,0874)	0,3253 (0,3449)
FD_u	+	3,6446* (2,9386)	4,3685* (4,7934)	4,2364* (3,6721)	4,2543* (3,6379)	3,0095* (2,1962)	2,8907 (1,5392)	4,3129* (3,1593)	4,1525* (2,9232)
R_u	·/.			-0,0652 (-0,0961)	-0,1594 (-0,2266)			-0,1029 (-0,1452)	-0,2353 (-0,3130)
PB_G	·/.					0,4752 (1,1721)	0,7274 (1,3020)	0,4018 1,2054)	0,4199 (1,2232)
PB_u	+					0,2669 (1,3645)	0,2423 (0,8492)	0,0459 (0,2460)	0,1009 (0,4877)
$\bar{R}^2$		0,8742		0,9296	0,9277	0,8877		0,9248	0,9206
$\hat{R}^2$			0,9626				0,9611		
F		19,53	43,56	27,43	12,84	16,81		20,67	6,96
DW		2,8718	2,5422	2,0392	2,1899	2,9249	2,5649	2,1102	2,3589
RHO			-0,5915 (-2,9342)				-0,5862 (-2,8945)		

Table 5: Estimates for the DM/$ Exchange Rate in the Case of Diversified CA Financing,[a)] Sample Period 1974.II - 1982.II, Quarterly Data.

		5-1	5-2	5-3	5-4	5-5	5-6
		OLS	OLS	2SLS	OLS	OLS	2SLS
C		390,18 (3,9950)	148,26 (1,5101)	136,73 (0,9699)	275,08 (2,5595)	128,13 (1,2657)	243,24 (1,3704)
$M1_G$	+	0,6446 (1,2578)	1,2649* (2,8120)	1,2896* (2,5818)	0,6934 (1,3427)	1,0839* (2,2827)	0,8552 (1,3276)
$M1_u$	./.	-0,7865* (-2,0338)	-0,1673 (-0,4962)	-0,1356 (-0,3100)	-0,6482* (-1,7638)	-0,1807 (-0,5503)	-0,5888 (-0,9772)
FD_G	./.	-0,0642 (-0,1033)	0,3195 (0,6347)	0,3454 (0,6249)	-0,0057 (-0,0099)	0,3083 (0,6306)	-0,0357 (-0,0499)
FM_G	./.	-1,0541* (-3,7047)	-1,3045* (-4,9666)	-1,3102* (-4,8953)	-1,4032* (-4,6118)	-1,4293* (-5,0871)	-1,4982* (-4,1635)
R_G	+		-2,5453* (-4,1234)	-2,6921* (-1,8872)		-2,3287* (-3,6386)	-0,0617 (-0,0240)
FM_u	+	-0,6002* (-2,0739)	-0,7660* (-3,3234)	-0,7744* (-3,1960)	-0,4652 (-1,6064)	-0,6153* (-2,5354)	-0,4886 (-1,5149)
FD_u	+	2,0223* (5,1491)	1,6040* (4,6376)	1,5739* (3,6165)	1,5868* (3,6959)	1,2734* (3,2233)	1,6805* (2,5397)
R_u	./.		0,6343 (1,1207)	0,7022 (0,8546)		0,7204 (1,2539)	-0,3407 (-0,2520)
PB_G	./.				0,0345 (0,1281)	0,1682 (0,7295)	0,0017 (0,0051)
PB_u	+				0,3293* (2,3855)	0,1813 (1,5130)	0,3180 (1,5111)
$\bar{R}^2$		0,9083	0,9435	0,9434	0,9206	0,9468	0,9164
F		53,81	67,85	50,01	47,35	57,90	24,11
DW		2,0716	1,9822	1,9670	2,2649	2,1590	2,3126

a) The exchange rate is defined as (DM/$)·100, that is, Pfennige per one US $. Subscripts G and u denote Germany and the US, respectively. In CORC and FAIR RHO is never significantly different from zero. Definitions of the varaibles and further explanations are given in the data appendix and in section 9.1.3.4.

α-ratios used in calculating the F variables are as follows: for the period from 1978 through 1982: see table 2 for both countries; for 1974 through 1977: see table 2 for Germany; for the US α_u^x = 0,036, α_u^{im} = 0,090.

Table 4. a) See footnote a) above. The α-ratios used in calculationg the F variables are those given in table 2.

Table 6: Estimates for the DM/$ Exchange Rate in the Case of Diversified CA Financing,[a] Sample Period 1973.I - 1982.II, Quarterly Data.

		6-1	6-2	6-3	6-4	6-5	6-6
		OLS	OLS	2SLS	OLS	OLS	2SLS
C		41,84 (0,2576)	61,92 (0,4543)	58,74 (0,4266)	-41,49 (-0,2027)	8,1332 (0,0470)	17,90 (0,1007)
$M1_G$	+	1,8684* (3,6351)	1,5195* (3,3996)	1,5662* (3,2166)	2,2490* (3,0305)	1,7235* (2,6715)	1,6296* (2,2475)
$M1_u$	·/.	0,0250 (0,0399)	0,1896 (0,3589)	0,1682 (0,3125)	0,2245 (0,3062)	0,3974 (0,6386)	0,4257 (0,6700)
FD_G	·/.	0,1925 (0,5123)	0,0216 (0,0574)	0,0623 (0,1513)	0,2935 (0,6287)	0,1900 (0,4227)	0,1530 (0,3251)
FM_G	·/.	-1,8413* (-5,8579)	-1,3462* (-4,6105)	-1,4206* (-3,3958)	-2,0160* (-4,4560)	-1,4996* (-3,7005)	-1,4011* (-2,6517)
R_G	+		-2,8103* (-3,9091)	-2,3801 (-1,2742)		-2,9309* (-3,7470)	-3,4949 (-1,6873)
FM_u	+	-3,7097* (-4,4039)	-2,6980* (-3,4550)	-2,8663* (-2,7695)	-4,2063* (-3,2808)	-3,1985* (-2,8070)	-2,9875* (-2,2048)
FD_u	+	2,1508* (6,2162)	1,0849* (2,7347)	1,2461 (1,6428)	2,3558* (4,5289)	1,2503* (2,3692)	1,0389 (1,1626)
R_u	·/.		1,4976* (1,9889)	1,3205 (1,2726)		1,5937* (2,0138)	1,8428 (1,5842)
PB_G	·/.				-0,3060 (-0,8877)	0,0811 (0,2631)	0,1538 (0,3872)
PB_u	+				-0,0058 (-0,0355)	-0,1118 (-0,7968)	-0,1314 (-0,8399)
$\bar{R}^2$		0,8867	0,9204	0,9194	0,8826	0,9166	0,9150
F		50,57	55,89	42,78	36,70	42,74	32,30
DW		1,5206	1,5404	1,5274	1,5379	1,5999	1,6432

a) The exchange rate is defined as (DM/$)·100, that is, Pfennige per one US $. Subscripts G and u denote Germany and the US, respectively. In CORC and Fair RHO is never significantly different from zero. Definitions of the variables and further explanations are given in the data appendix and in section 9.1.3.4.

α-ratios used in calculating the F variables are as follows:

$\alpha_G^x = 0,2$; $\alpha_G^{im} = 0,55$; $\alpha_u^x = 0,03$; $\alpha_u^{im} = 0,12$.

each other. The conjecture that multicollinearity represents a severe problem in our estimations is supported by the following observations:

- The inclusion or exclusion of asset variables in estimating the exchange rate equation affects primarily coefficients and t-ratios of the remaining variables and only to a minor extent R^2s.

- In many regressions we find low t-ratios for the coefficient estimates but high values for R^2.

- Estimation results react very sensitive to changes in the specification of variables and to alterations in the sample period.[1)]

To diminish the degree of multicollinearity and to increase thereby the reliability of the coefficient estimates we exclude PB_G and PB_u in a second group of regressions.

Next we turn to the results for the US and German money supply M1. The theoretical prediciton on the exchange rate impact of changes in the German money stock $M1_G$ finds some support in our estimations: apart from some estimation results for the short period from 1978.II to 1982.II,[2)] the coefficient on $M1_G$ is always positive in table 5 and 6 and always significant at the 95% level in table 6.

The empirical evidence for the US money supply $M1_u$ is more discordant and does not allow for clear conclusions on the validity of the theory. For the period from 1974.II to 1982.II, the $M1_u$ coefficient always takes the expected negative sign but is not significant when official foreign exchange reserves are included in the test. In the estimations for the time from 1973.I to 1982.II, the coefficient on $M1_u$ takes in all equations a theoretically wrong positive sign but is not significantly different from zero. A possible explanation for these unstable

---

1) A comparison of the estimates in tables 5 and 6, for example, shows that coefficients and t-ratios of many variables change considerably when CA variables are calculated differently. The sample period underlying the estimations of table 6 includes only nine more observations than the sample underlying the results in table 5.

2) Multicollinearity together with the small sample of 17 observations leads to very unstable estimates for this period. Because of the presumably low degree of reliability, it would, in our opinion, be inappropriate to give too great a weight to the single coefficient estimates of table 4.

and contradictory results may lie in the multicollinearity problem discussed above.

An examination of the coefficients of official foreign exchange reserves, R_G and R_u, confirms the negative estimation results in chapter nine. In almost all regressions shown in tables 5 and 6 the coefficients on R_G and R_u have signs opposite to those predicted by the theory.[1] The inclusion of a central bank reaction function for the German Bundesbank[2] does not lead to an essential change in results. As a consequence, we extend the estimations by additional regressions in which R_G and R_u are excluded to avoid possible distortions in the coefficient estimates of the other asset variables.

The cumulated German domestic-currency denominated CA, FM_G, is estimated with a significant negative coefficient in all equations of tables 5 and 6 and in most equations of table 4. The negative coefficient suggests that imbalances in the German DM-CA had a "normal" impact on the DM/$ rate over the investigation period. This result is backed up by the fact that the FM_G estimates prove to be relatively stable over all regressions in tables 5 and 6. They do not react very sensitive to differences in these sample periods and to differences in the α-ratios used in calculating FM_G. Thus, our estimations lend strong empirical support to the view that surpluses (deficits) in the German DM-CA lead to an appreciation (depreciation) of the DM against the dollar.

This outcome, however, stands in sharp contrast to the results for the cumulated German foreign-currency denominated CA. The coefficient of FD_G is never significantly different from zero. Its sign is frequently positive in tables 4 and 5 and always positive in table 6 seemingly indicating that a surplus in the dollar-part of the German CA tends to have a depreciation impact on the DM vis-à-vis the dollar.

---

1) For the short period from 1978.II to 1982.II, R_U is estimated with the theoretically correct negative coefficient which, however, is not significant.

2) We used the same reaction function as in chapter nine.

On the whole, our estimation results suggest that imbalances in the domestic-currency and the foreign-currency part of the German CA have different effects on the DM/$ rate. The hypothesis of equal exchange rate effects of FM_G and FD_G has to be rejected for our test specification and our investigation periods.

The empirical performance of the US CA variables leads to a very similar conclusion. The coefficient of the cumulated domestic-currency denominated CA of the US has a "normal" positive sign in all estimations given in tables 4, 5, and 6, and is in almost all cases significant at the 95% level: surpluses (deficits) in the dollar-CA of the US are estimated to have an appreciation (depreciation) impact on the dollar relative to the DM. A comparison of the results for FD_u in tables 5 and 6 shows, as in the case of Germany, a relatively high degree of stability in the estimates. Besides, it is interesting to note that the coefficient values of FD_u lie considerably higher than the values for the overall US CA in chapter nine.

The estimates for the cumulated foreign-currency part of the CA also stand in the case of the US in clear contradiction to estimates for the domestic-currency part. In tables 5 and 6 the coefficient on FM_u is estimated in all cases with a negative sign and is significant in almost all these cases. According to this negative coefficient, a surplus (deficit) in the DM-part of the US CA tends to depreciate (appreciate) the dollar against the DM. However, it is to be noted that the coefficient values of FM_u in table 5 are markedly lower than in table 6, and that FM_u takes, like FD_u, a positive coefficient in most estimations of the period 1978.II to 1982.II. But, as above for the German CA variables, the hypothesis of equal exchange rate effects of both currency parts of the US CA has to be rejected on our results.

Summing up, we repeat our empirical findings for the exchange rate impact of the different CA variables. Firstly, our results indicate a significant "normal" effect of imbalances in both the US and the German domestic-currency denominated CA on the DM/$ exchange rate.

On the other hand, there seems to be either no effect (for Germany) or a "perverse" effect (for the US) on the DM/$ rate of imbalances in the foreign-currency denominated part of the CA. However, for reasons that have been discussed at length above, it would most likely be misleading to attempt an explanation of this empirical outcome on the basis of the theoretical two-country model. On a more general level, we may say that our estimations do not support the view that the currency denomination of CA transactions is without significance for the exchange rate effect of CA imbalances.

11. Negative Net Foreign Asset Positions: Exchange Rate Stability in Portfolio Balance Models

11.1. The Theoretical Problem

This last chapter is devoted to a special problem inherent in stationary-expectations portfolio balance models: the signs of the comparative static multipliers as well as the stability properties of such models depend crucially on the sign of private net foreign asset positions of the countries included in portfolio balance considerations.

Empirical applications of portfolio balance models usually proceed from the (theoretically founded) assumption that a surplus in the home country's current account, causing an increase in the domestic net foreign asset position (NFP), leads to an appreciation of the home country's currency. Analogously, a decrease in the home country's NFP caused by a deficit in its CA is expected to bring about a depreciation of the domestic currency. This relationship is generally assumed to hold true regardless of the absolute levels of net foreign asset positions. Consequently, empirical estimations of portfolio balance exchange rate equations concentrate on changes in net foreign asset positions, that is, on CA imbalances, and neglect the absolute levels of net foreign asset positions.

In some recent papers, however, it has been argued that this approach may possibly be misleading. The main line of reasoning relates to the sign of private NFPs. If the private residents of the home country have a negative NFP (net debts denominated in foreign currency) a flexible exchange rate regime may be dynamically unstable even in the absence of destabilizing speculation.[1)]

To explain the problem let us first consider Martin and Masson's multi-country model. In this model there is only <u>one internationally traded asset</u>: US dollar bonds. As described in chapter eight, Martin and

---

1) The instability problem associated with negative net foreign asset positions is theoretically dealt with in Boyer (1977), Martin and Masson (1979), Kouri (1980, 1983), Henderson and Rogoff (1981, 1982). A good verbal description is given in Truman and Shafer (1982).

Masson assume a large country, the US, whose residents hold only dollar assets in their portfolios, and a number of n-1 other countries i (i = 2,...,n) whose residents hold domestic currency denominated assets and dollar bonds as well. Because there is only one internationally accepted financial instrument, country i's NFP corresponds to its net stock of dollar bonds.
In our empirical study in chapter nine we assumed that country i's private sector is a net creditor in dollar bonds ($PF_i > 0$, i = 2,..,n). It is however possible that country i's private sector borrows dollars (issues dollar bonds) to finance CA deficits either from the US or from third-countries. And therefore, it is likewise possible that country i's private sector is a net debtor in dollar internationally ($PF_i < 0$, i = 2,...,n). In the case of a negative NFP of country i's private residents Martin and Masson's model yields the following theoretical results.

a. The signs of most comparative static multipliers change compared with the creditor case meaning that the effect of changes in the exogenous variables on the bilateral dollar exchange rate is completely opposite depending on the sign of country i's private net foreign asset position.[1)] This implies, for example, that if country i's private sector is a net debtor in dollar, central bank interventions in the foreign exchange market will have a "perverse" exchange rate effect and a domestic CA surplus will lead to a depreciation of country i's currency relative to the dollar.

b. Portfolio and hence exchange rate equilibrium becomes unstable. Local stability of Martin and Masson's multi-country system requires that the private sectors of all countries i (i = 2,...,n) be net creditors in dollars (all $PF_i > 0$, i = 2,...,n): "...if any country is a net debtor in foreign currency (because it has a cumulated deficit on its current account forcing it to issue dollar bonds), then its currency will not return to its initial value when subject to a random shock." [2)]

---

1) Except for those cases where a positive private NFP does not permit to determine the sign of the multipliers unambiguously.

2) Martin and Masson (1979, p.16).

The economic rationale behind these mathematical results can be explained by comparing the portfolio-balance stability mechanism in the net creditor case with the net debtor case.

Assume that the private sector of country i is a net creditor in dollars. A rise in country i's dollar exchange rate (a depreciation against the dollar) induces a rise in the domestic-currency value of dollar denominated wealth. Since the increase in wealth will not in general be desired to be held solely in dollar bonds, the attempt to shift out of dollar bonds into domestic assets will tend to appreciate the domestic currency against the dollar. This appreciation increases domestic wealth again and establishes the mechanism that guarantees stability of the system.

If, however, the private sector of country i is a net debtor in dollars, this stabilizing wealth-valuation effect is reversed. A rise in the exchange rate induces a decline in the domestic-currency value of dollar denominated assets as the stock of foreign currency liabilities increases. Thus, wealth declines in terms of domestic currency units. As a consequence of the decrease in wealth domestic portfolio holders will try to scale down all assets and liabilities creating an excess supply of domestic assets and an excess demand for dollar assets (excess supply of dollar liabilities). The attempt to reduce the level of dollar liabilities leads to capital outflows and brings about a further rise in the exchange rate (a further depreciation of the domestic currency). It is this perverse valuation effect of exchange rate changes which causes instability in the case of a negative private NFP in Martin and Masson's model: a depreciation of the home currency lowers the home currency value of domestic wealth, rather than raising it as in the net creditor case, and hence reduces demand for home currency assets.

Conclusions a. and b. from Martin and Masson's model have to be modified when we consider the two-country model with two internationally traded assets that has been presented in chapter five. As mentioned earlier, in the case of two internationally traded assets denominated in different currencies there is no strict correspondence between a country's NFP and its net stock of foreign-currency denominated bonds.

Though a CA imbalance is associated with an equiproportional change in the NFP, this change may be embodied in domestic-currency and/or foreign -currency denominated assets. Nevertheless, perverse valuation effects do have major consequences also in this type of model. We can distinguish two cases.[1)]

a. One-sided perverse valuation effects. This first case occurs if either the home country's private sector is a net debtor in foreign assets but the foreign country's private sector is a net creditor in assets denominated in the home country's currency ($PF < 0$, $PB^* > 0$) or if the home country's private sector is a net creditor in foreign assets and the private sector of the foreign country is a net debtor in home country assets ($PF > 0$, $PB^* < 0$). In both cases the signs of the comparative statics and the stability of the system is indetermined as they depend on the relative size of the respective foreign-currency denominated asset stocks PF and PB^*.[2)] Perverse valuation effects which influence portfolio dispositions in one country may or may not be set off by stabilizing normal valuation effects in portfolios of the other country.

b. Two-sided perverse valuation effects. If the net stocks of respective foreign-currency denominated assets of both countries' private residents are negative ($PF < 0$, $PB^* < 0$), that is, if both countries' private residents are net debtors in the other country's currency, then we find similar results as in Martin and Masson's model: the signs of most comparative static multipliers are reversed and the model as a whole becomes unstable.[3)]

Thus, the analysis of both Martin and Masson's and the two-country model suggests that a country's actual debtor or creditor position in

---

1) The following distinction can also be derived from the models of Henderson and Rogoff (1981, 1982) and Kouri (1980, 1983).

2) In the two-country model described in chapter five the signs of the comparative static multiplieres become ambiguous as the sign of the system determinant D is not clear with either PF or PB^* negative.

3) The signs of the comparative static results change compared with those derived for positive NFPs as the system determinant D becomes negative. The system becomes dynamically unstable as the characteristic equation possesses positive real parts of the roots (x_3 is negative and x_1 and x_2 indetermined according to the Routh-Hurwitz condition).

foreign-currency assets has major implications for the applicability of the results of portfolio balance models and for the applicability of the model as a whole.

However, it should be mentioned that these critical properties of portfolio balance models relate strongly to the case with stationary expectations. Here the only stabilizing force incorporated in the model consists in the wealth-valuation effect of exchange rate changes. It has been shown that the unpleasant perverse properties can be ruled out if agents are assumed to form rational (model consistent) or strongly regressiv expectations.[1)]

Furthermore, it has been put forward in the literature that creditor and debtor cases are not necessarily symmetric. In both situations we may find different reactions of portfolio holders to changes in the domestic currency value of wealth. In particular, if valuation effects play no or only a minor part in the management of foreign-currency liabilities, instability may not be a serious problem in reality.[2)]

An additional problem arises from the compatibility of negative net foreign asset stocks with portfolio equilibrium. A net debtor position in portfolio equilibrium implies that the desired share of wealth which is planned to be held in foreign currency assets is negative ($f < 0$). This assumption is plausible if $f < 0$ reflects the desire to run CA deficits over a certain time period: net foreign debt is necessary to finance net imports. However, $f < 0$ implies, according to the logic of the model, that portfolio holders react to an increase in wealth with the attempt to increase their foreign currency liabilities ($f\,dW < 0$ with $dW > 0$). In other words, any increase in wealth, for example, due to an exogenous CA surplus causing a decrease in net foreign currency debt, is assumed to induce a desire to run a higher level of foreign currency debt. Such a mechanism which is implicit in the assumption $f < 0$ seems inplausible.[3)]

---

1) See Henderson and Rogoff (1981, 1982) and Kouri (1983).

2) Martin and Masson, for example, argue that "if the assets concerned are of longer term to maturity than just one period....debtors may not be concerned with the current value of their liabilities as they cannot repay them before maturity, while creditors can dispose of their assets." Martin and Masson (1979, p. 17).

3) In the extreme case the assumption $f < 0$ leads to a conclusion like "the wealthier the private sector of a country the higher is the planned level of its net foreign currency debt."

It is probably more realistic to assume that an increase in wealth induces the desire to reduce the level of net foreign currency debt ($f\ dW > 0$ with $dW > 0$). If we, however, accept this latter assumption, we either introduce an asymmetry in portfolio equilibrium conditions ($f < 0$ for the creditor case and $f > 0$ for the debtor case) or we have to take into account that an observed negative net foreign asset stock is not a portfolio equilibrium state. This argument does not change anything for the relevance of perverse valuation effects due to exchange rate changes in the case of a negative stock of net foreign assets; but it indicates that the conventional portfolio balance framework with stable and given demand functions might not be the adequate background for a discussion of portfolio adjustments in the case of a net debtor position in foreign assets.

All these objections suggest that perverse valuation effects arising from negative NFPs might not be of such crucial importance in the empirical application of the results from portfolio balance models. Nonetheless, the theoretical problems signify that stationary-expectations portfolio balance models should either not been applied to a situation in which a country's private sector is a net debtor in foreign currency or the estimation results should be interpreted with particular care as the observed values of the exchange rate may not reflect so much the effects of changes in asset stocks but effects of stabilizing forces not included in the model. It is surprising that in empirical applications of the portfolio model little attention has been paid so far to the problem involved in negative net foreign asset stocks.[1)]

The question whether negative net foreign asset stocks are relevant to the application of the portfolio model to a specific exchange rate can ultimately only be answered empirically. Therefore, in the next

---

1) An exception is Branson, Halttunen and Masson (1979). In their test of the $/DM rate they divide the sample period into those months where the German private stock of net foreign assets was, according to BHM's calculations, positive and those where it was negative. BHM's determination of the periods with positive and negative private net foreign asset stocks, however, differs from the empirical evidence we will discuss in the next section. Similar to BHM, also Martin and Masson test the portfolio model with reversed signs for those countries and time periods for which private net foreign asset stocks were negative in their computations. Assuming reversed signs for the coefficients whenever private NFPs are negative seems to us a very problematic procedure as in this case the model as a whole is unstable. The method employed by MM and BHM in calculating net private asset stocks will be discussed in the next section.

section we will discuss statistical data and estimates of private and total net foreign asset positions of the countries to which the portfolio model has been applied over the last chapters.

11.2. The Empirical Problem: Determining Private Net Foreign Asset Positions

The empirical question arising from the last section's discussion of perverse valuation effects depends on the underlying theoretical framework. When we, as in Martin and Masson's model, assume only one internationally traded asset - foreign-currency denominated bonds - a country's NFP equals its total net stock of foreign assets. One essential condition for ruling out perverse valuation effects [1] and thus for the stability of portfolio equilibrium is that the private NFP of the home country must be positive. In other words, we have to ascertain whether the home country's private sector is a net debtor or net creditor with respect to the foreign sector. Empirical evidence on this question will be presented for Germany, the United States, Japan, and the United Kingdom over the following pages.

In the more realistic case of two internationally traded assets - domestic and foreign-currency denominated bonds - the empirical problem is more complicated. In a two-country context perverse valuation effects can only be ruled out if it can be shown that both countries' net stocks of privately held foreign currency assets are positive. That is, both countries' private NFPs have to be decomposed in domestic and foreign currency parts. A reliable answer to this question, however, requires data which is not available for most countries. For this reason the discussion will be restricted to Germany.

Leaving aside for a moment the simplified theoretical models and considering the problem from a purely empirical perspective there are two further complications to observe.

---

1) A complete investigation of the stability of portfolio equilibrium in a multi-country framework would have to answer the question whether the private NFPs of all countries except the US are positive ($PF_i > 0$, $i = 2,\ldots,n$). Obviously, this would be too formidable a task to tackle empirically.

Firstly, perverse valuation effects always relate to a specific exchange rate and the net debtor position in this specific currency, for example, valuation effects due to changes in the DM/$ rate are related to German net holdings of dollar assets and not necessarily to German holdings of sterling, yen or Swiss franc assets. Ultimately, the empirical relevance of perverse valuation effects depends on the entire foreign currency structure in portfolios. Given the data available, such detailed investigation is not possible.

Secondly, perverse valuation effects in domestic portfolios may always be counterbalanced by normal valuation effects in the foreign country. As we cannot determine the relative strength of counteracting valuation effects, it is not possible to draw final conclusions from the home country's private NFP to the actual relevance of the instability problem.

Mainly for these two reasons the following data have to be considered as too crude to provide unambiguous evidence on the actual significance of perverse valuation effects for movements in the investigated exchange rates.

We start our investigation with Germany. Table 1 contains statistical data on the German NFP over the period from end-June 1974 to end-1982. The figures are taken in an aggregated form from three special benchmark surveys of the German Bundesbank on the asset position of the German Federal Republic vis-à-vis foreign countries (Vermögensstatus der Bundesrepublik Deutschland gegenüber dem Ausland).[1)]

---

1) Deutsche Bundesbank (1974, 1981, 1983). In calculating the German NFP the Bundesbank used whenever possible figures based on asset stocks as reported by domestic sectors. In cases in which stock data could not be obtained, data were computed by cumulation of balance of payments transaction values. Changes in the value of foreign claims and liabilities due to exchange rate movements and price changes are taken into account in their approximate magnitude. For further details see, in particular, Deutsche Bundesbank (1974, pp. 20-21). It should be pointed out that the figures reported in the above benchmark survey differ sometimes substantially from those given in the continuous report of the Bundesbank on short and long-term claims and liabilities of German banks and private enterprises (Deutsche Bundesbank, Statistische Beihefte zu den Moantsberichten, Reihe 3: Zahlungsbilanzstatistik, tables 7, 8, and 9). Judgements on German net foreign claims and liabilities based on this latter source, like in Henderson and Rogoff (1982, p. 86), yield an incomplete and distorted picture relative to the results given in the benchmark surveys.

Table 1: Net Foreign Asset Positions of German Domestic Sectors, June 1974 to December 1982, Billions of DM.

end of	Total Net Foreign Asset Position a)	Private Sector b)		Public Sector	Deutsche Bundesbank d)
		overall	financial c)		
	1	2	3	4	5
June 1974	89,0	-24,1	-13,7	21,5	91,7
Dec. 1975	103,2	-0,9	8,3	21,0	83,1
1977	107,8	5,6	12,1	15,3	86,8
1978	109,1	-5,1	-1,5	15,4	98,8
1979	88,5	-16,6	-16,9	13,8	91,3
1980	62,1	2,6	-9,0	-6,0	65,5
1981	56,9	15,2	-8,3	-25,3	66,9
1982	66,0	28,8	-0,4	-32,3	69,6

a) Columns 2, 4, 5 add up to column 1; differences may occur because of rounding.

b) Banks, private enterprises, and other private residents.

c) Overall net foreign asset position of the private sector (column 2) minus private net direct investments minus net real estate.

d) Net foreign asset position of the Bundesbank corrected for DM banknotes abroad.

Source: Deutsche Bundesbank, Monatsbericht der Deutschen Bundesbank, November 1974, pp. 13-21; May 1981, pp. 25-31; August 1983, pp.30-45.

According to the Bundesbank figures in column 1, Germany was over the entire time period a net creditor to foreign countries. An analysis of this net creditor position with respect to economic sectors, however, reveals that net foreign claims are largely concentrated at the German Bundesbank. Private asset holders, on the other hand, have been in a net debtor position at end-June 1974, at the end of 1975, 1978, and 1979 (column 2).

The figures in column 3 are based on an alternative definition of the private NFP. Here we consider only financial claims and liabilities. This restriction seems particularly relevant to portfolio balance models as they are usually formulated in terms of financial wealth components. Thus, in column 3 we exclude direct foreign investments and landed property from the definition of private net foreign wealth. On this measure the net debtor position at the end of 1975 changes to a net creditor position but an opposite change occurs for the benchmarks at end-1980, 1981, and 1982.

In both wealth definitions, overall and financial, the German private sector was a net debtor to the foreign sector at end-June 1974, end-1978, and end-1979. When we take Martin and Masson's theoretical model as basis, the figures in table 1 indicate that perverse valuation effects could have played a role for German private portfolio holders over the investigated time period.

In <u>table 2</u> we attempt a classification of Germany's total and private NFP according to currencies. Since official Bundesbank data on this currency subdivision are available only from 1978 on [1] we report in columns 9 and 11 own estimates of the currency parts in private (financial) NFPs for the complete investigation period.[2] As explained above, perverse valuation effects occur only with regard to net liabilities which are actually denominated in foreign currency. Hence, the distinction between domestic and foreign-currency denominated NFPs is most important to an assessment of the empirical relevance of such effects.

---

1) These figures are calculated from Deutsche Bundsbank, Der Auslansvermögensstatus der Bundesrepublik Deutschland Ende 1982, in: Monatsbericht der Deutschen Bundesbank, August 1983, pp. 30-45; see, in particular, the table on pp. 44 and 45.

2) The calculation method used in the currency division of foreign claims and liabilities is explained in footnote d. attached to table 2.

<u>Table 2</u>: Total and Private Net Foreign Asset Positions of Germany According to Currencies, June 1974 to December 1982, Billions of DM.

	Total Net Foreign Asset Pos.			Private Sector [a]							
				Overall Net Position			Net Financial Assets [b]				
								Net DM Position		Net Foreign Currency Position	
end of	Total	Net DM Position	Net Foreign Currency Position	overall	Net DM Position	Net Foreign Currency Position	overall	Actual [c]	Estimate [d]	Actual [c]	Estimate [d]
	1	2	3	4	5	6	7	8	9	10	11
June 1974	89,0	-	-	-24,1	-	-	-13,7	-	-4,2	-	-9,5
Dec. 1975	103,2	-	-	-0,9	-	-	8,3	-	11,5	-	-3,2
1977	107,8	-	-	5,6	-	-	12,1	-	0,3	-	11,8
1978	109,1	-65,6	174,7	-5,1	-71,4	66,4	-1,5	-25,0	-17,6	23,5	16,1
1979	88,5	-78,0	166,5	-16,6	-83,8	67,1	-16,9	-34,0	-28,8	17,0	11,9
1980	62,1	-93,3	155,5	2,6	-73,2	75,8	-9,0	-23,6	-22,8	14,4	13,8
1981	56,9	-113,8	170,7	15,2	-73,3	88,5	-8,3	-24,7	-25,8	16,4	17,5
1982	66,0	-128,9	194,9	28,7	-77,5	106,2	-0,4	-27,3	-27,4	26,9	27,0

For footnotes see next page.

Footnotes to table 2.

a) Banks, private enterprises, and other private residents.

b) Overall net foreign asset position of the private sector (columns 4 - 6) minus private net direct investments minus private real estate.

c) Taken in aggregated form from Deutsche Bundesbank, Monatsbericht der Deutschen Bundesbank, August 1983, pp. 44-45. Data series start in 1978.

d) The decomposition of net financial assets given in column 7 into currencies has been conducted as follows. The foreign-currency shares in short and long-term financial claims and liabilities of German banks and privates as well as the foreign-currency share in trade credits have been calculated on a yearly basis from figures reported by Deutsche Bundesbank, Statistische Beihefte zu den Monatsberichten, Reihe 3: Zahlungsbilanzstatistik, Tab. 7, 8, and 9 (the absolute figures given there differ quite considerably from the corresponding figures reported in the Bundesbank benchmark surveys on the German net foreign asset position used and quoted above). These ratios then have been applied to the figures given in the Bundesbank benchmark surveys, Deutsche Bundesbank, Monatsbericht der Deutschen Bundesbank, November 1974, May 1981, August 1983. To these figures we added the remaining asset positions reported by the Bundesbank assuming that:

(i) foreign securities held by German banks are denominated in foreign currency and domestic securities issued by German banks and held abroad are denominated in DM.

(ii) liabilities of the German private sector from equities and bonds held abroad are denominated in DM and German private claims from foreign equities and bonds are denominated in foreign currency.

Source: Deutsche Bundesbank, Monatsbericht der Deutschen Bundesbank, November 1974, pp.13-21; May 1981, pp. 25-31; August 1983, pp. 30-45.

The Bundesbank figures in columns 3, 6, and 10 of table 2 show that from 1978 on Germany has been a net creditor in foreign-currency denominated assets on all measures: total net foreign-currency positions as well as net foreign-currency positions of the private sector were positive at all benchmarks. Obviously, the negative private NFPs reported in table 1 accrued mainly in the form of DM denominated debt of German private residents. The general picture changes very little when we include our own, rather inexact, estimations for the complete period from June 1974 to December 1982 into the consideration. Taking into account the inaccuracy of our estimates, merely the benchmark for end-June 1974 in column 11 suggests that perverse valuation effects could have had a transitory influence on German private portfolios at the beginning of the investigation period.
All in all, the data in table 2 signifies that perverse valuation effects due to negative private net foreign asset stocks have been of negligible empirical importance in the case of Germany.

Before we continue the study with the empirical results for the NFPs of the United States, Japan, and the United Kongdom, we first turn to another,fairly central problem in calculating net foreign asset positions. So far we considered only yearly benchmark figures for total and private NFPs. These figures, however, give only a vague clue to the NFP within the time between two benchmark dates. Yet, such information may be essential as portfolio models are tested with monthly or quarterly data and private NFPs might fluctuate widely between positive and negative between the benchmarks. For this reason we look in the next step upon the calculation method employed by BHM (1977, 1979), MD (1980), and MM (1979) in generating monthly and quarterly figures for private NFPs.

The calculation method used by these authors is essentially based on the following fundamental accounting identity.

$$(1) \qquad NFP_t = \int_{-\infty}^{t} CAS\ (t)\ dt$$

According to eq. (1) the NFP of a country is determined by the sum of all past current account surpluses.

Equation (1) can be transformed into the more operational form of eq. (2).

$$(2) \qquad NFP_t = F_0 + \sum_{i=0}^{t} CAS_i$$

F_0 denotes a benchmark figure for the NFP on which the subsequent quarterly or monthly current account balances are cumulated.[1] To derive the private NFP eq. (2) has to be corrected for net foreign asset stocks held outside the private sector. Before we consider this step, however, we investigate the empirical validity of eq. (2) which builds the foundation of any furthergoing extension.

To examine eq. (2) we calculated the overall NFP of Germany, expressed in DM and dollars, with quarterly CA data. As benchmark figure we used the end-June 1974 values given in the Bundesbank survey (table 3, colums 1 and 2).[2] A comparison of the calculation results for the NFP at the end of 1981 from eq. (2) with the Bundesbank figures in column 1 and 2 revealed considerable discrepancies. When we cumulated the German CA in dollar [3] our calculations according to eq. (2) resulted in an overestimation of the German NFP at the end of 1981 of 7,3 billions of dollars compared with the figure reported by the Bundesbank. When eq. (2) was calculated with DM values, the overestimation of the German NFP amounted even to 47 billion DM.
The discrepancy between Bundesbank figures for the German NFP and estimates on the basis of cumulated current account balances can be explained by differences in the valuation of asset stocks.[4]

---

1) Eq. (2) corresponds to the formula used by the authors mentioned above. The benchmark figure F_0 used by BHM and MD is taken from the same source as the figures in table 1.

2) This is the benchmark date chosen by BHM and MD. The dollar values in column 2 of table 3 are calculated by dividing the DM figures in column 1 by end-of-period exchange rates given in footnote b. to table 3.

3) The DM values of the German CA were converted into dollars by multiplying with a quarterly average exchange rate (IFS, line rf) and cumulated afterwards.

4) Statistical deficiencies and omissions arising in both methods either in recording CA transactions or in recording asset stocks play also an important but less systematic role in explaining the different results. These problems are discussed in more detail in Deutsche Bundesbank (1974, 1981, 1983), United Kingdom Central Statistical Office (1982, 1983), International Monetary Fund (1983, chapter 11).

Empirically, a country's NFP consists of various types of assets denominated in different currencies. Exchange rate fluctuations and changes in the book or market value of asset stocks may lead to substantial deviations between NFP values created by cumulating CA balances and those calculated on the basis of stock data recorded by domestic asset holders. The Bundesbank figures are mainly based on the DM values of asset stocks actually held by German residents at a given point in time. In cases where transaction values are used to substitute missing stock data, valuation changes due to changes in exchange rates and market prices are approximately taken into account. Opposite to that, the valuation problem is ignored completely when the NFP is calculated by cumulating current account balances.[1] Thus, eq. (2) yields probably a relatively worse approximation to the actual level of a country's NFP.[2] [3]

The presumption that cumulated CA balances produce a very unreliable measure of actual NFPs is enhanced by the results of a second series of calculations. In columns 3 and 4 of table 3 we calculated the German NFP once more by cumulating CA balances but this time we took the respective last benchmark from columns 1 and 2, respectively, as basis for the cumulations between two benchmarks. Accordingly, a comparison between the figures shown in columns 1 and 2 and those in columns 3 and 4, for example, at the end of 1978 reveals the difference occuring in the time between the end of 1977 and end-1978. The difference between the so calculated estimates from eq. (2) in colums 3 and 4 and the Bundesbank figures in colums 1 and 2 are still rather large. In some cases the divergence between both even exceeds the NFP of the German private sector shown in table 1, column 2.

---

1) See on this point also Deutsche Bundesbank (1974), United Kingdom Central Statistical Office (1983).

2) The same result holds when transaction values of the capital account are cumulated, see Deutsche Bundesbank (1974).

3) When the German CA is cumulated in dollars, valuation changes in asset stocks due to fluctuations in the DM/$ rate are implicitly taken into account. Since a large part of German foreign claims and liabilities is likely to be denominated in dollars, this might be a reason for the relatively small divergence of the dollar cumulations from eq. (2) from the Bundesbank figures.

Table 3: The German Total Net Foreign Asset Position - A Comparison of Estimates from Cumulated Current Account Balances and Bundesbank Asset Stock Data, June 1974 to December 1981.

end of	Bundesbank Stock Data[a)] expressed in Bill. of		Cumulated Current Account[b)] Balances (F_G) expressed in Bill. of	
	DM	$	DM	$
	1	2	3	4
June 1974	89,0	34,8	-	-
Dec. 1975	103,2	39,4	111,7	44,0
1977	107,8	51,2	122,5	47,4
1978	109,1	59,7	126,0	60,4
1979	88,5	51,1	98,4	53,8
1980	62,1	31,7	59,9	35,3
1981	56,9	25,2	45,0	24,2

a) For source see table 1.

b) F_G was calculated according to $F_G = F_0 + \sum_{i=0}^{t} CAS_i$

where CAS denotes the quarterly balance in the German current account and F_0 denotes a (changing) benchmark for the total German net foreign asset position (taken from columns 1 and 2, respectively). In the case of dollar values CAS was converted into dollars by dividing through a a quarterly average exchange rate (IFS, line rf) and cumulated afterwards. The calculations for F_G were started with the respective last benchmark and stopped at the time when the next benchmark figure for NFP was available from colums 1 and 2, respectively. In the case of dollar values, F_0 from column 1 was converted into dollars by applying the following end-of-period exchange rates (IFS, line ae): 1974.6: 2,5550; 1975.12: 2,6223; 1977.12: 2,1050; 1978.12: 1,8280; 1979.12: 1,7315; 1980.12: 1,9590; 1981.12: 2,2548. Data Source: IMF, International Financial Statistics.

Summarizing the discussion so far, we have to concede that in most cases eq. (2) will produce only a very poor approximation to the actual level of a country's net foreign asset position.[1)]

The empirical content of the current account cumulation method is further reduced when eq. (2) is employed as foundation for the calculation of private NFPs. In this case the total NFP calculated according to eq. (2) has to be corrected for net foreign claims and liabilities held outside the private sector. The conventional method for determining private NFPs in empirical tests of portfolio models is described by the following formulas.

$$(3) \qquad NFP_t^p = F_0 + \sum_{i=0}^{t} CAS_i - R_t$$

In eq. (3) foreign exchange reserves held by the domestic central bank (R_t) are subtracted from the total NFP to arrive at the net foreign asset position of the private sector (NFP^p). This is the formula used by Branson, Halttunen, and Masson, and by Martin and Masson.[2)]

Alternatively, current account balances may first be cumulated on a benchmark for the NFP of the private sector, PF_0. This sum then has to be corrected for changes in official reserves from the benchmark date on. This is the approach of Murphy and Van Duyne.

$$(3') \qquad NFP_t^p = PF_0 + \sum_{i=0}^{t} CAS_i - \sum_{i=0}^{t} (R_i - R_{i-1})$$

Apart from the valuation problem discussed above, the main problem arising in eqs. (3) and (3') consists in the treatment of the public sector. From table 1 it can be seen that the total NFP is composed of net foreign asset holdings of the private sector including banks, private enterprises and other private residents, of the public sector, and the central bank. If NFP^p is calculated according to eq. (3), or

---

1) There may be, of course, purely accidental exceptions from this rule if valuation changes on the liability side are set off by valuation changes on the credit side.

2) Additionally, Martin and Masson correct for private direct investments.

according to eq. (3') with PF_0 denoting all net foreign asset stocks outside the domestic central bank, then the private and the public sector are grouped together: NFP^p includes net foreign asset stocks of banks, private enterprises and other private residents, and of the public sector and excludes only foreign assets held by the central bank. The portfolio model, however, is designed for the analysis of the asset allocation of private risk and profit oriented agents. The government - the public sector - appears in the model through its budgetary policy as supplier of interest-bearing assets. This net bond supply is not determined by the model but assumed to be an exogenous instrument of fiscal policy. Exchange rate changes which alter the domestic currency value of foreign asset stocks, also of those stocks held by the public sector,[1)] have in the context of the model no endogenous effects on the asset supply side. Wealth valuation effects due to exchange rate movements induce endogenous reactions on the asset demand side which is determined by the portfolio behaviour of private agents. Thus, it is neither in the sense of the model nor adequate to reality to apply the conventional theoretical portfolio balance system to the public sector.[2)]

The mix-up of net foreign assets held by the private and the public sector can be avoided when we define PF_0 in eq. (3') as NFP of the private sector only. In applying this definition to eq. (3'), however, we have to assume that the NFP of the public sector keeps unchanged over the complete investigation period; otherwise we would neglect changes in the private NFP due to asset shifts between the private and the public sector at a constant total NFP. If such changes take place - and the figures in table 1 suggest that this is the case - cumulating current account balances corrected for changes in central bank reserves

---

1) In conventional portfolio models it is assumed that the government issues domestic-currency denominated bonds. The more realistic case with governments holding also foreign-currency denominated claims and liabilities is normally not considered.

2) A disaggregation of the public sector's NFP suggests that it would most likely be inappropriate to apply the portfolio adjustment mechanism underlying portfolio balance models also to the public sector. For example, the positive NFP of the German public sector up to 1979 (table 1, column 4) was mainly due to development aid payments. These claims to foreign countries are highly illiquid with a very long-term maturity and thus certainly not subject to short run portfolio management. For further details see Deutsche Bundesbank (1974, 1982, 1983).

according to eq. (3') does not at all give a clue to developments in the private NFP. To illustrate this statement we calculated NFP^p according to eq. (3') with PF_0 defined as the NFP of the private sector (table 1, column 2). As expected, a comparison of the calculation results with the Bundesbank figures in table 1, column 2 revealed substantial differences. The sign of the NFP^p estimates from eq. (3') was frequently opposite to the sign indicated by the Bundesbank survey. Moreover, our calculations produced different signs for NFP^p of identical points in time when we started the calculations from different benchmark dates.
Thus, our analysis shows that there are very good reasons to distrust calculations of private NFPs which are based on either equations above.[1)] Judgements on the empirical relevance of perverse valuation effects may be seriously misleading if net foreign asset positions are calculated by cumulating current account balances.

This conclusion was confirmed by similar calculations for the United States, Japan, and the United Kingdom.[2)] Consequently, we leave aside in table 4 NFP estimates generated by cumulating current account balances and report only yearly data which have been taken in an aggregated form from official benchmark surveys. Furthermore, considering the insufficient data basis, a decomposition of net foreign asset

---

1) Apart from what has been said so far, there is an additional reason for divergencies between NFP^p estimates calculated according to eqs. (3) and (3') and private NFPs as reported by the Bundesbank. The definition of foreign exchange reserves used in the empirical studies of BHM and MD differs from the Bundesbank definition of its net foreign asset position (table 1, column 5). In BHM and MD official reserves R are defined as total reserves minus gold minus cumulated Special Drawing Rights whereas the Bundesbank includes these assets in its calculation of its net foreign asset position.

2) The large discrepancies between methods based on cumulated current account balances and asset stock recordings are also recognized by official statistical institutions. Differences occur already on the most fundamental level, namely for the identity of cumulated current account balances and total net foreign asset positions. In the US, for instance, the Interagency Committee on Balance of Payments Statistics established a work group in September 1980 to investigate possible sources of the large statistical deviations between the calculated change in the US international investment position and current account balances. Even when corrections have been made for valuation changes in asset stocks these discrepancies amounted in 1979 to 25 bill. dollars, in 1980 to 30 bill. dollars, in 1981 to 24 bill. dollars, and in 1982 even to 41 bill. dollars. Moreover, in 1978, 1979, and 1982 official calculations suggested an increase in the US net foreign investment position although the US current account was in deficit for these years; see Scholl (1981, 1983).

positions into currencies has not been attempted. Therefore, the figures in table 4 do not allow for strong conclusions on the actual empirical relevance of perverse valuation effects to the respective exchange rates.

The results for Japan in columns 5 and 6 suggest that Japanese private residents have been in a net debtor position to foreigners both on the overall and the financial measure during the whole investigation period from 1973 to 1981.[1) 2)] These figures can be taken as an indication that perverse valuation effects may have played a role in asset dispositions of Japanese portfolio holders - at least when we stick to the assumption of only one internationally traded asset.

In the case of the United Kingdom the data are not so straightforward. The figures in column 8 show that the UK private sector was in a net creditor position over the complete sample period if the private NFP is defined on an overall measure. When we include only financial claims and liabilities, the private NFP is slightly negative at the end of 1977 and otherwise positive. Considering the relative low values for the private NFP in column 9 and taking into account statistical inaccuracies, the financial NFP of the UK private sector is probably best described as balanced up to 1980. In any case, the data in columns 8 and 9 provide no support for the presumption of perverse valuation effect in UK portfolios.

In a two-country context with two internationally traded assets the empirical relevance of perverse valuation effects to movements in dollar exchange rates depends not only on the private NFP of the respective home country but in like manner on the NFP of the US private sector. Negative NFPs are unambiguously associated with inverted comparative static multipliers and model instability only in cases in which both the US and the home country's private foreign-currency denominated NFP is negative. The exchange rate impact of negative net foreign asset holdings of home country pr vates may be balanced out by normal valuation effects in US private portfolios.

---

1) With the exception of 1979 where the pr vate NFP of Japan was almost balanced.

2) This result confirms the calculations of Martin and Masson (1979).

<u>Table 4</u>: Net Foreign Asset Positions of the United States, Japan, and the United Kingdom, 1973 to 1982.

end of	United States a) (Billions of US dollars)			Japan b) (Billions of US dollars)			United Kingdom c) (Billions of Pound Sterling)		
	Total Net Foreign Asset Position	Private Sector		Total Net Foreign Asset Position	Private Sector		Total Net Foreign Asset Position	Private Sector	
		overall	financial		overall	financial		overall	financial
	1	2	3	4	5	6	7	8	9
1973	61,9	78,3	-7,1	13,0	-3,0	-5,9	4,9	6,1	1,8
1974	77,4	103,5	7,1	8,9	-8,3	-13,0	1,6	4,5	0,04
1975	93,6	122,5	16,1	7,0	-10,6	-16,8	1,0	5,1	0,19
1976	83,8	123,3	17,2	9,6	-11,7	-19,8	2,1	9,9	2,1
1977	71,3	143,2	31,9	22,0	-6,2	-15,9	3,0	5,3	-1,6
1978	76,2	176,3	56,1	36,2	-2,6	-14,0	10,4	10,8	3,3
1979	94,6	176,9	47,6	28,8	0,9	-13,0	13,8	10,8	1,0
1980	120,6	206,3	65,0	11,5	-16,7	-33,0	19,6	16,1	6,9
1981	156,4	238,8	87,8	10,9	-18,5	-39,1	31,1	29,0	13,0
1982	168,6	250,0	130,5	-	-	-	42,4	42,0	20,0

For footnotes see next page.

<u>Footnotes to table 4.</u>

a) Calculated from Scholl, R.B., The International Investment Position of the United States, Table 3, in: Survey of Current Business, August issues 1976, 1981, 1983.

Total net foreign asset position: net international investment position of the US (line 1).
Net foreign asset position of the private sector: US private assets abroad (line 13) minus foreign assets in the US excluding foreign official assets in the US (1976, 1981: line 32; 1983: line 28).
Financial net foreign asset position of the private sector: column 2 corrected for private net direct investments (1976, 1981: lines 14 and 33; 1983: lines 14 and 29).

b) Calculated from The Bank of Japan, Research and Statistics Department, Assets and Liabilities vis-à-vis Non-Residents of Japan, in: Economic Statistics Annual, 1977: Table 123, 1982: Table 127, 1983: Table 131.

Total net foreign asset position: total net assets vis-á-vis non-residents of Japan.
Net foreign asset position of the private sector: net assets of private sector vis-á-vis non-residents of Japan.
Financial net foreign asset position of the private sector: column 5 corrected for private net direct investments.

c) Calculated from United Kingdom Central Statistical Office, External Assets and Liabilities, in: United Kingdom Balance of Payments, December 1983, Tables 11.1 and 11.2.

Total net foreign asset position: total identified UK external assets minus total identified UK external liabilities.
Net foreign asset position of the private sector: total identified external assets of UK private sector minus total identified external liabilities of UK private sector.
Financial net foreign asset position of the private sector: column 8 corrected for net direct investments of privates and oil-companies.

Yet, we have no information on the currency composition of the NFPs of the countries included in table 4. If we, however, take the sign of the US private NFP as an indication of the net creditor or debtor position in foreign currencies, then the data in columns 2 and 3 suggest that a balancing out of perverse valuation effects is not an unreasonable assumption for the investigated dollar exchange rates: except for 1973, the NFP of US private residents was positive on all measures over the complete investigation period.

The main results of the previous analysis may now be summarized in the following tow points.

a. The empirical data set out above suggest that Japan's private sector was in a net debtor position internationally over the entire investigation period. The same holds for some time periods also for the German private sector. Under the (unrealistic) assumption of only one internationally traded asset, dollar bonds, these findings lead to the conclusion that perverse wealth-valuation effects may have had an influence on the yen/dollar and DM/dollar exchange rate over the time from 1973 to 1982.

b. When we consider the more realistic case of two internationally traded assets, the empirical presuppositions for exchange rate instability and perverse exchange rate reactions due to negative net foreign asset positions become more complicated. The available empirical data do not allow for a positive judgement on the empirical relevance of these phenomena to the investigated countries.

First, under conditions of international trade in assets it is not just the sign of the private NFP that matters but the sign of the foreign-currency denominated private NFP. Our results for Germany demonstrate that a negative NFP do not necessarily imply a net debtor position in foreign currency. On the contrary, the figures for Germany show that the German private sector was in fact in a net creditor position in foreign currency over most of the investigation period although its net foreign asset position was frequently negative.

Second, perverse valuation effects arising from a negative NFP of the home country's private sector may always be balanced by normal valuation effects occuring in US private portfolios. Although we have no information on the relative strenght of exchange rate influences from counteracting valuation effects, our data for the US NFP indicates that such offsetting forces represent a realistic possibility.

APPENDIX A

DEFINITIONS AND SOURCES OF THE DATA

The data were mainly taken from International Monetary Fund, International Financial Statistics (IFS) data tape, and OECD, Main Economic Indicators (MEI).

Variables used in chapter 9.

e : (home currency/US dollar) spot exchange rate, end-of-period market rate defined as units of DM, yen, pound sterling per one US dollar (IFS, line ae). For estimation purposes the DM/$ and £/$ exchange rate were multiplied by 100.

M1 : Money supply M1, seasonally adjusted and measured at the end of the period, billions of domestic currency units.

Quarterly series: all countries (IFS, line 34..b)
Monthly series : Germany, Japan, and United Kingdom (IFS, line 34..b), United States (MEI).

PF : Private net foreign asset stocks, end-of-period values, billions of US dollars. Calculated as the difference between total stocks of net foreign assets F and net foreign asset holdings of the central bank:

$$PF_t = F_t - R_t = \sum_{i=0}^{t} CAS_i - \sum_{i=0}^{t} (R_i - R_{i-1})$$

i = 0 denotes the beginning of the sample period.

F : total stocks of net foreign assets, calculated as cumulated current account surpluses, end-of-period, billions of dollars. The current account includes the trade account, the service account, and the balance of unrequited transfers.

Quarterly series: all countries, trade account surplus (IFS, line 77 aad + line 77 abd) plus service account surplus (IFS, line 77 acd + line 77 add) plus the balance of unrequited transfers (IFS, line 77 acd + line 77 agd).

Monthly series: Germany and Japan (MEI)

United States: monthly current account figures were interpolated from monthly figures on US exports and imports. The calculation was conducted according to the following method.

As data basis we used quarterly current account figures for the US (IFS, lines see above for quarterly series) and monthly figures on US exports fob (IFS, line 70x), called X in the following, and monthly figures on US imports cif (IFS, line 71), called IM in the following.

Step 1: Computation of a "corrected" monthly trade account.

First, we calculated quarterly trade account figures from the cumulated differences between X and IM (IFS, line 70x - line 71). The difference between the given quarterly trade account (IFS, line 77aad + line 77 abd) and the quarterly cumulated monthly figures for X-IM was divided by the quarterly cumulated monthly figures for X-IM to determine quarterly weights μ for the interpolation. $(1 - \mu)$ times the monthly figures for X-IM yields monthly trade account figures which sum up to the given quarterly trade account.

Step 2: Partition of the quarterly service account and transfer account figures.

Quarterly figures on services and transfers (IFS, lines see above) were equally distributed to the months within the quarter.

The so generated monthly figures for services and transfers were added to the monthly trade account figures from step 1 to arrive at the monthly current account of the US.

R : official net foreign exchange reserves, created as total reserves minus gold (IFS, line 1 l.d) minus Special Drawing Rights (IFS, line 1 b.d) minus the reserve position in the Fund (IFS, line 1 c.d).

PB : Private net stocks of domestic-currency denominated bonds. Quarterly and monthly figures for the US, Germany and Japan were created in the following way.

Central government debt (US and Germany: IFS, line 88; Japan: IFS, line 88b) minus central bank claims on the government (IFS, line 12a) plus government deposits at the central bank (IFS, line 16d). Billions of domestic currency units, end-of-period.

For the United Kingdom no direct data were available. Quarterly data for the UK were calculated from yearly (end-of-March) benchmark figures for the total (central government) national sterling debt (Bank of England, Quarterly Bulletin, various December issues, and Central Statistical Office, Financial Statistics, Supplementary Tables).

The total net stocks of sterling denominated bonds were created as follows. To the benchmark figure at the beginning of every year we added (or subtracted) quarterly figures for the increase or decrease in net domestic borrowing of the UK central government (IFS, line 84a). The difference between the so generated total central government debt at the end of the year and the new benchmark figure was equally distributed to the quarterly figures within the yearly calculation period.

From these quarterly figures we subtracted central bank claims on the government (IFS, line 12a) to derive private net stocks of sterling denominated bonds.

Δe : $(e_t - e_{t-1})/e_{t-1}$ rate of devaluation of the domestic currency vis-à-vis the US dollar between time t-1 and t.

TAR : $[(P_H/P_u)\cdot 100]_t - e_{t-1}$ where subscripts H and u denote "home country" and the US, respectively.

P : consumer price index (1975 = 100), (IFS, line 64).

Variables used in chapter 10.

The variables were defined in the same way as above with the following alterations and extensions.

R_U : Official net foreign exchange reserves of the US, defined as above but converted into billions of DM by multiplying with a period average DM/$ exchange rate (IFS, line rf).

FD_G : German net stocks of foreign-currency (US dollar) denominated assets resulting from imbalances in the German foreign-currency (US dollar) denominated current account. Calculated by cumulating imbalances in the foreign-currency part of the German current account:

$$FD_G = \sum_{i=0}^{t} (\alpha^x X_i - \alpha^{im} Im)_G$$

i = 0 denotes the beginning of the respective sample period. Billions of US dollars, end-of-quarter values.

α^x : share of "exports" which are denominated in foreign-currency in total "exports" (sources: see textual part).

α^{im}: share of "imports" which are denominated in foreign-currency in total "imports" (sources: see textual part).

X : total positive entries in the current account ("exports"), calculated as merchandise exports fob (IFS, line 77aad) plus other goods, services and income: credit (IFS, line 77 acd).

Im : total negative entries in the current account ("imports"), calculated as merchandise imprts fob (IFS, line 77 abd) plus other goods, services and income: debit (IFS, line 77 add) plus private and official unrequited transfers (IFS, lines 77 aed and 77 agd).

$\underline{FM_G}$: German net stocks of domestic-currency (DM) denominated assets resulting from imbalances in the domestic-currency (DM) denominated current account. Calculated by cumulating imbalances in the domestic-currency part of the German current account:

$$FM_G = \sum_{i=0}^{t} [(1 - \alpha^x) X_i - (1 - \alpha^{im}) Im_i]_G$$

Billions of DM, end-of-quarter values. Other definitions see FD_G.

$\underline{FM_u}$: US net stocks of foreign-currency (DM) denominated assets resulting from imbalances in the foreign-currency (DM) denominated current account. Calculated by cumulating imbalances in the foreign-currency part of the US current account:

$$FM_u = \sum_{i=0}^{t} (\alpha^x X_i - \alpha^{im} Im_i)_u$$

Billions of DM, end-of-quarter values. Other definitions and sources as for FD_G.

$\underline{FD_u}$: US net stocks of domestic-currency (US dollar) denominated assets resulting from imbalances in the domestic-currency (US dollar) denominated current account. Calculated by cumulating imbalances in the domestic-currency part of the US current account:

$$FD_u = \sum_{i=0}^{t} [(1 - \alpha^x) X_i - (1 - \alpha^{im}) Im_i]_u$$

Billions of US dollars, end-of-quarter values. Other definitions and sources as for FD_G.

APPENDIX B

TIME SERIES PLOTS OF ASSET VARIABLES USED IN THE ESTIMATIONS OF CHAPTER 9

Asset Variables:	Quarterly Data
Exchange Rates :	Monthly Data
Definitions :	See Appendix A
Data Sources :	Own Calculations from International Monetary Fund, International Financial Statistics Data Tape

Figures 1 - 3: United States and Germany: Exchange Rate, Total Net Foreign Asset Positions, and Central Bank Foreign Exchange Reserves

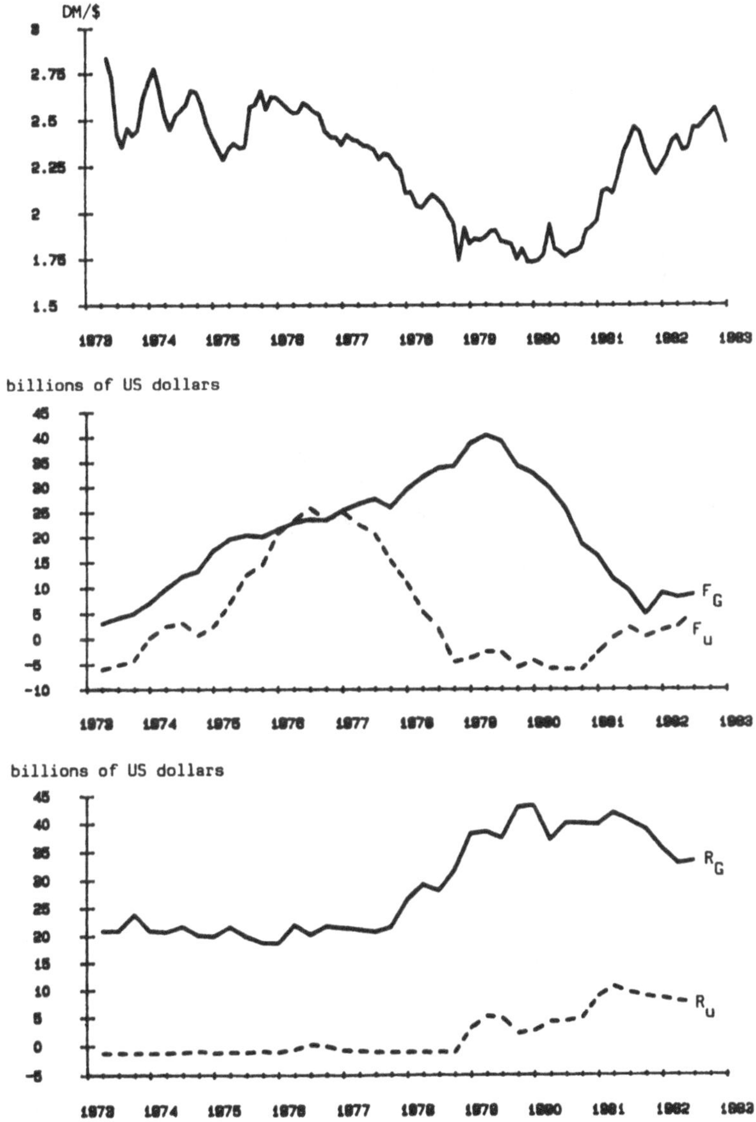

Figures 4 - 6: United States and Japan: Exchange Rate, Total Net Foreign Asset Position, and Central Bank Foreign Exchange Reserves

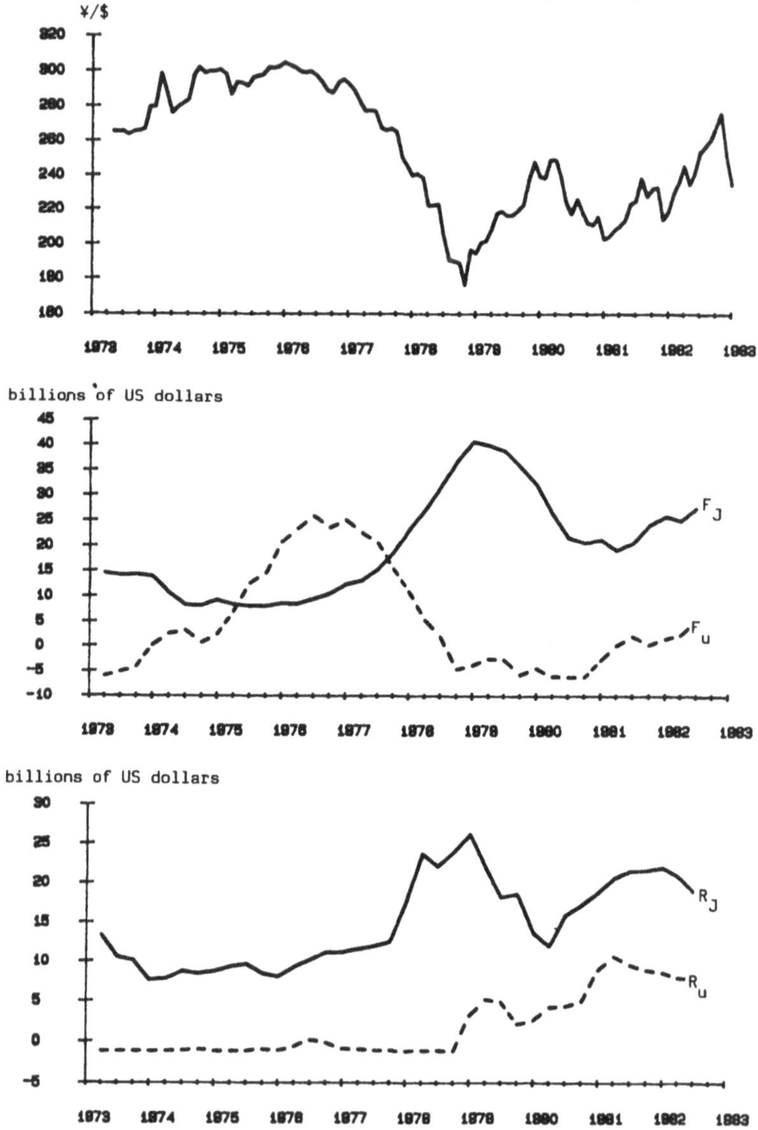

Figures 7 - 9: United States and United Kingdom: Exchange Rate, Total Net Foreign Asset Positions, and Central Bank Foreign Exchange Reserves

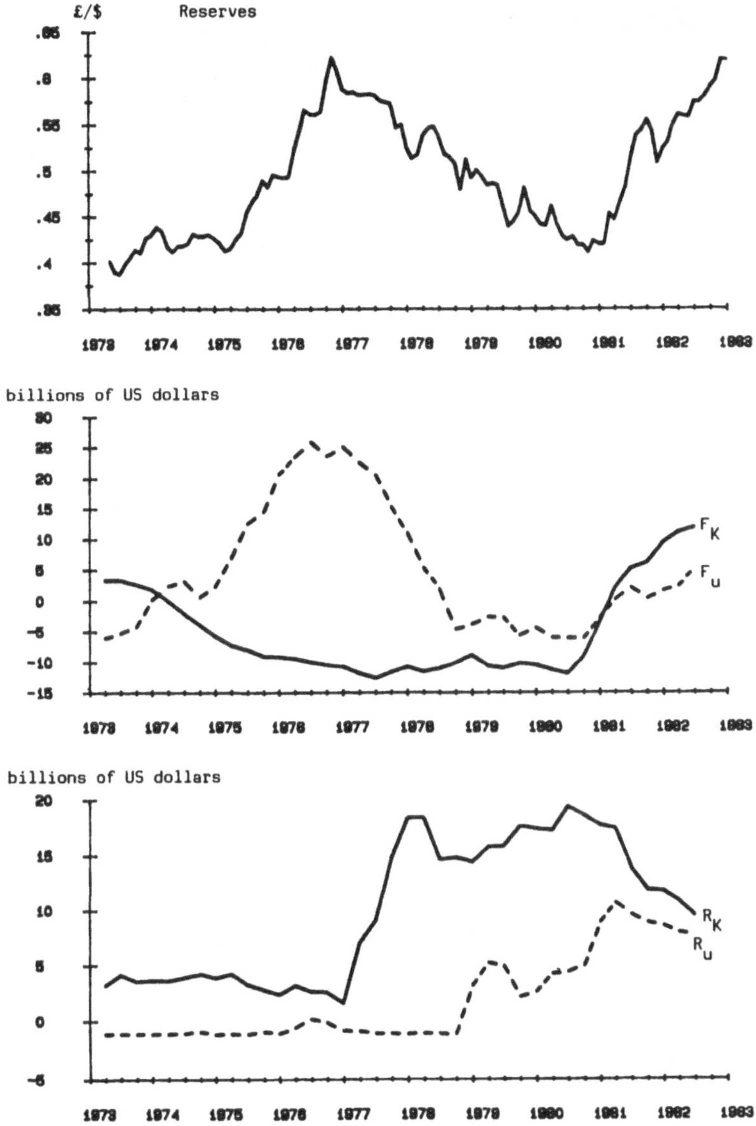

Figure 10: United States: Total and Private Net Foreign Asset Stocks

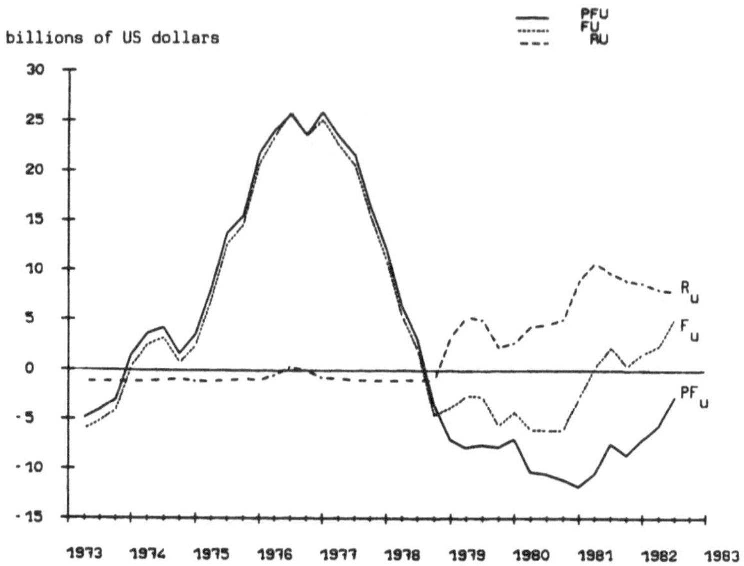

Figure 11: Germany: Total and Private Net Foreign Asset Stocks

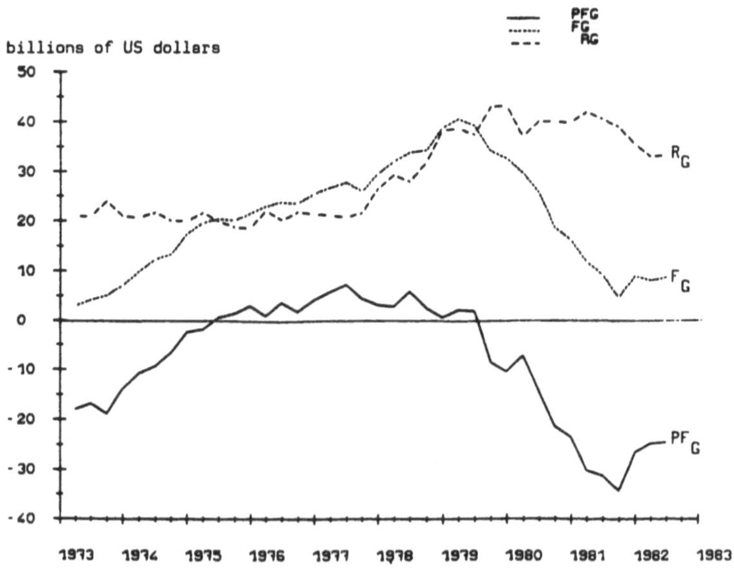

Figure 12: Japan: Total and Private Net Foreign Asset Stocks

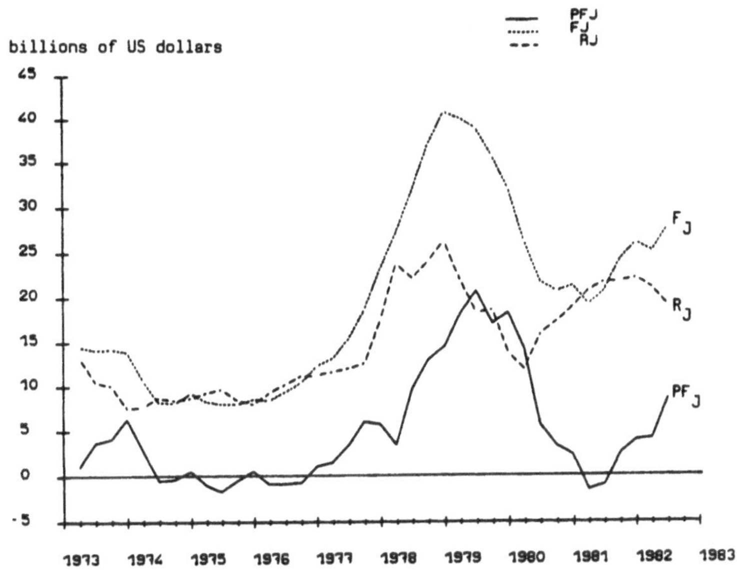

Figure 13: United Kingdom: Total and Private Net Foreign Asset Stocks

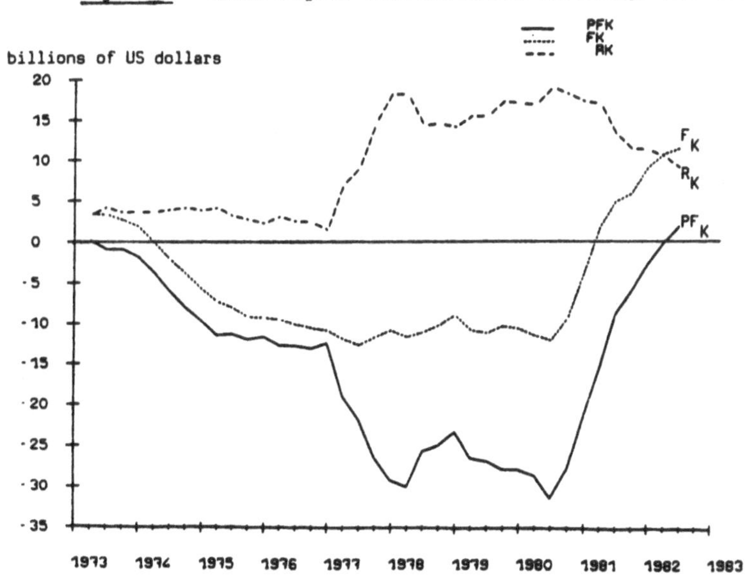

APPENDIX C

ESTIMATION RESULTS TO CHAPTER 9

For Definitions and Data Sources see Appendix A and Section 9.1.

C.1. Estimation Results for the DM/US Dollar Exchange Rate

Table 1: Estimates for the DM/$ Exchange Rate, Sample Period 1973.4 - 1978.10, Monthly Data.

Table 2: Error Statistics for the Ex-Post Forecasts of the DM/$ Exchange Rate over the Period from 1978.11 to 1982.8, Monthly Data.

Table 3: Estimates for the DM/$ Exchange Rate, Sample Period 1973.4 - 1982.8, Monthly Data.

Table 4: Estimates for the DM/$ Exchange Rate, Sample Period 1973.I - 1982.II, Quarterly Data.

Table 5: Consistent Estimates for the Reaction Function of German Foreign Exchange Reserves R_G, Sample Periods 1973.4 - 1982.8 (Monthly Data) and 1973.I - 1982.II (Quarterly Data).

<u>Table 1a</u>: Estimates for the DM/$ Exchange Rate, Sample Period 1973.4 - 1978.10, Monthly Data.

		Eq. (1.1)		Eq. (1.3)		Eq. (1.2)		Eq. (1.4)	
		OLS 1-1	CORC 1-2	OLS 1-3	CORC 1-4	OLS 1-5	CORC 1-6	OLS 1-7	CORC 1-8
C		465,62 (10,44)	522,84 (7,14)	446,08 (4,04)	491,18 (4,03)	325,24 (7,92)	322,59 (5,23)	190,87 (2,0779)	268,12 (2,5216)
$M1_G$	+	0,3370 (0,8632)	0,0880 (0,1807)	0,6143 (0,9367)	0,1514 (0,2891)	0,5902* (1,7263)	0,2845 (0,6147)	1,1020* (2,0927)	0,3363 (0,6865)
$M1_U$	./.	-0,9718* (-2,8050)	-1,0573* (-2,2271)	-1,0702* (-2,2657)	-0,9112 (-1,3972)	-0,2995 (-0,9808)	-0,1900 (-0,4603)	0,1870 (0,4616)	0,0857 (0,1504)
PF_G	./.	-0,1820 (-0,3636)	2,4984* (3,1782)	-0,2839 (-0,3000)	2,4567* (2,9493)				
F_G	./.					-1,8145* (-3,6221)	-1,1531 (-1,3476)	-3,0971* (-3,5065)	-1,4198 (-1,5483)
R_G	+					-4,2417* (-5,4323)	-3,9112* (-5,3205)	-3,5724* (-3,8514)	-3,7376* (-4,6581)
PF_U	+	0,8129* (3,5960)	0,2406 (0,5466)	0,8308* (1,6901)	0,3418 (0,6339)				
F_U	+					-0,1637 (-0,6414)	0,0822 (0,2644)	0,3916 (0,9475)	0,2702 (0,6343)
R_U	./.					11,7683* (2,3849)	6,1460 (1,2287)	10,1590* (2,0365)	6,3222 (1,2445)
PB_G	?			-0,3312 (-0,8246)	-0,0117 (-0,0484)			-0,0090 (-0,0288)	0,0213 (0,0970)
PB_U	+			0,1007 (0,5900)	-0,0627 (-0,3243)			-0,2405 (-1,6582)	-0,1062 (-0,6782)
$\bar{R}^2$		0,7785		0,7741		0,8672		0,8700	
$\hat{R}^2$			0,3993		0,3757		0,6792		0,6915
F		59,00	11,61	38,70	6,88	72,86	21,91	56,20	18,88
DW		0,6248	1,4498	0,6403	1,4482	0,7107	1,5291	0,8331	1,5621
RHO			0,7821 (10,20)		0,7857 (10,32)		0,6441 (6,84)		0,6180 (6,39)

Table 1b: Estimates for the DM/$ Exchange Rate, Sample Period 1973.4 - 1978.10, Monthly Data.

		Eq. (1.1)		Eq. (1.3)		Eq. (1.2)		Eq. (1.4)	
		2SLS 1-9	FAIR 1-10	2SLS 1-11	FAIR 1-12	2SLS 1-13	FAIR 1-14	2SLS 1-15	FAIR 1-16
C		447,22 (9,80)	425,67 (5,45)	222,50 (1,6428)	498,90 (4,09)	327,44 (7,49)	337,61 (5,1079)	179,20 (1,8128)	353,78 (3,3730)
$M1_G$	+	0,4724 (1,1847)	0,3169 (0,5953)	1,6887* (2,2040)	0,3176 (0,5583)	0,5936* (1,7319)	0,4954 (1,1294)	1,1912* (2,0003)	0,3750 (0,7477)
$M1_u$	./.	-0,9826* (-2,7887)	-0,8323 (-1,6447)	-0,5054 (-0,9607)	-1,0971* (-1,7650)	-0,3154 (-0,9737)	-0,3506 (-0,8278)	0,1932 (0,4757)	-0,3608 (-0,6734)
PF_G	./.	-0,9119 (-1,6672)	-1,1461 (-1,0031)	-2,5897* (-2,1069)	0,8221 (0,7011)				
F_G	./.					-1,8150* (-3,6224)	-1,5649* (-1,7317)	-3,2277* (-3,3176)	-1,1444 (-1,0940)
R_G	+					-4,1211* (-3,6456)	-3,5095* (-2,5545)	-3,2290* (-2,2833)	-4,4184* (-3,7586)
PF_u	+	1,0543* (4,4074)	1,2930 (2,4943)	1,9408* (3,1175)	0,5564 (0,9174)				
F_u	+					-0,1321 (-0,3964)	0,1449 (0,3169)	0,5154 (0,9126)	-0,1392 (-0,2763)
R_u	./.					11,4200* (2,0872)	4,6637 (0,8860)	9,4082* (1,7070)	5,4492 (1,0157)
PB_G	?			-0,7561* (-1,7116)	-0,1334 (-0,5012)			-0,0542 (-0,1576)	0,0200 (0,0880)
PB_u	+			-0,1276 (-0,6619)	0,0499 (0,2667)			-0,2521* (-1,6851)	0,0352 (0,2301)
$\bar{R}^2$		0,7709		0,7518		0,8672		0,8697	
$\hat{R}^2$			0,8158		0,8279		0,8952		0,8887
F		52,16	68,64	30,30	48,11	65,30	85,46	48,38	57,88
DW		0,6574	1,4180	0,8317	1,4447	0,7071	1,5955	0,8408	1,6146
RHO			0,6835 (6,96)		0,7489 (8,19)		0,6778 (6,96)		0,7021 (7,25)

Table 2: Error Statistics for the Ex-Post Forecasts of the DM/$ Exchange Rate over the Period from 1978.11 to 1982.8, Monthly Data. a)

Forecasting Model	RMSE	U^M	U^R	U^D	REG	CORR
BHM's Equation						
1-1	0,80	0,6140	0,3574	0,0287	-0,85	-0,85
1-2	1,44	0,6851	0,3047	0,0103	-0,37	-0,83
1-9	0,65	0,5760	0,3796	0,0444	-1,21	-0,85
1-10	0,58	0,6199	0,3167	0,0634	-1,89	-0,83
PF Divided						
1-5	0,67	0,8063	0,1634	0,0304	0,46	0,89
1-6	0,19	0,5198	0,1455	0,3347	0,77	0,91
1-13	0,64	0,8063	0,1605	0,0333	0,48	0,89
1-14	0,12	0,1153	0,1067	0,7780	0,85	0,91

a) Numbers of equations refer to tables 1a and 1b, last pages. For definitions and explanations see section 9.1.3.4.

Table 3a: Estimates for the DM/$ Exchange Rate, Sample Period 1973.4 - 1982.8, Monthly Data.

		Eq. (1.1)		Eq. (1.3)		Eq. (1.2)		Eq. (1.4)	
		OLS 3-1	CORC 3-2	OLS 3-3	CORC 3-4	OLS 3-5	CORC 3-6	OLS 3-7	CORC 3-8
C		251,74 (20,73)	7,93 (0,0840)	297,43 (6,49)	34,91 (0,4057)	314,81 (24,65)	288,46 (13,98)	322,29 (8,60)	253,68 (6,41)
$M1_G$	+	-1,5052* (-7,0576)	0,2274 (0,6167)	-1,5627* (-6,4117)	0,2058 (0,5553)	-0,1181 (-0,4963)	-0,0917 (-0,3130)	-0,1172 (-0,4314)	0,0276 (0,0900)
$M1_u$	./.	0,7484* (5,0534)	0,4240* (1,7012)	0,5808* (2,7801)	0,4087 (1,5800)	-0,0203 (-0,1447)	0,0341 (0,1889)	-0,0472 (-0,2729)	0,1379 (0,6559)
PF_G	./.	-0,4259 (-1,3843)	1,2551* (2,8942)	-0,3991 (-1,2410)	1,1772* (2,5254)				
F_G	./.					-1,1617* (-4,0448)	-1,2739* (-3,2193)	-1,1648* (-3,7612)	-1,3611* (-3,3827)
R_G	+					-2,4593* (-6,2414)	-2,1504* (-5,1912)	-2,3938* (-6,0062)	-1,9854* (-4,6542)
PF_u	+	1,3891* (9,0896)	0,6032 (1,1441)	1,3018* (6,7575)	0,7687 (1,4030)				
F_u	+					0,5093* (3,2398)	0,7245* (3,0843)	0,5308* (3,0779)	0,8670* (3,4318)
R_u	./.					2,7594* (3,8401)	1,6171* (1,7771)	2,8077* (3,8004)	1,6009* (1,7473)
PB_G	?			0,2032 (1,1131)	-0,0515 (-0,3087)			0,0409 (0,2847)	-0,1482 (-1,0502)
PB_u	+			0,0153 (1,0448)	-0,0086 (-0,9675)			-0,0134 (-1,2098)	-0,0099 (-1,2703)
$\bar{R}^2$		0,8329		0,8336		0,9052		0,9049	
$\hat{R}^2$			0,0642		0,0507		0,6665		0,6714
F		140,55	2,8227	94,54	1,9305	179,33	36,88	134,16	27,35
DW		0,5465	1,7289	0,5789	1,7461	0,6143	1,7278	0,6289	1,7383
RHO			0,9599 (36,24)		0,9528 (33,22)		0,6809 (9,8395)		0,6781 (9,7635)

Table 3b: Estimates for the DM/$ Exchange Rate, Sample Period 1973.4 - 1982.8, Monthly Data.

		Eq. (1.1)		Eq. (1.3)		Eq. (1.2)		Eq. (1.4)	
		2SLS 3-9	FAIR 3-10	2SLS 3-11	FAIR 3-12	2SLS 3-13	FAIR 3-14	2SLS 3-15	FAIR 3-16
C		261,84 (20,71)	-958,12 (-1,8654)	294,20 (6,39)	237,15 (3,0476)	315,10 (24,63)	296,54 (13,37)	322,98 (8,61)	259,95 (6,40)
$M1_G$	+	-1,2859* (-5,6920)	0,1894 (0,4282)	-1,3357* (-5,1677)	-0,2238 (-0,4486)	-0,1002 (-0,4161)	-0,0012 (-0,0038)	-0,0951 (-0,3475)	0,1237 (0,3862)
$M1_U$	·/.	0,5942* (3,7834)	0,2852 (0,8307)	0,4852* (2,2793)	0,2024 (0,5882)	-0,0240 (-0,1708)	-0,0249 (-0,1326)	-0,5277 (-0,3046)	0,0741 (0,3434)
PF_G	·/.	-0,7837* (-2,3726)	-0,1798 (-0,2304)	-0,7391* (-2,1359)	-1,7372* (-2,5284)				
F_G	·/.					-1,1431* (-3,9434)	-1,4472* (-3,4180)	-1,1368* (-3,6360)	-1,5926* (-3,5866)
R_G	+					-2,6020* (-5,3144)	-2,1788* (-2,7170)	-2,5941* (-5,2810)	-1,7404* (-2,2724)
PF_U	+	1,5018* (9,5052)	0,3530 (0,5671)	1,4347* (7,1889)	1,7477* (3,7125)				
F_U	+					0,4637* (2,5394)	0,6398* (1,9663)	0,4656* (2,3722)	0,8777* (2,5327)
R_U	·/.					2,8773* (3,7958)	1,5293 (1,5590)	2,9708* (3,8303)	1,4445 (1,4465)
PB_G	?			0,1559 (0,8457)	-0,1876 (-0,5921)			0,0415 (0,2882)	-0,1649 (-1,0822)
PB_U	+			-0,0181 (-1,2308)	-0,0419 (-1,4515)			-0,0126 (-1,1344)	-0,0097 (-1,1636)
$\bar{R}^2$		0,8308		0,8319		0,9051		0,9046	
$\hat{R}^2$			-0,2715		0,6490		0,8311		0,8246
F		132,57		87,42	32,66	168,54	88,59	123,31	61,10
DW		0,5476	1,7542	0,5769	1,7703	0,6190	1,7724	0,6344	1,7888
RHO			0,9994 (1686,54)		0,7691 (12,02)		0,7242 (10,29)		0,7369 (10,47)

Table 4: Estimates for the DM/$ Exchange Rate, Sample Period 1973.I - 1982.II, Quarterly Data.

		Eq. (1.1)		Eq. (1.3)		Eq. (1.2)		Eq. (1.4)	
		OLS 4-1	2SLS 4-2	OLS 4-3	2SLS 4-4	OLS 4-5	2SLS 4-6	OLS 4-7	2SLS 4-8
C		287,69 (11,32)	320,58 (11,24)	440,77 (5,91)	416,12 (5,25)	372,42 (14,50)	372,68 (13,40)	438,15 (7,11)	436,04 (6,90)
$M1_G$	+	-0,6600 (-1,2610)	0,2355 (0,3841)	-1,0970* (-2,0421)	-0,1777 (-0,2772)	0,6692 (1,5548)	0,6699 (1,5531)	0,3290 (0,6141)	0,2511 (0,4374)
$M1_U$	·/.	0,1397 (0,3778)	-0,4966 (-1,1456)	-0,4958 (-1,2247)	-0,8766* (-1,9681)	-0,5004* (-1,8498)	-0,4988* (-1,7927)	-0,6477* (-2,1131)	-0,7126* (-2,0691)
PF_G	·/.	-1,4637* (-2,4751)	-2,6098* (-3,6713)	-0,9404 (-1,6054)	-2,0607* (-2,8719)				
F_G	·/.					-1,7343* (-3,7010)	-1,7256* (-2,9295)	-1,4397* (-2,6449)	-1,5723* (-2,5017)
R_G	+					-2,6748* (-3,5012)	-2,7130 (-1,5528)	-2,6371* (-3,1679)	-1,6880 (-0,7474)
PF_U	+	1,6238* (5,0088)	2,0283* (5,5935)	0,8918* (2,2853)	1,3923* (3,1414)				
F_U	+					0,3778 (1,2692)	0,3658 (0,6322)	0,2584 (0,8105)	0,4986 (0,8021)
R_U	·/.					2,8920* (2,1149)	2,9255 (1,5061)	3,1342* (2,2416)	2,3978 (1,1088)
PB_G	?			0,2023 (0,5135)	0,0116 (0,0275)			0,2852 (0,9588)	0,2225 (0,6662)
PB_U	+			0,2656* (1,8408)	0,2622* (1,7184)			-0,0009 (-0,0070)	0,0509 (0,3015)
$\bar{R}^2$		0,7664	0,7398	0,8048	0,7818	0,8922	0,8923	0,8901	0,8852
$\hat{R}^2$									
F		31,35	23,46	26,43	18,51	52,07	42,79	38,45	27,94
DW		1,4562	1,4350	1,7542	1,6564	1,5201	1,5208	1,7200	1,7132

Table 5: Estimates for the Reaction Function of R_G, Monthly (1973.4 - 1982.8) and Quarterly (1973.I - 1982.II) Data.

together with :	Eq. (1.1)		Eq. (1.2)		Eq. (1.3)		Eq. (1.4)	
	Quarterly	Monthly	Quarterly	Monthly	Quarterly	Monthly	Quarterly	Monthly
	2SLS	2SLS	2SLS	2SLS	2SLS	2SLS	2SLS	2SLS
C	6,8184 (1,7575)	3,6717 (3,0058)	6,7966 (1,7678)	3,7646 (3,0647)	6,8226 (1,7526)	3,5982 (2,9327)	6,8019 (1,7678)	3,6797 (3,0222)
R_{t-1} +	0,9356* (16,33)	0,9664* (52,71)	0,9280* (16,39)	0,9627* (53,77)	0,9371* (16,32)	0,9693* (53,42)	0,9299* (16,42)	0,9661* (53,91)
$\Delta e(DM/\$)$ ./.	-30,3256* (-3,4224)	-18,2901* (-2,1612)	-26,0132* (-3,0844)	-13,4147* (-1,7607)	-31,1602* (-3,5777)	-22,1518* (-3,0671)	-27,0718* (-3,2309)	-17,8720* (-2,6601)
TAR +	0,0319* (1,7277)	0,0184* (3,1460)	0,0298 (1,6315)	0,0182* (3,0872)	0,0324* (1,7458)	0,0186* (3,1560)	0,0303 (1,6591)	0,0184* (3,1455)
$\bar{R}^2$	0,9317	0,9779	0,9329	0,9776	0,9312	0,9776	0,9328	0,9780
F	154,50	1610,31	157,53	1586,35	153,36	1587,93	157,25	1536,67
DW	2,0651	2,2185	2,0451	2,2074	2,0680	2,2212	2,0507	2,2179

C.2. Estimation Results for the Yen/US Dollar Exchange Rate

Table 1:	Estimates for the Yen/$ Exchange Rate, Sample Period 1973.4 - 1978.10, Monthly Data.
Table 2:	Error Statistics for the Ex-Post Forecasts of the Yen/$ Exchange Rate over the Period from 1978.11 to 1982.8, Monthly Data.
Table 3:	Estimates for the Yen/$ Exchange Rate, Sample Period 1973.4 - 1980.8, Monthly Data. (JAPAN SHORT including Net Domestic Bond Stocks)
Table 4:	Estimates for the Yen/$ Exchange Rate, Sample Period 1973.I - 1980.II, Quarterly Data. (JAPAN SHORT including Net Domestic Bond Stocks)
Table 5:	Consistent Estimates for the Reaction Function of Japanese Foreign Exchange Reserves R_J, Sample Periods 1973.4 - 1980.8 (Monthly Data) and 1973.I - 1980.II (Quarterly Data).
Table 6:	Estimates for the Yen/$ Exchange Rate, Sample Period 1973.4 - 1982.8, Monthly Data. (JAPAN LONG excluding Net Domestic Bond Stocks)
Table 7:	Estimates for the Yen/$ Exchange Rate, Sample Period 1973.I - 1982.II, Quarterly Data. (JAPAN LONG excluding Net Domestic Bond Stocks)
Table 8:	Consistent Estimates for the Reaction Function of Japanese Foreign Exchange Reserves R_J, Sample Periods 1973.4 - 1982.8 (Monthly Data) and 1973.I - 1982.II (Quarterly Data).

<u>Table 1a</u>: Estimates for the Yen/$ Exchange Rate, Sample Period 1973.4 - 1978.10, Monthly Data.

		Eq. (1.1)		Eq. (1.3)		Eq. (1.2)		Eq. (1.4)	
		OLS 1-1	CORC 1-2	OLS 1-3	CORC 1-4	OLS 1-5	CORC 1-6	OLS 1-7	CORC 1-8
C		421,86 (9,47)	532,54 (8,86)	255,73 (3,87)	280,27 (3,12)	185,17 (4,03)	199,64 (3,52)	130,20 (2,0246)	167,67 (2,2008)
$M1_J$	+	-0,0020 (-1,5371)	-0,0017 (-1,3879)	-0,0014 (-1,2250)	-0,0016 (-1,2827)	-0,0013 (-1,2472)	-0,0010 (-0,9472)	-0,0017 (-1,5402)	-0,0012 (-1,0535)
$M1_U$	·/.	-0,1660 (-0,4634)	-0,6729* (-1,8226)	0,7272* (1,8694)	0,6028 (1,1595)	0,6026* (1,9218)	0,4879 (1,4709)	0,8508* (2,1691)	0,6972 (1,5440)
PF_J	·/.	-3,0535* (-5,0886)	0,3414 (0,4274)	-1,5318* (-2,7811)	-0,7960 (-1,1244)				
F_J	·/.					-3,6066* (-8,9817)	-3,1909* (-5,3508)	-3,4833* (-6,0358)	-2,9630* (-4,1179)
R_J	+					-1,7682* (-2,7237)	-2,2524* (-2,7199)	-1,9784* (-2,5164)	-2,0874* (-2,3975)
PF_U	+	1,5659* (7,4914)	2,0299* (5,2900)	2,3518* (8,4591)	2,4070* (5,9743)				
F_U	+					0,0006 (0,0026)	0,1680 (0,5182)	-0,2098 (-0,3997)	0,3337 (0,6079)
R_U	·/.					7,4170* (1,9625)	3,6668 (0,9340)	7,8619* (2,0500)	4,0071 (1,0058)
PB_J	?			-0,000086 (-0,1143)	-0,00032 (-0,4009)			-0,00077 (-1,2149)	-0,00023 (-0,3428)
PB_U	+			-0,4162* (-5,3876)	-0,3520* (-2,7239)			0,0376 (0,3465)	-0,0606 (-0,4767)
$\bar{R}^2$		0,9291		0,9553		0,9700		0,9698	
$\hat{R}^2$			0,6091		0,8617		0,9237		0,9250
F		217,24	25,89	236,24	62,68	356,72	120,89	265,60	99,37
DW		0,7115	1,9888	0,9707	1,7454	1,1076	1,7274	1,1565	1,7395
RHO			0,8263 (11,92)		0,5807 (5,80)		0,4973 (4,65)		0,4832 (4,48)

Table 1b: Estimates for the Yen/$ Exchange Rate, Sample Period 1973.4 - 1978.10, Monthly Data.

		Eq. (1.1)		Eq. (1.3)		Eq. (1.2)		Eq. (1.4)	
		2SLS 1-9	FAIR 1-10	2SLS 1-11	FAIR 1-12	2SLS 1-13	FAIR 1-14	2SLS 1-15	FAIR 1-16
C		378,27 (8,03)	350,68 (5,66)	272,51 (3,99)	234,26 (2,8689)	206,29 (4,25)	271,17 (4,23)	164,96 (2,3558)	213,22 (2,75)
$M1_J$	+	-0,0027* (-1,9991)	-0,0032* (-2,0081)	-0,0017 (-1,5177)	-0,0022 (-1,6568)	-0,0016 (-1,4627)	-0,0020 (-1,4994)	-0,0019* (-1,6802)	-0,0021 (-1,5427)
$M1_u$	·/.	0,1311 (0,3486)	0,3163 (0,6845)	0,6967* (1,7360)	0,8861* (1,8333)	0,5768* (1,7977)	0,4088 (1,1215)	0,8584* (2,1277)	0,8112* (1,6965)
PF_J	·/.	-4,2756* (-6,2820)	-4,8380* (-4,0056)	-2,6099* (-4,1256)	-2,8876* (-3,3360)				
F_J	·/.					-3,9110* (-8,7485)	-4,1705* (-4,8510)	-3,4269* (-5,7622)	-3,2232* (-4,0265)
R_J	+					-0,6982 (-0,7675)	1,3306 (0,6811)	-0,5390 (-0,4316)	1,2685 (0,7551)
PF_u	+	1,3479* (6,0811)	1,2594* (3,4573)	2,1802* (7,5139)	1,9640* (5,0886)				
F_u	+					0,1554 (0,6404)	0,6436 (1,5689)	0,4204 (0,6164)	1,2196 (1,6645)
R_u	·/.					6,0069 (1,5207)	0,6503 (0,1386)	6,0174 (1,4575)	1,4141 (0,3131)
PB_J	?			0,00027 (0,3405)	-0,00027 (-0,3308)			-0,00042 (-0,6188)	-0,00024 (-0,3217)
PB_u	+			-0,3749* (-4,6625)	-0,3287* (-3,0890)			-0,0728 (-0,5456)	-0,1949 (-1,2946)
$\bar{R}^2$		0,9244		0,9525		0,9686		0,9680	
$\hat{R}^2$			0,8606		0,9146		0,9282		0,9326
F		189,43	95,70	200,42	107,13	308,98	129,21	219,42	100,34
DW		0,7940	1,7676	1,0137	1,7140	1,1124	1,7199	1,1138	1,7278
RHO			0,5914 (5,75)		0,5003 (4,54)		0,4970 (4,49)		0,4720 (4,12)

Table 2: Error Statistics for the Ex-Post Forecasts of the Yen/$ Exchange Rate over the Period from 1978.11 to 1982.8, Monthly Data. [a)]

Forecasting Model	RMSE	U^M	U^R	U^D	REG	CORR
BHM's Equation						
1-1	67,31	0,7754	0,1829	0,0418	-0,46	-0,55
1-2	104,20	0,8925	0,0861	0,0241	-0,26	-0,38
1-9	59,73	0,5322	0,4001	0,0677	-0,17	-0,34
1-10	57,83	0,3508	0,5736	0,0757	-0,11	-0,26
PF Divided						
1-5	97,70	0,7034	0,2690	0,0277	0,05	0,16
1-6	62,53	0,5752	0,3585	0,0663	0,09	0,22
1-13	83,33	0,6079	0,3534	0,0387	0,04	0,12
1-14	42,36	0,0096	0,8388	0,1515	-0,01	-0,02

a) Numbers of equations refer to tables 1a and 1b, last pages. For definitions and explanations see section 9.1.3.4.

Table 3a: Estimates for the Yen/$ Exchange Rate, Sample Period 1973.4 - 1980.8, Monthly Data.

		Eq. (1.1)		Eq. (1.3)		Eq. (1.2)		Eq. (1.4)	
		OLS 3-1	CORC 3-2	OLS 3-3	CORC 3-4	OLS 3-5	CORC 3-6	OLS 3-7	CORC 3-8
C		277,00 (6,07)	335,31 (3,10)	254,25 (3,62)	422,05 (4,20)	352,78 (17,41)	330,80 (10,73)	283,34 (6,68)	286,43 (5,35)
$M1_J$	+	-0,0042* (-2,5154)	-0,0012 (-1,2528)	0,0006 (0,4915)	-0,0011 (-1,1776)	0,0018* (1,9937)	-0,0006 (-0,6885)	0,0011 (1,3393)	-0,0003 (-0,3352)
$M1_u$	./.	0,6446 (1,6184)	-0,0763 (-0,2157)	0,8381* (2,0575)	-0,1826 (-0,4281)	-0,5550* (-2,8029)	-0,1100 (-0,5523)	0,1620 (0,6020)	0,2445 (0,7660)
PF_J	./.	-1,0478 (-1,5977)	0,9875 (1,6214)	-0,6409 (-1,5147)	1,0043* (1,6745)				
F_J	./.					-0,8888* (-3,0953)	-0,7636* (-1,7519)	-0,7358* (-2,8403)	-0,5985 (-1,5447)
R_J	+					-3,7509* (-8,8895)	-2,9158* (-5,0586)	-2,3518 (-4,9328)	-2,4684* (-4,2566)
PF_u	+	1,4074* (4,0681)	0,9024 (1,4910)	3,3864* (10,4640)	1,2159* (2,0542)				
F_u	+					0,5064* (2,5103)	0,9088* (3,2165)	1,6794* (4,7692)	1,6215* (4,4113)
R_u	./.					1,0098 (1,2882)	2,1751* (2,0104)	1,1678* (1,6789)	1,9192* (1,9191)
PB_J	?			0,00302* (4,2414)	0,00108* (2,2007)			0,00081 (1,6094)	0,00056 (1,2470)
PB_u	+			-0,9416* (-11,1241)	-0,2039 (-1,5717)			-0,3835* (-4,7029)	-0,2624* (-2,6168)
R^2		0,7442		0,9027		0,9515		0,9621	
$\hat{R}^2$			0,0480		0,1241		0,7486		0,8461
F		65,01	2,0213	126,79	2,9410	288,80	42,53	280,07	55,38
DW		0,2065	1,9467	0,6603	2,0143	0,7363	1,9225	0,8979	1,9137
RHO			0,9540 (29,84)		0,9384 (25,49)		0,7308 (10,04)		0,6334 (7,68)

Table 3b: Estimates for the Yen/$ Exchange Rate, Sample Period 1973.4 - 1980.8, Monthly Data.

		Eq. (1.1)		Eq. (1.3)		Eq. (1.2)		Eq. (1.4)	
		2SLS 3-9	FAIR 3-10	2SLS 3-11	FAIR 3-12	2SLS 3-13	FAIR 3-14	2SLS 3-15	FAIR 3-16
C		286,28 (6,23)	354,72 (6,02)	254,79 (3,61)	335,77 (4,37)	352,75 (17,41)	329,15 (10,95)	283,29 (6,68)	287,70 (5,77)
$M1_J$	+	-0,0036* (-2,1196)	-0,0007 (-0,6980)	0,0009 (0,7448)	-0,0006 (-0,6195)	0,0018* (1,9906)	-0,0006 (-0,6668)	0,0011 (1,3002)	-0,0001 (-0,1689)
$M1_U$	·/.	0,5341 (1,3276)	-0,1473 (-0,5211)	0,7948* (1,9424)	0,1230 (0,2980)	-0,5558* (-2,8000)	-0,1054 (-0,5311)	0,1727 (0,6325)	0,2078 (0,6676)
PF_J	·/.	-1,5660* (-2,2639)	-1,4133 (-1,6373)	-0,9703* (-2,1876)	-0,5285 (-0,6901)				
F_J	·/.					-0,8835* (-2,9254)	-0,9416* (-1,7757)	-0,7506* (-2,8131)	-0,5425 (-1,2405)
R_J	+					-3,7629* (-7,9660)	-2,5247* (-2,6712)	-2,2830* (-4,0652)	-2,6903* (-3,1302)
PF_U	+	1,2186* (3,4254)	0,8811* (1,7013)	3,2436* (9,8437)	1,5648* (3,1944)				
F_U	+					0,5060* (2,5075)	0,9414* (3,4048)	1,7062* (4,6035)	1,5708* (4,3707)
R_U	·/.					1,0007 (1,2506)	2,2672 (2,0422)	1,2010* (1,6909)	1,8150* (1,7860)
PB_J	?			0,0029* (4,1193)	0,0009* (1,7649)			0,0008 (1,6192)	0,0005 (1,1705)
PB_U	+			-0,9358* (-11,0113)	-0,2724* (-2,1467)			-0,3908* (-4,4687)	-0,2518* (-2,4430)
$\bar{R}^2$		0,7423		0,8948		0,9515		0,9621	
$\hat{R}^2$			0,5968		0,6804		0,8721		0,9072
F		60,50	31,09	116,26	29,10	268,18	93,16	250,46	96,58
DW		0,2096	1,7175	0,6610	1,9125	0,7373	1,8894	0,8979	1,9184
RHO			0,9044 (21,21)		0,8871 (19,15)		0,7367 (9,82)		0,6236 (7,10)

Table 4a: Estimates for the Yen/$ Exchange Rate, Sample Period 1973.I - 1980.II, Quarterly Data.

		Eq. (1.1)		Eq. (1.3)		Eq. (1.2)		Eq. (1.4)	
		OLS 4-1	CORC 4-2	OLS 4-3	CORC 4-4	OLS 4-5	CORC 4-6	OLS 4-7	CORC 4-8
C		255,44 (3,73)	300,58 (1,84)	240,63 (2,67)	423,56 (4,09)	414,95 (13,34)	417,52 (12,85)	371,10 (5,58)	354,90 (5,57)
$M1_J$	+	-0,0047* (-1,8473)	0,00002 (0,0084)	-0,0009 (-0,5498)	-0,0018 (-0,9928)	0,0026* (1,9956)	0,0031* (2,1649)	0,0021 (1,3189)	0,0027* (1,7252)
$M1_u$	./.	0,7864 (1,2932)	-0,2002 (-0,4096)	1,0559* (2,0329)	0,1118 (0,2379)	-0,7084* (-2,4880)	-0,7895* (-2,6348)	-0,3376 (-0,6842)	-0,2576 (-0,5687)
PF_J	./.	-0,5524 (-0,4383)	1,1228 (1,4123)	0,4454 (0,5688)	1,1406 (1,6293)				
F_J	./.					-1,3019* (-2,5283)	-1,2193* (-2,3214)	-1,0430 (-1,5748)	-0,7676 (-1,2056)
R_J	+					-3,4782* (-5,0631)	-3,7208* (-5,2026)	-2,9571* (-2,8939)	-2,9331* (-3,1417)
PF_u	+	1,6356* (2,7164)	1,5806* (2,1129)	3,5983* (6,6832)	2,6835* (3,8228)				
F_u	+					0,3007 (0,9732)	0,3180 (0,9855)	0,8414 (0,8437)	1,3128 (1,4346)
R_u	./.					1,3695 (1,0810)	1,0916 (0,8200)	1,2546 (0,9611)	0,6845 (0,5160)
PB_J	?			0,0026* (2,6023)	0,0026* (3,1811)			0,00024 (0,2248)	0,0006 (0,6464)
PB_u	+			-0,8715* (-6,6877)	-0,4533* (-2,3153)			-0,1609 (-0,7477)	-0,3080 (-1,4771)
$\bar{R}^2$		0,7179		0,8961		0,9537		0,9513	
$\hat{R}^2$			0,1386		0,4747		0,9373		0,9430
F		19,45	2,1263	42,69	4,2680	100,55	57,87	71,81	47,15
DW		0,5851	1,3531	1,1139	1,4447	1,4355	1,7744	1,4572	1,8587
RHO			0,9095 (11,78)		0,8013 (7,21)		0,2128 (1,1726)		0,1789 (0,9794)

Table 4b: Estimates for the Yen/$ Exchange Rate, Sample Period 1973.I - 1980.II, Quarterly Data.

		Eq. (1.1)		Eq. (1.3)		Eq. (1.2)		Eq. (1.4)	
		2SLS 4-9	FAIR 4-10	2SLS 4-11	FAIR 4-12	2SLS 4-13	FAIR 4-14	2SLS 4-15	FAIR 4-16
C		277,61 (3,44)	345,38 (4,83)	237,08 (2,55)	365,80 (5,07)	404,28 (11,16)	409,42 (11,59)	392,25 (5,16)	414,17 (6,48)
$M1_J$	+	-0,0009 (-0,2602)	-0,00003 (-0,0186)	-0,0002 (-0,1152)	-0,0011 (-0,7055)	0,0022 (1,4678)	0,0020 (1,4983)	0,0032 (1,4458)	0,0019 (1,1315)
$M1_U$	·/.	0,1635 (0,2192)	-0,2895 (-0,6504)	0,9504* (1,7701)	0,3131 (0,7060)	-0,6304* (-1,9210)	-0,6246* (-2,0764)	-0,7603 (-1,0113)	-0,5216 (-1,0271)
PF_J	·/.	-4,4392* (-2,2258)	-0,1910 (-0,1860)	-0,4517 (-0,4841)	0,6289 (0,7857)				
F_J	·/.					-2,1927* (-2,4070)	-1,4821* (-2,2411)	-1,1141 (-1,5618)	-0,6865 (-1,0000)
R_J	+					-1,7279 (-1,0935)	-2,6091* (-2,4685)	-4,7185* (-1,8982)	-3,4796* (-2,6208)
PF_U	+	0,2526 (0,2964)	1,3519* (2,1887)	3,2003* (5,4073)	3,0208* (4,9827)				
F_U	+					0,2723 (0,7768)	0,4121 (1,1959)	-0,3032 (-0,1684)	0,9192 (0,8556)
R_U	·/.					2,6839 (1,5183)	1,8298 (1,2368)	0,7218 (0,4658)	1,0476 (0,7264)
PB_J	?			0,0024* (2,3382)	0,0026* (3,2375)			-0,0008 (-0,4746)	0,0005 (0,4779)
PB_U	+			-0,8440* (-6,2629)	-0,5688* (-3,2316)			0,1070 (0,2610)	-0,1141 (-0,4678)
$\bar{R}^2$		0,6106		0,8902		0,9406		0,9444	
$\hat{R}^2$			0,7422		0,8569		0,9295		0,9293
F		9,8008	18,00	31,07	22,95	60,73	50,55	44,60	34,48
DW		0,8662	1,3650	1,1558	1,5087	1,3253	1,7089	1,6507	1,8030
RHO			0,8180 (8,24)		0,6722 (4,71)		0,3184 (1,5546)		0,3097 (1,4658)

Table 5: Estimates for the Reaction Function of R_J, Monthly (1973.4 - 1980.8) and Quarterly (1973.I - 1980.II).

together with :	Eq. (1.1)		Eq. (1.2)		Eq. (1.3)		Eq. (1.4)	
	Quarterly	Monthly	Quarterly	Monthly	Quarterly	Monthly	Quarterly	Monthly
	2SLS	2SLS	2SLS	2SLS	2SLS	2SLS	2SLS	2SLS
C	22,07 (3,80)	10,96 (3,16)	21,78 (3,83)	10,00 (3,73)	23,43 (4,20)	10,24 (3,67)	23,06 (4,19)	9,96 (3,77)
R_{t-1} +	0,4433* (3,1809)	0,7352* (8,7727)	0,4498* (3,2900)	0,7567* (11,6667)	0,4128* (3,0672)	0,7514* (11,1387)	0,4210* (3,1679)	0,7576* (11,8310)
$\Delta e(¥/\$)$ ·/.	-34,494* (-3,6942)	-42,144* (-2,6682)	-33,457* (-4,0764)	-24,747* (-3,0359)	-39,329* (-5,7708)	-29,019* (-4,3069)	-38,033* (-6,0546)	-24,049* (-4,6427)
TAR +	0,0809* (3,6164)	0,0415* (3,1121)	0,0797* (3,6529)	0,0373* (3,6595)	0,0863* (4,0480)	0,0382* (3,6141)	0,0849* (4,0385)	0,0371* (3,7001)
$\bar{R}^2$	0,9252	0,9496	0,9249	0,9689	0,9237	0,9660	0,9246	0,9692
F	107,19	533,85	106,77	881,37	104,97	805,01	106,23	891,71
DW	1,8167	2,0318	1,8116	1,7287	1,8155	1,8327	1,8198	1,7104

Table 6: Estimates for the Yen/$ Exchange Rate, Sample Period 1973.4 - 1982.8, Monthly Data.

		BHM's Equation (Eq. 1.1)				PF Divided (Eq. 1.2)			
		OLS	CORC	2SLS	FAIR	OLS	CORC	2SLS	FAIR
C		277,78 (16,69)	241,48 (2,5219)	280,86 (16,75)	305,68 (4,9220)	269,67 (15,66)	266,66 (7,11)	267,61 (15,43)	274,73 (8,28)
$M1_J$	+	-0,0047* (-5,7883)	-0,00002 (-0,0326)	-0,0045* (-5,4770)	-0,00014 (-0,1935)	-0,0019* (-3,3396)	-0,0002 (-0,3246)	-0,0018* (-3,3797)	-0,0003 (-0,5120)
$M1_U$	·/.	0,6731* (4,1775)	-0,0067 (-0,0275)	0,6359* (3,9030)	-0,1021 (-0,5243)	0,2454* (2,1076)	0,0323 (0,2110)	0,2546* (2,1798)	0,0299 (0,2005)
PF_J	·/.	0,5407 (1,2610)	1,0189* (2,0121)	0,3895 (0,8863)	-0,3158 (-0,4912)				
F_J	·/.					0,4171 (1,4903)	-0,4477 (-0,9206)	0,4686 (1,6654)	-0,3946 (-0,8361)
R_J	+					-4,7033* (-11,8603)	-3,4070* (-5,3279)	-4,8549* (-11,5415)	-3,5746* (-3,4126)
PF_U	+	1,9367* (8,2352)	0,9707* (1,8753)	1,8861* (7,9423)	0,9567* (1,8790)				
F_U	+					1,4107* (8,6113)	0,8882* (2,1794)	1,4181* (8,6430)	0,8458* (2,2890)
R_U	·/.					0,8539 (1,0875)	0,1666 (0,1538)	0,8590 (1,0931)	0,2402 (0,2402)
$\bar{R}^2$		0,7390		0,7387		0,9061		0,9060	
$\hat{R}^2$			0,0365 b)		0,6869		0,3627		0,7290
F		80,29	1,9948	76,34	59,22	181,14	11,20	170,23	47,51
DW		0,2448	2,0786	0,2395	1,9152	0,4661	2,0817	0,4716	2,0590
RHO			0,9674 (40,42)		0,9488 (35,16)		0,8681 (18,51)		0,8503 (16,33)

b) insignificant

Table 7: Estimates for the Yen/$ Exchange Rate, Sample Period 1973.I - 1982.II, Quarterly Data.

		BHM's Equation (Eq. 1.1)				PF Divided (Eq. 1.2)			
		OLS	CORC	2SLS	FAIR	OLS	CORC	2SLS	FAIR
C		279,96 (7,00)	174,69 (1,310)	337,64 (6,96)	292,91 (5,20)	372,83 (10,76)	315,41 (7,41)	374,52 (10,53)	335,73 (9,06)
$M1_J$	+	-0,0040* (-1,9351)	0,0003 (0,1587)	-0,0004 (-0,1601)	-0,0002 (-0,1073)	0,0012 (0,8156)	0,0015 (1,1301)	0,0031 (0,8382)	0,0011 (0,8697)
$M1_u$	·/.	0,5698 (1,3176)	0,1071 (0,3408)	-0,1602 (-0,2928)	-0,0947 (-0,3194)	-0,3631 (-1,1946)	-0,2424 (-0,9794)	-0,3896 (-1,1873)	-0,2379 (-0,9514)
PF_J	·/.	0,1637 (0,1558)	1,0129 (1,3854)	-2,0121 (-1,4127)	-0,0563 (-0,0605)				
F_J	·/.					-0,9831 (-1,3883)	-1,0502 (-1,4985)	-1,0936 (-1,2500)	-1,0490 (-1,4015)
R_J	+					-3,4684* (-4,4118)	-3,2915* (-4,0574)	-3,2759* (-2,7520)	-2,9690* (-2,3501)
PF_u	+	1,8640* (3,3527)	1,8785* (2,8053)	0,9620 (1,3833)	1,5770* (2,5508)				
F_u	+					0,7338* (1,7902)	0,8228 (1,6488)	0,6999 (1,5929)	0,7092 (1,4616)
R_u	·/.					1,6124 (1,1901)	0,0615 (0,0452)	1,5988 (1,1776)	0,2048 (0,1514)
$\bar{R}^2$		0,7127		0,6754		0,8904		0,8902	
$\hat{R}^2$			0,1342 b)		0,6745		0,6176		0,8410
F		23,95	2,395	17,17	17,10	51,10	10,69	41,88	27,33
DW		0,5079	1,7992	0,5351	1,7051	0,7726	1,9990	0,7668	1,9441
RHO			0,9230 (14,593)		0,8509 (10,443)		0,6950 (5,879)		0,6899 (5,089)

b) insignificant

Table 8: Estimates for the Reaction Function of R_J, Monthly (1973.4 - 1982.8) and Quarterly (1973.I - 1982.II).

together with :	BHM's Equation Eq. (1.1)				PF Divided Eq. (1.2)			
	Quarterly		Monthly		Quarterly		Monthly	
	2SLS	FAIR	2SLS	FAIR	2SLS	FAIR	2SLS	FAIR
C	11,83 (2,6438)	16,86 (3,2950)	4,45 (2,7973)	7,49 (3,3840)	11,83 (2,6440)	16,50 (3,2156)	4,47 (2,8618)	7,51 (3,4748)
R_{t-1} +	0,7279* (6,9462)	0,6096* (5,1336)	0,9069* (24,4940)	0,8253* (16,6630)	0,7279* (6,9455)	0,6132* (5,1460)	0,9060* (25,0320)	0,8253* (16,9290)
Δe(¥/$) '/.	-18,5176* (-2,0685)	-23,0562* (-2,6360)	-24,2377* (-2,2477)	-2,8228 (-0,4507)	-18,4982* (-2,1103)	-20,6277* (-2,4023)	-22,9900* (-2,6360)	-3,3508 (-0,6236)
TAR +	0,0440* (2,5030)	0,0627* (3,0549)	0,0174* (2,8091)	0,0276* (3,1214)	0,0440* (2,5042)	0,0607* (2,9550)	0,0174* (2,8619)	0,0277* (3,2240)
$\bar{R}^2$	0,9045		0,9703		0,9045		0,9712	
$\hat{R}^2$		0,8393		0,9378		0,8377		0,9389
F	107,33	59,18	1185,42	548,07	107,33	58,50	1224,52	558,44
DW	1,5348	1,9652	1,8645	2,0431	1,5347	1,9643	1,8313	2,0428
RHO		0,3056 (1,8939)		0,3758 (4,2466)		0,3063 (1,9005)		0,3734 (4,2184)

C.3. Estimation Results for the Sterling/US Dollar Exchange Rate

Table 1: Estimates for the £/$ Exchange Rate, Sample Period 1973.I - 1978.III, Quarterly Data.

Table 2: Estimates for the £/$ Exchange Rate, Sample Period 1973.I - 1982.II, Quarterly Data.

Table 3: Consistent Estimates (2SLS) for the Reaction Function of United Kingdom's Foreign Exchange Reserves R_K, Sample Period 1973.I - 1982.II, Quarterly Data.

<u>Table 1a</u>: Estimates for the £/$ Exchange Rate, Sample Period 1973.I - 1978.III, Quarterly Data.

		Eq. (1.1)		Eq. (1.3)		Eq. (1.2)		Eq. (1.4)	
		OLS 1-1	CORC 1-2	OLS 1-3	CORC 1-4	OLS 1-5	CORC 1-6	OLS 1-7	CORC 1-8
C		-5,41 (-0,1831)	6,381 (0,2071)	13,27 (0,4833)	15,40 (0,5198)	-23,68 (-0,8270)	9,67 (0,3151)	24,93 (0,8235)	26,15 (0,8606)
$M1_K$	+	0,4656 (0,4711)	0,6157 (0,5559)	-1,1407 (-1,1227)	-1,1185 (-1,0384)	-0,4318 (-0,4165)	0,1463 (0,1278)	-2,4895* (-2,3782)	-2,8243* (-2,9094)
$M1_U$	·/.	0,1579 (0,9909)	0,1015 (0,6055)	0,0658 (0,4449)	0,0545 (0,3425)	0,2822* (1,7690)	0,1215 (0,7294)	0,0566 (0,3553)	0,0547 (0,3452)
PF_K	·/.	0,2834 (1,6129)	0,1617 (0,8023)	0,2309 (1,0672)	0,2121 (0,8906)				
F_K	·/.					0,5711* (2,0370)	-0,3814 (-0,8385)	-0,0655 (-0,2186)	-0,0931 (-0,3106)
R_K	+					-0,0012 (-0,0058)	-0,2251 (-0,9280)	-0,3403 (-1,2226)	-0,3690 (-1,3148)
PF_U	+	0,3853* (7,8892)	0,3993* (5,6299)	0,3119* (3,6750)	0,2994* (2,7183)				
F_U	+					0,4539* (4,5275)	0,2234 (1,6591)	0,1462 (1,1689)	0,1264 (0,9534)
R_U	·/.					2,5841 (1,2942)	2,7985 (1,5609)	3,9367* (2,3467)	4,1155* (2,5846)
PB_K	?			0,2104 (0,4998)	0,1670 (0,3536)			0,6787 (1,3912)	0,7702 (1,4999)
PB_U	+			0,0786 (1,6247)	0,0857 (1,3334)			0,0763* (1,7845)	0,0812 (1,5491)
$\bar{R}^2$		0,8974		0,9265		0,9117		0,9430	
$\hat{R}^2$			0,7544		0,9139		0,4856		0,9594
F		49,09	16,12	47,19	30,52	38,88	3,4450	46,48	38,81
DW		1,1273	1,8752	1,9227	1,9423	1,5763	1,9059	2,2990	2,1685
RHO			0,4340 (2,2598)		0,0335 (0,1573)		0,6915 (4,4905)		-0,2249 (-1,0825)

Table 1b: Estimates for the £/$ Exchange Rate, Sample Period 1973.I - 1978.III, Quarterly Data.

		Eq. (1.1)		Eq. (1.3)		Eq. (1.2)		Eq. (1.4)	
		2SLS 1-9	FAIR 1-10	2SLS 1-11	FAIR 1-12	2SLS 1-13	FAIR 1-14	2SLS 1-15	FAIR 1-16
C		-2,8413 (-0,0914)	22,45 (0,7379)	13,55 (0,4926)	14,24 (0,5121)	-16,85 (-0,5484)	18,11 (0,6129)	25,48 (0,6715)	24,59 (0,8455)
$M1_K$	+	0,4689 (0,4739)	0,7219 (0,6488)	-1,1728 (-1,1416)	-1,0990 (-1,0630)	-0,7183 (-0,6424)	0,4023 (0,3552)	-2,4925* (-2,3635)	-2,7950* (-2,9956)
$M1_u$	./.	0,1474 (0,8980)	0,0358 (0,2164)	0,0662 (0,4473)	0,0615 (0,4109)	0,2706 (1,6040)	0,0850 (0,5220)	0,0536 (0,2639)	0,0624 (0,4106)
PF_K	./.	0,2505 (1,1727)	0,0265 (0,1123)	0,1949 (0,7171)	0,2059 (0,9265)				
F_K	./.					0,5273* (1,7692)	-0,2597 (-0,6133)	-0,0668 (-0,2192)	-0,0782 (-0,2833)
R_K	+					0,2801 (0,8953)	-0,3213 (-1,2618)	-0,3526 (-0,5987)	-0,3710 (-1,3178)
PF_u	+	0,3851* (7,8754)	0,3694* (4,9118)	0,3030* (3,2213)	0,3070* (3,5769)				
F_u	+					0,4872* (4,4661)	0,1921 (1,4046)	0,1447 (1,0409)	0,1353 (1,1575)
R_u	./.					3,5203 (1,5747)	2,6155 (1,4640)	3,9364* (2,3467)	4,0888* (2,6519)
PB_K	?			0,1614 (0,3386)	0,1729 (0,4054)			0,6960 (0,7943)	0,7736 (1,5557)
PB_u	+			0,0839 (1,5526)	0,0809 (1,6590)			0,0755 (1,4247)	0,0773* (1,8586)
R^2		0,8972		0,9263		0,9016		0,9430	
$\hat{R}^2$			0,7562		0,9191		0,7393		0,9682
F		61,07	13,96	33,53	30,31	24,44	7,56	28,94	53,27
DW		1,1106	1,8721	1,9135	1,9379	1,6118	1,8802	2,3009	2,1694
RHO			0,5083 (2,5866)		0,0366 (0,1494)		0,7196 (4,5468)		-0,2116 (-0,8306)

Table 2a: Estimates for the £/$ Exchange Rate, Sample Period 1973.I - 1982.II, Quarterly Data.

		Eq. (1.1)		Eq. (1.3)		Eq. (1.2)		Eq. (1.4)	
		OLS 2-1	CORC 2-2	OLS 2-3	CORC 2-4	OLS 2-5	CORC 2-6	OLS 2-7	CORC 2-8
C		61,29 (6,85)	46,49 (3,98)	76,11 (5,55)	67,22 (4,54)	55,35 (4,39)	37,90 (2,40)	76,05 (5,14)	68,37 (4,52)
$M1_K$	+	2,0550* (5,1440)	1,3490* (2,7879)	0,9430* (1,8533)	0,6435 (1,1089)	1,8442* (4,2490)	0,9679* (1,8041)	0,5353 (0,9853)	0,1997 (0,3268)
$M1_U$	./.	-0,1802* (-3,3757)	-0,0877 (-1,3301)	-0,2652* (-3,5850)	-0,2119* (-2,6526)	-0,1496* (-2,2190)	-0,0281 (-0,2940)	-0,2766* (-3,4395)	-0,2309* (-2,8079)
PF_K	./.	0,0647 (1,5938)	0,0645 (0,9674)	-0,0102 (-0,2353)	-0,0023 (-0,0420)				
F_K	./.					0,1909* (1,8971)	-0,0889 (-0,4114)	-0,0985 (-0,7943)	-0,1301 (-0,9578)
R_K	+					0,0913 (0,5078)	-0,5176* (-2,1345)	-0,2586 (-1,2950)	-0,3197 (-1,4980)
PF_U	+	0,4652* (11,2760)	0,4656* (6,3980)	0,3467* (6,0990)	0,3238* (4,0525)				
F_U	+					0,5062* (7,8849)	0,2460* (1,8611)	0,2490* (2,6648)	0,1939* (1,7278)
R_U	./.					-0,7569* (-2,3347)	-0,4053 (-1,1869)	-0,8793* (-2,7613)	-0,8004* (-2,3736)
PB_K	?			0,0251 (0,1740)	-0,0500 (-0,3405)			0,2077 (1,1915)	0,1168 (0,6960)
PB_U	+			0,0821* (2,9515)	0,0884* (2,5869)			0,0949* (3,1486)	0,1091* (3,0328)
$\bar{R}^2$		0,8478		0,8789		0,8481		0,8846	
$\hat{R}^2$			0,6119		0,7802		0,2476		0,7889
F		52,53	15,19	45,72	22,29	35,42	2,9690	36,46	15,27
DW		1,2621	2,0511	1,5288	1,8390	1,4174	2,1190	1,5678	1,8730
RHO			0,4912 (3,4299)		0,3019 (1,9263)		0,7827 (7,6489)		0,3079 (1,9688)

Table 2b: Estimates for the £/$ Exchange Rate, Sample Period 1973.I - 1982.II, Quarterly Data.

		Eq. (1.1)		Eq. (1.3)		Eq. (1.2)		Eq. (1.4)	
		2SLS 2-9	FAIR 2-10	2SLS 2-11	FAIR 2-12	2SLS 2-13	FAIR 2-14	2SLS 2-15	FAIR 2-16
C		61,28 (6,85)	48,38 (4,38)	77,27 (5,62)	66,60 (4,79)	62,42 (4,54)	54,40 (3,95)	69,93 (4,31)	64,51 (4,40)
$M1_K$	+	2,0516* (5,1317)	1,3713* (2,8641)	0,8817* (1,7265)	0,6697 (1,2098)	1,7904* (3,8743)	1,5320* (3,1071)	0,7940 (1,3141)	0,4709 (0,7947)
$M1_u$	·/.	-0,1804* (-3,3761)	-0,0952 (-1,4740)	-0,2718* (-3,6634)	-0,2115* (-2,7800)	-0,1781* (-2,4508)	-0,1325* (-1,7967)	-0,2348* (-2,5993)	-0,2078* (-2,5706)
PF_K	·/.	0,0559 (1,3625)	0,0476 (0,7352)	-0,0246 (-0,5591)	-0,0219 (-0,4029)				
F_K	·/.					0,3213* (2,6767)	0,2719* (1,9276)	0,0716 (0,3918)	-0,0215 (0,1376)
R_K	+					0,4531* (1,8604)	0,3340 (1,2198)	0,0960 (0,2825)	-0,0883 (-0,3237)
PF_u	+	0,4642* (11,2402)	0,4502* (6,9256)	0,3397* (5,9541)	0,3389* (5,1380)				
F_u	+					0,6004* (7,6216)	0,5610* (6,1564)	0,3716* (2,7561)	0,3014* (2,6494)
R_u	·/.					-0,6202* (-1,7746)	-0,6910* (-1,9529)	-0,6750* (-1,8303)	-0,7398* (-2,1402)
PB_K	?			0,0314 (0,2171)	-0,0367 (-0,2530)			0,0513 (0,2295)	0,0602 (0,3359)
PB_u	+			0,0863* (3,0861)	0,0854* (2,8206)			0,0776* (2,2597)	0,0888* (2,7026)
$\bar{R}^2$		0,8476		0,8784		0,8282		0,8721	
$\hat{R}^2$			0,6760		0,7886		0,7311		0,8012
F		45,88	17,21	37,32	19,27	24,90	14,05	24,71	14,61
DW		1,2618	2,0734	1,5371	1,8211	1,5666	1,9217	1,5598	1,8306
RHO			0,4874 (3,2988)		0,2878 (1,6948)		0,2623 (1,5348)		0,2634 (1,4802)

<u>Table 3</u>: Consistent Estimates (2SLS) for the Reaction Function of United Kingdom's Foreign Exchange Reserves R_K, Sample Period 1973.I - 1982.II, Quarterly Data.

together with		Eq.(1.1)	Eq.(1.2)	Eq.(1.3)	Eq.(1.4)
C		-2,1625 (-1,1506)	-2,1768 (-1,1594)	-2,1782 (-1,1583)	-2,1437 (-1,1467)
R_{t-1}	+	0,7527* (7,5705)	0,7518* (7,5761)	0,7517* (7,5576)	0,7539* (7,6399)
Δe(£/$)	·/.	-27,3656* (-3,4528)	-27,4967* (-3,4972)	-27,5097* (-3,4730)	-27,1921* (-3,5095)
TAR	+	0,0823* (1,8679)	0,0827* (1,8804)	0,0827* (1,8771)	0,0818* (1,8695)
$\bar{R}^2$		0,9366	0,9365	0,9365	0,9367
F		167,47	167,21	167,18	167,80
DW		1,7231	1,7258	1,7261	1,7196

REFERENCES

Alexander, S.S. — Wirkungen einer Abwertung auf die Handelsbilanz, in: Rose, K. (ed), Theorie der internationalen Wirtschaftsbeziehungen, Köln/Berlin 1965.

Aliber, R.Z. — Monetary Independence under Floating Exchange Rates, in: Journal of Finance, Vol. 30 (May 1975), pp. 365-376.

.... — The Firm under Pegged and Floating Exchange Rates, in: Scandinavian Journal of Economics, Vol. 78 (1976), pp. 309-322.

Allen, P., and Kenen, P. — Portfolio Adjustment in Open Economies, A Comparison of Alternative Specifications, in: Weltwirtschaftliches Archiv, Vol. 112 (1976), pp. 33-72.

Argy, V., and Porter, M. — The Forward Exchange Market and the Effects of Domestic and External Disturbances under Alternative Exchange Rate Systems, in: International Monetary Fund (IMF) Staff Papers, 19, No. 3., (1972).

Artus, J.R. — Exchange Rate Stability and Managed Floating: The Experience of the Federal Republic of Germany, in: IMF Staff Papers, 23 (July 1976), pp. 312-333.

.... — Monetary Stabilization With and Without Government Credibility, in: IMF Staff Papers, Vol. 28 (September 1981), pp. 495-533.

.... — Effects of U.S. Monetary Restraint on the DM-$ Exchange Rate and the German Economy, National Bureau of Economic Research, Working Paper No. 926, Cambridge, Mass. (July 1982).

Artus, J.R., and Crockett, A.D. — Floating Exchange Rates and the Need for Surveillance, Essays in International Finance, Princeton University, Princeton, New Jersey 1978.

Artus, J.R., and Young, J.H. — Fixed and Flexible Exchange Rates: A Renewal of the Debate, in: IMF Staff Papers, Vol. 26 (Dec. 1979), pp. 654-698.

Balassa, B. — The Purchasing-Power Parity Doctrine: A Reappraisal, in: Journal of Political Economy, 72 (Dec. 1964), pp. 584-596.

Baltensperger, E., and Böhm, P. — Stand und Entwicklungstendenzen der Wechselkurstheorie - Ein Überblick, in: Aussenwirtschaft, 37. Jahrgang (1982), pp. 109-157.

Bank of Japan — Reasearch and Statistics Department: Assets and Liabilities vis-à-vis Non-Residents of Japan, in: Economic Statistics Annual, 1977 (table 123), 1982 (table 127), 1983 (table 131).

Beach, C.M., and MacKinnon, J.G. — A Maximum Likelihood Procedure for Regression with Autocorrelated Errors, in: Econometrica 46 (1978), pp. 51-58.

Bender, D. — Externes und Internes Gleichgewicht in einem kurzfristigen Portfoliomodell internationaler Kapitalbewegungen, in: Jahrbücher für Nationalökonomie und Statistik, Bd. 192, 1977, pp. 244-264.

Bhandari, J.S. — A Theory of Exchange Rate Determination and Adjustment, in: Weltwirtschaftliches Archiv, Vol. 117 (1982), pp. 605-621.

Bickerdike, C.F. — The Instability of Foreign Exchange, in: Economic Journal, Vol. 30 (1920), pp. 118-122.

Bilson, J.F. — The Monetary Approach to the Exchange Rate: Some Empirical Evidence, in: IMF Staff Papers, (1978), pp. 48-75.

.... — Recent Developments in Monetary Models of Exchange Rate Determination, in: IMF Staff Papers, (Dec. 1979a), pp. 201-223.

.... — The Deutsche Mark/Dollar Rate, in: Brunner, K., and Meltzer, A.H., Policies for Employment, Prices and Exchange Rates, Carnegie-Rochester Conference Series on Public Policy, Supplement to the Journal of Monetary Economics, 1979b, pp. 59-101.

.... — The Choice of an Invoice Currency in International Transactions, in: Bhandari, J.S., and Putnam, B.H. (eds.), Economic Interdependence and Flexible Exchange Rates, Cambridge, Mass. (1983).

Black, S.W. — Flexible Exchange Rates and National Economic Policy, New Haven 1977.

Boyer, R.S. — Devaluation and Portfolio Balance, in: American Economic Review, Vol. 67 (1977), pp. 54-63.

Branson, W.H. — Asset Markets and Relative Prices in Exchange Rate Determination, Institute for International Economic Studies, Stockholm, Seminar Paper No. 66, December 1976.

.... — Asset Markets and Relative Prices in Exchange Rate Determination, in: Sozialwissenschaftliche Annalen des Instituts für Höhere Studien, Wien 1977.

Branson, W.H. Exchange Rate Dynamics and Monetary Policy, in: Lindbeck, A. (ed.), Inflation and Employment in Open Economies, North-Holland 1979, pp. 189-224.

.... Comment on Dornbusch, R.: Exchange Rate Economics: Where Do We Stand?, in: Brookings Papers on Economic Activity, No. 1 (1980), pp. 187-194.

.... Macroeconomic Determinants of Real Exchange Rates, National Bureau of Economic Research, Working Paper No. 801, Washington 1981.

.... Exchange-Rate Policy after a Decade of "Floating", National Bureau of Economic Research, Working Paper No. 909, Washington 1982.

Branson, W.H., and Buiter, W.H. Monetary and Fiscal Policy with Flexible Exchange Rates, Paper presented at a Seminar at the European University Institute, Florence (Feb. 1981).

Branson, W.H., Halttunen, H., and Masson, P. Exchange Rates in the Short Run: The Dollar - Deutschemark Rate, in: European Economic Review, 10 (1977), pp. 303-324.

.... Exchange Rates in the Short Run: Some Further Results, in: European Economic Review, 12 (1979), pp. 395-402.

Calvo, G.A, and Rodrîguez, C.A. A Model of Exchange Rate Determination under Currency Substitution and Rational Expectations, in: Journal of Political Economy, Vol. 85 (June 1977), pp. 617-625.

Carse, S., and Wood, G.E. Currency of Invoicing and Forward Covering, in: Martin, J.P., and Smith, A. (eds), Trade and Payments Adjustment under Flexible Exchange Rates, Trade Policy Research Centre, London 1979.

Caspers, R. Einflußgrößen der Wechselkursbildung und internationale Anpassungsmechanismen, Eine portfoliotheoretische und empirische Analyse des Devisenmarktes für US-Dollar in der Bundesrepublik Deutschland 1964-1971, Diss. Kiel 1977.

Cassel, G. Money and Foreign Exchange after 1914, London/Bombay/Sidney 1922.

Cézanne, W. Gleichgewichtstheorie und Wechselkurse, Schriften zur wirtschaftswissenschaftlichen Forschung, Bd. 62, Meisenheim/Glan 1974.

Chiang, A.C. Fundamental Methods of Mathematical Economics, Tokyo 1974.

Claassen, E.-M. Weltinflation, München 1978.

Claassen, E.-M. — Grundlagen der makroökonomischen Theorie, München 1980.

Clements, K.W. — The Monetary Approach to Exchange Rate Determination: A Geometric Analysis, in: Weltwirtschaftliches Archiv (1981), pp. 20-29.

Clements, K.W., and Semudram, M. — An International Comparison of the Price of Non-traded Goods, in: Weltwirtschaftliches Archiv, Vol. 119/2 (1983), pp. 356-363.

Deutsche Bundesbank — Vermögensstatus der Bundesrepublik Deutschland gegenüber dem Ausland, in: Monatsbericht der Deutschen Bundesbank, (Nov. 1974), pp. 13-21.

.... — Der Auslandsvermögensstatus der Bundesrepublik Deutschland Ende 1980, in: Monatsbericht der Deutschen Bundesbank, (May 1981), pp. 25-31.

.... — Der Auslandsvermögensstatus der Bundesrepublik Deutschland Ende 1982, in: Monatsbericht der Deutschen Bundesbank, (August 1983), pp. 30-45.

Dooley, M., and Isard, P. — The Portfolio-Balance Model of Exchange Rates, Federal Reserve Board, International Finance Discussion Papers No. 141, (May 1979).

.... — A Portfolio-Balance Rational Expectations Model of the Dollar-Mark Exchange Rate, in: Journal of International Economics 12 (1982), pp. 257-276.

.... — The Role of the Current Account in Exchange Rate Determination: A Comment on Rodríguez, International Finance Discussion Papers No. 191, (October 1981).

Dornbusch, R. — Exchange Rates and Fiscal Plicy in a Popular Model of International Trade, in: American Economic Review, 65 (December 1975), pp. 859-871.

.... — The Theory of Flexible Exchange Rate Regimes and Macroeconomic Policy, in: Scandinavian Journal of Economics, Vol. 78 (1976a), pp. 255-275.

.... — Expectations and Exchange Rate Dynamics, in: Journal of Political Economy, 84 (Dec. 1976b), pp. 1161-1176.

.... — Flexible Exchange Rates, Capital Mobility and Macroeconomic Equilibrium, in: Claassen, E.-M., and Salin, P. (eds.), Recent Issues in International Monetary Economics, Amsterdam 1976c, pp. 261-278.

Dornbusch, R. — Managed Floating: Eine Würdigung des internationalen Finanzsystems nach Bretton Woods, in: Zeitschrift für die gesamte Staatswissenschaft, 134 (1978), pp. 37-56.

.... — Open Economy Macroeconomics, New York 1980a.

.... — Exchange Rate Economics: Wher Do We Stand? in: Brookings Papers on Economic Activity, No. 1 (1980b), pp. 143-185.

.... — Exchange Rate Risk and the Macroeconomics of Exchange Rate Determination, National Bureau of Economic Research, Working Paper No. 493, (June 1980c).

.... — Equilibrium and Disequilibrium Exchange Rates, unpublished MIT, Massachusetts Institute of Technology, 1982a.

.... — Flexible Exchange Rates and Interdependence, National Bureau of Economic Research, Working Paper No. 1035 (October 1982b).

.... — Flexible Exchange Rates and Interdependence, in: IMF Staff Papers (May 1983).

Dornbusch, R. and Fischer, S. — Exchange Rates and the Current Account, in: American Economic Review, Vol. 70 (December 1980), pp. 960-971.

Dornbusch, R. and Krugman, P. — Flexible Exchange Rates in the Short-Run, in: Brookings Papers on Economic Activity, 3 (1976), pp. 537-575.

Driskill, R.A. — Exchange Rate Dynamics: An Empirical Investigation, in: Journal of Political Economy, Vol. 89/2 (1981), pp. 357-371.

Eaton, J., and Turnovsky, S.J. — Covered Interest Parity, Uncovered Interest Parity and Exchange Rate Dynamics, in: The Economic Journal, 93 (Sept. 1983), pp. 555-575.

Edison, H.J. — The Rise and Fall of Sterling: Testing Alternative Models of Exchange Rate Determination, International Finance Discussion Papers No. 224, (June 1983).

Einzig, P. — The History of Foreign Exchange, London 1970.

Enders, W. — Portfolio Balance and Exchange Rate Stability, in: Journal of Money, Credit, and Banking, 9 (1977), pp. 491-499.

Fair, R.C. The Estimation of Simultaneous Equation Models with Lagged Endogenous Variables and First Order Serially Correlated Errors, in Econometrica 38 (1970), pp. 507-516.

Fama, E.F. Efficient Capital Markets: A Review of Theory and Empirical Work, in: Journal of Finance (May 1970), pp. 383-417.

.... Foundations of Finance, New York 1976.

Fellner, W. The Bearing of Risk Aversion on Movements of Spot and Forward Exchange Relative to the Dollar, in: Chipman, J.S., and Kindleberger, C.P. (eds.), Flexible Exchange Rates and the Balance of Payments, Essays in Memory of Egon Sohmen, Amsterdam/New York/Oxford 1980, pp. 113-126.

Fleming, J.M. Domestic Financial Policies under Fixed and under Floating Exchange Rates, IMF Staff Papers, Vol.9 (November 1962), pp. 369-372.

Foley, D.K. On Two Specifications of Asset Equilibrium in Macroeconomic Models, in: Journal of Political Economy, Vol. 83 (April 1975), pp. 303-324.

Frankel, J.A. On the Mark: A Theory of Floating Exchange Rates Based on Real Interest Differentials, in: American Economic Review, Vol. 69 (1979a), pp. 610-622.

.... The Diversifiability of Exchange Risk, in: Journal of International Economics, Vol. 9 (1979b), pp. 379-393.

.... Monetary and Portfolio-Balance Models of Exchange Rate Determination, in: Bhandari, J.S., and Putnam, B.H. (eds.), Economic Interdependence and Flexible Exchange Rates, Cambridge, Mass. (1983), pp. 84-115.

Frenkel, J.A. A Monetary Approach to the Exchange Rate: Doctrinal Aspects and Empirical Evidence, in: Scandinavian Journal of Economics, Vol. 78 (1976), pp. 200-224.

.... Purchasing Power Parity, Doctrinal Perspective and Evidence from the 1920s, in: Journal of International Economics, Vol. 8 (1978), pp. 169-191.

.... Flexible Exchange Rates, Prices, and the Role of "News": Lessons from the 1970s, in: Journal of Political Economy, Vol. 89 (1981a), pp. 665-705.

.... The Collapse of Purchasing Power Parity during the 1970s, in European Economic Review (February 1981b), pp. 146-165.

Frenkel, J.A., and Levich, R.M. — Covered Interest Arbitrage: Unexploited Profits? in: Journal of Political Economy, Vol. 83 (April 1975), pp. 325-338.

.... — Transaction Costs and the Efficiency of International Capital Markets: Tranquil Versus Turbulent Periods, in: Sarnat, M., and Szegö, G.P. (eds), International Finance and Trade, Vol. I., Cambridge, Mass. 1979, pp. 53-81.

Frenkel, J.A., and Rodríguez, C.A. — Exchange Rate Dynamics and the Overshooting Hypothesis, in: IMF Staff Papers (March 1982), pp. 1-30.

Gaab, W. — Der Beitrag alternativer Finanzmarktmodelle zur Erklärung des DM/US-$ Wechselkurses von 1974(10)-1981(5), Vorläufige Fassung für die Tagung des Außenwirtschaftsausschusses vom 7.-8. Mai 1982 in Frankfurt a.M., Mannheim 1982.

Gandolfo, G. — Mathematical Methods and Models in Economic Dynamics, Amsterdam, North-Holland 1971.

Genberg, H. — Purchasing Power Parity under Fixed and Flexible Exchange Rates, in: Journal of International Economics, Vol. 8 (1978), pp. 247-276.

.... — Effects of Central Bank Interventions in the Foreign Exchange Market, in: IMF Staff Papers (September 1981), pp. 451-476.

Genberg, H., and Kierzkowski, H. — Impact and Long-Run Effects of Economic Disturbances in a Dynamic Model of Exchange Rate Determination, in: Weltwirtschaftliches Archiv, Vol. 115 (1979), pp. 605-628.

Girton, L., and Henderson, D. — Central Bank Operations in Foreign and Domestic Assets under Fixed and Flexible Exchange Rates, in: Clark, P.B., and Logue, D., and Sweeney, R.J. (eds.), The Effects of Exchange Rate Adjustments, Washington 1977, pp. 151-179.

Gleske, L. — Bestimmungsfaktoren und Wirkungen von Wechselkursbewegungen unter besonderer Berücksichtigung der Devisenpolitik der Bundesbank, Referat vor dem Ausschuß für Außenwirtschaft des Vereins für Socialpolitik, April 1982.

Goldstein, M. — Have Flexible Exchange Rates Handicapped Macroeconomic Policy? Special Papers in International Economics No. 14, Princeton University, Princeton, New Jersey 1980.

Graf, G. — Zur formalen Theorie des Devisenterminmarktes, Berlin 1971.

Grassman, S. — A Fundamental Symmetry in International Payment Patterns, in: Journal of International Economics, 3 (1973), pp. 105-116.

Greenwood, J. — Expectations, the Exchange Rate, and the Current Account, in: Journal of Monetary Economics, Vol. 12/4 (Nov. 1983), pp. 543-569.

Groß, A. — The Current Account and Current Account "News" in a Model of Nominal and Real Exchange Rate Determination: An Empirical Approach, Part I: The Theory, unpublished, European University Institute, San Domenico/Firenze (Feb. 1983).

.... — The Current Account and Current Account "News"... Part II: Empirical Results for the Deutsche Mark/US Dollar Rate, unpublished, Commission of the European Communities, DG II, Brussels (Feb. 1984).

Grubel, H.G. — Forward Exchange, Speculation, and the International Flow of Capital, Stanford/California 1966.

Hacche, G, and Townend, J.C. — Monetary Models of Exchange Rates and Exchange Market Pressure: Some General Limitations and an Application to Sterling's Effective Rate, in: Weltwirtschaftliches Archiv, Bd. 117 (1982), pp. 622-637.

Hammann, D. — Zahlungsbilanz, Konjunkturtransmission und Wechselkursbestimmung, Schriften zur monetären Ökonomie, ed. by Duwndag, D., Baden-Baden 1980.

Harbrecht, W. — Europa auf dem Wege zur Wirtschafts- und Währungsunion: theoretische und politische Probleme der Errichtung einer Wirtschafts- und Währungsunion in der EG, Habilitationsschrift, Nürnberg (Nov. 1979).

Harbrecht, W., and Neumann, M. — Zur Problematik der Kaufkraftparitätentheorie als Grundlage für Wechselkursanpassungen in einem Europäischen Währungssystem, Referat vor dem Wirtschaftspolitischen Ausschuß des Vereins für Socialpolitik, Nürnberg 1979.

Henderson, D.W. — Macroeconomic Theory: Modelling the Interdependence of National Money and Capital Markets, in: American Economic Review, Vol. 67 (Feb. 1977), 190-199.

Henderson, D.W., and Rogoff, K. — Net Foreign Asset Positions and Stability in a World Portfolio Balance Model, International Finance Discussion Papers, No. 178 (March 1981).

Henderson, D.W., and Rogoff, K. — Net Foreign Asset Positions and Stability in a World Portfolio Balance Model (revised version), in: Journal of International Economics, Vol. 13, No. 1/2, (August 1982), pp. 85-104.

Henderson, D.W., and Sampson, S. — Intervention in Foreign Exchange Markets, A Summary of Ten Staff Studies, in: Federal Reserve Bulletin, Vol. 69/11 (November 1983), pp. 830-836.

Hoffman, D.L., and Schlagenhauf, D.E. — Rational Expectations and Monetary Models of Exchange Rate Determination, in: Journal of Monetary Economics, Vol. 11/2 (March 1983), pp. 247-260.

Hooper, P., and Morton, J. — Fluctuations in the Dollar: A Model of Nominal and Real Exchange Rate Determination, Federal Reserve System, International Finance Discussion Papers No. 168, Washington 1980.

Ingram, J.C. — Expectations and Floating Exchange Rates, in: Weltwirtschaftliches Archiv, Vol. 114 (1978), pp. 422-477.

International Monetary Fund — World Economic Outlook, Occasional Paper No. 21, Washington D.C., (May 1983).

.... — Annual Report on Exchange Restrictions, various issues.

Isard, P. — How Far Can We Push the "Law of One Price"?, in: American Economic Review, Vol. 67 (December 1977), pp. 942-948.

.... — Exchange-Rate Determination: A Survey of Popular Views and Recent Models, Princeton Studies in International Finance No. 42, Princeton, New Jersey 1978.

.... — Expected and Unexpected Changes in Exchange Rates: The Role of Relative Price Levels, Balance of Payments Factors, Interest Rates and Risk, Federal Reserve System, International Finance Discussion Papers No. 156, Washington 1980.

.... — An Accounting Framework and Some Issues for Modelling how Exchange Rates respond to the News, Federal Reserve System, International Finance Discussion Papers No. 200, Washington 1982.

Jacob, K.-D. — Wechselkurs und Leistungsbilanz, Berlin/New York 1972.

Jurgensen Report — Report of the Working Group on Exchange Market Intervention, US Treasury, Washington 1983.

Keereman, F. — The Exchange Rate and the Banking System, unpublished, European University Institute, 1984.

Keynes, J.M. — A Tract on Monetary Reform, London 1923.

Kleinewefers, H. — Theorie und Politik der Abwertung, Basel/Tübingen 1969.

Kohlhagen, S. — The Behavior of Foreign Exchange Markets - A Critical Survy of Empirical Literature, New York University Series in Finance and Economics, New York 1978.

Kouri, P. — The Exchange Rate and the Balance of Payments in the Short Run and in the Long Run: A Monetary Approach, in: the Scandinavian Journal of Economics, Vol. 78 (1976), pp. 280-304.

.... — Monetary Policy, the Balance of Payments, and the Exchange Rate, in Bigman, D., and Taya, T. (eds.), The Functioning of Floating Exchange Rates: Theory, Evidence, and Policy Implications, Cambridge, Mass. (1980), pp. 79-111.

.... — Balance of Payments and the Foreign Exchange Market: A Dynamic Partial Equilibrium Model, in: Bhandari, J.S., and Putnam, B.H. (eds.), Economic Interdependence and Flexible Exchange Rates, Cambridge, Mass. (1983), pp. 116-156.

Kouri, P., and De Macedo, J.B. — Exchange Rates and the International Adjustment Process, in: Brookings Papers on Economic Activity, 1 (1978), pp. 11-157.

Laidler, D. — Comment on Myhrmann, in: Scandinavian Journal of Economics, Vol. 78 (1976), pp. 197-199.

Lapan, H., and Enders, W. — Devaluation, Wealth Effects, and Relative Prices, in: American Economic Review, Vol. 68 (1978), pp. 601-613.

Lee, M.H. — Purchasing Power Parity, Business Economics and Finance, ed. by Laffer, A., New York/Basel 1976.

Levich, R.M. — Overshooting in the Foreign Exchange Market, Group of Thirty, Occasional Papers No. 5, New York 1981.

Machlup, F. — Die Theorie des Devisenmarktes, in: Theorie der internationalen Wirtschaftsbeziehungen, ed. by Rose, K., Köln/Berlin 1966.

Machlup, F. Explaining Changes in Balances of Payments and Foreign Exchange Rates: A Polemic wihtout Graphs, Algebra and Citations, in: Chipman, J.S., and Kindleberger, C.P. (eds.), Flexible Exchange Rates and the Balance of Payments, Essays in Memory of Egon Sohmen, Amsterdam/New York/Oxford 1980, pp. 82-99.

Maddala, G. Econometrics, New York 1977.

Magee, S.P. Currency Contracts, Passthrough, and Devaluation, in: Brookings Papers on Economic Activity, 1/1973, pp. 303-323.

.... A Two-Parameter Purchasing-Power-Parity Measure of Arbitrage in International Goods Markets, in: Martin, J.P., and Smith, A. (eds), Trade and Payments Adjustment under Flexible Exchange Rates, Trade Policy Research Center, London 1979, pp. 152-173.

Magee, S.P., and Rao, R.K. Vehicle and Nonvehicle Currencies in International Trade, in: American Economic Review, Papers and Proceedings, Vol. 70 (May 1980), pp. 368-373.

Marshall, A. Money, Credit, and Commerce, London 1923, reprinted New York 1965.

Markowitz, H.M. Portfolio Selection, Efficient Diversification of Investments, 2nd ed., New Haven/London 1970.

Martin, J.P., and Masson, P.R. Exchange Rates and Portfolio Balance, National Bureau of Economic Research, Working Paper No. 377, Cambridge, Mass. (August 1979).

Masson, P.R. Portfolio Balance and Exchange Rate Stability, in: Journal of Money, Credit, and Banking, Vol. 12, No. 2 (May 1980), pp. 228-230.

McGregor, P.G. The Portfolio Selection Approach and Short-Run Econometric Models of Capital Flows and the Foreign Exchange Market: A Theoretical Analysis, in: Journal of Economic Studies 8,2 (1981), pp. 3-24.

McKinnon, R.I. Portfolio Balance and International Payments Adjustment, in: Mundell, R.A., and Swoboda, A.K. (eds.), Monetary Problems of the International Economy, Chicago and London 1969, pp. 199-234.

.... Fluctuating Exchange Rates, 1973 - 1978: A Qualified Monetary Interpretation, Chapter 8 of: Money in International Exchange: the Convertible Currency System, New York 1979, pp. 176-196.

McKinnon, R.I. — Instability in Floating Exchange Rates: A Money-Market Perspective, in: Bigman, D,, and Taya, T. (eds.), The Functioning of Floating Exchange Rates: Theory, Evidence, and Policy Implications, Cambridge, Mass., 1980, pp. 55-78.

Meade, J.E. — The Balance of Payments, London/New York/Toronto 1951, reprinted 1963.

Meese, R., and Rogoff, K. — Empirical Exchange Rate Models of the Seventies: Are They Fit to Survive? International Finance Discussion Papers, No. 184, Washington (June 1981).

Meese, R., and Singleton, K.J. — Rational Expectations, Risk Premia, and the Market for Spot and Forward Exchange, International Finance Discussion Paper, No. 165 (July 1980).

Metzler, L.A. — Wealth, Saving, and the Rate of Interest, in: Journal of Political Economy, Vol. 59 (1951), pp. 93-116.

Meyer, F.W. — Wechselkurse, in: Handwörterbuch der Sozialwissenschaften, Vol. 11 (1961), pp. 571-583.

Michaely, M. — Analysis of Devaluation: Purchasing Power Parity, Elasticities, and Absorbtion, in: Bigman, D., and Taya, T. (eds.), The Functioning of Floating Exchange Rates: Theory, Evidence, and Policy Implications, Cambridge, Mass. 1980, pp. 33-54.

Mundell, R.A. — Capital Mobility and Stabilization Policy under Fixed and Flexible Exchange Rates, in: Caves, R., and Johnson, H.G. (eds.), Readings in International Economics, London 1968, reprinted from the original articel in: Canadian Jounrnal of Economics and Political Science, 29 (November 1963), pp. 475-485.

Murphy, R.G., and Van Duyne, C. — Asset Market Approaches to Exchange Rate Determination: A Comparative Analysis, in: Weltwirtschaftliches Archiv, 116 (1980), pp. 628-656.

Mussa, M. — The Exchange Rate, the Balance of Payments and Monetary and Fiscal Policy under a Regime of Controlled Floating, in: Scandinavian Journal of Economics, Vol. 78 (1976), pp. 229-248.

.... — Empirical Regularities in the Behavior of Exchange Rates and Theories of the Foreign Exchange Markets in: Brunner, K. and Meltzer, A.H. (eds.), Policies for Employment, Prices and Exchange Rates, Carnegie-Rochester Conference Series on Public Policy, Supplement to the Journal of Monetary Economics, 1979, pp. 9-57.

Muth, J.F. Rational Expectations and the Theory of Price Movements, in: Econometrica, 29 (1961), pp. 315-335.

Myhrmann, J. Experience of Flexible Exchange Rates in Earlier Periods: Theories, Evidence and a New View, in: Scandinavian Journal of Economics, Vol. 78 (1976), pp. 169-196.

.... Strom-Bestands-Ansätze des internen und externen Gleichgewichts, in: Claassen, E.-M. (ed.), Kompendium der Währungstheorie, München 1977, pp. 75-105.

Neumann, M. Theoretische Volkswirtschaftslehre 1, Einführung und Theorie des Volkseinkommens, Heidelberg 1973.

Neumann, M.J.M. Intervention in the Mark/Dollar Market: The Authorities' Reaction Function, Paper prepared for a seminar at the Directorate-General for Economic and Financial Affairs, Commission of European Communities, Brussels (December 1983).

Niehans, J. Some Doubts about the Efficacy of Monetary Policy under Flexible Exchange Rates, in: Journal of International Economics, Vol. 5 (1975), pp. 275-281.

.... Exchange Rate Dynamics with Stock/Flow Interaction, in: Journal of Political Economy, Vol. 85 (1977), pp. 1245-1257.

.... Metzler, Wealth, and Macroeconomics: A Review, in: Journal of Economic Literature, Vol. 16 (March 1978), pp. 84-95.

.... Geldpolitik bei überschießenden Wechselkursen, in: Außenwirtschaft, Vol. 34 (1979), pp. 199-219.

.... Dynamic Purchasing Power as a Monetary Rule, in: Chipman, J.S., and Kindleberger, C.P. (eds.), Flexible Exchange Rates and the Balance of Payments, Essays in Memory of Egon Sohmen, Amsterdam/New York/Oxford 1980, pp. 213-230.

Obstfeld, M. Can We Sterilize? in: American Economic Review, Papers and Proceedings, Vol. 72, No. 2 (May 1982), pp. 45-50.

Officer, L. The Purchasing-Power-Parity Theory of Exchange Rates: A Review Articel, in: IMF Staff Papers, Vol. 23 (March 1976a), pp. 1-60.

Officer, L. — The Productivity Bias in Purchasing Power Parity: An Econometric Investigation, in: IMF Staff Papers, Vol. 23, (November 1976b), pp. 545-579.

Page, S.A.B. — Currency of Invoicing in Merchandise Trade, in: National Institute Economic Review, No. 81 (August 1977), pp. 77-81.

.... — The Choice of Invoicing Currency in Merchandise Trade, in: National Institute Economic Review, No. 98 (November 1981), pp. 60-72.

Penati, A. — Expansionary Fiscal Policy and the Exchange Rate, in: IMF Staff Papers, Vol. 30, No. 3, (September 1983), pp. 542-569.

Porter, M.G. — Exchange Rates, Current Accounts and Economic Activity - A Survey of Some Theoretical and Empirical Issues, Board of Governors of the Federal Reserve System, June 1979.

Riechel, K.-W. — Economic Effects of Exchange-Rate Changes, Lexington (Mass.)/Toronto 1978.

Robinson, J. — The Foreign Exchanges, in: Essays in the Theory of Employment, Oxford 1947, reprinted in: Ellis, H.S., and Metzler, L.A. (eds.), Readings in the Theory of International Trade, London 1958.

Rodríguez, C.A. — The Role of Trade Flows in Exchange Rate Determination: A Rational Expectations Approach, in: Journal of Political Economy, Vol. 88 (1980), pp. 1148-1158.

Roll, R.W., and Solnik, B.H. — A Pure Foreign Exchange Asset Pricing Model, European Institute for Advanced Studies in Management, Working Paper No. 75, August 1975.

Roper, D. — Two Ingredients of Monetarism in an International Setting, Seminar Paper No. 46, Stockholm Institute for International Economic Studies, April 1975.

Rose, K. — Theorie der Außenwirtschaft, Siebente, überarbeitete Auflage, München 1978.

Salter, W.E.G. — Internal and External Balance: The Role of Price and Expenditure Effects, in: Economic Record, 35 (August 1959), pp. 226-238.

Sargent, T., and Wallace, N. — Rational Expectations and the Dynamics of Hyperinflation, in: International Economic Review, 14 (June 1973), pp. 328-350.

Schadler, S. — Sources of Exchange Rate Variability: Theory and Empirical Evidence, in: IMF Staff Papers, Vol. 24 (July 1977), pp. 253-296.

Scharrer, H.-E., Gehrmann, D., Wetter, W. — Währungsrisiko und Währungsverhalten deutscher Unternehmen im Außenhandel, Veröffentlichung des HWWA-Institut für Wirtschaftsforschung, Hamburg 1978.

Scholl, R.B. — The International Investment Position of the United States, in: Survey of Current Business, August 1976 (pp. 29-33), August 1981 (pp. 52-57), August 1983 (pp. 42-48).

Shiller, R.J. — Rational Expectations and the Dynamic Structure of Macroeconomic Models: A Critical Review, in: Journal of Monetary Economics, 4 (1978), pp. 1-44.

Sohmen, E. — The Theory of Forward Exchange, Princeton Studies in International Finance No. 17, Princeton, New Jersey 1966.

Solnik, B. — International Parity Conditions and Exchange Risk, in: Sarnat, M., and Szegö, G.P. (eds.), International Finance and Trade, Vol. I, Cambridge, Mass. 1979, pp. 83-97.

Stackelberg, H.v. — Die Theorie des Wechselkurses bei vollständiger Konkurrenz, in: Jahrbücher für Nationalökonomie und Statistik, Vol. 161, 1949.

Stein, J.L. — The Dynamics of Spot and Forward Prices in an Efficient Foreign Exchange Market with Rational Expectations, in: American Economic Review, Vol. 70, No. 4 (1980), pp. 565-583.

Steuer, W. — Leistungsbilanz - Kein sinnvoller Kompaß, in: Wirtschaftswoche Nr. 47, 18.11.1983, pp. 86-90.

Stockman, A.C. — Risk, Information, and Forward Exchange Rates, in: Frenkel, J.A., and Johnson, H.G. (eds.), The Economics of Exchange Rates: Selected Studies, Reading, Mass. 1978, pp.159-178.

Sreit, M.E. — Information Processing in Futures Markets - An Essay on the Adequacy of an Abstraction, European University Institute Working Paper No. 9, San Domenico, Firenze (March 1982).

Suss, E.C. — The Trade-Off between Exchange Rate and Reserve Changes: Theoretical and Empirical Evidence, in: Bigman, D., and Taya, T. (eds.), The Functioning of Floating Exchange Rates: Theory, Evidence, and Policy Implications, Cambridge, Mass., 1980, pp. 221-242.

Sweeney, R.J. — Report on Technical Studies on Speculation and Market Efficiency, in: Exchange Rate Flexibility, ed. by Dreyer, J.S. (et all), American Enterprise Institute for Public Policy Research, Washington 1978.

Tobin, J. — A General Equilibrium Approach to Monetary Theory, in: Journal of Money, Credit, and Banking, 1 (1969), pp. 15-29.

.... — The State of Exchange Rate Theory, Some Skeptical Observations, in: Cooper, R.N. et all (eds.), The international Monetary System under Flexible Exchange Rates, Essays in Honor of Robert Triffin, Combridge, Mass. 1982, pp. 115-128.

Tobin, J., and De Macedo, J.B. — The Short-Run Macroeconomics of Floating Exchange Rates: An Exposition, in: Chipman, J.S., and Kindleberger, C.P. (eds.), Flexible Exchange Rates and the Balance of Payments, Essays in Memory of Egon Sohmen, Amsterdam/New York/ Oxford 1980, pp. 5-28.

Truman, E.M., and Shafer, J.R. — International Portfolio Disturbances and Domestic Monetary Policy, in: Cooper, R.M., et all (eds.), The International Monetary System under Flexible Exchange Rates, Essays in Honor of Robert Triffin, Cmbridge, Mass. 1982, pp. 129-144.

Tsiang, S.C. — The Theory of Forward Exchange and Effects of Government Intervention on the Forward Exchange Market, in: IMF Staff Papers, Vol. 7 (1959/60), pp. 75-106.

Ueda, K. — Permanent and Temporary Changes in the Exchange Rate and Trade Balance Dynamics, in: Journal of International Economics, Vol. 15, No. 1/2 (August 1983), pp. 27-43.

United Kingdom Central Statistical Office — Financial Wealth of the Non-Bank Private Sector, in: Economic Trends (July 1981), pp. 105-118.

.... — External Assets and Liabilities, in: United Kingdom Balance of Payments, December 1983, pp. 51-61.

Whitmann, M.v.N. — Comment on Kouri, P., and De Macedo, J.B.,: Exchange Rates and the International Adjustment Process, in: Brookings Papers on Economic Activity, 1 (1978), pp. 153-156.

Wihlborg, C. — Currency Risk in International Financial Markets, Priceton Studies in International Finance No. 44, Princeton, New Jersey 1978.

Williamson, J. The Exchange Rate System, Policy Analysis in international Economics 5 (Institute for International Affairs), Washington 1983.

Wilson, C.A. Anticipated Shocks and Exchange Rate Dynamics, in: Journal of Political Economy, Vol. 87 (1979), pp. 639-647.

Kolibri 360 GmbH
Ferdinand-Jühlke-Straße 7
99095 Erfurt, Deutschland
produktsicherheit@kolibri360.de